Eighteenth-Century Coffee-House Culture

Volume 1

Eighteenth-Century Coffee-House Culture

Volume 1
Restoration Satire

Edited by
Markman Ellis

Routledge
Taylor & Francis Group

LONDON AND NEW YORK

First published 2006 by Pickering & Chatto (Publishers) Limited

Published 2016 by Routledge
2 Park Square, Milton Park, Abingdon, Oxfordshire OX14 4RN
711 Third Avenue, New York, NY 10017, USA

First issued in paperback 2015

Routledge is an imprint of the Taylor & Francis Group, an informa business

BRITISH LIBRARY CATALOGUING IN PUBLICATION DATA

Eighteenth-century coffee-house culture
  1. Coffeehouses – England – History – 18th century – Sources
2. Coffeehouses – England – History – 17th century – Sources   3. English
literature – 18th century   4. English literature – Early modern, 1500–1700
5. Satire, English   6. England – Social life and customs – 18th century
– Sources   7. England – Social life and customs – 17th century –
Sources   8. England – Intellectual life – 18th century – Sources   9. England
– Intellectual life – 17th century – Sources
  I. Ellis, Markman
820.9'3559'09033

ISBN-13: 978-1-138-66059-5 (pbk)
ISBN-13: 978-1-1387-5285-6 (hbk)
ISBN-13: 978-1-85196-829-9 (set)
Typeset by P&C

CONTENTS OF THE EDITION

The complaint of all the she-traders ... against the city cheats, or the new coffee-houses ([1682–93])

'Letter from a French gentleman in London to his friend in Paris ... Containing an Account of Will's Coffeehouse, and of the Toasting and Kit-Kat-Clubs' (1701)

Edward Ward, *The Humours of a Coffee-House: a Comedy* (1707)

Edward Arwaker, 'Fable XXIX: The Coffee-House: Or, A Man's Credit, is his Cash' (1708)

Edward Ward, *Vulgus Britannicus: or, the British Hudibras* (1710)

John Macky, *A Journey Through England. In Familiar Letters. From a Gentleman Here, to his Friend Abroad* (1714)

Lewis Theobald, 'Coffee-House Humours Exposed' (1717)

Volume 2: The Eighteenth-Century Satire
Introduction

Coffee: a tale (1727)

The Velvet Coffee-woman (1728)

Coffee-man, *The Case of the Coffee-men of London and Westminter [sic]* ([1728])

The case between the proprietors of news-papers, and the subscribing coffee-men, fairly stated (1729)

The case between the proprietors of news-papers, and the coffee-men of London and Westminster, fairly stated ([1729])

James Salter, *A catalogue of the rarities to be seen at Don Saltero's Coffee-house in Chelsea* (1729)

Anthony Hilliar, *A Brief and Merry History of Great Britain* ([1730])

The Life and Character of Moll King, late mistress of King's Coffee-house in Covent-garden ([1747])

Arthur Murphy, '[Account of Jonathan's Coffee-House]'; '[Proposal for a Female Coffee-House]' ([1753–4])

George's coffee house. A poem (1761)

Memoirs of the Bedford Coffee-House (1763)

The British coffee-house. A poem (1764)

A Sunday Ramble; or, Modern Sabbath-Day Journey ([1776])

Johann Wilhelm von Archenholz, *A Picture of England* (1789)

Volume 3: Drama
Introduction

[John Tatham], *Knavery in all Trades: or, The Coffee-House. A Comedy* (1664)

Thomas Sydserf, *Tarugo's Wiles: or, the Coffee-House. A Comedy* (1668)

Elkanah Settle, *The New Athenian Comedy* (1693)

Charles Johnson, *The generous husband: or, the coffee house politician* ([1711])

Exchange-Alley: or, the stock-jobber turn'd gentleman (1720)

James Miller, *The Coffee-House. A Dramatick Piece* (1737)

The Usurpers: or the Coffee-House Politicians. A farce (1749)

CONTENTS

GENERAL INTRODUCTION

A coffee-house, as Samuel Johnson defined it the *Dictionary* (1755), is 'A house of entertainment where coffee is sold, and the guests are supplied with newspapers'.[1] In his estimation, a coffee-house is a business which not only retails coffee, but also makes available newspapers. As this suggests, the coffee-house has long been more than a commercial enterprise: it is also an arena for culture and politics. This collection of texts on English coffee-house culture of the late seventeenth and early eighteenth centuries gives evidence of the material history of the coffee-houses, coffee drinking and the habits of those people who went there. But the texts in this collection also contribute to a debate or contest over the meaning of the coffee-house and the unique sociability of its clientele. As a novelty in the society of this period, the coffee-house was an institution open to numerous interpretations: the texts assembled here offer competing languages and discourses for comprehending the coffee-house experience, each located within a generic or disciplinary matrix.

As an idea, the coffee-house has been the subject of a considerable amount of interest from social historians, literary critics and sociologists since the nineteenth century. As such, they have come to be seen as a central locus for understanding the social and cultural history of Britain in the eighteenth century: closely associated with the consumption of news, whether in the form of printed news-sheets and newspapers, political and religious tracts and satires, commercial market currents, or manuscript newsletters and correspondence. The coffee-house was also constituted as the central locus of newly egalitarian practices of discussion and conversation, including forms of structured discourse, such as lectures and debates, as well as unregulated discourse, such as gossip and chatter. In this heady combination of news, literature, debate and writing, many commentators have identified the coffee-house as an important arena for publicness – the origin of that sense of the political will of the ordinary people known as public opinion, central to modern notions of civil society and democratic culture. The

---

1.   Samuel Johnson, *A Dictionary of the English Language* (London, W. Strahan, 1755). See also William Rider, *A New Universal English Dictionary: or, a compleat treasure of the English language* (London, W. Griffin, 1759): 'a place where coffee is sold, if near change, to transact business, and the daily papers are taken in for the accommodation of customers'.

texts included in the collection constitute the evidence for such a claim, and in as much as this evidence supports it or not, so that claim must fall short.

In the eighteenth century, the coffee-house was central to the social life of British cities. Visitors to London in the mid-eighteenth century were often struck by the extraordinary number of coffee-houses – some estimated there were over two thousand – and the extraordinary fondness Londoners had for their three products: coffee, company and conversation. Staying in London in the 1730s, the Prussian nobleman Charles Lewis Pollnitz remarked that the coffee-houses were among the most typical of the 'Pleasures of this great City'.[2] He observed that is was a 'Sort of Rule with the *English*, to go once a Day at least, to Houses of this Sort, where they talk of Business and News, read the Papers, and often look at one another'. The role played by the coffee-house was central to the social and commercial life of the city, with a social significance that extended beyond entertainment or sustenance. Another commentator observed that 'these Coffee-Houses are the constant Rendezvous for Men of Business, as well as the idle People, so that a Man is sooner ask'd about his Coffee-house than his Lodgings. They smoak Tobacco, game and read Papers of Intelligence: here they treat of Matters of State ... and transact Affairs of the last Consequence to the whole World.'[3] As he makes clear, the coffee-house was only incidentally a place to drink coffee: primarily it was a place for conversation. Everything about the coffee-house was organized to facilitate this congenial conversation. A French traveller, Henri Misson, in London in 1698, remarked that coffee-houses were 'extremely convenient. You have all manner of news there; you have a good Fire, which you may sit by as long as you please; you have a Dish of Coffee; you meet your Friends for the transaction of Business, and all for a penny, if you don't care to spend more.'[4]

Intellectual interest in the coffee-house has been reinforced by the revival of the coffee-house within urban culture in the last two decades. The seemingly irresistible rise of Starbucks and their numerous branded imitators have seen the high streets and malls of modern cities reanimated by legions of coffee-shops. Many commentators, including those employed by the branded coffee-shop chains themselves, have pointed to the continuities between these establishments and the coffee-houses of the eighteenth century. These coffee-shops, it is claimed, have forged a new social space somewhere between home and office, between private and public, where the

2.   *The Memoirs of Charles-Lewis, Baron de Pollnitz,* 2 vols (London, Daniel Browne, 1737), vol. II, pp. 462–3.

3.   Anthony Hilliar, *A Brief and Merry History of Great Britain* (London, J. Roberts, J. Shuckburgh, J. Penn and J. Jackson, [1730]), pp. 21–2 (Volume 2, pp. 191–2).

4.   Henri Misson de Valberg, *Mémoirs et observations faites par un voyageur en Angleterre* (La Haye, 1698); trans. by Ozell, *Memoirs and Observations in his Travels over England* (London, D Browne et al., 1719).

sense of urban community can be renewed or made apparent.[5] Yet in their ubiquity, and uniformity, the branded coffee-shops also seem to reinforce the feelings of emptiness and alienation caused by modern life.

The coffee-house enlightenment

After the Second World War, amidst the ruins of the enlightenment ideal of progress and liberty, sociologists identified in the coffee-house an important and forgotten lesson about sociability and civic community. In an essay entitled 'Historical Development of Public Opinion', which first appeared in 1950 in *The American Journal of Sociology*, the American sociologist Hans Speier argued that the eighteenth century held the key to modern notions of public opinion. His article outlined some important structural transformations in British and French society in the eighteenth century: especially the expansion of the reading public, and the emergence of new social institutions in the coffee-house and salon. Speier, an exile from Nazi Germany trained in the German sociological tradition, was employed at the time by the American strategic military research organisation called the Rand Corporation: at this time he was writing extensively on American policy in occupied Germany, especially the so-called 'Re-education'. The article makes use of the speculative mode of German sociology in the Simmel tradition, and marries it to Anglophone history of enlightenment culture. In this example, Speier makes use of a tradition of English historical writing on the coffee-houses. He makes the coffee-house the agent of bourgeois political emancipation, arguing that 'The English middle classes began to accomplish their own education'. Coffee-houses 'became popular as centers of news gathering and news dissemination, political debate, and literary criticism'.[6] The discussions and debates of the coffee-houses of England, and the salons of France, Speier argued, helped to forge the prominent role of public opinion in democratic politics.

The most influential expression of Speier's hypothesis was that by the German philosopher and sociologist Jürgen Habermas in his first book, *The Structural Transformation of the Public Sphere*, published in German in 1962 but not translated into English until 1989.[7] This book has had an enormous influence on historical, literary and political debate on eighteenth-century culture, although this fame should not mask the nature and problems of the book itself. It is in a way quite untypical of Habermas's work: it avoids the technical and abstract language of his later works, its argument is essentially his-

---

5. Ray Oldenburg, *The Great Good Place* (New York, Marlowe & Co., 1989).
6. Hans Speier, 'Historical Development of Public Opinion', *American Journal of Sociology*, 55: 4 (January 1950), pp. 376–88, 376, 381.
7. Jürgen Habermas, *The Structural Transformation of the Public Sphere: an inquiry into a category of Bourgeois society*, trans. by Thomas Burger (Cambridge, Polity, 1992); *Strukturwandel der Öffentlicheit* (Darmstadt and Neuwied, Hermann Luchterhand Verlag, 1962).

torical in its structure, and he lards the theoretical with thought-provoking and even charming examples. The book originated as Habermas's *Habilitationschrift*, the post-doctoral dissertation required in the German academy, submitted to Wolfgang Abendroth in the philosophy department at the University of Marburg, having been intended for Max Horkheimer and Theodor Adorno at Frankfurt.[8] The long gap between publication and translation has occasioned much commentary: despite the early uptake by Eagleton and others, the book became well known in English in the 1990s after many related works (by Habermas and others) for which it laid the groundwork; as such, it no longer accurately represented its author's opinions.[9] In addition, as Ken Hirschkop had suggested, during the decades of the publication/translation gap, a great deal had changed in the debate, not least the rise of cultural studies.[10] In its original formation, the book was embedded in arguments about the rebirth of democratic culture in post-war Germany, and especially the role of public opinion, critical debate and the media in this period, whereas in the 1990s, in Britain and America, it has just as often been read as a commentary on the information revolution and the internet.

The public sphere, Habermas says, is 'a realm of our social life in which something approaching public opinion can be formed'.[11] A public sphere is constituted, he suggests, when individuals gather together to participate in an open discussion uncontaminated by hierarchy or status. The public sphere does not have concrete materiality (it is not a place): it is an ideal condition only approximated by lived historical experience. Nonetheless, Habermas suggests that in the early eighteenth century certain institutional innovations briefly gave rise to something that approximated a public sphere. The 'new institutions' he notes are coffee-houses in England in the period 1680–1730, salons in France and the *Tischgesellschaften* (table or dining societies) in Germany in the mid-eighteenth century. The first two institutions are those of Speier: Habermas's key revision is to find a German example, and so to undo Speier's hostility to German political culture. Where Speier sees German history as the exception to the enlightenment hypothesis, Habermas sees it as part of the continuum. Speier argued that in the absence of the institutions of public opinion, German political culture continued to be dominated by the military, the aristocracy and by secret soci-

---

8.   Craig Calhoun, 'Introduction', in *Habermas and the Public Sphere*, ed. by Craig Calhoun (Cambridge, MA, and London, The MIT Press, 1992), pp. 1–48; p. 4.

9.   Nick Crossley and John Michael Roberts 'Introduction', in *After Habermas: new perspectives on the public sphere*, ed. by Nick Crossley and John Michael Roberts (Oxford, Blackwell Publishing/ The Sociological Review, 2004), pp. 1–27. See also Peter Uwe Hohendahl, 'The Theory of the Public Sphere Revisited', in *Sites of Discourse – Public & Private – Legal Culture*, ed. by Uwe Böcker and Julie Hibbard (Amsterdam, Rodopi, 2002), pp. 13–23.

10.   Ken Hirschkop, 'Justice and Drama: on Bakhtin as a complement to Habermas', in *After Habermas*, ed. by Crossley and Roberts, pp. 49–66.

11.   Jürgen Habermas, 'The Public Sphere', *New German Critique*, 3 (1974), p. 49.

eties (the Masons), a situation that left the way free in the twentieth century for the rise of German fascism. As this reminds us, while Habermas's account is designed to rehabilitate German civil society of the 1950s, Speier's argument attempts to locate the origins of the German tragedy of the twentieth century. Habermas uses the same argument about English history to make the opposite conclusion, that German society also contains within itself the origins of democratic culture.

Habermas broadly recapitulates Speier's hypothesis that the English coffee-house was the primary and originary paradigm for the public sphere. Like Speier, Habermas's treatment of the English coffee-houses is a brief section, establishing it as a model for his other examples. Habermas offers a brief history of the coffee-houses in what he calls their 'golden age': their first establishment in the 1650s by Levantine merchants, their ubiquity in the city by the first decade of the eighteenth century, and the favour they found with poets and critics. In coffee-houses, like salons, the nobility had intercourse with 'intellectuals' of the middling sort, mediated by the literary culture (Habermas says 'literature had to legitimate itself in these coffee houses'[12]). Habermas sees the coffee-houses allowing a particular mixing of classes and interests: the nobility mix with intellectuals, but in the particular case of England, the 'nobility' combine with the 'upper bourgeois stratum' from the landed and moneyed interest. It was in the free mixture of the coffee-house, Habermas argues, that 'critical debate ignited by works of literature and art was soon extended to include economic and political disputes'. In Habermas's account literature and art have a central role in catalysing critical debate, which soon expands from the merely literary to what Habermas sees as the more serious issues of economics and politics. Despite local differences, Habermas argues that the coffee houses, the salons and the *Tischgesellschaften* had a number of 'institutional criteria' in common: (i) a non-hierarchical type of social interaction ('they preserved a kind of social intercourse that, far from presupposing the equality of status, disregarded status altogether'); (ii) an unfettered range to their debate and conversation ('discussion ... presupposed the problematization of areas that until then had not been questioned'); and (iii) an inclusivity and accessibility ('everyone had to *be able* to participate').[13] Although he notes the exclusion of women, he turns this potential objection into evidence for the cultural influence of the coffee-houses.

The coffee-house example is arguably a minor part of Habermas's argument. Nonetheless, in the book's reception in English-speaking intellectual circles, and in eighteenth-century studies especially, the coffee-house digression has come to have a curious force of its own. In numerous studies that deploy Habermas's public sphere argument, the coffee-house example is enlisted to explain the theory

12. Habermas, *Structural Transformation*, p. 33.
13. Ibid., pp. 36–7.

of the public sphere, whether positively or critically, often in disciplines or subjects at some distance from eighteenth-century historical sociology, such as musicology, post-modern sociology, media studies, geography and literary criticism.[14] Some readers might object that the coffee-house section is merely an historical digression: arguing that although Habermas's account dwells on the eighteenth century, and on the Enlightenment, it is clear that in his historical schema, the eighteenth century provides the best examples, but not the only ones. Habermas's historical writing has its defenders too. In Calhoun's *Habermas and the Public Sphere*, published in 1992, Geoff Eley suggests that 'Habermas's perspective has been fundamentally borne out by recent social history', concluding that the argument's historical grounding is secure and imaginative – an assessment Habermas noted with approval in his own 'Further Reflections on the Public Sphere' published in the same volume.[15] Nonetheless, it is clear that Habermas does not claim that the historical argument is his own research. Writing in the late 1950s, Habermas's research was restricted to a narrow range of generalist secondary texts: two works by significant English social historians and critics (Leslie Stephen and George Macaulay Trevelyan); two short review essays; and a German reworking of English coffee-house historiography.[16]

Habermas's excursion into history on *The Structural Transformation of the Public Sphere* was undertaken to clarify the origin and thus structure of democratic cultures of debate, with the intention that such an understanding might be used to increase discursive rationality in the social practice of the present. Habermas's sociology relies on the account of the coffee-houses celebrated – and perhaps invented – by the nostalgic accounts in nineteenth-century English social history of the civilised values of the reign of Queen Anne. The weakness of Habermas's historical digression on coffee-houses is in that sense irrelevant: his argument did not address

14. Michael Chanan, *From Handel to Hendrix: the composer in the public sphere* (London, Verso, 1999), p. 9; Mike Hill, 'Of Multitudes and Moral Sympathy: E.P. Thompson, Althusser, and Adam Smith', in *Masses, Classes and the Public Sphere*, ed. by Mike Hill and Warren Montag (London, Verso, 2000), p. 210; Alan McKee, *The Public Sphere: an introduction* (Cambridge, Cambridge University Press, 2005), p. 198; Monroe Edwin Price, *Television, the Public Sphere, and National Identity* (Oxford, OUP, 1995), p. 28; Mimi Sheller, *Consuming the Caribbean: from Arawaks to zombies* (London, Routledge, 2003), p. 84; John Jervis, *Exploring the Modern* (Oxford, Blackwell, 1998), p. 326; Terry Lovell, *Consuming Fiction* (London, Verso, 1987).

15. Geoff Eley, 'Nations, Publics and Political Cultures: placing Habermas in the nineteenth century', in *Habermas*, ed. by Calhoun, pp. 298–339; p. 294; Jürgen Habermas, 'Further Reflections on the Public Sphere', in *Habermas*, ed. by Calhoun, pp. 421–61; p. 424.

16. Leslie Stephen, *English Literature and Society in the Eighteenth Century: Ford Lectures, 1903* (London, Duckworth and Co., 1904); George Macaulay Trevelyan, *English Social History: a survey of six centuries from Chaucer to Queen Victoria* (London, Longmans, 1944), in the German translation of 1948 (*Kultur-und sozialgeschichte Englands: ein ruckblick auf sechs jahrhunderte von Chaucer bis Queen Victoria* (Hamburg, Claassen & Goverts, 1948)); [Tom Taylor], 'The Clubs of London', *National Review*, 4:8 (April 1857), pp. 295–334; Helmut Reinhold, 'Zur Sozialgeschichte des Kaffees und des Kaffeehauses', *Kölner Zeitschrift für Soziologie und Sozialpsychologie*, 10 (1958), pp. 151ff; Hermann Westerfrölke, *Englische Kaffeehäuser als Sammelpunkte der literarischen Welt von Dryden und Addison* (Jena, Frommannschen Buchhandlung, 1924).

eighteenth-century England, but Germany in the 1950s and 60s. Nonetheless, the argument transforms the eighteenth-century coffee-house into a kind of pastoral, a golden age of communicative rationality. As the texts in this collection demonstrate, this story is not only inaccurate, but also relies on and embeds another argument, the Whig mythology of English liberty and its foundation in good manners. In a commentary on the English reception of Habermas's theory of the public sphere, Peter Hohendahl reproaches social and cultural historians for having 'misunderstood' Habermas's approach to the eighteenth century 'because they disregarded the larger structure of Habermas' theory and, in particular, the political agenda which grew out of the political problems of the 1950s in the federal Republic of Germany. They mistook for an historical account what was meant as a normative intervention.'[17] Hohendahl suggests that the attractiveness of Habermas's argument was the tension between the historicist and normative arguments: although contradictory, the one makes the other tenable. In making the textual evidence for this historical argument available to readers, this collection is intended to show that the historical dimension of that normative argument is not simply contradictory but untenable.

The historiography of the coffee-house

Coffee-houses became of interest to historians around the same time that their decline became apparent to all. The end of the age of the coffee-house – roughly the long eighteenth century – ushered in the age of the coffee-house history. Beginning with Macaulay, a parade of historians found in the coffee-house the epitome of English politics and society in the Restoration and eighteenth century. The first coffee-houses had opened in London in the early 1650s, and the idea spread rapidly, both across the city, and around the provincial towns of the empire, so that by the end of the century there were as many as 500 in London alone, as well as many more in Oxford, Bristol and Boston. The first histories of this phenomenon emerged in the late 1690s amongst antiquarians and virtuosi associated with the Royal Society.[18] Such writing located coffee-house history at the boundary between the discourse on trade and the botanical history of coffee (*Coffea Arabica*), a tradition that extended through the century.[19] Coffee-houses do not figure in the great eighteenth-century narrative histories of England except as incidental locations for plots and plotters during the Exclusion Crisis:

17. Peter Uwe Hohendahl, 'The Theory of the Public Sphere Revisited', in *Sites of Discourse – Public & Private – Legal Culture*, ed. by Uwe Böcker and Julie Hibbard (Amsterdam, Rodopi, 2002), pp. 13–23; p. 14.

18. See texts by John Houghton, Richard Bradley and James Douglas in Volume 4.

19. Adam Anderson, *An Historical and Chronological Deduction of the Origin of Commerce, From the Earliest Accounts to the Present Time. Containing, an history of the great commercial interests of the British Empire,* 2 vols (London, A. Millar, J. and R. Tonson, J. Rivington, R. Baldwin, W. Johnston et al., 1764). See also John Ellis in Volume 4.

the exception here is the issue of Charles II's attempt to suppress the coffee-houses in 1675, which David Hume and Catherine Macaulay, for example, read as evidence of the king's subversion of popular liberties.[20] Historical writing on coffee-houses remained an antiquarian interest through to the early decades of the nineteenth century. A series of essays and notices published in the popular periodicals of 1790s explored the origins of coffee and the coffee-houses in surveys of seventeenth and early eighteenth-century travel writing.[21] Such accounts were laced with nostalgia, for, as many commentators noted, the coffee-houses of their own day appeared to be in decline. The antiquarian Isaac D'Israeli wrote in this tradition: in *Curiosities of Literature* in 1817 he wrote that he was 'surprised in fact that coffee was ever more popular than tea'. Nonetheless, he discerned that coffee-houses were once of great influence in English society. As he concluded, 'the history of coffee-houses is often that of the manners, the morals, and the politics, of a people'.[22]

The most important early contribution to the history of the coffee-houses was that of Thomas Babington Macaulay in his *History of England from the Accession of James the Second* (1849).[23] His account of them is the centrepiece of an innovative section of social history describing the everyday life of London around 1685 (the urban milieu of that signal event in his history, the Whig coup of 1688). As well as discourse on fashion, shopping, street lighting, and the taste for scandal and rumour, Macaulay dwells on the coffee-house, which was, he thought, the most characteristic social innovation of the period.

> The coffee house must not be dismissed with a cursory mention. It might indeed at that time have been improperly called a most important political institution. No Parliament had sat for years. The municipal council of the City had ceased to speak the sense of the citizens. Public meetings, harangues, resolutions, and the rest of the modern machinery of agitation had not yet come into fashion. In such circumstances, the coffee houses were the chief organs though which the public opinion of the metropolis vented itself. These gregarious habits had no small share in forming

20. David Hume, *The History of Great Britain. Vol. II. Containing the Commonwealth, and the Reigns of Charles II. and James II.* (London, A. Millar, 1757), p. 245; Catherine Macaulay Graham, *The History of England from the Accession of James I to the Revolution [of 1688],* 8 vols (London, A. Hamilton, 1763–83), vol. VII (1781), p. 31.

21. 'Historical Anecdotes reflecting Coffee', *The Literary Magazine, and British Review,* IV, (April 1790), pp. 247–50; C., 'The Coffee-Room, No. 1', *The Universal Magazine,* n.s. VII (March 1807), pp. 205–7; C., 'The Coffee-Room, No. 2', *The Universal Magazine,* n.s. VII (April 1807), pp. 314–17; 'Coffee and Chocolate', *The Cabinet; or, Monthly Report of Polite Literature,* III (May 1808), pp. 312–17. Nostalgia for the decline of the coffee-houses is seen in William Hazlitt, 'On Coffee-House Politicians' (1822), in *The Selected Writings of William Hazlitt,* ed. by Duncan Wu, 9 vols (London, Pickering & Chatto, 1998), vol. VI, pp. 170–82.

22. Isaac D'Israeli, 'Introduction of Tea, Coffee and Chocolate', *Curiosities of Literature,* 3 vols (London, John Murray, 1817), vol. III, pp. 365–80; p. 374.

23. Thomas Babington Macaulay, *The History of England from the Accession of James the Second,* 4 vols (London, Longman, Browne, Green and Longmans, 1849–1855), vol. I, pp. 366–70.

the character of the Londoner of that age. He was, indeed, a different being from the rustic Englishman.

After this introduction, Macaulay spends several pages investigating the phenomenon of the coffee-house, noting the first to be established, their utilisation in daily life, their ubiquity, variety and smokiness, and finally, the fondness for them shown by writers and critics: all this before he segues into his next topic, the rivalry between the city and the country. In these pages Macaulay has offered a substantial prose portrait of the coffee-house as a symbol of eighteenth-century city life, and as such, located the coffee-house at the heart of Whig historiography.

There are many reasons to object to the facts as Macaulay presents them (not least his suggestion that the coffee-houses were not scenes of agitation and harangue in 1685). Nonetheless, what is innovative here is Macaulay's methodology: firstly his richly-detailed social history – his study of manners – offered in support of an argument that was essentially political; and secondly, his use of sources. Eighteenth-century coffee-house history practiced by the virtuosi of the Royal Society relied on a useful but limited set of materials, especially the first-hand evidence derived from the recollections of early coffee-men and coffee-drinkers (as collected by Houghton and Douglas and 'remembered' by Wood). By the early nineteenth century, the chance to collect such evidence had long gone, but in its place historians had new tools and techniques. New kinds of evidence about coffee-houses were found in contemporary diaries, such as those by John Evelyn and Samuel Pepys, first published in 1818 and 1825 respectively.[24] But Macaulay's most innovative research was his reading of the popular literature of the late seventeenth century in the British Museum. A long footnote supplies a list of those he found relevant: alongside some biographies of statesmen, he also notes a series of short vulgar satires, such as Ned Ward's *London Spy* (1698–1700) and *The Character of a Coffee House* (1673).[25]

Macaulay's approach to the coffee-houses, and his perception of their role in shaping the manners of the age, changed the way they were represented thereafter: they became a favourite topic in Whig social history.[26] Coffee-houses were rehabilitated in the cause of English national identity, which proposed the coffee-house and the club as the best expression of the nation's manners, those core values of gentility, politeness and civility. Coffee-houses were lauded in this way in an influential review article on the history of club-life in London, published

24. *Memoirs Illustrative of the Life and Writings of John Evelyn*, ed. by William Bray (London, Henry Colburn, 1818); *Memoirs of Samuel Pepys comprising his Diary from 1659 to 1669*, ed. by Richard Braybrooke (London, Henry Colburn, 1825).

25. *The Character of a Coffee-House* appears in this volume, pp. 81–90. For Macaulay's bibliography on coffee houses, see *History of England*, pp. 368–9n.

26. Bill Schwarz, '*Philosophes* of the Conservative Nation: Burke, Macaulay, Disraeli', *Journal of Historical Sociology*, 12:3 (1999), pp. 183–217.

in 1857 in the Unitarian journal *The National Review*. The writer of this essay, cited by Habermas, was Tom Taylor (1817–80), described as the leading comic playwright of the day, and also a prodigious writer of columns in *Punch* and popular comic journals. A genial review of some genial books, Taylor's article is not driven by argument as much as sentiment: nonetheless, to him, the coffee-house was above all a convivial and pleasant location: 'To these coffee-houses men of all classes, who had either leisure or money, resorted to spend both; and in them politics, play, scandal, criticism, and business, went on hand in hand'.[27]

The first monograph coffee-house histories were undertaken in the wake of Macaulay, perhaps answering Tom Taylor's opening gambit, a call for a history of clubs. 'The history of London Clubs', he declared, 'is the history of London manners'.[28] The same spirit of gentlemanly antiquarianism is seen in the first coffee-house history, written by the omnivorous hack John Timbs (1801–75), published as the second volume of his encyclopaedic *Club Life of London* in 1866.[29] Timbs offers an exhaustive survey of coffee-houses derived from a wide variety of archival and anecdotal sources, organised to focus on the particular, with an eye for the eccentric and the peculiar – both a history of the coffee-house and a defence of the model of gentlemanly politeness advanced by *The Spectator*. If Timbs has a theory of the coffee-house – and it is hard to tell amongst this barrage of detail and anecdote – it is that Whig version preferred by Macaulay: coffee-houses are the location for egalitarian and convivial gentlemanly sociability.[30] Timbs was followed by other antiquarian historians using a similar gentlemanly language: most notably the young schoolmaster Edward Forbes Robinson in 1893, in his *The Early History of the Coffee-Houses in England*;[31] but also the

27. Tom Taylor, 'The Clubs of London', *National Review*, 4:8 (April 1857), pp. 295–334; p. 302. Attribution from the Martineau file, in the University of Reading Library, compiled by Russell Martineau, son of James and himself a contributor. Walter Houghton (ed.), *Wellesley Index to Victorian Periodicals*, 5 vols (Toronto, University of Toronto Press, 1979), vol. III, pp. 135–60. See also Richard D. Fulton, '*The National Review* (1855)', in *British Literary Magazines: The Victorian and Edwardian Age, 1837–1913*, ed. by Alvin Sullivan (Westport, CN, Greenwood Press, 1984), pp. 236–42.

28. Taylor, 'The Clubs of London', p. 295.

29. John Timbs, *Club Life of London with Anecdotes of the Clubs, Coffee-Houses and Taverns of the Metropolis During the 17th, 18th, and 19th Centuries*, 2 vols (London, Richard Bentley, 1866).

30. See Timbs's biography in *ODNB*. See also *The Times*, Saturday 6 March 1875, p. 5: 'the worthy and painstaking antiquary John Timbs ... has died in harness, almost with his pen in his hand ... Though not gifted with any great original powers he was one of the most industrious of men'.

31. Edward Forbes Robinson, *The Early History of the Coffee-Houses in England: with some account of the first use of coffee and a bibliography of the subject* (London, Kegan Paul, Trench, Trübner & Co., 1893). Robinson was 29 years old when the book was published, employed at Haverford West Grammar School, having graduated from Cambridge with a BA in 1886, and a third-class degree in the Theology Tripos in 1886. This was his only published book: he subsequently emigrated to South Africa, working as a school-teacher until his death in 1921. *Biographical History of Gonville and Caius College: 1349–1897. Vol II. Admissions 1713–1897*, comp. by John Venn (Cambridge, the University Press, 1898), p. 467.

histories of taverns written by the retired stock-broker Edward Callow in 1899 and Henry Shelley in 1909.[32]

The antiquarian research was consolidated by a parade of popular social historians. John Ashton (fl. 1882–1904) brought an antiquarian's habits of scholarship to his history of the social life of the reign of Queen Anne in 1882, describing the coffee-house as 'the centre for news, the lounge of the idler, the rendezvous for appointments, the mart for businessmen … They were alike the haunt of the wit and the man of fashion – a neutral meeting-ground for all men, although they naturally assorted themselves, like to like, by degrees'. An appendix to his book lists the names of more than 500 coffee-houses, drawn, he says, from the newspapers and 'light literature' of the eighteenth century, but without references.[33] In this way coffee-houses became a standard topic of histories of the early eighteenth century. William Henry Davenport Adams (1828–91), in his *Good Queen Anne; or, men and manners, life and letters in England's Augustan age*, remarked that 'The Coffee-Houses played so prominent a part in the literary life of London *sub tempore Annæ*, that some reference to them is indispensable', before going on to give nearly fifteen pages to their description.[34]

In this kind of historical writing, the evidence of the quotidian world of the coffee-house was primarily drawn from literary evidence: satires, burlesques, lampoons, including those by Ned Ward and Tom Brown, but also numerous anonymous seventeenth-century hacks. The literariness of these works was often down-played, suppressed or ignored. But in the work of literary critics of the same period, the close links between the coffee-houses and the literary world came to have creative force. In his posthumously published lectures on eighteenth-century literature, Leslie Stephen (1832–1904) argued that there is a 'necessary connection between the social and the literary departments of history'. Stephen recognised – somewhat wearily – that 'One of the familiar features of the day, we know, was the number of coffee-houses'. For him coffee-houses were the model and example of his necessary connection between social and literary history. He noted how the coffee-houses facilitated 'the

32. Edward Callow, *Old London Taverns: historical, descriptive and reminiscent with some account of the coffee houses, clubs etc.* (London, Downey & Co, 1899); Henry Shelley, *Inns and Taverns of Old London setting forth the historical and literary associations of those ancient hostelries, together with an account of the most notable coffee-houses, clubs, and pleasure gardens of the British metropolis* (London, Sir Isaac Pitman & Sons, 1909). Also see John Timbs, *Clubs and Club Life in London with Anecdotes of its famous coffee houses, hostelries, and taverns from the seventeenth century to the present time* [a new edn with 41 illustrations] (London, Chatto & Windus, 1908).

33. John Ashton, *Social Life in the Reign of Queen Anne, taken from original sources*, 2 vols (London, Chatto & Windus, 1882), vol. I, p. 214; vol. II, pp. 262–8.

34. W. H. Davenport Adams, *Good Queen Anne; or, men and manners, life and letters in England's Augustan age*, 2 vols (London, Remington & Co., 1886), vol. II, ch. 6: 'The Coffee-Houses and Clubs, etc.', pp. 357–73; p. 357. William Connor Sydney, *Social Life in England from the Restoration to the Revolution 1660–1690* (London, Ward and Downey, 1892), pp. 409–24.

characteristic fraternization of the politicians and the authors', an effect with important and far-reaching consequences he felt. The result was something he identifies as 'the town', a commonality of opinion created within the conversations, debates and correspondences between coffee-houses, clubs, literary journals, in their collective judgements on literature and politics. As Stephen says, 'The "town" was the environment of the wits who produced the literature generally called after Queen Anne. We may call it the literary organ of the society.'[35]

Stephen's lead was taken up by Harold Victor Routh (1878–1951), then a young lecturer at Goldsmith's College of the University of London. In his chapter on Steele and Addison for the early eighteenth-century volume in *The Cambridge History of English Literature* published in 1913, Routh pursued Stephen's suggestion that Steele finds in the coffee-house the 'world of thought', exploring the coffee-house's role in the new social consciousness of urban life. Like Macaulay, to whom he refers directly, Routh finds the coffee-house the most striking feature of London life.

> Men who gathered day after day in these resorts were not only interested in their companions' ideas and demeanour; they cultivated an eye for trivial actions and utterances, a gift for investigating other people's prejudices and partialities, and they realized the pleasure of winning their way into the intricacies of another man's mind. Hence, they acquired a new attitude towards their fellow creatures.

The coffee-houses, Routh suggested, acted as an agent of social reformation: through them

> the middle classes were accomplishing their own education. They were becoming thinkers with a culture and a standard of manners born of conversation and free from pedantry of thought or expression. Coffeehouses had given them a kind of organisation; a means of exchanging ideas and forming the public opinion of their class ... Coffee-houses had unconsciously become fraternities for the propagation of a new humanism.

Routh argues that Steele's innovation in *The Tatler* is to appeal to the coffee-house clientele as an audience for politeness, rather than for sedition, pedantry or vulgarity. Steele 'knew how confused and misguided their political discussions often were, thanks to the irresponsible news-sheets which flooded London': Routh argues that his account of the coffee-houses is in this way a wilful revision of the lived reality of the coffee-house so as to represent them, or remember them, as the location of polite, rational, public discourse.[36]

35. Stephen, *English Literature and Society in the Eighteenth Century,* pp. 5, 37, 39.
36. H. V. Routh, 'Steele and Addison', *From Steele and Addison to Pope and Swift*, in *The Cambridge History of English Literature, vol. IX* (Cambridge, Cambridge University Press, 1913), pp. 31, 33, 35.

The culmination of this approach to the coffee-house history was that of George Macaulay Trevelyan (1876–1962) in his enormously popular three-volume social history *England Under Queen Anne*, first published between 1930 and 1934. The nephew of Thomas Babington Macaulay, Trevelyan made considerable use of his uncle's work in his social history writing, including his taste for literary evidence of everyday life. Appointed to the Regius chair at Cambridge in 1927, Trevelyan wrote his social history of Queen Anne as an act of Whig resistance to German fascism, celebrating historically-enduring Whig myths of English liberty and prosperity. The coffee-houses, which he describes as 'the centre of social life', are emblematic of these grand themes:

> The 'universal liberty of speech of the English nation' [an unsourced quotation from John Macky, 1714[37]] uttered amid clouds of tobacco smoke, with equal vehemence whether against the Government and the Church, or against their enemies, had long been the wonder of foreigners; it was the quintessence of Coffee House life.

The coffee-house represents the golden age of gentlemanly conviviality: informal, egalitarian, inclusive, rational. As Trevelyan suggests 'The Coffee House filled the place now occupied by the Club, but in a more cheap and informal manner, and with greater admission of strangers. In days when men stood much on their rank, it had a levelling influence.'[38] Through the coffee-house's close association with political and commercial news, Trevelyan places it in the centre of his whiggish defence of English civic virtues. The book, written against the rise of the Nazi threat, was revised to serve the war effort in the 1940s, when the coffee-house example was incorporated almost verbatim in his later *English Social History: a survey of six centuries from Chaucer to Queen Victoria* (1942). Paper shortages meant the first edition, now described as celebrating the values of 'the common cause' between Britain and America, was printed in New York in 1942, with several further editions in successive years in Britain from 1944. The book's considerable influence over the post-war period led to its translation into German in 1948, the edition consulted by Habermas.[39]

These acts of history writing remember the coffee-house in a particular way, memorialising it as a normative expression of English good manners and civility. The fondness for the reign of Queen Anne in the Whig school of social history paints the early eighteenth century as an idyllic Augustan age, an island of civility and politeness, contrasted with the smoky mechanical vulgarity of the industrialised age of the nineteenth and twentieth centuries. The Whig histori-

37. John Macky, *A Journey Through England. In familiar letters. From a gentleman here, to his friend abroad* (London, J. Roberts for T. Caldecott, 1714), p. 208.

38. George Macaulay Trevelyan, *England Under Queen Anne: Blenheim* (London, Longmans, Green and Co., 1930).

39. George Macaulay Trevelyan, *Kultur- und sozialgeschichte Englands: ein ruckblick auf sechs jahrhunderte von Chaucer bis Queen Victoria* (Hamburg, Claassen & Goverts, 1948).

ans' pastoral recapitulation of the coffee-house re-imagines the period as good-natured, egalitarian and sociable; an act of remembering that shears off the recalcitrant complexity of coffee-house history, where the coffee-house was equally the home of sedition, sectarian strife, domestic spies, incendiary rhetoric, dissension and discord. It is this version of the coffee-house that Habermas appeals to in his public sphere argument.

The rise of the coffee-house

The coffee-house, and also the practice of drinking coffee, are comparatively recent innovations. The origin of coffee-drinking is an event outside history: the first records of the practice refer to the southern regions of the Arabian peninsula in the early fourteenth century, although it can be conjectured that the people of Ethiopia had knowledge of the coffee bean and the coffee shrub some centuries before that. The Ottoman, and before that, the Arab, history of coffee relies on little firm evidence (edicts and opinions given by jurists and judges on the legality of its consumption), alongside some oft-repeated fables. What hard evidence there is suggests that as a beverage, coffee was first consumed by Sufis living in Yemen, in the southern reaches of the Arabian peninsula (the area known since the classical period as Arabia Felix).[40] In the fourteenth century, the Sufi adopted coffee consumption into their religious ceremonies, for they found that its propensity to keep them awake helped incite their mystical raptures. A legal opinion dated to 1438 records that coffee was being consumed in Aden, while another implies that coffee was known in Mecca by the end of the fifteenth century. As with the Sufi, coffee was primarily a medicinal simple that enabled the pious and the studious to stay awake during their devotions. Other Arabic documents confirm the spread of coffee drinking beyond the Arabian peninsula in the sixteenth century. Coffee is known to have been consumed in Cairo in the first decade of the sixteenth century by Sufis inhabiting the Azhar quarter of the city. As well as legal judgements, coffee was the subject of essays, dissertations and even poems considering its effects. This Ottoman discourse on coffee – the best guide to which is Ralph Hattox's *Coffee and Coffeehouses: the origins of a social beverage in the Medieval Near East* (1988) – was not unknown to eighteenth-century scholarship.[41] For example, a copy of Abdalcader Alanzari's legal judgement on coffee written in the year 996 Hegira, or AD 1587, was purchased by the Marquis de Nointel while he was the French Ambassador to the Ottoman court in 1672, and on his return from Istanbul in 1679 was deposited in the *Bibliotheque du Roy* of Louis XIV. The document discussed the etymology of

40. Cornelis Van Arendonk, 'Kahwa', in *Encyclopaedia of Islam*, 12 vols (Leiden, E.J. Brill, 1954–2005).
41. Ralph Hattox, *Coffee and Coffeehouses: the origins of a social beverage in the Medieval Near East* (Seattle, University of Washington Press, 1988).

the word *Cahouah* (coffee), its properties and history, surveyed the religious controversy on its legality in Islamic law, and finished with a collection of verses in praise of coffee.[42] The manuscript was subsequently translated into French by the Arabic scholar and traveller Antoine Galland, later author of *The Thousand and One Nights* (1704–17). Galland's translation formed the basis of his treatise *De L'Origine et du Progrez du Café,* published in a small edition in Caen in 1699, which became central evidence in subsequent treatises on coffee by the French travel writer Jean de La Roque in 1716, and the Scottish physician James Douglas in 1727 (see Volume 4).[43] By this method then, Arabic coffee lore was brought to the Europe of the Enlightenment.

Businesses dedicated to retailing fresh roasted coffee drink were unknown in Istanbul until the year 1554 (962 Hegira) during the reign of Suleiman the Magnificent (1520–66), according to the Turkish historian Ibrahim-I Peçevi (also translated by James Douglas). Peçevi stated that 'two Men, nam'd *Schems* and *Hekim*, the one from *Damascus*, the other from *Aleppo*, set up each of them a Coffee-House in that Quarter of *Constantinople* call'd *Takhtacalah*'. Situated near a bustling *kapan* or market near the port and the Rustem Pasa mosque, their coffee houses were 'furnish'd with very neat Couches and Carpets, on which they receiv'd their Company', attracting a clientele of 'studious Persons, Lovers of Chess, Trictrac [an early form of backgammon], and other sedentary Diversions; and as the generality of the Turks came soon to relish this sort of Meeting-Places, call'd in their Language *Cahveh Kaneh*, the number of them multiplied insensibly'. The Kahveh Kaneh of Istanbul sold coffee and sociability, especially associated, Peçevi argued, with knowledge workers and indolence: students, professors, and out of work *kadis* (judges).[44]

In the Christian West, coffee came to notice first amongst men of science and merchants, especially those with a direct connection to or interest in the Ottoman lands. In London, the renowned physician William Harvey, famous for his account of the circulation of the blood, was one of the first habitual drinkers of coffee in London, from perhaps as early as 1627, receiving supplies of coffee from his brothers, Daniel and Eliab, who were established members of the Levant Company.[45] By 1630 it is probable that London merchants trad-

---

42. Al-Shaykh Abd al-Câder Ibn Mohammad al-Ansârî al-Djazîrî al-Hanbali, 'Umdat al-Safwa fi hilli al-qahwa', Bibliotheque Nationale, MSS Arabe, No. 971.

43. Antoine Galland, *De L'Origine et du Progrez du Café* (Caen, Jean Cavelier; Paris, Florentin & Pierre Delaulne, 1699); Jean La Roque, *Voyage de L'Arabie Heureuse* (Paris, André Cailleau, 1716), trans. by Jean de La Roque, *A Voyage to Arabia the Happy* (London, G. Strahan and R. Williamson, 1726), pp. 217–306 (see Volume 4, pp. 277–312); James Douglas, *A Supplement to the Description of the Coffee-Tree* (London, Thomas Woodward, 1727), pp. 12–21 (Volume 4, pp. 219–76; pp. 234–43).

44. Douglas, *Supplement*. For a modern translation see Bernard Lewis, *Istanbul and the Civilisation of the Ottoman Empire* (Norman, OK, University of Oklahoma Press, 1963), pp. 132–3.

45. Louis Chauvois, *William Harvey: his life and times: his discoveries: his methods* (London, Hutchinson Medical Publications, 1957), p. 173; Geoffrey Keynes, 'Harvey's Use of Coffee', in *The Life of William Harvey* (Oxford, Clarendon Press, 1966), pp. 406–9.

ing with the Ottoman Empire were privately importing small quantities of coffee, primarily for consumption within their own circles. John Evelyn wrote (in 1697) that he remembered that in 1637, a Greek Orthodox priest, Nathaniel Conopios, studied at Balliol College, Oxford, where he 'was the first that I ever saw drink *Caffe*', suggesting that it was already possible to purchase the product for domestic consumption. As he remarked, coffee was 'not heard of then in England, nor til many yeares after made a common entertainment all over the nation'.[46] Merchants trading with Ottoman ports in other cities in Europe, such as Venice, Leghorn, Marseilles and Amsterdam are also likely to have developed a domestic taste for coffee.[47]

The first coffee-house in Christian Europe, however, opened in London at some time between 1652 and 1654 (most plausibly 1652), in a simple shed in the churchyard of St Michael's in Cornhill, at the centre of London's commercial community. It was opened at the behest of a Levant Company trader, Daniel Edwards, who had recently returned from Smyrna (Izmir) in Anatolia, where he had been his family's chief representative in the trade in silks and fine woollen textiles. When returned he brought with him a young man called Pasqua Rosee, probably a Greek Orthodox Christian from Ragusa (Dubrovnik), who acted as his clerk, valet and agent. In London they spied an opportunity to open a retail coffee shop: some commentators have suggested they were motivated by the numbers of their acquaintances who came to their shop to drink coffee gratis,[48] while it is equally possible that the particular historical moment of 1652 in London suggested something new might work (the puritan government of the English Republic actively campaigned against drunkenness and public houses, while the depressed economic climate perhaps promoted innovatory retail opportunities).[49] Using Rosee's specialist knowledge of coffee preparation, and Edwards's connections in the Levant trade, their coffee-shop in St Michael's Alley soon became well known amongst merchants and traders on the Royal Exchange (London's bourse). The business was not initially a grand affair: the shed might have had a pentice shutter to shelter under, and a brazier to heat water. Their business also came to the notice of a young virtuoso, the term then widely used to describe a gentleman interested in scientific matters. William Brereton, an enthusiast for experimental science

    46. John Evelyn, 'De Vita Propria' (1697), in *The Diary of John Evelyn*, ed. by E.S. de Beer, 6 vols (Oxford, Clarendon Press, 1955), vol. I, pp. 14–15.

    47. La Roque, *Voyage to Arabia*, pp. 280–1.

    48. William Oldys, 'Notes on Trees', BL Add. MS 20724, fol. 90r.

    49. *General Sessions of the Publick Peace holden for the City of London 16 August 1654*: CLRO: Alchin Coll. Box H/103.(7) [printed]; David Underdown, *Revel, Riot, and Rebellion: popular politics and culture in England, 1603–1660* (Oxford, Clarendon Press, 1985), pp. 268–9; Christopher Durston, 'Puritan Rule and the Failure of Cultural Revolution, 1645–1660', in *The Culture of English Puritanism, 1560–1700*, ed. by Christopher Durston and Jacqueline Easles (Houndsmills, Basingstoke, Macmillan Press, 1996), pp. 210–33.

and novelties in trade, informed the intelligencer Samuel Hartlib (*c.* 1600–62) on 4 August 1654 that 'A cuphye-house or a Turkish – as it were – Ale-house is erected near the Old Exchange' in Cornhill. Hartlib operated the most extensive network of scientific correspondence in the period, collecting information in his *Ephemerides*, a unique archival database. This 'cophye-house drinke', Hartlib noted, was 'a Turkish-kind of drink made of water and some berry or Turkish-beane ... It is somewhat hot and unpleasant but [has] a good after relish and caused some breaking of wind in abundance'.[50] The coffee retailing business soon outgrew this simple shed. By 1656, the partnership opened a more permanent coffee-house across the alley, in a building owned by the churchwardens of St Michael's Church (so leaving records in the vestry minutes of leases and parish business).[51] The new coffee-house had a substantial coffee-room located up one pair of stairs. After Rosee had to leave the business (perhaps because as an alien he was disqualified from trading in the City), he was replaced by another of Edwards's apprentices, Christopher Bowman, although the coffee-house continued to trade under Pasqua Rosee's sign-board. A one-page advertising handbill, probably folded up and enclosed in parcels of retail coffee beans, was entitled *The Vertue of the Coffee Drink. First publiquely made and sold in England, by Pasqua Rosee*: it explained the authentic Ottoman method of preparing the beans, and made a series of extravagant medical claims for the drink's properties. At the bottom of the page it explained that coffee is 'Made and Sold in *St. Michael's Alley* in *Cornhill*, by *Pasqua Rosee*, at the Signe of his own Head'.[52]

Coffee-houses modelled on Rosee's soon spread across the city. A survey made by the magistrates in May 1663 recorded that there were 82 coffee-houses in the City alone, with no fewer than six in Cornhill ward all competing for the same customers. The Rainbow Coffee-house was in operation by 1657, when the Wardmote inquest book of the parish of St Dunstan's recorded that James Ffarr, a barber, was presented for causing annoyance to his neighbours from the 'evil smells' and fire associated with coffee-making.[53] During the final years of the English republic, the coffee-houses became firmly associated with the tumultuous political culture of the Commonwealth. Thomas Rugg, a barber of Covent Garden, wrote in his *Diurnal* in 1659 that 'theire ware also att

50. Samuel Hartlib, *Ephemerides*, No. 254, 4 August 1654, *The Hartlib Papers*, 2nd edn (Sheffield, HROnline, Humanities Research Institute, 2002), HP 29/4/29A–B.

51. Vestry Minutes (Guildhall Library MS 04072), Churchwardens' Accounts (Guildhall Library MS 04071), and a contemporary copy-book of the deeds and leases of the church property (Guildhall Library MS 04083). See Markman Ellis, 'Pasqua Rosee and the First English Coffee House', *London Journal*, 29:1 (2004), pp. 1–25.

52. *The Vertue of the Coffee Drink. First publiquely made and sold in England, by Pasqua Rosee* ([London], n.p., [1666?]). BL: C.20.f2.(372).

53. Wardmote Inquest Book, St Dunstans in the West, Guildhall Library, MS 3018/1. Monday 21 December 1657.

this time a Turkish drink to bee sould, almost in evry street, called coffee'.[54] James Harrington held the meetings of his famous Rota Club at the Turk's Head Coffee-house in New Palace Yard, Westminster, in the last months of the republic, where they debated around a specially-constructed table provided by the proprietor, Miles.[55] As one of the few social or political innovations of the Interregnum to survive virtually unaltered into the Restoration, the coffee-house to many contemporaries seemed to have been strongly marked by the Republic. Yet the coffee-houses were also quickly subsumed into Restoration institutions. The Excise Act of 1660, modelled on the system established by Parliament during the Interregnum, had extended the excise to coffee (along with tea and chocolate), with the tax being levied on coffee-house keepers.[56] But although Royal revenues relied on the coffee-house, Royalist commentators continued to associate the coffee-houses with republican London. John Evelyn, writing in May 1659, thought them a clear sign of London's republican depravity. The city was, he said, 'a very ugly Town, pestred with *Hackney-Coaches*', a 'pestilent Smoak', and obsessed and 'universally besotted' by coffee and tobacco: it was 'most deplorable', he continued, that 'the gentlemen sit, and spend much of their time ... drinking of a muddy kind of *Beverage*, and *Tobacco*'.[57]

Coffee-houses soon spread to other cities with close connections to London: Oxford, Cambridge, Bristol, Yarmouth, Amsterdam, Hamburg, Boston.[58] In Oxford, for example, the apothecary Arthur Tillyard opened an establishment selling coffee on the High Street opposite All Souls in 1655 or 1656: accord-

54. *The Diurnal of Thomas Rugg, 1659–1661*, ed. by William L. Sachse, Camden Third Series, vol. 91 (London, Offices of the Royal Historical Society, 1961), pp. 29, 10.

55. Aubrey, *Brief Lives*, p. 136. See also Markman Ellis, *Coffee-House*, ch. 4.

56. 12 Car. II (1660): A Grant of Certain Impositions upon Beer, Ale and other Liquors, For the Encrease of His Majesties Revenue during his Life.

57. John Evelyn [?], *A Character of England. As it was lately presented in a letter, to a noble man of France* (London, Jo. Crooke, 1659), pp. 28–9.

58. It has often been claimed that the first coffee-house opened in Oxford in 1650, although there is no positive evidence – such as building leases or licenses issued by regulatory authorities – to back up the assertion. The claim rests on the antiquarian writings of Anthony Wood: in 1671, he wrote in his diary that public coffee-selling was initiated in Oxford in 1650 (a trade in coffee-beans that had by then been active in London amongst Levant company circles for decades). In the earliest version of Wood's diary, written up to the end of 1659, Wood claims that coffee was first consumed in private in Oxford in 1650 and, at an unstated date between 10 August 1654 and 25 April 1655, he claims that coffee was 'publickly solde at or neare the Angel within the East Gate of Oxon ... by an outlander or a Jew' ('The Diarie of the Life of Anthony à Wood Historiographer and Antiquarie', BL Harley MS 5409, fol. 43). In 1671, Wood redrafted his diary, now called his 'Secretum Antonii' (in the Bodleian Library), now claiming that that 'Jacob a Jew opened a coffey house at the Angel in the parish of S. Peter, in the East Oxon' (without supplying a date), and that 'When he left Oxon he sold it in Old Southampton buildings in Holborne neare London', a building first constructed in 1664 (*Life and Times of Anthony Wood, antiquary, at Oxford, 1632–1695*, ed. by Andrew Clark, 5 vols (Oxford, Clarendon Press, 1891–1900), vol. I, pp. 168–9). In the late nineteenth century, this undated addition was conjecturally dated by Wood's editor Andrew Clark at 'March 1650/51', but there is no evidence to support this earlier date.

ing to the garrulous antiquarian Anthony Wood, 'He was encouraged so to do by som royallists, now living in Oxon, and by others who esteem'd themselves either *virtuosi* or *wits*', offering these men space for their Chemical Club for the practice of the new experimental science.[59] In later decades, Paris (1671), Venice (1683) and Vienna (1684) also saw the establishment of coffee-houses. In Europe and America, the coffee-house idea was established on an English model, later transmuted into the café in France, the caffè in Italy, and the kaffee-haus in Vienna, each of which developed their own distinct character.

By the end of the seventeenth century, coffee-houses were numerous in London and, although precise figures are difficult to estimate, contemporary observers were quick to make the computation. In 1714, John Macky noted that coffee-houses were 'innumerable', before going on to make the 'modest Computation' that there were 'above Eight Thousand of them ... in and about *London*'.[60] Ephraim Chambers, in his *Cyclopaedia* of 1727, 'computed' that there were 'three thousand Coffee-houses' in London alone, as had Edward Hatton in 1708.[61] The estimate that there were two to three thousand is of course a guess, but one that has often been followed by twentieth-century historians.[62] A more accurate estimate would suggest a number closer to four to five hundred, which is, of course, still a substantial number for a city of around half a million people.[63] In 1739, the topographer and historian William Maitland quantified the number in his topographical survey for his *History of London*, compiled over eleven months with 'unwearied Application' and 'incredible Pains' by walking every street, square, lane and alley in the city. Maitland counted a total of 551 coffee-houses, concentrated especially in comparatively

59. 'The Diarie of the Life of Anthony à Wood', fol. 45. See also *The Life and Times of Anthony Wood*, vol. I, p. 201. Norma Aubertin-Potter and Alyx Bennet, *Oxford Coffee Houses, 1651–1800* (Oxford, Hampden Press, 1987).

60. Macky, *A Journey Through England*, p. 208.

61. Ephraim Chambers, *Cyclopaedia or an Universal Dictionary of Arts and Sciences*, 2 vols (London, James and John Knapton, 1727), vol. I, p. 246; Edward Hatton, *A New View of London, or, an ample account of that city* (London, John Nicholson, 1708), vol. I, p. 30.

62. The figure of 3,000 is stated by Walter Besant, *London in the Eighteenth Century* (London, Adam & Charles Black, 1902), p. 308; Leslie Stephen, *English Literature and Society in the Eighteenth Century* (1903; London, Methuen & Co, 1966), p. 22; Jürgen Habermas, *Structural Transformation*, p. 32; Pat Rogers (ed.), *The Eighteenth Century: the context of English literature* (London, Methuen, 1978), p. 46; and E. J. Clery, 'Women, Publicity and the Coffee-House Myth', *Women: a cultural review*, 2:2 (1991), pp. [168]–77; p. 169. The figure of 2,000 is stated by Aytoun Ellis, *The Penny Universities: a history of the coffee-houses* (London, Secker & Warburg, 1956), p. xiv; and Peter Stallybrass and Allon White, *The Politics and Poetics of Transgression* (London, Methuen, 1986), p. 95. Bryant Lillywhite's *London Coffee-Houses* identifies 2,033 different coffee-houses that operated between the mid-seventeenth and mid-nineteenth centuries, but many of these were short-lived businesses of which only a subset were ever open at the same time.

63. John Ashton collected a list of about 500 coffee-houses mentioned in newspapers during the reign of Queen Anne (John Ashton, *Social Life in the Reign of Queen Anne* (London, Chatto & Windus 1882), Appendix B; see also George Rudé, *Hanoverian London 1714–1808* (London, Secker & Warburg, 1971), p. 77.

prosperous parts of town, especially the City, St James's, and in the corridor between the two around Covent Garden and Fleet Street.[64] By comparison, districts such as Wapping, Southwark, and the area outside the walls between Moorgate and Whitechapel, where large numbers of poorer people lived, had few coffee-houses and an enormous number of gin shops and taverns.

London remained famous for the number of its coffee-houses until the nineteenth century. A German traveller, Johann Wilhelm von Archenholz, visiting London in 1788 commented

> The English live in a very remarkable manner. They rise late, and spend most of the morning, either in walking about town or sitting in the coffee-houses. There they not only read the newspapers, but transact business. Associations, insurances, bets, the trade in foreign bills; all these things are not only talked of, but executed in these public places. They there form connections, conclude bargains, talk of the intrigues and the cabals of court, criticise works of genius and art, and enter into patriotic resolutions concerning the good of the state.[65]

Nonetheless, in the same period, per capita consumption of coffee had remained stable or declined, while that of tea increased rapidly. Coffee quality, never high in England, became notoriously poor. Another German visitor, Charles Motitz, complained

> I would always advise those who wish to drink coffee in England, to mention before hand how many cups are to be made with half an ounce; or else the people will probably bring them a prodigious quantity of brown water.[66]

Despite the peevish edge to Moritz's complaint, poor quality coffee may be the answer to the decline of the coffee-house in the late eighteenth century. Coffee consumption was eclipsed by tea during the latter half of the eighteenth century.[67] The relative decline of coffee, and the unprecedented rise of tea drinking, reflects macroeconomic changes in the global economy in luxury beverages. By this period, the market for coffee was international: competition for Arabian coffee was offered by coffee from European colonies in the West Indies and South

---

64. William Maitland, *The History of London, from its Foundation by the Romans, to the Present Time* (London, Samuel Richardson, 1739), bk II, pp. 519–20. There were about 300 cafés in Paris at this time, Thomas Brennan, *Public Drinking and Popular Culture in Eighteenth-Century Paris* (Princeton, NJ, Princeton University Press, 1988), pp. 86–7.

65. Johann Wilhelm von Archenholz, *A Picture of England: containing a description of the laws, customs and manners of England,* 2 vols (London, Edward Jeffery, 1789), pp. 105–6 (Volume 2, pp. 371–2).

66. Charles P. Moritz, *Travels, Chiefly on Foot, through Several parts of England, in 1782. Described in letters to a friend, by Charles P. Moritz, a literary gentleman of Paris, translated from the German, by a lady* (London, G. G. and J. Robinson, 1795), p. 26.

67. Elizabeth Boody Schumpeter, *English Overseas Trade Statistics* (Oxford, Oxford University Press, 1960), table XVIII.

East Asia.[68] Competition between coffee importers, and coffee-producing colonies, drove the coffee price low, and did not encourage high quality, whereas the near monopoly on tea imports enjoyed by the East India Company meant it was able to use its market dominance to guarantee quality, and its political influence to manipulate the system of tariff preferences so as to distort the trade. As coffee production in British colonies in the West Indies increased, taxes and tariffs were manipulated so as to make their trade less profitable. A vicious spiral resulted: low consumption led to a falling price of coffee, to which growers responded by using high-yield/low-cost cultivation techniques, further driving down the quality of the coffee on the market.[69]

The decline in the coffee-house in the late eighteenth century was apparent to many. Isaac D'Israeli noted in 1817 that 'The frequenting of coffee-houses is a custom which has declined within our recollection'. He ascribed this to increasing competition in the market for sociability: 'institutions of a higher character, and society itself' he said, have 'much improved within late years'. D'Israeli's nostalgia for the old coffee-houses – 'the common assemblies of all classes of society' – suggests not only that the golden age of the coffee-house had past, but that so too had the golden age of the idea of the coffee-house.[70] William Hazlitt lamented in 1826 that 'I never pass Covent Garden ... without thinking of all the old coffee-houses and the wits', where there had been, he added, a 'humane openness of intercourse': instead 'there are no such meetings now, and no coffee-room that looks as if it would suit them'.[71]

68. See John Ellis, *An Historical Account of Coffee* (London, Edward and Charles Dilly, 1774), in Volume 4, pp. 363–400.

69. Simon Smith, 'Accounting for Taste: British coffee consumption in historical perpsective', *Discussion Papers in Economics*, No. 14 (York, University of York, 1994), pp. 19–30.

70. D'Israeli, *Curiosities of Literature*, vol. III, p. 378.

71. William Hazlitt, 'Coffee-Houses and Smoking', *New Monthly Magazine and Literary Journal*, 16 (1826), pp. 50–2.

BIBLIOGRAPHY

'A Coffee-House Scene', *British Museum Quarterly*, 6:2 (1931/2), pp. 43–4

Adams, W. H. Davenport, *Good Queen Anne; or, men and manners, life and letters in England's Augustan age*, 2 vols (London, Remington & Co., 1886), vol. I, pp. xi–xxiii, 357–73

Allan, D. G. C., 'Coffee Houses, Taverns and Great Rooms: the homes and houses of the Society 1754–1957', *Royal Society of Arts Journal*, 146:5485 (1998), pp. 119–21

Alvaraz-Detrell, Tamara, 'Goldoni's View of Venetian Society: *La bottega de caffè*', *Language Quarterly*, 22:1–2 (Fall–Winter 1983), pp. 44–6

Andia, Beatrice de (ed.), *Paris et ses cafés* (Paris, Action artistique de la Ville de Paris, 2004)

Arendonk, C. van, 'Kahwa', in *Encyclopedia of Islam*, 12 vols (Leiden, E. J. Brill, 1954–2005)

Ashton, John, *Social Life in the Reign of Queen Anne* (London, Chatto & Windus, 1882), Appendix B

Bayles, William Harrison, *Old Taverns of New York* (New York, Frank Allaben Genealogical Company, 1915)

Berry, Helen, '"Nice and curious questions": Coffee houses and the representation of women in John Dunton's *Athenian Mercury*', *Seventeenth Century*, 12:2 (Fall 1997), pp. 257–76

—, 'An Early Coffee House Periodical and its Readers: the *Athenian Mercury*, 1691–1697', *London Journal*, 25:1 (2000), pp. 14–33

—, 'Rethinking Politeness in Eighteenth-Century England: Moll King's coffee house and the significance of "Flash Talk"', *Transactions of the Royal Historical Society*, 6th ser., IX (2002), pp. 65–81

—, *Gender, Society and Print Culture in Late-Stuart England: the cultural world of the 'Athenian Mercury'* (Aldershot, Hampshire, Ashgate, 2003)

Besant, Walter, *London in the Eighteenth Century* (London, Adam & Charles Black, 1902)

Bradshaw, Steve, *Café Society: Bohemian life from Swift to Bob Dylan* (London, Weidenfeld and Nicolson, 1978)

Braun, Stephen, *Buzz: the science and lore of alcohol and caffeine* (New York and Oxford, Oxford University Press, 1996)

Brennan, Thomas, *Public Drinking and Popular Culture in Eighteenth Century Paris* (Princeton, NJ, Princeton University Press, 1988)

Brown, Peter B., *In Praise of Hot Liquors: the study of chocolate, coffee and tea-drinking, 1600–1850* (York, York Civic Trust, 1995)

Calhoun, Craig, *Habermas and the Public Sphere* (Cambridge, MA, and London, MIT Press, 1992)

Castro, Jean Paul de, 'London Eighteenth-Century Coffee-Houses', *Notes and Queries*, 12th ser., 6 (January–June 1920), pp. 29, 59, 84, 105, 125, 143, 162; 7 (July–December 1920), ppp. 26, 67, 103, 145, 185, 464; 9 (July–December 1921), pp. 85, 105, 143, 186, 226, 286, 306, 385, 426, 504, 525; 10 (January–June 1922), pp. 26, 66, 102, 164, 202

Chaudhuri, K. N., *The Trading World of Asia and the English East India Company, 1660–1760* (Cambridge, Cambridge University Press, 1978)

Clarke, R. J., and R. Macrae (eds), *Coffee*, 6 vols (London, Elsevier Applied Science, 1988)

Clay, Mike, *Café Racers: rockers, rock'n'roll and the coffee-bar cult* (London, Osprey Publishing, 1988)

Clayton, Antony, *London's Coffee Houses, a stimulating story* (London, Historical Publications, 2003)

Clery, Emma, 'Women, Publicity and the Coffee-House Myth', *Women: a cultural review*, 2:2 (1991), pp. [168]–77

—, 'The *Athenian Mercury* and the Pindarick Lady', in *The Feminization Debate in the Eighteenth Century: Literature, Commerce and Luxury* (Basingstoke, Palgrave, 2004), ch. 2

Connery, Brain, 'IMHO: authority and egalitarian rhetoric in the virtual coffeehouse', in *Internet Culture*, ed. by David Porter (New York and London, Routledge, 1997), pp. 161–79

Cope, Jackson I., 'Honor among the Denizens of Goldoni's *Botteghe da caffè*', *Annali D'Italianistica*, 11 (1993), pp. 159–72

Cope, S. R., 'The Stock-Brokers Find a Home: how the Stock Exchange came to be established in Sweetings Alley in 1773', *Guildhall Studies in London History*, II:4 (April 1977), pp. 213–19

Cowan, Brian, 'What Was Masculine About the Public Sphere? Gender and the coffeehouse milieu in post-Restoration England', *History Workshop Journal*, 51 (February 2001), pp. 127–57

—, 'Mr. Spectator and the Coffeehouse Public Sphere', *Eighteenth-Century Studies*, 37:3 (2004), pp. 345–56

—, 'The Rise of the Coffeehouse Reconsidered', *Historical Journal*, 47:1 (2004), pp. 21–46

—, *The Social Life of Coffee: the emergence of the British coffeehouse* (New Haven and London, Yale University Press, 2005)

Dawson, Warren, 'The London Coffee-Houses and the Beginnings of Lloyd's', *The Journal of the British Archaeological Association*, n.s. 40 (1935), pp. 104–34

Deghy, Guy, and Keith Waterhouse, *Café Royal: ninety years of Bohemia* (London, Hutchinson, 1955)

Delle, James A., *An Archaeology of Space: analyzing coffee plantations in Jamaica's Blue Mountains* (New York, Plenum Press, 1998)

—, 'The Landscapes of Class Negotiation on Coffee Plantations in the Blue Mountains of Jamaica: 1790–1850', *Historical Archaeology*, 33:1 (1999), pp. 136–58

Dobranski, S. B., '"Where Men of Differing Judgments Croud": Milton and the culture of the coffee-houses', *Seventeenth Century*, 9:1 (1994), pp. 35–56

Eagleton, Terry, *The Function of Criticism: from the 'Spectator' to post-structuralism* (London, Verso, 1984)

Earle, Peter, *The Making of the English Middle Class: business, society and family life in London, 1600–1730* (London, Methuen 1989)

Ellis, Aytoun, *The Penny Universities: a history of the coffee-houses* (London, Secker & Warburg, 1956)

—, *No 15. Fleet St, 1657–1957: the coffee house story* (London, Augustine Press for the Coffee House Ltd, 1957)

Ellis, Markman, 'The Coffee-women, *The Spectator* and the Public Sphere in the Early-Eighteenth Century', in *Women and the Public Sphere*, ed. by Elizabeth Eger and Charlotte Grant (Cambridge, Cambridge University Press, 2001), pp. 27–52

—, 'The Coffee-house, a Discursive Model', in *A Coffee-House Conversation on the International Art World and its Exclusion*, ed. by Hatice Abdullah and Geoff Cox (http://www.kahve-house.com/society/, pdf format; London, Kahve-Society, 2002)

—, 'The Devil's Ordinary: consuming public culture in the coffee-house and the (re)invention of modern culture', *Cabinet Magazine* (New York), 8 (Fall 2002), pp. 28–33

—, 'Shipley's Study', *Royal Society of Arts Journal* (October 2003), pp. 32–5

—, 'Pasqua Rosee's Coffee House 1652–1666', *London Journal*, 29:1 (2004), pp. 1–25

—, *The Coffee House: a cultural history* (London, Weidenfeld & Nicolson, 2004)

Fenton, Alexander, 'Coffee-drinking in Scotland in the 17th–19th Centuries', in *Kaffee im Spiegel europäischer Trinksitten/Coffee in the Context of European*

Drinking Habits, ed. by Daniela Ball (Zurich, Johann Jacobs Museum, 1991), pp. 93–102

Goodman, Jordan, 'Excitantia, or how Enlightenment Europe took to soft drugs', in *Consuming Habits: deconstructing drugs in history and anthropology*, ed. by Jordan Goodman (London, Routledge, 1995), pp. 126–47

Gürsoy-Naskali, Emine, 'Pococke's Turkish Exercise', *Bodleian Library Record*, 13:2 (1989), pp. 156–6

Gutzke, David W., 'A History of Private Clubs and Coffee Houses in Britain: an annotated bibliography' *Social History of Alcohol Review* (1995), pp. 30–1

Habermas, Jürgen, *The Structural Transformation of the Public Sphere: an inquiry into a category of Bourgeois society*, trans. by Thomas Burger (Cambridge, Polity, 1992)

Haine, W. Scott, *The World of the Paris Café: sociability among the French working class, 1789–1914* (Baltimore, Johns Hopkins University Press, 1996)

Harris, Brice, 'Captain Robert Julian, Secretary to the Muses', *ELH*, 10:4 (1943), pp. 294–309

Hattox, Ralph, *Coffee and Coffeehouses: the origins of a social beverage in the Medieval Near East* (Seattle, University of Washington Press, 1988)

Hess, Alan, *Googie: fifties coffee shop architecture* (San Francisco, Chronicle Books, 1996)

Hünersdorff, Richard Von, and Holger G. Hasenkamp, *Coffee: a bibliography: a guide to the literature on coffee* (London, Hünersdorff, 2002)

Iliffe, Rob, 'Material Doubts: Hooke, artisan culture and the exchange of information in 1670s London', *British Journal for the History of Science*, 28:3:98 (September 1995), pp. 285–318

Illy, Ernesto, 'The Complexity of Coffee', *Scientific American*, 286:6 (June 2002), pp. 86–91

Isherwood, Robert, *Farce and Fantasy: popular entertainment in eighteenth-century Paris* (New York, Oxford University Press, 1986), pp. 25–6, 240–5

Jacob, Heinrich Eduard, *The Saga of Coffee: the biography of an economic product* (London, George Allen & Unwin, 1935); American title *Coffee: the epic of a commodity* (1935); translation of *Sage und Siegezug des Kaffees, die Biographie eines weltwirtschaftlichen Stoffes* (Berlin, Rowohlt, 1934)

James, Jack E., *Understanding Caffeine: a biobehavioral analysis*, Behavioural Medicine and Health Psychology, 2 (London, Sage Publications, 1997)

Kaye, Alan S., 'The Etymology of "Coffee"; the dark brew', *Journal of the American Oriental Society*, 106:3 (1986), pp. 557–8

Klein, Lawrence, 'Coffeehouse Civility, 1660–1714: an aspect of post-courtly culture in England', *Huntington Library Quarterly*, 59:1 (1997), pp. 30–51

Kümin, Beat, and B. Ann Tlusty (eds), *The World of the Tavern: public houses in early modern Europe* (Aldershot, Ashgate, 2002)

Leclant, Jean, 'Le café et les cafés à Paris', *Annales, economies, societés, civilisations*, 6 (1951), pp. 1–14; trans. in *Food and Drink in History*, ed. by Robert Forster and Orest Ranum (Baltimore, Johns Hopkins University Press, 1979)

Lecoq, Benoît, 'Le café', in 'Singularities', 'Traditions', ed. by Pierre Nora, *Les Lieux de mémoire*, 7 vols (Paris, Gallimard, 1992), vol. III, pp. 855–83

Levere, Trevor H., 'Natural Philosophers in a Coffee House: dissent, radical reform, and pneumatic chemistry', in *Science and Dissent in England, 1688–1945*, ed. by Paul Wood (Aldershot, Hampshire, Ashgate, 2004), pp. 131–46

Levere, Trevor H., and G. Turner, *Discussing Chemistry and Steam: the minutes of a coffee house philosophical society 1780–1787* (Oxford, Oxford University Press, 2002)

Lillywhite, Bryant, *London Coffee Houses: a reference book of coffee houses in the seventeenth, eighteenth and nineteenth centuries* (London, George Allen and Unwin, 1963)

Macaulay, Thomas Babington, *The History of England from the Accession of James the Second* (London, Longman, Browne, Green and Longmans, 1849)

Matthee, Rudi, 'Exotic Substances: the introduction and global spread of tobacco, coffee, tea, and distilled liquor, 16th to 18th centuries', in *Drugs and Narcotics in History*, ed. by Roy Porter and Mikulás Teich (Cambridge, Cambridge University Press, 1995), pp. 24–51

McCalman, Iain, 'Ultra-radicalism and Convivial Debating-clubs in London, 1795–1838', *English Historical Review*, 102 (1987), pp. 309–33

McEwen, Gilbert D., *The Oracle of the Coffee House: John Dunton's Athenian Mercury* (San Marino, CA, The Huntingdon Library, 1972)

Melton, James van Horn, *The Rise of the Public in Enlightenment Europe* (Cambridge, Cambridge University Press, 2001)

Menninger, Annerose, *Genuss im kulturellen Wandel: tabak, kaffee, tee und schokolade in Europa (16.–19. Jahrhundert)* (Stuttgart, F. Steiner, 2004)

Merrick, Jeffrey, 'Society Needs Women "Like Coffee Needs Sugar": André Morellet on the female sex', in *André Morellet (1727–1819) in the Republic of Letters and the French Revolution*, ed. by Jeffrey Merrick and Dorothy Medlin (New York, Peter Lang, 1995), pp. 95–113

Morton, Timothy, *The Poetics of Spice: Romantic consumerism and the exotic* (Cambridge, Cambridge University Press, 2000)

Moura, Jean, and Paul Louvet, *Le Café Procope* (Paris, Perrin et Cie, 1929)

Pelzer, John, and Linda Pelzer, 'The Coffee Houses of Augustan London', *History Today*, 32 (October 1982), pp. 40–7

Pendergrast, Mark, *Uncommon Grounds: the history of coffee and how it transformed our world* (New York, Basic Books, 1999)

Pincus, Steven, '"Coffee politicians does create": coffeehouses and restoration political culture', *Journal Of Modern History*, 67:4 (1995), pp. 807–34

Raymond, Joad, 'The Newspaper, Public Opinion, and the Public Sphere in the Seventeenth Century', in *News, Newspapers and Society in Early Modern Britain*, ed. by Joad Raymond (London, Frank Cass, 1999), pp. 109–40

Reato, Danilo, *The Coffee-House: Venetian coffee-houses from 18th to 20th century* (Venice, Arsenale Editrice, 1991)

Reinders, Pim, and Thera Wijsenbeek (eds), *Koffie in Nederland: vier eeowen cultuursgeschiedenis* (Zutphen, Walburg Pers; Delft, Gemeente Musea Delft, 1994)

Robinson, Edward Forbes, *The Early History of the Coffee-Houses in England* (London, Kegan Paul, Trench, Trübner & Co., 1893)

Rogers, Pat, *The Eighteenth Century: the context of English literature* (London, Methuen, 1978)

Rudé, George, *Hanoverian London 1714–1808* (London, Secker & Warburg, 1971)

Schivelbusch, Wolfgang, *Tastes of Paradise: a social history of spices, stimulants, and intoxicants*, trans. by David Jacobson (New York, Pantheon Books, 1992)

Schulze, Hans-Joachim, '"Ey! How Sweet the Coffee Tastes": Johann Sebastian Bach's *Coffee Cantata* in its time', trans. by Alfred Mann, *Bach: Journal of the Riemenschneider Bach Institute*, 32:2 (2001), pp. 1–117

Sennett, Richard, *The Fall of Public Man* (1977; London, Faber and Faber, 1986)

Shapin, Steven, and Simon Schaffer, *Leviathan and the Air-Pump: Hobbes, Boyle, and the experimental life* (Princeton, Princeton University Press, 1985)

Smith, Simon, 'Accounting for Taste: British coffee consumption in historical perpsective', *Discussion Papers in Economics*, No. 14 (York, University of York, 1994), pp. 19–30

—, 'Accounting for Taste: British coffee consumption in historical perspective', *Journal of Interdisciplinary History*, 27:2 (Autumn 1996), pp. 183–214

—, 'Coffee and the "Poorer Sort of People" in Jamaica during the Period of African Enslavement', in *Slavery without Sugar: diversity in Caribbean economy and society since the 17th century*, ed. by Verene Shepherd (Gainesville, FL, University Press of Florida, 2002)

Smith, Woodruff, 'From Coffee-House to Parlour: the consumption of coffee, tea, and sugar in north-western Europe in the seventeenth and eighteenth centuries', in *Consuming Habits: deconstructing drugs in history and anthropology*, ed. by Jordan Goodman (London, Routledge, 1995), pp. 148–63

Sommerville, C. John, *The News Revolution in England: cultural dynamics of daily information* (New York, Oxford University Press, 1996), pp. 75–84

—, 'Surfing the Coffeehouse: networking in 17th-century English coffeehouses', *History Today*, 47:6 (June 1997), pp. 8–10

Speier, Hans, 'Historical Development of Public Opinion', *American Journal of Sociology*, 55:4 (January 1950), pp. 376–88

Stallybrass, Peter, and Allon White, *The Politics and Poetics of Transgression* (London, Methuen, 1986)

Stephen, Leslie, *English Literature and Society in the Eighteenth Century* (London, Duckworth and Co., 1904)

—, *The Rise of Public Science: rhetoric, technology and natural philosophy in Newtonian Britain, 1660–1750* (Cambridge, Cambridge University Press, 1992)

Stewart, Larry, 'Other Centres of Calculation, or, Where the Royal Society didn't Count: commerce, coffee-houses and natural philosophy in early modern London', *British Journal for the History of Science*, 32:113 (June 1999), pp. 133–53

Thomson, Gladys Scott, *Life in a Noble Household 1641–1700* (London, Jonathan Cape, 1937)

Timbs, John, *Club Life of London with Anecdotes of the Clubs, Coffee-Houses and Taverns of the Metropolis During the 17th, 18th, and 19th Centuries*, 2 vols (London, Richard Bentley, 1866)

Tlusty, B. Ann, *The Culture of Drink in Early Modern Germany* (London, University Press of Virginia, 2001)

Toussaint-Samat, Maguelonne, 'Coffee and Politics', in *A History of Food*, trans. by Anthea Bell (Oxford, Blackwell, 1992), pp. 581–95

Trevelyan, George Macaulay, *England Under Queen Anne: Blenheim* (London, Longmans, Green and Co. 1930)

—, *English Social History: a survey of six centuries from Chaucer to Queen Victoria* (1942; London, Penguin Books, 2000)

Trouillot, Michel-Rolph, 'Coffee Planters and Coffee Slaves in the Antilles: the impact of a secondary crop', in *Cultivation and Culture: Labor and the Shaping of Slave Life in the Americas*, ed. by Ira Berlin and Philip Morgan (Charlottesville, VA, University Press of Virginia, 1993), pp. 73–98

Ukers, William, *All about Coffee* (New York, Tea and Coffee Trade Journal, 1922)

—, *All about Tea*, 2 vols (New York, Tea and Coffee Trade Journal, 1935)

Varey, Simon, 'Three Necessary Drugs [coffee, tea and chocolate]', 1650–1850: *Ideas, Aesthetics, and Inquiries in the Early Modern Era*, 4 (1998), pp. 3–51

Weatherill, Lorna, *Consumer Behaviour and Material Culture in Britain, 1660–1760* (London, Routledge, 1988)

Weinberg, Bennett Alan, and Bonnie K. Bealer, *The World of Caffeine: the science and culture of the world's most popular drug* (New York and London, Routledge, 2001)

Westerfrölke, Hermann, *Englische Kaffeehäuser als Sammelpunkte der literarischen Welt im Zeitalter von Dryden und Addison* (Jena, Frommannschen Buchhandlung, 1924)

Wrightson, Keith, 'Alehouse, Order and Reformation in Rural England, 1590–1660', in *Popular Culture and Class Conflict, 1690–1914*, ed. by Eileen Yeo and Stephen Yeo (Brighton, Harvester, 1981)

ABBREVIATIONS

Biographical Dictionary of Actors

    A Biographical Dictionary of Actors, Actresses, Musicians, Dancers, Managers and other stage personnel in London, 1660–1800, ed. by Philip Highfill, Kalman Burnim and Edward Langhans (Carbondale, IL, Southern Illinois University Press, 1973)

BL   British Library

CSPD   *Calendar of State Papers Domestic*

Ellis, *Coffee-House*   Markman Ellis, *The Coffee-House: a cultural history* (London, Weidenfeld & Nicholson, 2004)

ESTC   English Short Title Catalogue

Hünersdorff   Richard Von Hünersdorff, and and Holger G. Hasenkamp, *Coffee: a bibliography: a guide to the literature on coffee* (London, Hünersdorff, 2002)

Lillywhite   Bryant Lillywhite, *London Coffee Houses: a reference book of the coffee houses of the seventeenth, eighteenth and nineteenth centuries* (London, George Allen and Unwin, 1963)

London Stage   *The London Stage, 1660–1800: Part IV: 1747–1776*, ed. by George W. Stone, 3 vols (Carbondale, IL, Southern Illinois University Press, 1962)

LE   *London Encyclopædia*, ed. by Ben Weinreb and Christopher Hibbert (London, Macmillan, 1983)

KJV   King James Version

OED   *Oxford English Dictionary*, 2nd edn, online

ODNB   *Oxford Dictionary of National Biography*, online

Pepys, *Diary*   Samuel Pepys, *The Diary*, trans and ed. by Robert Latham and William Matthews, 11 vols (London, Bell & Hyman, 1970)

Plomer   H. R. Plomer et al., *Dictionaries of the Printers and Booksellers who were at Work in England, Scotland and Ireland, 1557–1775* (London, The Bibliographical Society, 1977)

PRO	Public Records Office
Smith	William Smith, *A New Classical Dictionary of Biography, Mythology and Geography* (London, John Murray, 1853)
Ukers	William Harrison Ukers, *All about Coffee* (New York, Tea & Coffee Trade Journal Co., 1922)
Wing	*Short-title Catalogue of books printed in England, Scotland, Ireland, Wales, and British America and of english books printed in other countries, 1641–1700*, compiled by Donald Wing, 3 vols (New York, Index Society, 1945–51)

INTRODUCTION

The first coffee-houses in Britain – or for that matter anywhere in Christian Europe – opened in London during the English republic, where they rapidly gained a renown for public debate and the circulation of news. In consequence, the coffee-house in its early years was associated by contemporaries with puritan, republican and refractory politics. To many it seemed as if the coffee-house was a symbol of all the constitutional novelties and disruptions of the republic. As an anonymous satirist quipped in 1665:

> *Coffee* and *Commonwealth* begin
> With one letter, both came in
> Together for a *Reformation*,
> To make's a free and sober *Nation*.[1]

Supporters of the King remained wary of the bitter hot drink that had invaded the city during their exile. One of Henry Bold's Royalist drinking songs (published in 1664), extolling the loyal virtues of cider, declared that '*Sherbet, Coffee, and Chocolate,* / Are *Heathenish Drinks*, compar'd to *this*', the '*Nobler Juice*' of 'King Pippin'.[2] Contemporaries, however, also saw that their appeal was to those of high status and education. When the agricultural improver John Beale (1608–83) wrote to the intelligencer Samuel Hartlib (c. 1600–62) in December 1658 lamenting the 'wantonesse' or popularity of the 'Coffa-drinke', he predicted that it 'will growe into generall use having already obtain such a general reception by young & old in our Innes of Courts'.[3]

After the Restoration in 1660, it was not clear that Charles II would tolerate the coffee-houses, although he was in no position to dictate terms. The authorities of the City of London were in no mood to countenance their suppression. The coffee-houses had already changed the City, ushering in a lasting and important revolution in social interaction. On the evening of Monday 10

---

1. *The Character of a Coffee-House* (1665), see below, pp. 59–72; p. 68.
2. Henry Bold, *Poems: Lyrique, Macaronique, Heroique, &c.* (London, Henry Brome, 1664).
3. John Beale to Hartlib, 14 December 1658, Hartlib MS 51/43A–B, *The Hartlib Papers Second Edition* (Sheffield, HROnline, Humanities Research Institute, 2002).

December 1660, for example, Samuel Pepys, then a young clerk in the Navy Office, went with his colleague, Colonel Robert Slingsby, to 'the Coffee-house in Cornhill'. He commented in his diary, this was 'the first time that ever I was there. And I find much pleasure in it through the diversity of company – and discourse.'[4] As Pepys notes, the attraction of the coffee-house was not coffee, but company and conversation. When Pepys describes the sociable practices of coffee-house-going in his diary, he is describing an activity for which there was no settled convention of representation. Pepys's diary records the construction, elaboration and revision of a substantially new form of social encounter. The activity itself bore similarities to Pepys's sociable encounters in taverns, ale-houses and ordinaries (dining houses), yet it was also marked by some striking revisions, especially his detailed records of conversations he encountered there about sober and serious topics: scientific curiosity, commercial business, news and politics.

Pepys was a very sociable man: friendly, affable and generous, even though his diaries also reveal a self-interested side given to Machiavellian strategising. Although he was always keen on fellowship and company – what his age called 'sociality' or 'sodality'[5] – he was always careful to search out the company of those who he thought could be useful to him. Over the course of the diary, which runs for nearly ten years from 1 January 1660 to 31 May 1669, Pepys records 99 visits to the coffee-house, making his diary the first and the fullest contemporary record of coffee-house sociability. In the years 1663 and 1664 the coffee-house became a central part of Pepys's daily routine. While he was also an inveterate drinker in taverns, the coffee-house in these years came to have a special significance for him. The attraction was never simply the coffee, rather it was the potential the coffee-house offered for social intercourse and companionship with one's fellows. As an ambitious young man, Pepys recognised that in the coffee-house he had an opportunity to meet with and talk to men of influence and acuity whose expertise would be advantageous to him. Yet even by the later 1660s, Pepys left off visiting the coffee-houses: in part because he had learned what he needed to know about commerce, and in part because his now elevated position in the court and Navy circles made the coffee-houses seem demeaning, both too vulgar and tainted with republican excess. Pepys's practice, both in his everyday life and his diary, shows how the coffee-house idea remained dangerously ambiguous, confused and uncertain. This was not for want of debate.

Early satires on the coffee-house registered this sense of innovation in their construction of coffee as a kind of foreign and superfluous luxury, variously

---

4. Pepys, *Diary*, vol. I, p. 315.

5. 'Sociality' was defined in Edward Phillips's dictionary of 1658 as 'fellowship, company', a near homonym for sodality, defined as 'fellowship, brotherhood or society'. Edward Phillips, *The New World of English Words: or, a general dictionary* (London, E. Tyler for Nath. Brooke, 1658).

described as unpalatable and unhealthy. Furthermore, all consumers of coffee could recognise the important differences between its physiological properties and those of beer or wine. Where a few dishes of coffee made you awake, conversational and alert, a few pints of alcohol made you confrontational, garrulous, immoderate, lustful and sleepy. Just as coffee was associated with wakefulness, conversation, and commerce, so was the coffee-house.

'A paper scuffle in print': the Restoration coffee-house controversy

Throughout the Restoration period, the coffee-house was the subject of a bad-tempered battle to control its meaning. In part this was conducted at the highest levels: Charles II's ministers repeatedly debated the merits and meaning of the coffee-houses, and on several occasions contemplated methods to control or suppress them (see Volume 4). Sir Thomas Player, the chamberlain of the Paper Office, wrote to the secretary of state Sir Joseph Williamson in November 1673 complaining that 'the common people talke anything, for every carman and porter is now a statesman; and indeed the coffee-houses are good for nothing else'. Court circles regularly attributed to coffee-houses the high level of public debate on affairs of state – the equivalent, they thought, of libel and sedition. As Player lamented, 'It was not thus when wee dranke nothing but sack and claret, or English beere and ale. These sober clubbs produce nothing but scandalous and censorious discourses, and at these nobody is spared.'[6] When debate was fuelled by wine and beer, Player argued, discussion was loyal to the King. Coffee made men sober but also seditious – an argument whose latent irony he did not declare.

But the debate on coffee was also undertaken in a more creative mode by satirists. The coffee-house was the subject of a significant 'paper scuffle in print', as Pepys called it.[7] Despite the pre-publication censorship of the press instituted by the 1663 Licensing Act, the Restoration saw the publication in print and manuscript of a huge number of satires. Many fall under the category of 'small merry books', as Margaret Spufford has called them.[8] Like contemporary chapbooks or penny merriments, these coffee-house texts relate amatory fictions of courtship, infidelity, intemperance and impotence, and depict rogues and fools in a riotously carnivalesque mode of vulgar language and indecorous expressions. The head-notes to this edition consider the diverse forms and genres taken by these satires,

6. *Letters to Sir Joseph Williamson*, ed. by W. D. Christie, 2 vols ([London], Camden Society, new ser. VIII and IX, 1874), vol. II, p. 68.

7. Samuel Pepys, *Pepys's Later Diaries*, ed. by C. S. Knighton (Stroud, Sutton Publishing, 2004).

8. Margaret Spufford, *Small Books and Pleasant Histories: popular fiction and its readership in seventeenth-century England* (Cambridge, Cambridge University Press, 1981). See also Peter Burke, *Popular Culture in Early Modern Europe* (London, Temple Smith, 1978).

both in prose and verse, as well as determining, as far as possible, their location within a typology of Restoration vulgar satire, such as mock forms, low travesties, jest-book histories, chapbook burlesques and broadside ballads. Locating these texts in the cultural context of popular fiction, and exploring these forms as literary genres of Restoration satire, allows the reader a more nuanced analysis of the place of the coffee-house in late seventeenth-century culture.

These texts have been of central importance to historians' understanding of coffee-houses, providing much of the colour, flavour and nuance to their construction of coffee-house sociability. Lord Macaulay, in his *History of England* (1849–55), made use of these texts for his innovative account of the manners of the English nation in 1685.[9] They remained the staple of Whig histories of the coffee-house throughout the twentieth century: Habermas, for example, used *The Women's Petition Against Coffee* (1674) to argue that the women of London waged a 'vigorous but vain struggle' against the coffee-houses, a claim that any reader of this libertine squib (see pp. 109–18 below) would find hard to believe. But despite their ubiquity in historical accounts, the status of these satires as texts has been often overlooked. They have been routinely examined by positivist readers believing that these are documents that will reveal facts about the coffee-house, its manners and everyday materiality, in a simple and transparent fashion. A consideration of their literary form, and the context of their publication and dissemination, should be central to their analysis. The purpose of this collection is to make available these fugitive texts. But by making them more widely known to scholars and researchers, the purpose is not to make them better evidence for the material history of the coffee-house, but rather as a contribution to the history of ideas.

The distinctive formal feature of these Restoration satirical burlesques on the coffee-house is the contrast they stage between the vulgar and undignified representation of coffee-house manners and conversation, and the adoption of a mock form derived from the discourse of authority, such as the petition, complaint, news report, travel journal, character or dialogue. These hybrid forms defy easy categorisation: perceived within a classical literary matrix they bear some allegiance to forms of Menippean and Varronian satire; while at times they also adopt innovative satiric forms like the hudibrastic or the complaint. The mock-complaint, for example written as if by ironically over-amorous maidens, ale-wives and she-traders, burlesques the genre of the complaint – a statement of grievance laid before a judiciary authority.[10] In John Crouch's *The maidens*

9.   Thomas Babington Macaulay, *The History of England from the Accession of James the Second*, 4 vols (London, Longman, Browne, Green and Longmans, 1849–55), vol. I, pp. 368–69n. Macaulay noted: 'Lettres sur les Anglois; Tom Brown's Tour; Ward's London Spy; The Character of a Coffee House, 1673; Rules and Orders of the Coffee House, 1674; Coffee Houses Vindicated, 1675; A Satyr Against Coffee ... The liveliest description of Will's is in the City and Country Mouse'.

10.   Kirk Combe, 'The New Voice of Political Dissent: the transition from complaint to satire', in *Theorising Satire: essays in literary criticism*, ed. by Brian Connery and Kirk Combe (Basingstoke,

complain[t] against coffee (see pp. 45–54 below), the satire is directed against the new form of male sociability found in the coffee-houses, especially its voluble and gossipy sobriety. Mock petitions, such as the *The Women's Petition Against Coffee* (see pp. 109–18 below) and *The Mens Answer to the Womens Petition* (see pp. 199–26 below), adopt similar burlesque strategies by marrying a genre associated with the diction of authority with the unconventional and coarse language of the people. All these forms imagine an audience imbricated in and knowledgeable about the popular discourses of the street, but also to some extent educated in and about intellectual debates. In this sense they are addressed downwards, to a reader below the writer in status, but also curious, sincere and to some extent polite.

The form of the 'character', a short prose satire detailing the nature and qualities that make some person distinctive, is the form that was most commonly adapted to address the coffee-house, beginning with *A Character of Coffee and Coffee-Houses* in 1661 (pp. 1–14 below, but see also pp. 59–72, 81–90 and 91–9). A classical form imitating Theophrastus (373–284 BC), the character was given to schoolboys as a Latin exercise in grammar schools. English imitations abound in the seventeenth century, including those by Joseph Hall, Sir Thomas Overbury and John Earle, who innovated characters addressing particular places such as the tavern and bowling alley. The character by Samuel Butler (1612–80), addressing 'A Coffee-Man', satirises his immoderate pretensions to learning and status:

> Keeps a coffee market, where people of all qualities and conditions meet, to trade in foreign drinks and newes, ale, smoak, and controversy. He admits of no distinction of persons, but gentleman, mechanic, lord, and scoundrel mix, and are all of a piece, as if they were resolv'd into their first principles. His house is a kind of *Athenian* school, where all manner of opinions are profest and maintain'd to the last drop of coffee … If it were not for news and the cheapness of company he would be utterly abandon'd: for that, with the freedom to vapour, lye, and loiter upon free cost, draws more company than his coffee, or the *Turk* that drinks it on his sign, though that be the better of the two.[11]

When Butler penned this character, every adult could remember a time when there were no coffee-houses at all: the character sees this innovation as an abrogation and confusion of confirmed social values.

Macmillan, 1995), pp. 73–94; John Peter, 'The Moral Themes of Complaint', in *Complaint and Satire in Early English Literature* (Oxford, Clarendon Press, 1956); Steven Zwicker, *Lines of Authority: politics and English literary culture, 1649–1689* (London, Cornell University Press, 1993).

11. Samuel Butler, *Characters*, ed. by Charles Daves (Cleveland, Press of Case Western Reserve University, 1970), pp. 256–8. Although Butler wrote more than 200 characters between 1667 and 1669, they were not published until 1759 in *The Genuine Remains of Mr Samuel Butler*, ed. by Robert Thyer (London, Tonson, 1759).

The Restoration satires in this volume are almost entirely hostile to the new forms of sociability and manners associated with the coffee-house. The consistency and longevity of this assault on the coffee-houses suggests more political coherence than is perhaps justified: nonetheless, it would not be excessive or inaccurate to identify in these satires common motives and associations with Tory political circles in the period. It is ironic that this Tory resistance to coffee-house culture is used as central evidence in the Whig re-evaluation of the coffee-house in the nineteenth and twentieth centuries. Even the few exceptions to the Tory hegemony over discourse on coffee-houses are unable to escape the burlesque satiric forms established by their opposition: the anonymous *Coffee-houses Vindicated* (see pp. 91–9 below) burlesques the debased intellectual attitudes exhibited by those who write satires attacking coffee-houses. By contrast, *A Bridle for the Tongue* (see pp. 145–53 below), which expresses Puritan resistance to the coffee-house, especially its licentious nature, its tendency to 'scoff at religion', and 'repeat prophane, debauch'd or scurrilous Language', adopts the form of a religious tract.

Nonetheless it remains clear that the historical coffee-house was closely associated with sedition and anti-court sentiment, and after the rise of party in the late 1670s, with the Whig political interest. Government ministers had considered acting against coffee-house debate as a locus of sedition since the first days of the Restoration. After the fire in London in September 1666, the King was the subject of 'Pasquils and Libels', despite his every effort to have himself cast in a heroic mould. The Earl of Clarendon, the chancellor, noted that Charles II 'complained very much of the Licence that was assumed in the Coffeehouses, which were the Places where the boldest Calumnies and Scandals were raised, and discoursed amongst a People who knew not each other, and came together only for that Communication, and from thence were propagated over the kingdom'.[12] Clarendon concurred that the unprecedented 'Impunity' from the law assumed by the coffee-houses, 'where the foulest Imputations ... laid upon the Government ... were held lawful to be reported and divulged to every Body'. In short, Clarendon concluded, 'people generally believed that those Houses had a Charter of Privilege to speak what They would, without being in Danger to be called in Question', and counselled the King to 'apply some Remedy to such a growing Disease'. Clarendon advised either a proclamation to suppress the coffee-houses, or the organisation of 'some Spies, who, being present in the Conversation, might be ready to charge and accuse the Persons who had talked with the most Licence in a Subject that would bear a Complaint'. While the King liked both expedients, the former proposal was brought forward to the Privy Council by Clarendon. There, however, he was opposed by secretary of state

12. *The Life of Edward Earl of Clarendon ... Written by Himself*, 3 vols (Oxford, Clarendon Printing-House, 1759), vol. III, pp. 675–8.

Sir William Coventry (who already operated an extensive network of domestic spies in the coffee-houses). Coventry argued 'that Coffee was a Commodity that yielded the King a good Revenue, and therefore it would not be just to receive the Duties and inhibit the Sale of it, which many Men found to be very good for their Health' and that the King owed the coffee-houses an obligation, because during the Interregnum the 'King's Friends had used more liberty of Speech in those Places' than in any other. After this, the proposal fell into desuetude. A newsletter noted on 19 February 1672 that 'the King having been informed of the great inconveniences arising from the great number of persons that resort to coffee houses, has desired the Lord Keeper and the Judges to give their opinion in writing how far he may lawfully proceed against them'.[13] A series of royal proclamations in the 1670s (see Volume 4, pp. 89–101) were intended to regulate coffee-house discourse, most notably the attempt to suppress them all in December 1675.

As Steven Pincus, Brian Cowan and others have shown, the widespread popular debate on political and religious matters in the coffee-house was identified as a specifically Whig discourse: an association that extended to the coffee-house itself.[14] The force of this association was underwritten by the coffee-houses' provision of news. It was news that made coffee-houses popular, for it was news that gave the conversations there their importance and value, and it was the circulation of this news that so distressed the authorities. News was of course a flexible category: as well as domestic and foreign news (including everything from the movements of the monarch and accounts of debates and votes in parliament to revelations of state secrets), the category included commercial intelligence, scientific and philosophical matters, literary and critical writing, as well as scurrilous gossip and defamatory rumour. By the end of the seventeenth century, after the Whig revolution of 1688, this association with news began to be recast in a more loyal mode.

13. No 1292, 20 February 1671/2, Historical Manuscripts Commission, *The Manuscripts of S.H. Le Fleming, Esq., of Rydall Hall* (London, HMSO, 1890), p. 88.

14. Steven Pincus, '"Coffee politicians does create": coffeehouses and restoration political culture', *Journal Of Modern History*, 67:4 (1995), pp. 807–34; Brian Cowan, 'The Rise of the Coffeehouse Reconsidered', *Historical Journal*, 47:1 (2004), pp. 21–46; see also Ellis, *Coffee-House*, pp. 86–105.

M. P., *A Character of Coffee and Coffee-Houses* (London, John Starkey, 1661), [2], 10pp.; 4°. Worcester College Library, Oxford University. ESTCR28769. Hünersdorff.

This short 10-page prose satire of 25 numbered paragraphs is the first of several coffee-house 'Characters', but as such it continues an enduring literary tradition. Ralph Johnson, in *The Scholars Guide* (London, Tho. Pierrepoint, 1665), defined a Character as 'a witty and facetious description of the nature and qualities of some person, or sort of person' (p. 15). From the 1640s, the Character was widely adopted in political and religious controversies. The form was derived from the practice of Theophrastus (373–284 BC), who wrote thirty sketches gently satirizing contemporary types in Athenian society using a neutral and detached tone. The best-known early English imitator was Sir Thomas Overbury, whose Characters mixed in samples of characteristic speech and behaviour, and satirised occupations and places. Character-writing was often given to schoolboys as a Latin exercise in grammar schools. See Benjamin Boyce, *The Theophrastan Character in England to 1642* (Cambridge, MA, Harvard University Press, 1947).

The first eleven paragraphs of the satire investigate the medical properties of coffee: noting various physiological effects it was supposed to have, including impotence and migraine, discussed using the humoural theory prevalent at the time. The remaining paragraphs explore the regime of the coffeehouse, making a number of observations that have strongly marked subsequent representations of coffee-house sociability, such as the notion that each man takes the next available chair (equality); and that there is no limit to topics of discussion, nor rules governing behaviour. These points make extensive use of ironic ambiguity and make a heterogeneous list, so that the same properties that make coffee-house discourse enticing lead equally to dullness and faction. As the writer suggests in paragraph 19, the limitless contestation of coffee-house argument implies that it is politically neutered. A scientific context of the satire is signalled in the postscript 'Apology' where the 'Describer' identifies several of his friends who resort to the coffee-house as '*Virtuosi* and *Ingenuosi*', men associated with the nascent Royal Society for Improving Natural Knowledge (1661).

The author has not been identified. The initials 'M.P.' had been adopted by a prolific ballad writer who published more than a hundred songs in the first half of the seventeenth century. He died in 1656, but his works continued to be published thereafter. Perhaps the name is meant to recall the abbreviation for member of parliament, or again, the initials of one of the mercuries or newspapers of the period, such as Marchemont Nedham's *Mercurius Politicus* (6 June 1650 to 5 April 1660), the official organ of the Protectorate state, or Henry Muddiman's *Mercurius Publicus*, the continuation published during and after the Restoration (29 December 1659 to 13 August 1663).

The pamphlet was published by the Anabaptist bookseller John Starkey, who kept shop in Fleet Street by Temple Bar, next to the Devil Tavern. His printing house was close to the location of the second known coffee-house in London, James Ffarr's Rainbow Coffee-house, known to have been in business since 1657 (noted in the St Dunstan's Wardmote Inquest Book, 21 December 1657, Guildhall Library MS 3018/1, fol. 140r).

This is a very rare text: only three copies survive: this one from Worcester College Library, Oxford University, and further examples in the Houghton Library, Harvard University and the Johann Jacobs Museum, Zurich.

A

CHARACTER

O F

COFFEE

A N D

Coffee-Houſes.

By M. P.

LONDON,
Printed for *John Starkey,* neer the *Devil-Tavern,* by
Temple-Barr. 1661.

[1]

A
CHARACTER
OF
COFFEE
AND
COFFEE-HOUSES.

Coffee-houfe is free to all Comers, fo they have Humane fhape, where a Liquor made of an *A-rabian* Berry called *Coffee* is drunk. Six or feven years ago was it firſt brought into *England*, when the Palats of the Englifh were as Fanatical, as their Brains. Like Apes , the Englifh imitate all other people in their ridiculous Fafhions. As Slaves they fubmit to the Cuſtomes even of *Turky* and *India*. Doth the French-man wear Feathers in his Hat, and Pantaloons to hide his ſtrad-ling? Believe it , the Englifh-man will be *a la mode de France*. With the Barbarous *Indian* he fmoaks Tobacco. With the *Turk* he drinks Coffee.

A 2   *The*

[2]

b.
*some
alte-*

The Englifh-man, might be himfelf mifplace,
Sure to be croffe, would fhift both feet and face.

2. Thefe capricious Iflanders, of the Hop, Malt, Cock, China, Rafh-berry, and other ingredients, make and fwallow as many and as various forts of Drink, as they amongft them have Sects and Opinions. They drink as much Canary, as its native Countrey produceth. 'Tis faid, they devoure down a greater quantity of Wine, (called Canary) than the *Canaries* afford. All Countries fend in hither their feveral forts of Wine and other Liquors. This variety of drink fatisfies not the voraginous Palat of the Englifh. Even the Deferts of *Arabia* are ranfackt for a Berry, which made into a drink, is as thick as puddle-water, and fo ugly in colour and taft, that Poets hereafter will undoubted y choofe it, as the beft refemblance to defcribe the *Stygian* Lake by. Oh Heavens, how do the Englifh Palats differ from thofe of more fober Nations? Thefe preferve Snow to temper their Liquor with, thofe gulch down Coffee even boyling in the Difh, more eagerly, than an almoft ftarved Dog doth lick up Pottage, juft then taken from the fierce fire. In time (fure) the Englifh-man will fwallow down burning Coals.

3. Coffee is a Dryer, and therefore with fucceffe is drunk by thofe Gentlemen, who are infected with the French-pox, which is now become the Charactieriftal difference between the plumed Noblefs and the highfhoon. Alas, Vertue is a pedantical and vulgar quality.

4. 'Tis extolled for drying up the Crudities of the Stomack, and for expelling Fumes out of the Head. Excellent Berry! which can cleanfe the Englifh-man's
Stomack

[3]

Stomak of Flegm , and expel Giddineffe out of his Head.
Yet it is certain , that for the fmall fpace of an hour or
thereabouts it hath expelled out of an Englifh head and
Stomack thefe infirmities. But after fuch a little interval,
they return again.   And the houfe being thus fwept and
cleanfed , feven Devils enter it. For Phyficians fay, that
Coffee caufeth the *Meagrim* and other Giddineffes in the
Head, &c. Of this dayly experiment may be made : For
if you fet Short-hand-writers to take down the Difcourfe of the Company , who prattle over Coffee , it
will be evident on reading the Notes , that the talk is
extravagant and exactly like that of the Academians of
Bedlam, and fuch, as any others , would be afham'd of,
but themfelves.

5 . Coffee makes no man drunk. But for this , it is no
more to be commended , than a Neates-tongue , a difh
of Anchovaes , or a falt Bit , which never yet intoxicated
any man. For Coffee being mixt with the more drying
fmoak of Tobacco makes too many run to the Tavern or Ale-
houfe to quench their thirft , which they cannot fatisfy,
till out of their gorged ftomacks, they fend up rich facrifi-
ces to *Liber Pater*.

6 . This forein Liquor in truth qualifies the Vapours
of Wine, which makes your Good Fellows refort thither
to heat their Stomacks made cold and infirm by their having powred thereinto too too much Wine, and thus they
inable their weak Stomacks to receive a new *Load*. But
hereby in part may be made a Judgment of the good Company of this place. O Heavens ! how well will the Barrels
of Herings (impofed on thefe houfes) agree with Coffee.

7. Coffee being dry, in proportion , dryes up the Radical

[4]

cal moifture. By conftant ufe thereof, a man becomes,

——— *ad unum*
Mollis opus ————

The other Sex hath juft caufe to curfe the day, in which it was brought into *England*; Had Women any fenfe or fpirit, they would remonftrate to his Majeftie, that Men in former times were more able, than now, They had ftronger Backs, and were more Benevolent, fo that *Hercules* in one night got fifty Women with Child, and a Prince of *Spain* was forc'd to make an Edict, that the Men fhould not repeat the act of Coition above nine times in a night, for before that Edict, belike Men did exceed that proportion; That in this Age, Men drink fo many Spirits and Effences, fo much Strong-water, fo many feveral forts of Wine, fuch abundance of Tobacco, and (now at laft) pernicious Coffee, that they are grown as impotent as Age, as dry and as unfruitful, as the Deferts of *Africk*. Having remonftrated this, they then would (were they wife) petition his Majefty to forbid Men the drinking of effeminating Coffee, and to command them inftead thereof to drink delicious Chocolate.

8. 'Tis the Intereft alfo of Women to have this drink damn'd, left the Men bereave them of one of their moft excellent and appropriated Qualities, that is Garrulity and Talkativenefs. In this Age Men tattle more than Women, and particularly at the Coffee-houfe, when the number hath been but fix, five of them have talkt at one time. The Company here have out-talk'd an equal number of Goffipping Women, and made a greater noife than a Bake-houfe. Men are here born down by clamour, which refembles at times the noife of the Cataracts of *Nilus*, but alwayes refembles a School, fili'd with Children, every one conning his Leffon aloud.

9. Here

[5]

9. Here Men carried by inftinct fipp muddy water, and like Frogs confufedly murmur Infignificant Notes, which tickle their own ears, and to their inharmonious fenfe, make Mufick of jarring ftrings. *Hic fluvius Verborum, vix gutta Mentis.*

10. In this confufed way of gabbling the Coffee-drinkers fondly imagine, that they make a better Confort, than four and twenty Violins. They run from point to point, from one fubject to another, as infenfibly and as fwifty, as *Polewheel* runs divifion on the Bafe Viol.

11. The day fufficeth not fome Perfons to drink 3. or 4 difhes of Coffee in. They borrow of the night, though they are fure, that this drink taken fo late, will not let them clofe their Eyes all night. Thefe men are either afraid to be alone with themfelves, or they to excefs love Company, fo that they never fet apart any time to converfe with themfelves. This ill-tafted Liquor (by what charms I know not) makes Men to neglect and forfake themfelves ; for

> *who cannot reft, till he good Fellows find,*
> *He breaks up houfe, turns out of dores his mind.*   Herb.

12. At this place a man is cheated of what is, by far more valuable than Mony, that is, Time. A conftant Companion of this Houfe going in all hafte for a Midwife, or to fave the life of a Friend then dying, muft call in, and drink at leaft his two difhes of Coffee and his two Pipes of Tobacco. And which is yet more wonderful, many perfons prefer Coffee, (and the Company, which love it) before the gain of money, for many men neglect their Callings and Voca-tion, to tattle away their time over two or three difhes of Coffee.

13. Here is no refpect of perfons. Boldy therefore let any perfon, who comes to drink Coffee fit down in the very
                                                        Chair

[6]

Chair., for here a Seat is to be given to no man. That great privilege of *equality* is only peculiar to the *Golden Age*, and to a *Coffee-house*. However even here, a small portion of Wit, gilded over with an Eftate, hath an influence. Mony! *Thou art the Man, and Man but Drofs to thee.* Or with *Juvenal* I may fay,

> ----*O nummi vobis hunc præftat honorem*
> *Vos eftis fratres*-----

So alfo is it here in refpect of Titles; Children do not more for a time value their Babies, than Titles are for a while here gazed on. Even a ----- as fuch, gains as good an opinion as the place is capable of. Light things weigh much in thofe Scales, which are here ufed, *Heavy*, little or nothing. Wifedom and Vertue are every where ufed, as fanatical -----

14. Such is the humour of the Coffee-meetings, that that perfon fhall gain more love and refpect, who gives to the Company a Sugcr-plum, than he who beftows gifts more befitting men to receive, and he who hath attained the Art of making an agreeable * addreffe to the Company, and knows, how by empty Complements to flatter them into a good opinion of themfelves, or to tattle to them little pleafing things, fhall affuredly thereby infinuate himfelf into their good opinion more than if he difcourfed to them of the moft Profitable Subjects with the deepeft Judgment.

* by words.

15. Very critical and very difcerning is the Affembly here. The Company within a very fhort while will look thorow and thorow the Prudenteft and moft cryed-up Perfon. A Weak part will quickly be found in him, and not only Real but Imaginary Faults will be laid to his charge. A Man of Reputation is fo tender a Creature, that he fhould in a manner alwayes keep within dores, and never come into the Air, unlefs chofen, and cleer. But by all means let him beware of the Coffee-houfe, for here there is alwayes a thick fmoak, which will fully a fair colour. In plain terms, an affiduous

fre-

[7]

frequenting the Coffee-houfe, and expofing reafon, parts and eftimation, by converfation, to the open view of the Society, renders them hereby firft familiar, then contemptible. Here a man too late will be taught, that the moft excellent Jewels, to wit, the Nobleft Speculations, the Divineft Truths, the moft Exquifite Fancies, the moft Meritorious Actions, and the moft Complacential Humours prodigally thrown away amongft a mixt number of perfons, become as common, as Gold was once in *Jerufalem*, that is, as common, as Stones.

16. Such is the mixture of Perfons here, that me thinks I cannot better exprefs it, than by faying, That at thefe Waters meet all forts of Creatures. Hence follows the Production of diverfe monftrous Opinions and Abfurdities. Here is a congrefs of old *Rome* and of new, of *Turky*, *Geneva*, and *Amfterdam*. A Coffee-houfe, like Logick, the Lawyer, and the Switzer, will maintain any Caufe.

17. Infinite are the Contefts, irreconcileable the Differences here. The Society hath been divided about the manner of the creeping of a Loufe. Were there not here, a conftant contention amongft the Elements of this Body, it could not fubfift. *For fhould all agree, and be of one Judgment, they would as it were become but one Perfon, the Houfe would be folitary, and at laft one or two Perfons would be the whole Company.*

18. However, though it refemble *Amfterdam*, being divided into innumerable different Opinions, yet is it free from effects of Sedition or War. For there are no bloody Challenges here made, much lefs Duels fought, or Blows given. Will you know the reafon? The Company in this are more Couragious than wife, that they contend about triffles only, but they are more Wife than couragious, in that they fight not for the Victory: fo that in a true fenfe the Lion and the Lamb ly down together here.

B   19. Such

[8]

19. Such being the differences of Opinion, and such the Tameness of the Company, how can any one in reason, think, that a Coffee-house is dangerous to the Government, that seeds of Sedition are here sown, & Principles of Liberty infinuated? A Coffee-house hath alwayes been as great a Friend to Monarchy, as an Enemy to Liberty. The Principles of a Popular Government at the *Rota* were weakne'd, and rendred contemptible. Men of such Contrary Judgments as here meet, cannot justly be feared to Agree in a Conspiracy. And in truth they talk too much, to be lookt on as dangerous, and active Persons.

20. Rather say the Fanaticks, that this is not a place in which a great and generous Truth can be maintain'd, that a Person full of such a Truth, not being able to contein it, is forc'd to whisper it in the ear of some Ingenuous, if he can find such a one. This is certain, that who ever intends here to discourse of Worthy Subjects judiciously, ought carefully not only to chuse his Time, but to pack the Company; that so he may be heard but with patience.

11. On the other side, who ever is troubled with impertinent Fancies and ridiculous Notions, is here quietly heard and sometimes heraunged. The Relater hereof hath heard a young Gentleman affirm, that he used to go to the Coffee-house purposely to vent his strange and wild Conceits, and to rid himself of such bad Guests. An opinion, how foolish or fond soever, here receives entertainment. To this Coast, as to the *West-Indies*, you carry not rich Merchandises to Trade with, but only Beads, Looking-glasses, Knives, and such like, nor shall the Merchant make returns of any other Commodities, than such as are fit for the Pedlars box.

22. Though the Coffee-house may be condemned for ill choice of Subjects, on which they discourse, yet are the Company by many persons commended for this, that every one of
them

[9]

them abounds in his own fenfe, and fubmits to the reafon of
no other Mortal, following herein that great Example of the
Men who inhabit the Lunary World, who put the Monfieur in a Cage, for difcourfing like a Parrat in the words of
Ariftotle. Every one over Coffee difcourfeth thofe things,
which his own reafon or fancy infpire him with, and he, who
cants in the terms of *Ariftotle,* or argues by Book, is lookt on
to want terms and reafon of his own, *& jurare in verba
Magiftri.*

23. Yet here being neither Moderators, nor Rules, (were
there no other reafon) a Man fhall as foon fill a Quart Pot
with Difcourfe, as Profit by it. He may as rationally expect
to carry a Ship from the River of *Thames* to the *Eaft-Indies*
without a Pilot or Rules of Navigation, as to manage a difcourfe fuccefefully, or in this School to bring it to a good
Iffue.

24. A School it is without a Mafter. Education is here
taught without Difcipline. Learning (if it be poffible) is here
infinuated without Method. Good Manners and commen-
dable Humors are here infufed into Men by the contempla-
tion of the Deformity of their contrarie's, as the *Sparta* s infufed into their Children hatred of Drunkennefs by fetting
before them their drunken Helots.

25. The Company, (that their intertainment man appear
in its native colours) at times divert themfelves with the
controverting fuch points as thefe.
Utrum corpus eft immateriale.
*Utrum chimæra bombinans in vacuo poffit commedere fecundas
intentiones.*
Utrum antiqua Roma a Chriftianis *fundata fuit.*
Utrum beftia honoranda fit.

26. A facetious or merry Story is preferred by the Gentlemen here before a Banquet of Philofophy. The Auditors
                                                            liffen

[10]

liffen to him, who tells a Tale gracefully, with as great an attention, as *Orpheus* his Beafts did to his Charming Mufick. And good reafon fuch a perfon fhould be attentively heard.

> -----*nam quæ comœdia ? Mimus*
> *Quis melior ?*

One relates he took thirty and thre   thoufand Pipes of To-bacco in one night. He tickles the Auditors. They laugh heartily. Another informs the Company, that the night be-fore having fwallow'd a vaft quantity of Ale, he flinkt home, and crept into Bed, and that in the midft of the night he was wak'd by an Alarum made in his Guts by reafon of an In-furreét on therein. Hereupon he rifeth to expel the Rebel, but his weighty A---- being too ponderous for an earthen Chamber-pot to bear, the Pot broke, and his A --- unluckily fell on the bedighted ground. At this Story the Company laugh *majore cachinno.*

Here I at prefent ftop, having run (methinks) a long race in dirty way, concluding with *Juvenal,*

> *Afpice quid faciunt commercia------*

An Apology to thofe Ingenuous Perfons, who frequent the Coffee-houfe, for this defcription.

THe *Defcriber knows, there are feveral* Virtuofi *and* Ingenuofi, *refort to the Coffee-houfe, whom, he hath the honour to be acquainted with, others are his Friends. Yet all the Elements here being confufedly mixt, this Houfe ap-pears to him as a meer Chaos, fo that (in contemplating it) he cannot prefer even Light before Darknefs, not being here feparated or diftinguifhable one from another, amidft confu-fion it felf.*

> *Verbum fat.*

FINIS.

Woolnoth, *The Coffee Scuffle, Occasioned by a Contest Between a Learned Knight, and a Pitifull Pedagogue. With The Character of a Coffee-House* (Lodon [sic], printed and are to be sold at the Latine Coffee House near the Stocks, 1662), [18]pp.; 8°. BL: 11622.bb.11. ESTCR186857.

A ballad satire detailing a vociferous dispute about the works of Hugo Grotius between two coffee-house debaters, that casts light on the nature of coffee-house discussion and, *inter alia*, learning, philosophy and puritan politics in the early years of the Restoration. The text comprises 93 numbered 4-line stanzas in the typical form of the oral ballad, with alternating four-stress and three-stress lines (with the first and third line having an internal rhyme). The verses are mock heroic, using the high style of the romance ballad to ridicule the protagonists' claims to learning. The first 27 stanzas describe in satirical terms the topics discussed in the coffee-house, mocking especially the diversity and range of subjects addressed there, from politics to science, from quotidian events to sectarian disputes. After describing the coffee-man and his wares (stanzas 27–31) the main protagonists are introduced. On one side is a 'dull Pedagog' or school master called Evans (described stanzas 35–54), sitting at a table in the coffee-room like a King surrounded by petitions and paper. The rest of the poem concerns his dispute (stanzas 55–93) with the 'learned Knight', Sir James Langham, who poses the coffee-house a query, asking why Holland produced such good scholars compared to England. This leads to a panegyrical description of the poetry, philosophy and scholarship of Hugo Grotius, a Dutch Arminian Calvinist influential in English intellectual circles (stanzas 65–75). The poem concludes with Evans's intemperate attack on Grotius and Langham.

The debaters are identified internally as 'Sir J' (stanza 89) and 'E', a Welsh pedagogue or schoolmaster (stanza 87). The copy in the British Library has a contemporary manuscript addition on the verso of last blank leaf: 'This is thought to be made and by one Woolnoth, on Evans a schoole mr [master] & Sr James Langham'. Sir James Langham (1621–99) of Lincoln's Inn and

Cottesbrooke, Northamptonshire, was a member of a notable Dissenter family in the City of London. Langham had represented Northamptonshire in the second Protectorate Parliament, and was elected again in 1661, only to have his election declared void in April 1662 after agitation by the sheriff, Sir William Dudley, who subsequently purged the corporation of Dissenters by modifying the charter. Langham was later described by Burnet (in *Bishop Burnet's History of his Own Time* (London, Thomas Ward, 1724–34) as a very weak man, famous only for speaking florid Latin at every opportunity. In reply to Woolnoth's satire, Evans wrote *The Juniper Lecturer corrected and his Latin, pagan, putid [sic] nonsense paraphrazed; also, The coffee scoffer cussed and kicked, or, The pittifull paedagoog's Latin vindication* (London, n.p., 1662), a 16-page pamphlet attack on Langham and Woolnoth in Latin verse. Woolnoth's counter-reply followed, entitled *Orbilius vapulans [The Flogger Scourged] or A juniper lecture for a moth-eaten scholar. By the authour of the Coffee scuffle* (London, n.p., 1662), eighteen pages of English verse in self-vindication, followed by three pages in Latin (and further identifying 'E' as 'Evans ap Shone's, ap Morgan' from Penmaenmawr in North Wales). Nothing is known of Woolnoth, although Evans's reply perhaps makes a pun on his name ('A Riddle: What [...] Doth Scribble Lies, and filthy flies doth feed? Solution: Woollen breeds Moths', 'The coffee scoffer cussed and kicked', in *The Juniper Lecturer*, p. 11).

The coffee-house is identified as the Latine Coffee-house near the Stocks, presumably a pseudonym describing the learned pretensions on the clientele (no such coffee-house is identified in Lillywhite).

THE
Coffee Scuffle,

Occasioned by a

CONTEST

Between a

Learned Knight,

AND A

Pitifull Pedagogue.

WITH

The Character of a COFFEE-HOUSE.

LODON,
Printed and are to be fold at the Latine Coffee
Houfe near the Stocks. 1662.

THE
Coffee. Scuffle.

[1]

O F Gyants and Knights, and their terrible
Fights
We have ſtories enough in Romances,
Of *Hercule*'s Beam, and one ey'd *Polipheme*,
With *Don Quixot*'s attempts and miſchances:

[2]

But Il' tell you a tale, worth a Noggin of Ale
Of a Combate was lately begun
Between a brave Knight, and a pitiful Wight
That out of th' Arena did run.

[3]

I was t'other day, in a place as they ſay
Where Doctors and Schollars aſſemble :
Where the folk do ſpeak, nought but Latin & Greek
O' twould make a poor Vicar to tremble !

[4]

For hither reſort, a throng of each ſort,
Some clad in blew-aprons, ſome ſattin ;
And each Prentice-boy, and brave Hobedehoi
Doth call for his Coffee in Latine.

A 2   5. But

[5]

But did you but hear, their Latin I fear,
    You'd laugh till you'd burſt your brechees;
To ſee with what ſtate, they break Priſſians pate
    And yet do but ſcratch where it itches.

[6]

One talks, I ſuppoſe, of *Ovid*'s great Noſe,
    With a Bridge as broad as a Biliad;
A third breaks his tooth, with cracking forſooth
    a nutſhel to get out an Iliad.

[7]

One ſtands on his head, ſo Stateſmen are ſaid
    To kick their heels up in the Air
Another Ile be ſwore, doth crawle on all four,
    And lick up the duſt with great care.

[8]

The former man he, cries up Philoſophy
    Admireth brave *Euclid, Diſcartis* ;
The one he crumps roots, and the other he moots,
    And he's a good Lawyer, a fart he'is.

[9]

The one talks of News, the other of Stews,
    And a third of pick-pockets and Bears,
A fourth doth always curſe Maſques, Balls and Plays
    Great *Belzebubs* markets he ſwears.

[10]

One loves Mathematicks, the other Fanaticks
    Store of *Mercuries* here to be found;
A third's for a Lecture, a fourth a Conjecture,
    A fift for a penny in the pound.

11. One

[11]

One Quack doth pretend to foretell the laft end,
    Of Antichrift even to an hour ;
And dares to prefix the year fixty fix
    As the period of the Beafts power.

[12]

The one is for canting the other for ranting,
    With laughing indangers his crupper ;
A fourth's for a Faft, eight hours to laft
    But with a good Breakfaft and Supper.

[13]

The one bids apox, upon *Beza* and *Knox*
    And the reft of that damnable Crew,
Crys up *Blundel* and *Grotius*, *Arminius* and *Voffius*
    As the Doctors that only fpeak true.

[14]

Another's for *Lockier*, fweet *Powel* and *Knocker*,
    Brother *Jeffe* and honey mouth'd *Brook*,
Who's a licenfe of late, to break Priffians pate
    And fay that his Printer miftook.

[15]

Some are for *Taylor*, and fome are for *Naylor*
    And others do cry up the Whipper ;
A third is for *Kiffin*, a fourth is for *Giffin*,
    And a fifth for *Paul Hobs* the Dipper.

[16]

One's for a *Teazar*, anothers for *Keyser*,
  A third doth his *Gildas* adore,
The Counteſſes Uſher, and *Babylons* puſher
  That can't pay his debts he's ſo poor.

[17]

Which was the viler, *Jack Straw* or *Wat Tyles*,
  Or the mad Fifth-monarchy vermine ?
Whether *Harringtons Rota* or *Boyls Vertuoſa*
  Be the nobler deſign they determine ?

[18]

Other ſit and tell tales, of Wakes and Wiſſon Ales,
  and the Whore of *Romes* bauble the Maypole,
The reſt vent their whimſeys, concerning theChim-
  upon which the Parliament lay tole.   (neys,

[19]

And others I find do diſcourſe of the Wind,
  And how the Trees kickt up their heels :
How ChriſtChurch at *Norwich*, theBuſſes at *Harwich*
  was blown down, and turn'd up their keels.

[20]

How the Countryman ſmil'd to ſee's Cock-loft un-
  and theSun peep thorough the rafters,   (til'd
And how't blew the rug, from off *Robin* and *Jug*,
  and turn'd topſeturvey the Wafters.

                                                  21. Onc

[21]

The one fwaggers and fwears, againſt Altars and
   And bleſſeth the Convocation;   (prayers
Saith 'tis a bad wirk, to make coſtive the Kirk,
   Conformitie's no Reformation.

[22]

There are many that fear, the plague will be here
   Before the fourth next month is over.
Another ſays may this choke me, if *Corbet* and *Okey*
   And *Bárkſtead* an't landed at *Dover.*

[23]

The one fee's an Aſſe within a fine glaſs,
   And ſmickers and grins at the ſame ;
And wonders I ſwear which way he came there,
   Into that fine Ebony frame.

[24]

The other talks louder, for Sr. *Kenelms* powder ;
   more ſovereign than that of Steel,
Makes uſe of the fiction of pitifull I*xion*,
   And alwaies is turning the wheel.

[25]

The one he doth ſmoke, and the other good foke,
   Say Tobacco's a ſtinking vapour;
Another can dandle, a Theife in a **Candle**,
   But crucifie *Chriſt* in a **Taper.**

26. And

[27]

And thus are they all, both great, wife and fmall'
  Ingag'd in fuch tattle if not worfe:
And evr'y one doth fpeak, like the members of *Feak*,
  or the Goffips that follow a Courfe.

[28]

The Hoaft on my Soul's an ingenious Pole,
  Like *John* in the Wildernefle di'ght,
The man is fo pirt, and his loynes are begirt,
  And the Locufts fwarm there every night.

[29]

Good Coffee he draws, and fhirbets becaufe,
  They'r pleafant, and fweet Chockalet,
The former doth fpe'd all fumes from the head,
  And the laft makes the P-- to curvet.

[30]

No fack is here drunk, her's no Baud', Whore or Punk
  But pimping fanaticks good ftore:
The Stocks are too neer, for good Ale, and ftrong
  And the Counter to keep e'r a Whore.   (Beer

[31]

Here come loyal Souls, and fanaticall Fools,
  The fons both of God and the Devil:
Where Loyalifts brew, there fanaticks bake too,
  And the good will be mixt with the evil.

35. Yet

[35]
Yet none of them dare fpeak *Latine* I fwear,
 But a Quack, the more is the wonder:
And a dull *Pedagog* with a fnout lik a hogg,
 And a face as flat as a Flounder.

[36]
He whips his boyes Affes and tickles their Taffes,
 Sees which is a man which a woman:
And the poor Schollars nock, is his Dyal and Clock;
 But his own pocky nofe is the *Gnomon.*

[37]
He fits like a King, a Tyrannical thing ,
 His Desk is his Chair and his Throne :
His Scepters a rod, and his globe is a clod,
 And an old *Oxford* Cuftard his Crown.

[38]
Verfes and Theams, the petitions it feems,
 which the Shcollars do bring, and he teares :
And whether he doth break, I cannot well fpeak,
 Poor priffians pate oftner or Theirs.

[39]
The Welfh man Cot tam her, doth Kenn not the
 Defires *Ap Williams* direction,   *Grammar:*
His mony he earns, but the firft thing her learns,
 I dare fay is an *Interjection.*

[40]
But if fo he fome of his Schollars are com'e,
 To that part, which is called *Syntaxe* ;
The *Concords* do reach to the Rod and the Breech,
 And *figura* is read on their backs.

           B   41. He

[41]

He has a forehead of brass, and eares like an Aſs
    And he uſes the Welſhmans houlter :
His noſe and his ſnout, jet forth like a ſpout,
    Or if you pleaſe like a Plow Coulter.

[42]

His breath's muckle ſtrong, and his eye brows are
    Yet hath never a hair on his chin: (long,
His wide mouth hath ſwallow'd his cheeks that are
    And his bones do crump in his ſkin.   (hollow'd

[43]

His eyes are as little as thoſe of a Beetle,
    But O when he ſettles to ſpeak:
I dare ſay you may welly, look into his belly,
    Another devils arſe a peeke.

[44]

His breath would even fill, a ſail drive a mil,
    His Countenance hollow and meager;
Yet his buttocks below, very liking do ſhow,
    And his ſtomach is coming and eager.

[45]

His face doth look Callous, like one dropt from the
    Or ſome of your Newgate Cattel,   (Gallows,
But when he ſpeaks plumbs, fill his wizzin and
    I'd as live hear my Grannums breach twattle.(gums

[46]

The man would be kickt, that ſhould think him a
    For all his thin jaws and courſe grain,   (pickt:
Since the Carrets I trow that do on his head grow,
    Do rather declare him a Dane.

                                        47. Hee

[47]
He hath never a beard, and wel't may be fear'd,
  That the Gentleman wants a Bobin,
Let me be asperst if hee's not hoperarc't,
  Like Aniseed water *Robin*.

[48]
He's a Batchelor, as some do aver,
  And solitarily doth live:
He's too nee'r on my life, to marry a wife,
  Too gluttoning chastly to live.

[49]
Whither's hand, or his foot, his glove or his boot
  Are the bigest I cannot well tell:
Of which of the two make the greatest adoe,
  I ken not the dog or his bell.

[50]
Should *Egypt* I say, thy face but survey,
  Thy uglines they would adore.:
And think thee some odde, old *Memphian* god,
  Found lately cast upon the shoar.

[51]
Let *Africa* see her Monsters in thee,
  The *Crockod'ile*, *Pardus*, and *Iaccall*:
A kennel of those, doth thy person disclose,
  More deformed then those that are black all,

[52]
Sure the Curtaines were rung, with monsters were
  Or thy Father and Mother were Meager;   (hung,
So *Dames* heretofore, by phancying a *More*,
  Have been brought to bed of a *Neager*.

B 2   53 He's

[53]

He's a *Socinian* in fome mens opinion,
　Denyes the divinity of our Saviour:
But I am fure He, hath no humanity,
　If I underftand but behaviour.

[54]

One night above others he met his gude Bro-
　And down to the Table he fits:　　　　(thers,
Falls a talking of Latine, like ruffling of Satine,
　Excepting his hums, and his hits.

[55]

It chanced that night, that a Learned Knight,
　The glory and fhame of the Citty,
Came into the Room as he ufed to come,
　A perfon both ferious and witty.

[56]

Rome never did know, nor *Athens* I trow,
　One fpeak pvrer Latine and Greek,
If *Tully* were here, or *Demofthenes* neer,
　They could not more fluently fpeak.

[57]

That Schollars are Clowns, and flovings in Gowns
　My Grannum I oft have heard fay;
Call 'em blunt tooles, and dogmaticall fooles,
　Good only to preach and to pray.

[58]

But Sir I is a Shollar, Ill wage you a doller,
　A Gentleman both born and bred :
Bloud, vertue, or either, no buskin or feather,
　Have made him to be fo. I ded.

59, Tapfters

[59]

Tapsters and Groomes, and men that sell broomes,
   Did see his accomplishments thorough,
And had not the spie been blind with one eye,
   He had been *Burgess* for the Burrough.

[60]

Yet neverthelefs none but will confess,
   Sir *I*'s of a generous temper:
Who know's how to obey, can rule I dare say,
   Subjectio'ns the way to an Empire.

[61]

The Knight, of no worse did begin to difcourse,
   then of books and of Tongues and of arts:
But firft in the way he a Query did lay,
   And after his judgment imparts.

[62]

His Queries were not fuch as *Harrington* wrote,
   That deferved a frown and a fearch:
Nor were they indeed fuch as Captain *Mead*,
   Did make at *St. Alhallows* Church.

[63]

The query was this, what the reafon is,
   That *Holland*, a thick and grofs aire,
Should breed as good wits, if not better by hits,
   Than *England* a Region more fair:

[64]

He inftanc'd in *Voffius, Erafmus,* and *Grotius,*
   In *Heinfius* and *Schurman* the wonder:
Spanhemius, Barleus, Vanhelmonty Walleus,
   Whofe fame hath refounded like Thunder.

65 But

[65]

But *Grotius* alone, is sufficiently known,
   Great Master of Tongues, and of Arts;
Whom Papists deplore, Protestants adore,
   For his profound learning and parts.

[66]

Grotius, whose Name, on the wings of fame,
   Hath been carried where *Grotius* is dumb:
The talk of these dayes the wonder and maze,
   Of all generations to come.

[67]

Athens and *Syracuse*, *Smarta*, and famous *Greece*,
   Jerusalem live in his story:
And he that shall read his Latine indeed,
   Will swear he sees *Rome* in his glory.

[68]

His Poems do prove how the *Muses* did love,
   The babe, when it lay in its Cradle;   (knees
How they hung like fond bees, on his lips and his
   As Historians of *Plato* do fable.

[69]

Before ever (we know) that *Grotius* could goe,
   Or the least of a man could discover :
His fancie and wit on *Poeticall* feet,
   Had travel'd the Vniverse over.

[70]

Princes and great ones, owe their Scepters and
   To him for his learned defence,   (Crownes,
Of their honour, and power, the Buckler and
   Of *Monarchy*, Allegiance.   (Tower

71. Who

[71]

Who fee's not his learning hath little difcerning,
    Bu't as blind as an Owle or a Widgon;
Dull *Atheift* for why, who his worth doth deny,
    Muft alfo the Truth of Religion.

[72]

But leaft I fhould ftain, fhould wound or prophane,
    So precious and facred a thing,
As *Grotius*, his name, by blending the fame,
    With fuch trifles as thefe that I bring.

[73]

Ile leave him to reft after ftormes at the beft,
    Good marble lie light on his head:
Holland brags of his birth, and *France* of his earth,
    And the World of his bookes it is faid.

[75]

But the fhade dogs the Sun, and the dog bates the
    No vertue without its difgraces: (*Moon*
Though fuch ftories and flams, are but foiles unto
    Or black patches to beautiful faces.   (Gems,

[76]

The *Thredbeare* pedant, gan to ftrut and to vaunt,
    Cals *Grotius*, a Gobernole Preift;
A rotten *Arminian*, and wicked *Socinian*,
    And the fhort pufhing Horne of the Beaft.

[77]

Bafe vile Runegado, francifcan Bravado,
    Idolater, Cavaleer, what not:
Apoftate, bad liver, and reprobate filver,
    And the ftripling his Second a hot fhot.

                         78. His

[78]
His Difcourfes are weak, and his Arguments eke,
  But his Tenents and principles Hideous,
His Lattine with al and his eloquence fmall,
  But his pride and ambition prodigious.

[79]
Nor doth he admire *Hugo* or the Squire,
  But rather demires them both :
Gramercy good Joke, tis a quible is fpoke,
  And the man is a wit by my troth.

[80]
But fuch was the fting of the zealous thing,
  That he called as many bad names,
As the Papifts did *Parry*, the monk did Old *Harry*,
  And the boatfwain the *Billings-gate* dames.

[81]
Sir I doth ingage, 'thought paffion or rage,
  To vindicate *Grotius* his fame ;
But as for himfelf let the whippiting elfe,
  Talk himfelf out of breath a Gods name.

[82]
Tis beneath a great Soul, to regard what a fool
  His perfon or learning fhall ftile,
From a Hector or Drab, 'twould call for a ftab
  From a Gentleman only a fmile.

[83]
A fmile fometime will, as fatally kill
  as a Poniard, a Sword or a Dagger,
Not to mind or regard, an affront's a reward
  Sufficient to make a fool fwagger.

84. His

[84]
His blood was too thin, and his perfon too mean
   to merit revenge from Sir J.
His boys fhall chaftife, his bafe contumelies ;
   what Eagle will cope with a Flye ?

[85]
Let the dogs bough-wough foon, our Knight like
   fhall move in his orbe and his fphear,   (the Moon
His fame fhall be hurl'd,thorough the *Brittifh* world
   and his light maugre clouds fhall appear.

[86]
Sharpe tongues, blubber lips, no more can eclipfe
   his worth then a punctum of earth,
Then a cloud or a fhade, can skreen and invade
   the Sun in his glory and mirth.

[87]
Let *E.* and his train go learn *Cato* again,
   and then let 'em come and difcourfe ;
Though the Coffee-houfe can't of much comple-
   yet its dialect is not fo courfe.   (ment vant

[88]
But who would have thought, that a bufinefs of
   fhould occafion fuch words with a p——(nought
When 'twas only I trow, which fhould uppermoft
   An Englifh tale or Butterbox.   (go

[89]
Sir J. God forbid, he did no way recede
   from Nature, from Honor or Reafon :
Nor did he forfwear his own Climate and air,
   which would amount almoft to treafon.

                                    90.He

[·90]

He acknowledged then, that no learneder men
   have ever been bred on the main,
Then have flourisht some while in this troublesom
   and may so for all this again.   (Isle

[91]

Yet 'tis justice say you, to give all men their due,
   Hugo Grotius wrote rarely well,
And what we can't reach to condemn and impeach
   is the pride of the Angels that fell.

[92]

Then let pitiful *E* crouch down on his knee,
   and to the Knight pardon implore:
His boys you may swear, with many a tear
   for lesser mistakes have done more.

[93]

So thus together they came, like two Cocks of the
   But what was the issue say you sirs?   (game,
F. had the best beak, if I may so speak,
   But Sir *J.* had the sharper Spurs.

F I N I S.

The Tryall of the Coffee-Man: Wherein He is Indicted,
Arraigned, Convicted, and Condemned, by Sir Benjamin
Bacchus, Sir Mathew Malt, Sir Henry Hop, Sir Francis
Froth, judges of the court. Mr. Antidote, Mr. Purge, Mrs.
Dorothy, Mrs. Jone, Witnesses. Simon Swift, Clark to
the Court. Four Maids, Four Wives, and Four Widows,
Gentlewomen of the Jury. Also, the Petition and Desires
of many Thousands Maids, Wives, and Widows, in
and about the city of London, in behalf of themselves,
and all their sex. With the Coffee-mans Confession;
and the heavy Sentence pronounced against him by
Judge Bacchus. Published for the benefit of all Vintners,
Brewers, Victuallers, Cooks, Alewives, Tapsters, and
true Companions to the Pot, Pipe, and Can ([London],
printed for J[ohn] Jones, in the Arabian Kalender,
1662/3), [2], 6pp.; 4°. Worcester College Library, Oxford
University. ESTCR185503.

A mock trial report detailing a fictional case brought by the purveyors of traditional English beverages against the coffee-man, who they accuse of being an
interloper on their trade, a harmful innovation, and the cause of the corruption
of morals in the city. The satire offers a consistent and extended imitation of
a legal report, making entertaining use of legal diction and forms of writing,
including a copy of an indictment and a judicial sentence. The tract's comedy
derives from the ridiculous contrast between the associations of authority pertaining to these legal forms of writing and the often vulgar and obscene language
of the protagonists.

The satire begins with the arrest of the coffee-man, Don Ballingo Blackburnt, by a group of London tradesmen involved in the food and beverage trades, including a vintner, a brewer and a victualler. These men accuse the coffee-man of stealing their trade, and bring him before a court presided over by magistrates associated with their own trades (Sir Benjamin Bacchus, Sir Mathew Malt, Sir Henry Hop and Sir Francis Froth), with a jury of London women. In the course of the brief trial, Blackburnt and his coffee are found guilty not only of encroaching upon the trade of the brewer and vintner, but also of rendering the men of the city impotent. Two witnesses, Dorothy and Jone (Joan), give testimony to the deleterious effect of coffee on the virility of the city's men-folk. After the jury finds Blackburnt guilty, he is condemned to a remarkable and vicious execution: he is to be stained black by immersion in coffee, have his sexual organs cut off, carried naked through the streets, beaten with bull's penises, until finally, at Billingsgate market, he is to be stoned to death with sheep's testicles. In as much as the coffee-man is found guilty, and is condemned to death, the satire would seem to be written against coffee. But as the charges laid against the coffee-man and his coffee by the traditional beverage tradesmen are also clearly trumped up, their complaints are also shown to be self-interested and insubstantial.

The anonymous pamphlet was published by John Jones (fl. 1658–65), a bookseller in Cornhill near the Royal Exchange (*ODNB* and Plomer). He was also the publisher of John Crouch's Royalist anti-coffee-house tract *The maidens complain[t]* (see pp. 45–54 below), published in 1763, a tract which elaborates on some of the concerns of *The Tryall*, uses some of the same characters, and has some of the same literary flavour. Unlike *The maidens complain[t]*, however, there is no evidence that *The Tryall* was written by John Crouch. The title suggests that the implied author is the clerk to the court, Simon Swift.

THE

TRYALL

OF THE

Coffee-Man :

Wherein He is Indicted, Arraigned,
Convicted, and Condemned, by

Sir *Benjamin Bacchus*,			Mr: *Antidote*,	
Sir *Mathew Malt*,	Judges of		Mr. *Purge*,	Witnesses.
Sir *Henry Hop*,	the Court.		Mrs. *Dorothy*,	
Sir *Francis Froth*,			Mrs. *Jone*,	
Simon Swift, Clark to the Court.		Four Maids, four Wives, and four Widows,		Gentlewomen the Jury.

ALSO,

The *Petition* and *Desires* of many Thousands Maids, Wives, and
Widows, in and about the City of *London*, in behalf of themselves,
and all their Sex. With the *Coffee-mans* Confession; and
the heavy Sentence pronounced against him by
Judge *BACCHUS*.

Published for the Benefit of all Vintners, Brewers, Victuallers, Cooks, Ale-wives, Tapsters, *and true Companions to the Pot, Pipe, and Can.*

Printed for *F. Jones*, in the *Arabian Kalender*, 166$\frac{2}{3}$.

(1)

The Tryal of the Coffee-man.

Vintner.

VVEll overtaken Sir, whither away in such haft ?

Coffee-man. I am posting Home Sir, my Trade being in it's prime near *Change*-time.

Vint. You have a brave time on't, nothing like to quick Trading ; it can't choose but go well with you, for he muft needs go the Devil drives ; it seems Hell-broth is a Thriving Commodity, when good *Canary* lies by the *Lee*.

Coff. Pray be content Sir, your Trade's good enough.

Vint. I wifh my gain were like yours, for if I want Cuftom, my Sack devours it felf, which cannot be reviv'd or preferv'd without great charge, though you with a little fair Water replenifh your lofs ; fo that your new-tempting Liquor is as great a Cheat to the City, as the crafty VVhore of *Canterbury* was to the Lawyers Clark.

Brewer. 'Tis very true, for we have no way to help our felves, though he can cozen the Excize-man at pleafure ; if we do but get a falfe Guile 'tis found out, the Excize-man every Brewing attending to gage our Coppers, and if he finds us to play faft and loofe, he makes us to pay througo the Nofe ; yet there's no finding him out, unlefs they attend his Houfe, drink *coffee*, and wait all day ; fo that if he gives an account of one Gallon in Ten, he comes off like an honeft man, for, *Tom Colling* Law, he efcapes free, right or wrong.

Victualler. Come Brothers, there's more ways to the *wood* then one, we fhall never thrive till we have beat up his Quarters.

Coffee-man. You have no caufe to complain, you can nick
and

(2)

and froth luftily, though I fill my Difhes brim-full, & cheat no man of his Meafure.

Victualler. We'l fhew you a Trick for your Learning ; let's Indict him, for if we can but cut him off, our Trade will flourifh gallantly.

Coffee-man. Not too faft Mt. *Nimble*, pray who fhall Indict you Mr. *Vintner*, for felling your Wine contrary to the Act at 12 d. a Pint, fmothering your Knavery with a Plate of Olives, or 2 or 3 Oranges, which brings you off like an honeft man; yet I muft fuffer, although I give many a Pipe of Smoak to a Difh of *Coffee*.

Victualler. We'l Sir ! When you are Condemn'd & executed, take a Legal Tryal if you can ; in the mean time, we'l feize you.

The Plot being laid, they apprehend him, and fend him Prifoner to the *Brewers* Stoak-hole.

The Court being call'd, Sir *Benjamin Bacchus*, Sir *Mathew Malt*, Sir *Henry Hop*, and Sir *Francis Froth*, appeared on the Bench, where the Jaylor Mr. *Stoaker* brought the Prifoner to the Bar; And a Jury was pannel'd of 4 Widows, 4 Wives, and 4 Maids, Mrs. *Troublefom* being chofen Fore-woman of the jury. The Clerk having Order (after *O Yes*, made three times) fpake as followeth, *Don Ballingo Blackburn, Hold up thy Hand at the Bar, and hearken to the Charge whereof thou ftandest Indicted.*

The Copy of the Indictment.

Don Ballingo Blackburn, Thou ftandeft Indicted, for that thou haft contrary to Law brought in and put to publick Sale that New-Invented and Black Liquor called Coffee, *not onely to the deftruction of the lawful Trade of Vintners, Brewers, Victuallers, Ale-wives, Tapfters, Cooks, and others ; but alfo infected many young Batchelors, Widowers, and marryed men, to the great injury and un-doing of Maids, Widows, and Wives ; fo that they have been difa-*
bled

(3)

bled from reaching the Line of Communication, and. also unfit to enter their S onces by way of Battery, or otherwise.

What can'st thou say for thy self, art thou Guilty of the Felony whereof thou standest Indicted.

Blackburnt. Not Guilty my Lord.

Clerk. How wilt thou be try'd ?

Blackburnt. By all the *Coffee-men* in *England.*

Clerk. You must be try'd by the Court, and a lawful Jury provided for the same end and purpose.; What can you say for your self?

Blackburnt. I say that the Liquor I provided was for the good of this Nation, not onely for the restoring Drunkards to their Sences, but the Sick to their Health, it being an infallible Medicine for the Cure of all Diseases.

The Witnesses being call'd and sworn, gave Evidence as follows.

Antidote. I know him to be the man that hath done much good for my Profession, by poysoning the People, which is not for my profit to declare, were not I sworn, though it infects the whole Body with Diseases.

Judge. What say you *Purge* ?

Purge. Since *Coffee* came up, I have utter'd more Syrups, Pills, and Ingredients, than I did before.

Judg. *Jone,* What can you say against the Prisoner at the Bar, speak, for now he stands upon his Deliverance ?

Jone. I'm sure for my part he's been my destruction ; for honest *Tom* before that Liquor came up, was as kind to me as heart could desire; but now he's much alter'd, & brought into such a condition, that though I am always ready to serv him, he is notwithstanding as backward, as a Thief to take Cart.

Judge. And what canst thou say *Dorothy* ?

Dorothy. Marry I can say enough, had he been hang'd 7 years

years ago it had bin better for me ; **For our** *Dick* **is undone** by this Drink, he is as lank as a Dish-clout, and absolutely Standard-fallen, being not fit for **Service ;** so that whatever she be that marryes such a one, *Poor Soul,* what greater sorrow can befall her.

Judge. Mr. *Blackburnt,* you hear the Witnesses have given Evidence against you, can you say any thing more for your self ?

Coffee. I desire the mercy of the Bench ; for what I did, I was driven to through Poverty, Trading being dead, I knew this way would take with all sorts of People, who delight in new Fancies more then that which may be for their Health and Happiness.

Judge. **Gentlewomen** *of the Jury,* You hear what the Witnesses have Evidenced against the Prisoner at the Bar, and what he can say for himself ; you are, according to your Oaths, to bring in your Evidence according to Law, for or against the Prisoner at the Bar.

The Jury withdraw.

Judg. Officer, look that none do prompt the Jury, or pervert them.

Their private Discourse.

The **4** *Wives.* For our parts we find him guilty, in regard we have not the love of our Husbands as formerly , but are forced to use young Gallants at home, whilst they spend their Estates at the *Coffee,* smoaking their Noses like *Indians,* till their Inwards are like to a *Westphalia* Ham.

The 4 *Widows.* Truly, formerly we were in hopes of good rich Widowers, having brought them to such a Point, that we had them at pleasure ; but now give them a Dish of *Coffee,* and the Case is alter'd.

The 4 *Maids,* Indeed, for our parts, we have sufficient cause to complain, for this sad Liquor hath so shortned the
                                                                   Abilities

(5)

Abilities of Batchelors, that we are compell'd to live fingle; leaft we dye without Iffue, and our Portions be confumed in a *Coffee-houfe* ; befides, fince this Liquor came up, we enjoy not the pleafure we had formerly; for now when we fhould go with Young-men to *Iflington*, *Holloway*, *Lambeth*, or other places of Recreation; to be merry with a Bott'e of Sack,or a Pot of Ale and a Cake, they are fometimes at a *Coffee-houfe* drinking that black-burnt Broth, and fmoking of their Nofes ; fo that we are much prejudic'd thereby : Let us therefore cut him off, whileft the Power is in our Hands, for it is dangerous to detract time.

All the Jury. Come, we are all agreed, he is Guilty, let's give in our Verdict.

Cryer. Room for the Gentlewomen of the Jury.

Clark. Gentlewomen of the Jury, Are you agreed in your Verdict ?

Jury. We are all agreed.

Clark. Who fhall fpeak for you ?

Jury. Miftrifs *Troublefome* our Fore-woman.

Clark. Don Ballingo Blackburnt., Hold up thy Hand ; *Gentlewomen of the Jury*, Look upon the Prifoner at the Bar, is he guilty of the Injuries and Wrongs whereof he ftands Indicted, or not Guilty ?

Fore-woman. Guilty of all.

Clark. Hearken to your Verdict: You fay that *Don Ballingo Blackburnt* is guilty of all and every one of the Wrongs and Injuries whereof he is Indicted, and fo you fay all.

Jury. Yes, we do fo.

Clark. Gentlewomen of the Jury, the Court do difcharge you for this time.

The Jury being difcharg'd, a Petition was deliver'd to the Bench, in the Names of many Thonfands Maids, Widdowes,

(6)

dows, and Wives, in and about the City of *London*; which was to this effect ; *That whereas their Sex had bin the greatest sufferers by the Invention of this Enemy to Women ; so they desired the Favour, that one of them might appoint the punishment that should be pronounced against the Prisoner at the Bar.*

The Petition was granted, and Mrs. *Troublesome* call'd into the Court, who deliver'd the Sentence in writing to Judg *Bacchus.*

Clark. O yes, O yes, O yes, Silence in the Court, whilest Sentence is giving to the Prisoner at the Bar.

Judge. Mr. *Blackburnt*, You are here found guilty by the Jury, upon Evidence of several Witnesses ; hearken therefore to your Sentence.

You are to be caryed back to the Stoke-hole, from whence you came, and from thence to be carryed to the next *Brewers* Copper, being fill'd with thy own Liquor, to stand there up to thy Neck, till thy Skin be as black as thy *Coffee*, then to have thy principal Members cut off, afterwards to go stark naked through the City, and be beaten by the Maids of *London* with Bulls Engines, till thou comest to *Billinsgate*, where the Fish-wives, Oyster-Lasses, and Orange-Girls, shall pelt thee with Ram-stones, till thou art *Dead, Dead, Dead.*

F I N I S.

Merc. Democ. [John Crouch], *The maidens complain[t]
against coffee. Or, The coffee-house discovered, beseiged,
stormed, taken, untyled and lai[d] open to publick view, in a
merry couference [sic] between Mr. Black-burnt the coffee-man.
Mr. Suck-soul the userer. Mr. Antidote the mountibank. Mr.
Purge the apothecarier. Mris. Troublesome the userers wife.
Snap-short the usurers man. Toby the brokers man. Dorothy
the userers maid. And Joane the brokers maid. Being very
pleasant and delightsome for old and young, lads and lasses,
boyes and girles, Omnium gatherum, as the devout ironmonger
quotes it, in his annotations upon Toby and his dog* (London,
printed for J. Jones and are to be sold at the Royal Exchange
in Cornhil, 1663). [2], 6pp.; 4°. Houghton Library, Harvard
University: *EC65 A100 663m2. Hünersdorff.

The maidens complain[t] is a satirical mock complaint by the Royalist hack John
Crouch (*c.* 1615–*c.* 1680). The mock complaint was one of the ephemeral verse
forms of the mid-seventeenth century, the kind Pepys collected in his 'penny merriments'. Burlesques of petitions and complaint literature proliferated in the heated
controversies and pamphlet wars of the Interregnum and Restoration literary scene.
A complaint was a legal device, an utterance of grievance or injustice laid before a
court or judicial authority. Writers had long made use of its satirical potential, as
is seen in works such as *The Maidens Complaint of her Love's Inconstancie*, a popular broadsheet song first published in 1620, and G.M., *The Citizens Complaint for
Want of Trade* (London, n.p., 1663), a satirical verse complaint on the shortage of
coin. In the case of *The maidens complain[t]*, the complaint concerns the impotence
in men caused by coffee, ironically delivered by some highly libidinous women.
   The idea that coffee caused impotence in men was not without scientific cred-
ibility in this period: Ottoman sources making this claim had been noted by the
German physician Adam Olearius (Oehischlaeger) (1603–71) in his embassy
to Persia in 1634, published in German in 1647 and translated into English in

1663. In his *Voyages and Travells ... to the King of Persia*, Olearius states that 'the Persians are perswaded this water [Cahwa or Coffee] is able absolutely to smother all Natural heat, and to take away the power of engendering' (trans. by John Davies (London, John Starkey and Thomas Basset, 1662), p. 240). But the satire is not directly concerned with medical theory: rather the topic is the transformation in the sociable manners of men occasioned by and celebrated in the coffee-house, which stands as a synecdoche for cultural change. Dorothy and Joan, the highly sexed servant women, both lament that their men have lost interest in them since they started attending the coffee-house. The tenor and the vehicle of these complaints demonstrate that the writer's rejection of the coffee-house is also a rejection of the values of the new urban culture that emerged in the Interregnum, and which had proliferated in the Restoration.

The pamphlet is ascribed to 'Merc. Democ.' or Mercurius Democritus, the pseudonym of Royalist newsbook writer John Crouch from the 1640s to his death. Crouch was a bookseller during the 1640s who came to notice as the writer of anti-puritan pamphlets in 1648 (see Gerard Jason McElligott, 'Propaganda and Censorship: the underground royalist newsbooks, 1647–1650' (PhD dissertation, University of Cambridge, 2000), pp. 203–42). From 1649–50 he wrote a Royalist newsbook called the *Man in the Moon*, which contained mainly obscene stories and rhymes discreditable to parliamentarians and army officers. In 1652 he began *Mercurius Democritus*, a satirical Royalist newsbook that ran for 86 weekly numbers and was revived for 10 issues between April and May 1659, and again in 1661 (connections with *The maidens complain[t]* are reinforced by the full title of the periodical in 1659, *Mercurius democritus, or, A perfect nocturnal. Communicating many strange wonders out of the world in the moon, the Antipodes, Maggy-land, Tenebris, Fary-land, Greenland, and other adjacent countries; published for the right understanding of all the mad-merry people of Great-Bedlam* (May 1659)). *The Man in the Moon* was also revived in 1663. Crouch's printer, for both newsbooks and *The maidens complain[t]*, was John Jones (fl. 1658–65), a bookseller who published political pamphlets and satires, and who kept shop in or near the Royal Exchange between 1658 and 1665 (*ODNB* and Plomer). Copies are available in Houghton Library, Harvard, the library of Christ Church, Oxford, and the Bayerische Staatsbibliothek, Munich.

Jones published an eight-page satirical reply to *The maidens complain[t]* in the same year, *The Coffee-Mans Granado Discharged Upon the Maidens Complaint Against Coffee. In a dialogue between Mr. Black-Burnt and Democritus; Wherein is Discovered severall Strange, Wonderful, and Miraculous Cures Performed by Coffee, (the like never heard of since the Creation)* (London, J. Johnson, 1663); BL: 1038. i.45; ESTCR171418). Notionally written by a Spanish gentleman, Don Bollicosgo Armuthaz, it presents a satirical apology for chocolate, a competitor with coffee sold in similar establishments, and often advertised together. The greater part of the reply is a dialogue between Black-burnt, the coffee-man from *The maidens complain[t]*, and Democritus, which is to say, John Crouch. In their discussion, Black-burnt attempts to defend coffee by retailing its supposed medical properties, but ironically each story reveals how coffee has rendered men impotent. In response, two milkmaids from Islington, Cissy and Peg, discuss the restorative and priapic properties of chocolate.

THE

Maidens Complain

Againſt COFFEE.

OR, THE

COFFEE-HOUSE

DISCOVERED,

Beſieged, Stormed, Taken, Untyled and laid

Open to publick view, in a merry Conference between

Mr. *Black-burnt* the Coffee-man.		*Snap-ſhort* the Uſurers man.
Mr. *Suck-ſoul* the Uſerer.		*Toby* the Brokers man.
Mr. *Antidote* the Mountibank.		*Dorothy* the Uſerers maid.
Mr. *Purge* the Apothecaries.		And
Mrs. *Troubleſome* the Uſerers wife.		*Joane* the Brokers maid.

BEING

Very pleaſant and delightſome for Old and Young, Lads and Laſſes, Boyes and
Girles, *Omnium gatherum*, as the devout *Ironmonger* quotes
it, in his Annotations upon *Toby* and his Dog.

Written by Merc. Democ. *at his Chamber in the World in the Moon, for the benefit
of all the mad-merry-conceited people under the Sun.*

L O N D O N, Printed for J. Jones and are to be ſold at the *Royal Exchange*
in *Cornhil*, 1663.

(1)

THE

COFFEE-HOUSE

UNTYL'D.

Black-burnt

Who's at dore?

Troublesom. Is my Husband here?

Blak. He is juft come in. Pray Mris *Trouble-*
some go into the Coffee-room, there's none but
a Broker with him.

Troubl. Truly Mr. *Suck-soul* you drive a fine
Trade here, you I ene make your body as black with this curfed liquor,
as your Soul is with extortion; but efaith I'le beat up your quarters
a little oftner then I have done; for if your haunt be here *Black-burnt*
will Soul-fuck you with his Coffee more than you do the poor with
extortion.

Black. Indeed Mris *Troublesome* you judge very uncharitably, for
my gain is but ten pence in the fhilling, and I am as well contented
with that as he that gets pounds.

Troubl. I marry, that you may well be, for ten pence in the fhilling
is juft 83 pound, 6 fhillings and 8 pence *per cent.* and if my husband
get but 30 or 40 pound in the hundred hee's as fafe as a thief in a mill,
Come *Suck-soul*, let's be gone.

Suck-soul. Prethee love be patient, I'le follow the prefently.

Troubl. You fhall go with me, or the houfe fhall be to hot to hold
you or any of your Companions, before *Black-burnt* fhall keep you

A 2 up

(2)

up in his Hell-black Ordinary, I'le make h'm fly his houfe, I and his Country too.

Black. Pray Mris. *Troublefome* don't make fuch a ratling noife here to d fturb my houfe, and frignt away my cuftomers, if you do, I fhall be forced to turn you out a dores.

Troubl. Ufe better languæge, Sirrah, be more Civil,
   Or I fhall fling you: Coffee to the Devil.

Suck. Mr. *Black-burt* I muft needs go, or there will be fuch a peal of thunder by and by, as will far exceed the heat of your Coffee ; for this is but one of my Wives preaubles fhe will enlarge prefently, to prevent that da, ger fa evil.

Antidote and *Purge.*

Ant. Well overtaken Mr. *Purge,* 'Whether away fo faft ?

Purg. In footh I'me going to the Devils O dinary call'd the Coffee Houfe.

Ant. I faith Change time is almoft paft. Let's away w to all dexterity, agility and celerity leaft we lofe our oportunity ; for I intend to perfwade as man, a, I can to drink that Indian liquor, 'twill make work enough for me.

Purg. I and for me too I hope, if your trade go forward

Ant. And that it fhall do, for what Ingredients I want, I'le have of none but your felf.

Purg. Come then, let's enter this Coffee-houfe.

Ant. Mr. *Black-burnt*, Have you any Coffee ready ?

Black. Yes Sir, the beft in *London.*

Ant. Give me a difh. Oh it's rare liquor, good for feveral difeafes, an infallible Medicine I'le promife you for the Gout, Confumption, Dropfie, Ptifick and all other Maladies.

All the Cuftomers. Truly Sir we have found fome good in it, but if it be infallible, and fo rare for all difeafes, wee'l make this our head-quarters.

Ant. Do you fee Mr. *Purge* how it takes with them, I fhall have imployment enough ; for I know it is the only liquor in the univerfe, to fill the body with difeafes, it drys up the brains, putrifies the blood, fhrinks up the Sinews, Nerves, Arteries and corodes upon every part of the body, that I am fure to have patients enow infected to fill my Coffers.

Purg. Sil, I hope as fortune favours you with ftore of patients,
                                                          you

(3)

you will be pleased to favour me with your Custome, fo: I can fit you with Unguents, Syrups, O,ls, Pills, Plaisters, Powders, and other In gredients of all sorts.

Ant. I know thou'rt an able fellow, be confident of my custome, till when farewell.

Enter Dorothy and Jone.

Dorothy. Honest *Ione*, how fares it with you these hard times ?

Ione. Worse then ever I expected; for I believe I shall never en-joy any comfort from our man *Snapshort* since he went with my Ma-ster to the *Coffee-house*, he is so dry as a kix, that damn'd liquor will shorten his life and ability at least five in the fifteen.

Dorothy And truly our *Toby* is come to the same passe ; for since he drank *Coffee*, he is no more like the man he was then an apple's like an O,ster.

Ione. In truth *Dorothr* my Mistris complains as much of my Master; for now, if she look him, she finds him no where but at a *Coffee-house* forsooth, with a dish in his hand and a pipe at his nose, where there's a smoak like a Brewers Stoak-hole.

Dorothy. Verily *Ioane* my Miis. dos cry out as much against my Master, for formerly she was wont to find him at a Taverne, where she could have a glasse of Canary to refresh her languishing spirits, but now (since this black-broth came up) if she look him, hee's at a *Coffee house*, making a chimney of his noddle, where there is such an odious scent; fogh, fogh, fogh it makes my heart ake to think what a Jaques he makes of his brains.

Ioane. I believe the Devil first invented this liquor , on purpose to plague our Sex.

Dor. I imagine so too, but rather then I'le dote upon a man that drinks *Coffee*, I am resolv'd to leod Apes in Hell.

Ioane. And Devils to rather then I will chink,
Upon such sots as Hell-burn'd Liquors drink.

Dorothy. I protest *Ione* there's a little comfort in *Chocolate* , but before I'le fling my self away upon any such dry horson as drinks *Coffee*, I'le wrap my Maiden-head in my smock, and fling it into the Ocean to be bugger'd to death by young Lobsters.

Ioane. And for my part, I'le hang my Maiden-head on a Wind-mill to be bated to death by the four Winds, rather then be poyson'd with the scent of old crusts, and shreads of Leather burn'd and beaten to
powder,

(4)

powder, of which I believe this curfed *Coffee* is made ; fome decayed
Marchant has doubtlefs breught this in fafhion to replenifh his crack'd
eftate ; and without queftion blind *Hewfon* was the firft inventer of
this liquor, who converted his old fhoes to powder, and fent them over
on purpofe to poyfon the *Englifh* , but I'le do the beft I can to preferve my felf from being infected with the fcent of the Devils ordinary, and fo farewel fifter *Dorothy*.

Dorothy. Adieu till to morrow, and then, if we meet, inftead of
Coffee, wee'l have a cup of wholfom Ale and a toft, till when let us be
gone for yonder comes *Snapfhort* and *Toby*.

Toby. Heav'ns affift me ' What's this ? a vifion ' Sure 'tis honeft
Snapfhort the Uferers man ' Efaith 'tis he in his own likenefs, How
fairs it with you?

Snap. So ftrangely that I am ready to ftagger with thinking, as much
as the moft diftemper'd fot in the world can be with fwallowing a
whole brewing of *Englifh Ale*.

Toby. Prethee *Snapfhort* what's the caufe of thy fuddain diftemper?

Snap. Caufe enough to make thee mad if there were no more men
in the world but thy felf ; for upon *Thurfday* laft, I travel'd to the
Royal Exchange, to collect certain fums of mony due to my Mafter
from fome decayed Marchants ; and by the confufed noife of feveral
Languages, I was fo confounded in my noddle that my brains ran to
and fro like a foot-boy ; and paffing from thence into *Lothbury*, I
went into a *Coffee-houfe*, took a difh of that Hell-burn'd liquor, thinking to fettle them in their right Center, with the ratling noife of Kettles, Skimers and Ladles amongft the Brafiers, my brains run round fo
fwift as a Wind-mill, and all my joynts were as num as a old Wo-
mans troubled with the dead Palfy 30 years togather, till I went into
Moor-fields, took a turn or two in the Uferers walk, and drank a cup of
good wholfome Ale, with which I was revived, enlivened and reftored
to my memory, fo perfectly, that I had an account in my pate of every
penny due to my Mafter fince the Creation.

Toby. Sfoot *Snapfhort*, I'me not a little joyful of thy recovery to
thy fences, but for that curfed Indian liquor, 'twill poyfon a horfe, it
is a drench for the Devil ; for fince I drank *Coffee*, twice I adventer'd
to ftorm the Fortreffe of our maid *Joane*, with as much eagernefs as
ever the Great Turk did attempt to gain *Conftantinople* ; yet all my
hopes were fruftrated, and I did but juft fling away a nights lodging or

two

(5)

two, to as little purpose as if I had run my Head into a Kitching-stuff Tub;

> But I'le leave *Coffee*, for a cup of *Bracket*
> Will fit a youngman for a Maidens Pl———

Snap. I that, that, that's the liquor I fancy; for I've as great an ambition to try our maid *Dorothy* as ever I had to satisfy my hungry maw with a breakfast of poach'd Eggs.

Toby. Honest *Snapshort*, I'le help the to a cup of the best about *London*, for a cunning Landaberis of mine invited me (not long ago) to a house in *Petty-France*, where after a bottle or two, I grew so strong, that I call'd for a more convenient room, went up staires, had a fresh bottle, flung her on the bed, and gave her as good a meales meat as ever she eat since the prime of her understanding; these are the effects of *Bracket*, but for *Coffee*, that curs'd liquor disables the most valiant Hectors in the universe. Nay, I dare pawn my honesty, had *Coffee* been made in the days of fair *Hellen* of *Greece*, so many heroick Champions would not have been so lusty, to adventur their lives and fortunes for a *Nunquam satis.*

> Rather than I will such damn'd liquor take,.
> I'le drink the waters of the *Stygian Lake.*

Snap. But to leave off this dispute, where shall we pacifie the fury of our angry Stomacks with a good dinner?

Toby. If you'l accept of such faire as I have provided for a friend or two of mine, you shall be as welcome as Maycrel in *May*; Go with me to the *Labour in Vain*, I have bespoke a Shoulder of Veal stufft with Cockles, a Lobster-tart, a Goose-giblet Custard, net'e a bone of Bief, a Lack of Mutton and two Wood-cocks, if you'l make a third you'l find as good company as your self; for there's *Donpancratone*, the Spanish Postelion, and Mounsieur *La Flamsted* the Plank-weavet of *Tenebrosa*, as good company as ever mortal mouth'd meat withal, besides a rare eccho of invissible musick.

Snap. Never was gentleman of quality better pleas'd with a dinner than I am in election to be. Divine chear! Oh how pomper'd my poor panch is like to be by honest *Toby!* Veal, Cockles, Lobsters, Mutton, Bief. Wood-cocks, Goose-giblets, Musick and pure company; the gods themselves could not have more variety of dainties for fish and flesh; But among all this chear is there no *Coffee*?

Snap.

(8)

Toby. Not a drop comes in my mouth or any mans there. What, poyſon my gueſſe, no honeſt *Snapſhort*, there's a cup of good wholeſome *Engliſh* Ale,

        'Twill ſting your Noſe like Nector, and will raiſe
        Rich Rubies to your everlaſting praiſe.

Snap. Come noble *Toby* let's away to dine,
        And ſteep our drowſie ſouls in ſparkling Wine.

    The Mountebanks Poſtcript to the Reader.

Reader, this drink call'd Coffee, *it is good*
To dry the Brains, and putrefie the Blood :
It Cures the Body of its health, no doubt
The ſight alſo, if that it put not out
The eye:, its full of Gravel, and there's none
That uſe it, but may ſoon obtain the Stone,
The Palſie, Dropſie, Gout, Feaver and Ptiſick ,
So that in fine, they'l come to me for Phyſick :
It dryes up moiſture, ſhortens precious life,
And makes a man unkind unto his Wife :
It makes a Chriſtian blacker far within,
Then ever was the Negars outward skin :
Its of a Berry, men, this liquor make ,
Which is tranſported from the Stygion Lake,
Upon the Banks of it theſe buſhes growes,
The which the Stygion waters overflows,
(Like Nilus *) and ſo nouriſht is this Weed,*
That now hath gain'd the name of Coffee ſeed :
If't be not brought from Styx, *no man can tell,*
(It is ſo black) except it grow in Hell.

FINIS

A Cup of Coffee: or, Coffee in its Colours (London, n.p.,1663). BL: C.20.f.2(373). ESTCR33428. Hünersdorff.

A broadsheet verse satire is a single-sheet publication printed on one side, in three columns of closely printed text. It is more likely that such broadsides were intended to be read alongside other printed volumes rather than displayed on the wall. The satire extends to 154 lines in rhymed pentameter couplets, and is broadly burlesque in its strategy, imitating a serious, even heroic, manner to discuss a vulgar, quotidian and fraudulent topic, coffee and coffee-houses. As a target of satire, coffee-houses and coffee-men – 'these sons of nothing' (l. 47) – are emblematic of the profound political and cultural revolution that was occasioned in London by the restoration of the monarchy in 1660. But the satire further explores coffee's medicinal properties and physiological effects, which had been widely inflated by medical writers (surveyed in Volume 4 of this edition). These claims are ridiculed here, and coffee are revealed to be a fraudulent and inefficacious quack remedy that (contradictorily) encourages syphilis and other morbid conditions. The taste and flavour of coffee are given extensive analysis, denigrated by repeated and diverse associations with excrement. In part this curiosity about the 'hogo of sirreverence', not only in coffee but also China ale and other spiced drinks, suggests a search for, and curiosity about, a critical language for new bitter flavours (see Ellis, *Coffee-House*, pp. 116–17).

Nothing is known of the writer or publisher. Two copies are extant, one in the collection of ballads assembled by Narcissus Luttrell (1657–1732) in the British Library, and the other in the Houghton Library, Harvard University. Lines from this satire (ll. 1–33) were quoted in Isaac D'Israeli, *Curiosities of Literature*, 3 vols (London, Frederick Warne, 1866), vol. II, p. 323; and the poem has been widely cited in the twentieth century.

A Cup of

COFFEE:

OR,

Coffee in its Colours.

FOr Men and Christians to turn Turks, and think
T' excuse the Crime becaufe 'tis in their drink,
Is more then Magick, and does plainly tell
Coffee's extraction has its heats from Hell.
Pure English Apes! ye may, for ought I know,
Would it but mode, learn to eat Spiders too.
Should any of your Grandfires Ghofts appear
In your Wax-Candle-Circles, and but hear
The name of Coffee fo much call'd upon,
Then fee it drank like fcalding *Phlegeton* ;
Would they not ftartle, think ye, all agreed,
'Twas Conjuration both in Word and Deed ;
Or *Catiline's* Confpirators, as they ftood
Sealing their Oaths in Draughts of reeking Blood ?
The merrieft Ghoft of all your Sires would fay,
Your Wine's much worfe fince his laft yefterday :
He'd wonder how the Club had giv'n a Hop
O'er Tavern-Bars, into the Farriers Shop ;
Where he'd fuppofe, both by the fmoak and ftench,
Each Man a Horfe, and each Horfe at his Drench.
That y' are no Poets, nor their Friends, I vow
Without an Oath I'd credit : for fhould now
Ben Johnfon's ftrenuous Spirit, or the rare
Beaumont and *Fletcher's* in your Rounds appear,
They would not tinde the Air perfum'd with one
Caftalian Drop, nor Dew of *Helicon* ;
But fleeing, cry out, *Sulphur, Liquid Fire,*
Fetcht from *Cocytus,* and the *Stygian Mire* :
When they but men, would fpeak as the Gods do ;
They drank pure Nectar as the Gods drink too,
Sublim'd with rich Canary ; they would move
Difcourfe i' th' Language fpoke i' th' world above.
But pray Sirreverence Sirs, what wonder drops
Nuncle *Johns* Kettle-houfe in the Coffee-fhops ?
Your Servant, Sir, what News from Tripoly ?
Do the Weekly Pamphlets in their Works agree ?
Then Dame *Diurnal* goes to th' Pot ; if you
But fay fhe fcoulds, fhe's duck'd in Coffee too :
Oft at your Seffions b'ing arraign'd and caft
For petty Thefts, pleading her Book, at laft
She's with Wax-Candle, or Tobacco-fnuff,
But burnt i' th' hand, and fo ferv'd well enough.
Hear, and admire, Oh Men! thefe are the new
Admirabilia of the Coffee-Crew.
Fie, Friends to the grofs Turky-fhore, fhall then
Thefe lefs then Coffee's felf, thefe Coffee-men,
Thefe fons of nothing, that can hardly make
Their Broth, for laughing how the Jeft does take ;
Yet grin, and give ye for the Vine's pure Blood,
A loathfome Potion, not yet underftood,
Syrrop of Soot, or Effence of old Shoops,
Daſht with Diurnals, and the Books of News ?

Nay, for ought I know, (I'd not be abfurd)
A meer Decoction of the Devils —— [Affakerida.
If, as the fafhion of your Cloaths, you change
Your Drinks as often, to as new and ftrange,
Let Pothecaries then your cuftom thank,
And not thefe Munkeys of a Mountebank.
Have by misfortune your crofs-cap'ring Brains
Got either Clap, or Running of the Reins ?
Guaicum's infufion take, and *Turpentine,*
Which but compar'd with Coffee, drink like VVine.
Are ye with Surfeits ftomach-full ? Take then
Warm *Treacle-water,* fweat, and well apen.
Does *Venus* heat your Bloods too high ? Allay
That fire with drops of *Malden Camphora.*
Drink whole *Pharmascopeia* o'er, know this,
No Draught fo loathfome as foul Coffee is,
Of which this onely is a tafte, and thofe
Would know its Vertue, may go look't in Profe,
For 't cannot ftand in Verfe, (though 't lye in Print)
Becaufe there's neither Rime nor Reafon in 't.
Yet I have heard a grave Grand-Signior tell,
Coffee does dull and yawning Sleeps expel.
Why Frenzie, Fevers, or the Poor Mans Gout,
Will do this feat as well, and that without
A God-a-mercy; nay, 'twill make 'en do
And talk as idly and as franticky too.
Though in the power of this Turkifh Spell
I'm faithlefs as a Jew or Infidel,
Yet I believe I eafily might confefs
Coffee potential in fuch Cures as thefe.
Firſt, (for example) are there 'mongſt ye fome
Have foundly had the *Morbum Gallicum* ?
Let 'em drink Coffee, and from Whores abftain,
I'll pawn my Pen they're Pocky well again.
From *Venus* Racks, let's fall to *Bacchus* Stocks :
Are ye dead drunk ? ha' ye caught a catching Fox ?
Take me then Coffee, drink it fcalding hot,
(For though it fcalds, yet know, it burneth not)
Sleep upon 't foundly ; when you re-awake,
Y' are a lives man again, I'll undertake.
Is any of your fober Signiors ta'en
With Maggot-Meagroms, or the Worm i' th' Brain ?
(For though fuch Worms in Ages heretofore
Sought their forc'd fortunes at mens Poftern Door)
Yet as the Moon and humane Humours change,
They alter too, and now through th' head do range,
If any be thus craz'd, and by the Rimples
About his Nofe, you fear he'll fall i' th' Simples,
Well worm him firft, and take a fpecial heed
No fpawn remain of the fly Serpents feed ;
Then to the Miftrefs of the great *Mogul*
Let him carroufe a Coffee-Kettle full;

And rife a wonder of the Turkey-fhore,
As wife and well as ere he was before.
Such cures can Coffee work. I could afford
Ye many more; but *to the wife a word.*
And now Stew'd Prewen-mongers, and all you
Drink-dablers, that have fo long kept ado
With *China-Ale, Stupent, Virgin-Wine,*
Mum and *Metheglin,* and a hundred fine
Devices more, all to no purpofe, know,
Ye ha' mt the way ; thefe are all things that grow
Here, here at home, when as a forraign Fart,
Mixt and mifcall'd according unto Art,
Sells quick as the new Perukes now adays,
Goes off as well, and takes the felf-fame place.
But whine not, Dunces, nor defpair, ye Fools;
Ye have Back-fides left yet, and good Clofe ftools,
Large as the Coffee-Kettles; make good ufe
Of thefe; they fhall an equal gain produce.
Remember Coff', can ye but Pifs and Cack ?
Jumble't together, call it *Scythian Sack,*
Tantavelin, Fogofarto, or but fome
New name, not known in English *Chriftendome,*
Or let fome Jew derive its ftock and ftem
At leaft as far as fro n *Jerufalem,*
That fo it be at firelt out ; let him but frame
Ought but to call 't out of it's Chriftian Name ;
Pofte up it. Vertues ev'ry where in good
Strange Hebrew-English, which not underſtood
Makes much the better; there lies all the knack,
The Jeft's pure Hogo, and the Conceit's fmack :
For in this Age, nothing's fcry'd up for good,
Save what's ftark naught, or what's not underftood.
So that, I fear, thefe very Rules may run
I' th' compafs of fome commendation.
But to the fcope : There muft be got mad Boys
For your firft fetters, or as't were Decoys,
I'ſ intice the Novifts, till they've made a Rode
Unto your Door, and your Knack 'gins to mode ;
When you'll, I fear, be forced to have wait
Some tall-gown'd-Porter at your thronged Gate
To make diftinction of your Ouefts, left none
Enter but friends, and men of fafhion ;
And this will take the Youngfters fo, you'll fee
A Leaguer dayly at your Door will be ;
You'll be befieg'd with Money and good Words
For the rare Juyce that your Back-fides affords;
Ye fhall make Coffee ftink. In fhort, be all
Made men at length, for to make men withal.
'T fhall ne'er be faid, a Turdy Turk could do
More with a meer Sirreverence then you.

London, Printed in the year 1663.

The Character of a Coffee-House. Wherein Is contained a Description of the Persons usually frequenting it, with their Discourse and Humors, As also, The Admirable Vertues of Coffee. By an Eye and Ear Witness ([London], n.p., 1665), [2], 10pp.; 4°. BL: 11626.bb.11. ESTCR32619. Hünersdorff.

A quarto pamphlet satire of ten pages of rhymed verse couplets in irregular quatrameter (the form made famous by Butler's *Hudibras*, the first two parts of which were published in 1662 and 1663, though dated a year later respectively). In form, the verse also appeals to the genre of the Theophrastan 'Character', a satiric sketch of the characteristic speech and behaviour of a specified occupation or place. The poem first describes the typical shop signs that identify coffee-houses, which often employed Turkish iconology, before briefly surveying the virtues of coffee. As the poem argues, the physiological effects of coffee make it particularly congenial to the business of 'news-mongers' – a new term signifying men who circulate true and false news. The rest of the poem burlesques several conversations around three separate coffee-house tables, between different kinds of men. The poem's depiction of coffee-house conversations celebrates two key aspects. The first is that men from radically different interests come together around a coffee table, where they conduct one conversation. The second is that their conversation is intemperate, and each only has a mind for their own interests and topics, so that the discussion is atomistic, unprofitable and collapses in failure. Formally, this description of conversation around the coffee-house table recalls the *cena* or dinner table scene of Juvenal's *Satire* V.

Nothing is known of the author or publisher, although the pseudonym 'Eye and ear witness' is not widely used in the period. The six extant copies are listed on the ESTC.

THE
CHARACTER
OF A
Coffee-House.

WHEREIN
Is contained a Defcription of the Perfons
ufually frequenting it , with their Difcourfe and Humors,

AS A.LSO
The Admirable Vertues of
COFFEE.

By an Eye and Ear Witnefs.

When Coffee once was vended here,
The Alc'ton fhortly did appear :
For (our Reformers were fuch Widgeons,)
New Liquors brought in new Religions.

Printed in the Year, 1665.

THE
CHARACTER
OF A
Coffee-Houſe.

Coffee-houſe, the learned hold
It is a place where *Coffee's* ſold ;
This derivation cannot fail us,
For where *Ale's* vended, that's an *Ale-*
 This being granted to be true, (*houſe.*
'Tis meet that next the *Signs* we ſhew
Both *where* and *how* to find this houſe
Where men ſuch *cordial broth* carowſe.
And if *Culpepper* woon ſome glory
In turning the *Diſpenſatory*
From *Latin* into *Engliſh*, then,
Why ſhould not all good *Engliſh men*
Give him much thanks who ſhews a *cure*
For all *diſeaſes* men endure ?
 As you along the ſtreets do trudge,
To take the pains you muſt not grudge,

The deri-
vation of
a Coffee-
houſe.

Signs how
to find it
out.

A 2   To

(2)

To view the Posts or Broomsticks where
The Signs of *Liquors* hanged are.
And if you see the great *Morat*
With Shash on's head instead of hat,
Or any *Sultan* in his dress,
Or picture of a *Sultaness*,
Or *John*'s admir'd curled pate,
Or th' great *Mogul* in's Chair of State,
Or *Constantine* the *Grecian*,
Who fourteen years was th' onely man
That made *Coffee* for th' great *Bashaw*,
Although the man he never saw :
Or if you see a *Coffee*-cup
Fil'd from a Turkish pot, hung up
VVithin the clouds, and round it *Pipes*,
Wax Candles, *Stoppers*, these are types
And certain signs (with many more
VVould be too long to write them 'ore,)
VVhich plainly do Spectators tell
That in that house they *Coffee* sell.
Some wiser than the rest (no doubt,)
Say they can by the smell find't out ;
In at a door (say they,) but thrust
Your Nose, and if you scent *burnt Cruss*,
Be sure there's *Coffee* sold that's good,
For so by most 'tis understood.

    Now being enter'd, there's no needing
Of complements or gentile breeding,
For you may seat you any where,
There's no respect of persons there ;
Then comes the *Coffee-man* to greet you,
VVith welcome Sir, let me entreat you,
To tell me what you'l please to have,
For I'm your humble humble slave ;

But

(3)

But if you ask, what good does Coffee ?
He'l anfwer, Sir; don't think I fcoff yee,
If I affirm there's no difeafe
Men have that drink it but find eafe.
Look, there's a man who takes the fteem
In at his Nofe, has an extreme
Worm in his pate, and giddinefs,
Ask him and he will fay no lefs.
There fitteth one whofe Droptick belly
VVas hard as flint, now's foft as jelly.
There ftands another holds his head
'Ore th' *Coffee*-pot, was almoft dead
Even now with Rhume; ask him hee'l fay
That all his Rhum's now paft away.
See, there's a man fits now demure
And fober, was within this hour
Quite drunk, and comes here frequently,
For 'tis his daily Malady.
More, it has fuch reviving power
'Twill keep a man awake an houre,
Nay, make his eyes wide open ftare
Both Sermon time and all the prayer.
Sir, fhould I tell you all the reft
O'th' cures 't has done, two hours at leaft
In numb'ring them I needs muft fpend,
Scarce able then to make an end.
Befides thefe vertues that's therein,
For any kind of *Medicine*,
e *Commonwealth — Kingdom* I'd fay,
Has mighty reafon for to pray
That ftill *Arabia* may produce
Enough of Berry for it's ufe :
For 't has fuch ftrange magnetick force,
That it draws after't great concourfe

The ver-
tues of
Coffee.

Of

(4)

Of all degrees of perfons, even
From high to low, from morn till even;
Efpecially the *fober Party*,
And News-mongers do drink't moft hearty.
Here you'r not thruft into a *Box*,
As *Taverns* do to catch the *Fox*,
But as from th' top of *Pauls* high fteeple,
Th' whole *City's* view'd, even fo all *people*
May here be feen; no fecrets are
At th' *Court* for *Peace*, or th' *Camp* for *War*,
But ftraight they'r here difclos'd and known;
Men in this Age fo wife are grown.
Now (Sir) what profit may accrew
By this, to all good men, judge you.
VVith that he's loudly call'd upon
For *Coffee*, and then whip he's gone.

Here at a Table fits (perplext)
A griping *Ufurer*, and next
To him a gallant *Furiofo*,
Then nigh to him a *Virtuofo*;
A *Player* then (full fine,) fits down,
And clofe to him a *Country Clown*.
O'th' other fide fits fome *Pragmatick*,
And next to him fome fly *Phanatick*.

The gallant he for *Tea* doth call.
The *Ufurer* for nought at all.
Pragmatick he doth intreat
That they will fill him fome *Beau cheat*,
The *Virtuofo* he cries hand me
Some *Coffee* mixt with *Sugar-candy*,
Phanaticus (at laft) fays come,
Bring me fome *Aromaticum*.
The *Player* bawls for *Chocolate*,
All which the *Bumpkin* wond'ring at,

The company.

The feveral liquors

Cries,

(5)

Cries, ho, my *Masters*, what d'ye speak,
D' ye call for drink in Heathen Greek?
Give me some good old *Ale* or *Beer*,
Or else I will not drink, I swear.
Then having charg'd their *Pipes* around,
They silence break; First the profound
And sage *Phanatique*, Sirs, what news?
Troth says the *Us'rer* I ne'r use
To tip my tongue with such discourse,
'Twere news to know how to disburse
A summ of mony (makes me sad)
To get ought by't, times are so bad.
The other answers, truly Sir
You speak but truth, for I'le aver
They ne'r were worse; did you not hear
VVhat *prodigies* did late appear
At *Norwich*, *Ipswich*, *Grantham*, *Gotam*?
And though prophane ones do not nor'em,
Yet we —— Here th' *Virtuoso* stops
The current of his speech, with hopes
Quoth he, you will not tak't amiss,
I say all's lies that's news like this,
For I have Factors all about
The Realm, so that no *Stars* peep out
That are unusual, much less these
Strange and unheard-of *Prodigies*
You would relate, but they are tost
To me in letters by first Post.
At which the *Furioso* swears
Such chat as this offends his ears,
It rather doth become this Age
To talk of bloodshed, fury, rage,
And t'drink stout healths in brim-fill'd *Nogans*,
To th' Downfall of the *Hogan Mogans*.

With

Their dis-
course.

(6)

VVith that the *Player* doffs his Bonnet,
And tunes his voice as if a Sonnet
VVere to be fung; then gently fays,
O what delight there is in *Plays* !
Sure if we were but all in *Peace*,
This noife of *Wars* and *News* would ceafe;
All forts of people then would club
Their pence to fee a Play that's good.
You'l wonder all this while (perhaps)
The *Curtofo* holds his chaps,
But he doth in his thoughts devife,
How to the reft he may feem wife ;
Yet able longer not to hold,
His tedious tale too muft be told,
And thus begins, Sirs unto me
It reafon feems that liberty
Of fpeech and words fhould be allow'd
VVhere men of differing judgements croud,
And that's a *Coffee-houfe* , for where
Should men difcourfe fo free as there ?
Coffee and *Commonwealth* begin
Both with one letter, both came in
Together for a *Reformation*,
To make's a free and fober *Nation*.
But now——With that *Phanaticus*
Gives him a nod, and fpeaks him thus,
Hold brother, I know your intent,
That's no difpute convenient
For this fame place, truths feldome find
Acceptance here, they'r more confin'd
To *Taverns* and to *Ale-houfe* liquor,
VVhere men do vent their minds more quicker ,
If that may for a truth but pafs
VVhat's faid, *In vino veritas*.

VVith

(7)

With that up ſtarts the *Country Clown*,
And ſtares about with threatning frown,
As if he would even eat them all up,
Then bids the boy run quick and call up
A *Conſtable*, for he has reaſon
To fear their Latin may be *treaſon*.
But ſtraight they all call what's to pay,
Lay't down, and march each ſeveral way.

The com-
pany.

At th'other table ſits a *Knight*,
And here *a grave old man* ore right
Againſt his *worſhip*, then perhaps
That *by* and *by* a *Drawer* claps
His bum cloſe by them, there down ſquats
A dealer in old ſhoes and hats ;
And here withouten any panick
Fear, dread or care a bold *Mechanick*.

Their diſ-
courſe.

The *Knight* (becauſe he's ſo) he prates
Of matters far beyond their pates.
The grave old man he makes a buſtle,
And his wiſe ſentence in muſt juſtle.
Up ſtarts th' *Apprentice boy* and he
Says boldly ſo and ſo't muſt be.
The dealer in old ſhoes to utter
His ſaying too makes no ſmall ſputter.
Then comes the pert *mechanick blade*,
And contradicts what all have ſaid.
The end of all their *Chat* is this,
Each for the *Dutch* have *rods* in *piſs*.

There by the fier-ſide doth ſit,
One freezing in an *Ague* fit;
Another poking in't with th' tongs,
Still ready to cough up his lungs.
Here ſitteth one that's melancolick,
And there one ſinging in a frolick.

B   Each

(8)

Each one hath such a prety gesture,
At Smithfield fair would yield a tester.
Boy reach a pipe cries he that shakes,
The songster no Tobacco takes,
Says he who coughs, nor do I smoak,
Then *Monsieur Mopus* turns his cloak
Off from his face, and with a grave
Majestick beck his pipe doth crave.
They load their guns and fall a smoaking,
Whilst he who coughs sits by a choaking,
Till he no longer can abide,
And so removes from th' fier side.
Now all th s while none calls to drink,
Which makes the *Coffee boy* to think
Much they his pots should so enclose,
He cannot pass but tread on toes.
With that as he the *Nectar* fills
From pot to pot, some on't he spills
Upon the *Songster*, Oh cries he,
Pox, what dost do? thou'st burnt my knee ;
No says the boy, (to make a bald
And blind excuse,) *Sir 'twill not scald.*
With that the man lends him a cuff
O'th' ear, and whips away in snuff.
The other two, their pipes being out,
Says *Monsieur Mopus* I much doubt
My friend I wait for will not come,
But if he do, say I'm gone home.
Then says the *Aguish man* I must come,
According to my wonted custome,
To give ye' a visit, although now
I dare not drink, and so *adieu*.
The boy replies, O Sir, however
You'r very welcome, we do never

Our

(9)

Our *Candles, Pipes* or *Fier* grutch
To daily cuftomers and fuch,
'They'r *Company* (without expence,)
For that's fufficient recompence.
Here at a table all alone,
Sits (ftudying) *a fpruce youngfter,* (one
VVho doth conceipt himfelt full witty,
And's 'counted *one o'th' wits o'th' City,*)
Till by him (with a ftately grace,)
A Spanifh *Don* himfelf doth place.
Then (cap in hand) a brisk *Monfieur*
He takes his feat, and crowds as near
As poffibly that he can come.
Then next a *Dutchman* takes his room.
The Wits glib tongue begins to chatter,
Though't utters more of noife than matter,
Yet 'caufe they feem to mind his words,
His lungs more tattle ftill affords.
At laft fays he to *Don,* I trow
You underftand me ? *Senner no*
Says th' other. Here the Wit doth paufe
A little while, then opes his jaws,
And fays to *Monfieur,* you enjoy
Our tongue I hope ? *Non par ma foy,*
Replies the *Frenchman*: nor you, Sir ?
Says he to th' *Dutchman, Neen mynheer* :
VVith that he's gone, and cries, why fho'd
He ftay where *wit's* not underftood ?
There in a place of his own chufing
(Alone) fome *lover* fits a mufing,
VVith arms acrofs, and's eyes up lift,
As if he were of fence bereft,
Till fometimes to himfelf he's fpeaking,
Then fighs as if his heart were breaking.

B 2   Here

(10)

Here in a corner fits a *Phrantick*,
And there ftands by a frisking *Antick*.
Of all forts fome and all conditions,
Even *Vintners, Surgeons* and *Phyficians*.
The *blind*, the *deaf*, and *aged cripple*
Do here refort and Coffee tipple.

Now here (perhaps) you may expect
My *Mufe* fome *trophies* fhould erect
In high flown verfe, for to fet forth
The *noble praifes* of its *worth*.

Truth is, *old Poets* beat their brains
To find out high and lofty ftrains
To praife the (now too frequent) ufe
Of the bewitching *grapes ftrong juice*.
Some have ftrain'd hard for to exalt
The *liquor* of our *Englifh Mault*,
Nay *Don* has almoft crackt his *nodle*
Enough t' applaud his *Caaco-Caudle*.
The *Germans Mum, Teag's Ufquebagh*,
(Made him fo well defend *Tredagh*,)
Metheglin, which the *Brittains* tope,
Hot *Brandy wine*, the *Hogans* hope.
Stout *Meade* which makes the *Rufs* to laugh,
Spic'd *Punch* (in bowls,) the *Indians* quaff.
All thefe have had their pens to raife
Them *Monuments* of lafting praife,
Onely poor *Coffee* feems to me
No fubject fit for *Poetry*.
At leaft 'tis one that none of mine is,
So I do wave't, and here write——

F I N I S.

News from the Coffe-House; In which it is shewn their several sorts of Passions, Containing Newes from all our Neighbours Nations. A Poem (London, E. Crowch for Thomas Vere, 1667). BL: C.20.f.2.(374). ESTCR220393. Hünersdorff.

A broadside ballad satirising the close relationship between coffee-houses and news. An orthodox ballad in form, it comprises fourteen eight-line stanzas in alternating tetrameter and trimeter, rhymed abab, with the last line of each stanza an evolving refrain repeating with variation 'It cannot but be true'. The narrative relates the function of news in the coffee-house, and the role of the coffee-house in the dissemination and production of news. The satire is directed against excessive regard for novelty and fresh intelligence in Restoration urban life, of which the coffee-house is emblematic. To the satirist, the coffee-house is the natural home of the news-monger, a person busily involved in the collecting and narrating of news. The satire testifies to the close relation between coffee-houses and the dissemination of news, both printed in the form of newsbooks, diurnals and pamphlets, and unprinted news such as rumour and gossip, and manuscript newsletters. The topic of the satire, and the nature of its production, suggest that this ballad was Royalist and counter-republican.

A second edition, omitting the fifth stanza with its hostile references to the French, was published in 1672 by the same printer and bookseller, under the title *The Coffee House or Newsmongers Hall. In which it is shewn their several sorts of Passions, Containing News from all our Neighbour Nations. A Poem* ((London, E. Crouch for Thomas Vere, 1672); BL: C.20.f.2(375); ESTCR226933). A nine-stanza version of the ballad was employed at a pageant for the Lord Mayor of London in October 1675, and republished in the printed account by the actor and playwright Thomas Jordan (*c.* 1614–85), where it was performed by a musician as a song accompanied by a pipe, at the conclusion of the dinner at Guildhall (Thomas Jordan, *The Triumphs of London: Performed on Friday, Octob. 29. 1675* (London, printed by I. Macock, for John Playford, 1675), pp. 22–4). The ballad was published by the cartel of 'Ballard Partners', a group of three wealthy stationers (Thomas Vere, Francis Coles and J. Wright) who had cooperated since the 1620s to produce large numbers of ballads, which they sold through a network of itinerant ballad-pedlars and chapmen for an established market of readers who wanted cheap, accessible and entertaining literature. Thomas Vere's shop was at the Cock in St John Street. The printer employed in this ballad was Edward Crouch of Hosier Lane, Snow Hill, a poor printer of many chapbooks and ballads, who had gained some notoriety for publishing Royalist newsbooks and satires during the Civil War. The ballad was published 'With Alowance' [sic], which is to say that it has been licensed or approved for publication by Roger L'Estrange, the official licenser of the press. The only copy of the first edition survives in the collection of ballads assembled by Narcissus Luttrell (1657–1732) now in the British Library. The second edition is extant in two copies, one also in the Luttrell Collection at the British Library, the other at the Boston Athenaeum, Boston, Massachusetts.

NEWS from the COFFE-HOUSE;

In which is shewn their several sorts of Passions, Containing Newes from all our Neighbour *Nations*.

A POEM.

YOu that delight in Wit and Mirth,
    And long to hear such News,
As comes from all Parts of the *Earth*,
    Dutch, *Danes*, and *Turks*, and *Jews*,
I'le send yee to a Rendezvouz,
    Where it is smoaking new ;
Go hear it at a *Coffe-house*,
    It cannot but be true.

There Battles and Sea-Fights are Fought,
    And bloudy Plots display'd ;
They know more Things then ere was thought
    Or ever was betray'd :
No Money in the Minting-house
    Is halfe so Bright and New ;
And comming from a *Coffe-house*,
    It cannot but be true.

Before the *Navyes* fall to Work,
    They know who shall be Winner ;
They there can tell ye what the *Turk*
    Last Sunday had to Dinner ;
Who last did Cut *Du Ruitters* Corns,
    Amongst his jovial Crew ;
Or Who first gave the *Devil Horns*,
    Which cannot but be true.

A *Fisherman* did boldly tell,
    And strongly did avouch,
He Caught a Shoal of Mackarel,
    That Parley'd all in *Dutch*,
And cry'd out *Yaw*, *yaw*, *yaw Mynt Here* ;
    But as the Draught they Drew,
They Stunk for fear, that *Monck* was there,
    Which cannot but be true.

Another Swears, by both his Ears,
    Mounsieur will cut our Throats ;
The *French King* will a Girdle bring,
    Made of Flat-bottom'd Boats,
Shall Compas *England* round about,
    Which' must not be a few,
To give our *Englishmen* the Rout .
    This sounds as if, t'were true,

There's nothing done in all the World,
    From *Monarch* to the *Mouse*
But every Day or Night 'tis hurld
    Into the *Coffe-house.*
What *Lillie* or what *Booker* can
    By Art, not bring about,
At *Coffe-house* you'l find a Man,
    Can quickly find it out.

They'l tell ye there, what Lady-ware,
    Of late is grown too light ;
What Wise-man shall from Favour Fall,
    What Fool shall be a Knight ;
They'l tell ye when our Fayling Trade,
    Shall Rise again, and Flourish ,
Or when *Jack Adams* shall be made
    Church-Warden *of the* Parish.

They know who shall in Times to come,
    Be either made, or undone,
From great St. *Peters-street* in *Rome*,
    To *Turnbull-street* in *London* ;
And likewise tell, at *Clerkenwell*,
    What *Whore* hath greatest Gain ;
And in that place, what Brazen-face
    Doth wear a Golden Chain.

At Sea their Knowledge is so much,
    They know all Rocks and Shelves,
They know all Councills of the *Dutch*,
    More then they know Themselves ;
Who 'tis shall get the best at last,
    They perfectly can shew
At *Coffe-house*, when they are plac'd,
    You'd scarce beleive it true.

They know all that is Good, or Hurt,
    To Dam ye, or to Save ye ;
There is the *Colledge*, and the *Court*,
    The *Country*, *Camp*, and *Navie* ;
So great a *Vniversitie*,
    I think there ne're was any ;
In which you may a Schoolar be
    For spending of a Penny.

A *Merchants Prentice* there shall show
    You all and every thing,
What hath been done, and is to do,
    'Twix *Holland* and the *King* ;
What *Articles* of *Peace* will bee,
    He can precizely show ;
What will be good for *Them* or *Wee*,
    He perfectly doth know.

Here Men do talk of every Thing,
    With large and liberal Lungs,
Like *Women* at a Gossiping,
    With double tyre of Tongues ;
They'l give a Broad-side presently, :
    Soon as you are in view,
With Stories that, you'l wonder at,
    Which they will swear are true.

The Drinking there of *Chockalat*,
    Can make a *Fool* a *Sophie* :
'Tis thought the *Turkish Mahomet*
    Was first Insoir'd with *Coffe*,
By which his Powers did Over-flow
    The Land of *Palestine* :
Then let us to, the *Coffe-house* go,
    'Tis Cheaper farr then Wine.

You shall know there, what *Fashons* are ;
    How Perrywiggs are Curl'd ;
And for a Penny you shall heare,
    All Novells in the World.
Both Old and Young, and Great and Small,
    And Rich, and Poore, you'l see :
Therefore let's to the *Coffe* All,
    Come All away with Mee.   *Finis.*

London, Printed by *E. Crowch* for *Thomas Vere* at] the Cock in St. *John's-street* 1667. With Allowance.

A Broad-side against Coffee; Or, the Marriage of the Turk (London, J. L., 1672). BL: C.20.f.2(376). ESTCR226934. Hünersdorff.

A 62-line broadsheet verse satire in pentameter rhyming couplets. The satire adapts the conventional attack on coffee as an emblem of the cultural innovations of the Restoration by elaborating a complex and extended analogy to relations between Christian Europe and the Ottoman Empire. The trope plays at several levels, one of which is a metaphor of coffee as a profane marriage between a brown Islamic bean and innocent Christian water. As well as the by now conventional burlesque of medical writing on coffee, the poem weaves together intricate layers of cultural stereotype, cross-cultural curiosity and transculturated practices around coffee and Turkey, making this a telling symbol for Anglo-Turkish relations in the seventeenth century. In addition, the poem makes some historical notes on the first arrival of coffee and coffee-houses in England (ll. 35–40), perhaps a sign that, by 1672, Londoner's had become so habituated as to think of it as having a history, no longer an innovation.

Nothing is known of the author or the printer (the initials J. L. were used by several different printers in the later seventeenth century). The satire was reprinted in a slightly revised form, without the final couplet, as 'A Broad-Side against Coffee, or, the Marriage of the Turk', in two compilations by John Hancock: *Two Broad-Sides against Tobacco, The first given by King James of Famous memory; His Counterblast to Tobacco. The Second Transcribed out of that learned Physician Dr. Everard Maynwaringe, His Treatise of the Scurvy ... Concluding with Two Poems Against Tobacco and Coffee* (London, John Hancock, 1672), pp. 58–60 [licensed on June 6 1672]; and *The touchstone, or, Trial of tobacco whether it be good for all constitutions: with a word of advice against immoderate drinking and smoaking: likewise examples of some that have drunk their lives away, and died suddenly: with King Jame's [sic] opinion of tobacco, and how it came first into England: also the first original of coffee: to which is added, witty poems about tobacco and coffe* (London, printed and sold by several booksellers, 1676), pp. 58–60. In this edition, Hancock appends the following note to the text:

I have heard it is good for one thing (and that falls out too often) when men are drunk with *Wine, Beer* or *Ale*, or *Brandy*, that they are unfit to manage their Imployment; then a Dish of hot *Coffee* is a present Remedy to settle their Heads. No doubt but a Dish of Broth, or Beer, will work the same Cure, if it be drunk as hot. (p. 60)

In its broadsheet state, the poem is represented by examples in the collection of ballads assembled by Narcissus Luttrell (1657–1732) in the British Library and in the Bodleian Library, Oxford. Examples of Hancock's tobacco compilations are held in a number of libraries.

A Broad-fide againſt COFFEE;

Or, the

Marriage of the Turk.

COFFEE, a kind of *Turkiſh Renegade*,
Has late a match with *Chriſtian water* made;
At firſt between them happen'd a Demur,
Yet joyn'd they were, but not without great *ſtir*;
For both ſo cold were, and ſo faintly met,
The *Turkiſh Hymen* in his *Turbant* ſwet.
Coffie was cold as *Earth*, *Water* as *Thames*,
And ſtood in need of recommending Flames;
I or each of them ſteers a contrary courſe,
And of themſelves they ſue out a Divorce;
Coffee ſo brown as berry does appear,
Too ſwarthy for a Nymph ſo fair, ſo clear:
And yet his ſails he did for *England* hoiſt,
Though cold and dry, to court the cold and moiſt,
If there be ought we can, as love admit;
'Tis a hot love, and laſteth but a fit.
For this indeed the cauſe is of their ſtay,
Newcaſtle's bowels warmer are than they:
The melting Nymph diſtills her ſelf to do't,
Whilſt the Slave *Coffee* muſt be *beaten* to't:
Incorporate him cloſe as cloſe may be,
Pauſe but a while, and he is none of he;
Which for a truth, and not a ſtory tells,
No Faith is to be kept with Infidels.
Sure he ſuſpects, and ſhuns her as a Whore,
And loves, and kills, like the *Venetian Moor*;
Bold Aſian Brat! with ſpeed our confines flee;
Water, though common, is too good for thee.
Sure *Coffee's* vext he has the breeches loſt,
For ſhe's above, and he lies undermoſt;
What ſhall I add but this? (and ſure 'tis right)
The Groom is *heavy*, cauſe the Bride is *light*.

This canting *Coffee* has his Crew enricht,
And both the *Water* and the *Men* bewitcht.
   A Coachman was the firſt (here) *Coffee* made,
And ever ſince the reſt *drive on* the trade;
Me no good Engalaſh! and ſure enough,
He plaid the Quack to ſalve his Stygian ſtuff;
Ver boon for de ſtomach, de Cough, de Ptiſick,
And I believe him, for it looks like Phyſick.
Coffee a cruſt is charkt into a coal,
The ſmell and taſte of the Mock *China* bowl;
Where huff and puff, they labor out their lungs,
Leſt *Dives*-like they ſhould bewail their tongues.
And yet they tell ye that it will not burn,
Though on the Jury Bliſters you return;
Whoſe furious heat does make the water riſe,
And ſtill through the Alembicks of your eyes.
Dread and deſire, ye fall to't ſnap by ſnap,
As hungry Dogs do ſcalding porrige lap,
But to cure Drunkards it has got great Fame;
Poſſet or *Porrige*, will't not do the ſame?
Confuſion huddles all into one Scene,
Like *Noah's* Ark, the clean and the unclean.
But now, alas! the Drench has credit got,
And he's no Gentleman that drinks it not;
That ſuch a *Dwarf* ſhould riſe to ſuch a ſtature!
But Cuſtom is but a remove from Nature.
A little Diſh, and a *large* Coffee-houſe,
What is it, but a *Mountain* and a *Mouſe*?
   From Bawdy-houſes differs thus your hap;
They give their tails, you give their tongues a clap:
Mens humana novitatis avidiſſima.

London, Printed for *J. L. Anno Dom.* 1672.

The Character of a Coffee-House, with the Symptomes of a Town-Wit. With Allowance, April 11th 1673 (London, Jonathan Edwin, 1673), [2], 7pp.; 2°. BL: 12330.k.5. ESTCR20219. Hünersdorff.

This six-page folio tract comprises a 'Character' or satiric description of an unspecified, and hence generic, coffee-house in the City of London, together with several of its principal inhabitants, including the coffee-man, and the 'town-wit', a social and intellectual gad-fly. As a 'Character', the satire abides by the key conventions of that genre (see pp. 1–2 above for elaboration). This example is typical for the extraordinary mixture of discourses canvassed in its satire, reflecting a view that in the coffee-house disciplines, languages and attitudes that ought to remain separate are mixed uncritically. To reflect this loss of values, the satire's language is enthusiastic and excessive, mixing medical language, political jargon, religious cant and classical erudition. The coffee-man is described as having a swarthy appearance, perhaps caused by the smoky effects of his product. He is a commercial pragmatist: where once he affected a turban, so as to appear Turkish, he now wears a broad brimmed hat, like a Royalist cavalier: in both guises, he is as inauthentic and fraudulent as the brew he retails. The text further describes the range of drinks served in the coffee-house; a 'hodge-podge' comprising not only coffee but also tea, aromatique (spiced eggnog), betony (a drink flavoured with the herb of that name), rosade (rosa solis, a liqueur flavoured with the plant sun-dew), Herefordshire redstreak (cider or scrumpy), chocolet (chocolate) and mum (wheat beer flavoured with herbs). The text then surveys some of the clients: first a sycophant know-it-all, a retailer of old news and exaggerated rumour whose ignorance is betrayed by poor geographical knowledge; and secondly a stirrer of religious dissent, clandestinely revealing sham plots and counterplots against the church and state. The king or arch-devil of these coffee-house habitués is the town-wit: a man driven by contrarieties and contradictions, memorably described as 'a *Squib* on a rope, a *meteor* composed of self-conceit and noise'. These portraits of new urban character types point to the chaotic cultural, intellectual and commercial climate of Restoration London, in which established social roles and hierarchies were overturned and debased. In this fevered atmosphere, men consumed by ambition and emulation grew wealthy, just as others saw opportunities for self-advancement offered by the new science, by sectarian struggles, and by commercial speculation.

The writer is not known, although *The Character* has been attributed to Joseph Glanvill (1636–80) on the strength of some textual similarities with Glanvill's *A Blow at Modern Sadducism* (1668), explored by Samuel Weiss in 'Joesph Glanvill and *The Character of a Coffee-house*', *Notes and Queries*, 197 (1952), pp. 234–5; and accepted by Jackson Cope, *Joseph Glanvill, Anglican Apologist* (St Louis, MO, Washington University Committee on Publications, 1956), p. 36. Glanvill was a Church of England clergyman who wrote extensively on theological controversies and scientific method, including the relation between reason and supernatural matters such as the occult and witchcraft. Nonetheless, the attribution is not secure, as the text, which is unlike most of Glanvill's output, also borrows from works by a number of other writers (see James Jacob, *Henry Stubbe, Radical Protestantism and the Early Enlightenment* (Cambridge, Cambridge University Press, 1983)). *The Character* was published by Jonathan Edwin, a bookseller at the Three Roses in Ludgate Street, who published a wide variety of literature from pamphlet satires to folio classics, and who by reputation was a staunch Royalist and churchman (Plomer). In 1745, it was reprinted in the *The Harleian Miscellany* (8 vols (London, T. Osborne, 1744–6), vol. VI, pp. 429–33); and was consulted by Thomas Babington Macaulay in his research for the coffee-house section in his *The History of England from the Accession of James the Second*, 5 vols (London, Longman, Browne, Green and Longmans, 1849), vol. I, pp 366–70. At least thirteen copies of the text survive.

THE

CHARACTER

OF

A Coffee-Houſe,

WITH THE

SYMPTOMES

OF A

TOWN-WIT.

With Allowance, April 11ᵗʰ 1673.

LONDON,

Printed for *Jonathan Edwin*, at the three Roſes in
Lud-Gate-Street, 1673.

THE
CHARACTER
OF
A Coffee-Houſe, &c.

A Coffee-Houſe is a *Lay-Conventicle*, Good-fellowſhip turn'd *Puritan*, Ill-husbandry in *Maſquerade*, whither people come, after *Toping* all day, to purchaſe, at the expence of their laſt peny, the repute of *ſober Companions*; a *Rota-Room* that (like *Noahs* Ark) receives Animals of every ſort, from the preciſe *diminutive Band*, to the *Hectoring Cravat* and *Cuffs* in *Folio* ; a *Nurſery* for training up the ſmaller Fry of *Virtuoſi* in confident Tattling, or a Cabal of *Kittling Criticks* that have only learn't to *Spit* and *Mew* ; a Mint of *Intelligence*, that to make each man his *peny-worth*, draws out into petty parcels, what the Merchant receives in Bullion : He that comes often ſaves *two pence* a week in *Gazets*, and has his News and his Coffee for the ſame charge , as at a *three peny Ordinary* they give in Broth to your Chop of Mutton; 'tis an *Exchange* where Haberdaſhers of *Political ſmall wares* meet , and mutually abuſe each other, and the Publique, with bottomleſs ſtories, and headleſs notions ; the Rendezvous of *idle Pamphlets*, and perſons more idly imployd to read them ; a *High Court of Juſtice*, where every little Fellow in a *Chamlet-Cloak* takes upon him to tranſpoſe Affairs both in Church and State , to ſhew reaſons againſt *Acts* of Parliament , and condemn the Decrees of *General Councels* ; 'Tis impoſſible to deſcribe it better than the moſt ingenious of the *Latine Poets* has done it to our hand , and that ſo excellently , we cannot but tranſcribe it:

    " *Unde quod eſt uſquam quamvis Regionibus abſit*
    " *Inſpicitur, penetrátque cavas vox omnis ad Aures;*
    " *Nocte Diéque patet, Tota eſt ex Ære ſonanti,*
    " *Tota Fremit, Vocéſque refert, Iterátque quod Audit.*
    " *Nulla Quies intus, nulláque ſilentia parte,*
    " *Nec tamen eſt Clamor, ſed parvæ Murmura Vocis:*
    " *Qualia de Pelagi (ſi quis procul audiat) undâ*
    " *Eſſe ſolent, qualemve ſonum cum* Jupiter *atras*
    " *Increpuit nubes, Extrema Tonitrua reddunt ;*
    " *Atria Turba tenet, veniunt Leve vulgus, Euntque,*
    " *Miſtáque cum veris paſſim Commenta vagantur,*
    " *Millia Rumorum, confuſáque verba volutant ;*
    " *E quibus Hi vacuas Implent ſermonibus Aures,*
    " *Hi narrata ferunt alio, Menſuráque ficti*
    " *Creſcit, & Auditis aliquid novus Adjicit Author.*
    " *Illic Credulitas, Illic temerarius Error*

                                                    Vanáque

2   *The Character of a Coffee-House.*

" *Vanáque Lætitia est, Consternatique Timores*
" *Seditióque recens, dubióque Authore Susurri*
" *Ipsa quid in Cælo Rerum, Pelagóque geratur*
" *Et Tellure videt, Totúmque Inquirit in Orbem.*
                         Thus strictly Englisht.

Here *all that's done*, though far remote, appears,
And in close whispers penetrates our ears ;
As built of *Brass*, the *House* throughout resounds,
Reports things *heard*, and every word rebounds.
No rest within, nor *silence*, yet the noise
Not loud, but like a hallow murmuring voice ;
Such as from far by Rowling Waves is sent,
Or like *Joves* fainting Thunder almost spent :
Hither the *idle vulgar* come and go,
Carrying a thousand Rumours to and fro ;
With *stale reports* some listening ears do fill,
Some *coyn fresh tales*, in words that vary still ;
Lies mixt with Truth, all in the telling grows,
And each *Relator* adds to what he knows :
Here dwells rash error, light credulity,
Sad panick fears, joys built on vanity ;
New rais'd sedition, secret whisperings,
Of unknown Authors, and of doubtful things :
All Acts of Heav'n and Earth it boldly views,
And through the spacious World enquires for *News*.

The Room stinks of *Tobacco* worse than Hell of *Brimstone*, and is as full of *smoak* as their Heads that frequent it , whose humours are as various as those of *Bedlam* , and their discourse oft-times as *Heathenish* and *dull* as their Liquor ; that Liquor, which by its looks and taste, you may reasonably guess to be *Pluto*'s *Diet-drink* ; that Witches tipple out of *dead mens Skulls,* when they ratifie to *Belzebub* their Sacramental Vows.

This *Stygian-Puddle-seller,* was formerly notorious for his ill-favour'd *Cap*, that Ap'd a *Turbant* , and in Conjunction with his *Antichristian face* , made him appear perfect *Turk* : But of late his *Wife* being grown acquainted with Gallants, and the provocative virtue of *Chocolet* , he finds a *Broad-brim'd Hat* more necessary: When he comes to fill you a Dish , you may take him for *Guy Faux* with a *dark Lanthorn* in's hand , for no sooner can you taste it, but it scalds your throat, as if you had swallowed the *Gunpowder-Treason* : though he seem never so demure, you cannot properly call him *Pharisee,* for he never *washes* either out or Inside of his *pots* or *dishes* , till they be as black as an Usurers Conscience ; and then only scraping off the contracted *Soot* , makes use of it, in the way of his Trade, instead of *Coffee-powder* ; their taste and virtue being so near of Kin, he dares defie the veriest *Coffee-Critick* to distinguish them : Though he be no great *Traveller*, yet he is in continual *motion*, but 'tis only from the fire side to the Table, and his *tongue* goes infinitely faster than his *feet* , his grand study being readily to eccho an answer to that thredbare question, *What News have you Master ?* Then with a grave whisper (yet such as all the Room may hear it) he discovers some mysterious *Intrigue* of State told
                                                                    him

The *Character* of a *Coffee-House.*

him laſt night by *one* that is *Barber to the Taylor of a mighty great Courtiers man.* relating this with no leſs formality than a young *Preacher* delivers his *firſt Sermon*, a ſudden *Hickup* ſurprizes him, and he is forced twenty times to break the thred of his Tale with ſuch neceſſary Parentheſis's, *Wife, ſweep up thoſe looſe Corns of Tobacco, and ſee the Liquor boil not over:* He holds it as part of his Creed, that the *Great Turk* is a very good Chriſtian, and of the Reformed Church, becauſe he drinks Coffee , and ſwears that *Pointings* for celebrating its virtues a *doggerel* deſerves to be *Poet Laureat :* yet is it not only this hot *Hell-broth* that he ſells, for never was Mountebank furniſht with more variety of poyſonous *drugs;* then he of *liquors, Tea* and *Aromatique* for the ſweettooth'd Gentleman, *Betony* and *Reſade* for the *addle-headed Cuſtomer* , Back-recruiting *Chocolet* for the Conſumptive Gallant, *Herefordſhire Redſtreak* made of rotten apples at the *three Cranes,* true *Brunſwick-Mum* brew'd at S. *Katherines,* and *Ale* in peny *Mugs,* not ſo big as a Taylors Thimble.

As you have a *hodge-podge* of Drinks, ſuch too is your Company, for each man ſeems a Leveller, and ranks and files himſelf as he liſts, without regard to degrees or order ; ſo that oft you may ſee a ſilly *Fop*, and a worſhipful *Juſtice,* a griping *Rook,* and a grave *Citizen,* a worthy *Lawyer*, and an errant *Pickpocket,* a Reverend *Nonconformiſt,* and a Canting *Mountebank;* all blended together, to compoſe an *Oglio* of impertinence.

If any *Pragmatick,* to ſhew himſelf witty or eloquent, begin to talk high, preſently the further *Tables* are abandon'd, and all the reſt flock round (like ſmaller birds to admire the gravity of *Madge-Howlet*) They liſten to him a while with their *mouths,* and let their *Pipes* go out, and *Coffee* grow *cold,* for pure zeal of attention, but o'th' ſudden fall all a yelping at once with more noiſe, but not half ſo much harmony as a *Pack of Beagles* on the full Cry, to ſtill this bawling, **U**pſtarts

Captain *All-man-ſir,* the man of mouth, with a face as bluſtring as that of *Eolus* and his four Sons in Painting, and a voice louder than the ſpeaking *Trumpet,* he begins you the ſtory of a Sea-fight ; and though he never were further by water than the *Bear-garden,* or *Cuckolds-Haven,* yet having pyrated the names of Ships and Captains, he perſwades you himſelf was preſent, and performed Miracles; that he waded *Knee-deep* in blood on the upper Deck, and never thought *ſerenade* to his Miſtreſs, ſo pleaſant as the Bullets *whiſtling ;* how he ſtopt a *Vice-Admiral* of the Enemies under full ſail, till ſhe was boarded, with his *ſingle arm* inſtead of *Grapling Irons,*
* and puſt out with his breath a *Fire-ſhip* that fell foul on   *Vide Juſtin. l 2.* them. All this he relates ſitting in a *Cloud* of Smoak, and   *de Cynagiro..* belching ſo many common *Oaths* to vouch it, you can ſcarce gueſs whether the real Engagement, or his Romancing account of it, be the more *dreadful :* However, he concludes with railing at the Conduct of ſome *Eminent Officers,* (that perhaps he never ſaw) and proteſts, had they taken *his adviſe* at the Councel of War, not a *Sail* had eſcap'd us.

He is no ſooner out of breath, but another begins a Lecture on the *Gazet,* where finding ſeveral *Prizes* taken, he gravely obſerves, if this Trade hold, we ſhall quickly rout the Dutch *Horſe* and *Foot* by *Sea :* He nick-names the *Poliſh Gentlemen* where ever he meets them , and enquires, whether *Gayland* and *Taffaletta* be *Lutherans* or *Calviniſts : Stilo Novo* he interprets a vaſt new
       B.   *Stile,*

4   *The Character of a Coffee-House.*

Stile or *Turn-pike* erected by his Electoral Highnefs on the borders of *Weft-phalia* to keep Mounfieur *Turenes* Cavalray from falling on his retreating Troops; He takes words by the found without examining their fenfe: *Morea* he believes to be the Country of the *Moors*, and *Hungary* a place where famine alwayes keeps her Court, nor is there any thing more certain, than that he made a whole Roomful of Fops, as wife as himfelf, fpend above two hours in fearching the *Map* for *Ariftocracy* and *Democracy*, not doubting but to have found them there, as well as *Dalmatia* and *Croatia*

Next Seigniour *Poll* takes up the Cudgels, that fpeaks nothing but *Defigns*, *Projects*, *Intrigues*, and *Experiments*, One of thofe in the old *Comedian*, *Plautus*, *Sctunt id quod in Aurem Rex Reginæ dixerit*, *Quod* Juno *confabulata eft cum* Jove, *Sciant quæ neque futura neque facta funt, tamen illi fciunt*, &c. All the Councels of the *German* Dyet, the *Romifh Conclave*, and *Turkifh Divan*, are as well known to him as his *Laundreffes Smock*. He kens all the Cabals of the Court to a hairs breadth, and (more then an hundred of us do,) which Lady is not painted; you would take his mouth for a *Limbéck*, it diftills his words fo niggardly, as if he was loath to enrich you with lies, of which he has yet more plenty than *Fox*, *Stowe*, and *Hollingfhead* bound up together; He tels you of a Plot to let the *Lyons* loofe in the Tower, and then blow it up with *white-powder*; of five hundred and fifty *Jefuits* all mounted on *Dromedaries* feen by Moonfhine on *Hampfteadheath*, and a terrible defign hatch'd by the Colledge of *Doway*, to drain the narrow Seas and bring Popery over *dry fhod*, befides he has a thoufand inventions dancing in his brain-pain; an *Advice-boat* on the Stocks, that fhall go to the Eaft-Indies, and come back again in a *Fortnight*, a trick to march *under water*, and bore holes through the *Dutch-fhips* Keele with Augurs, and fincke them, as they ride at Anhor, and a moft excellent *purfuit to catch Sunbeams*, for making the Ladies new fafhioned *Towrs*, that *Poets* may no more be damn'd for telling lies about their *Curls* and *Treffes*.

But thefe are puny *Pugs*, the *Arch-Devil*, wherewith this *Smoke-hole* is haunted, is the *Town-wit*, one that playes *Rex* where ever he comes, and makes as much hurry as *Robin Goodfellow* of old amongft our *Granams Milk-bouls*; He is a kind of a *Squib* on a Rope, a *meteor* compos'd of Self-conceit and noife, that by *blazing and crackling* engages the wonder of the ignorant, till on a fudden he vanifhes and leaves a *ftench*, if not *infection* behind him; he is too often the *ftain* of a good Family, and by his debaucht life blots the noble *Coat* of his Anceftors, A *wilde unback'd Colt*, whofe *brains* are not half *codled*, indebted for his *cloaths* to his Tailor, and for his wit (fuch as it is) to his Company: The School had no fooner 'dued him with a few fuperficial befprinklings, but his *Mothers indulgence* pofted him to Town for *Genteeler breeding*, where three or four *wilde* Companions, half a dozen bottles of *Burgundy*, two leaves of *Leviathan*, a brisk encounter with his *Landlords Glafswindowes*, the charms of a little *Mifs*, and the fight of a new *Play* dub'd him at once both a *Wit* and a *Hero*, ever fince he values himfelf mainly for *underftanding the Town*, and indeed *knows* moft things in it, that are not *worth knowing*. The two *Poles* whereon all his difcourfes turn are *Atheifm* and *Bawdry*; Bat him from being prophane or obfcene, and you *cramp* his Ingenuity, which forthwith *Flags* and becomes *ufelefs*, as a meer *Common Lawyer* when he has crofs'd the *Channel*.

He is fo refractory to *Divinity* that Morality it felf cannot hold him, he affirms

The Character of a Coffee-House. 5

firms humane Nature knows no such things as *principles* of Good and evil, and will swear *all women* are *whores*, though his *Mother* and *Sister* both stand by : Whatever is sacred or serious he seeks to render Ridiculous, and thinks Government and Religion fit objects for his *idle* and fantastick *Buffoonry*, his humor is proud and assuming, as if he would palliate his ignorance by *Scoffing* at what he understands not, and therefore with a *pert* and *pragmatique* scorn depreciates all things of nobler moment, but most passionately affects *pretty a-lamode* words, And is as covetous of a *New Song* or Ayre, as an Antiquary of *Cato's Statue* with ne'r an arm, and but half a nose, These keep him alwaies imployd, and fill up the *Grotesco's* of his conversation, whilst with a stately Gallantry once in every half hour he *Combes out his Wig*, *Carreens* his breeches, and new marshalls his *Garniture*, to the Tune of *Methinks the poor Town has been troubled too long*.

His mind used to *whistle* up and down in the levities of Fancy, and effeminated by the childish *Toyings* of a rampant imagination finds it self indisposed for all solid imployment, especially the serious exercises of *Piety* and *Virtue*, which begets an aversion to those *Lovely Beauties*, and that prompts him on all occasions to expose them as ridiculous and vain : Hence by degrees he comes to abuse *Sacred Scripture*, makes a mock of eternal Flames, Joque on the venerable Mysteries of Religion, and in fine, scoffe at that *All Glorious* and *Tremendous Majesty* before whom his brother *Wits below* tremble ; Tis true he will not confess himself *Atheist*, yet in his heart the Fool hath said it, and boasts aloud that he holds his *Gospel* from the *Apostle of Malmsbury*, though it is more than probable he ne'r read, at least understood *ten* leaves of that *unlucky Author* ; Talk of *Witches* and you Tickle him, speak of *Spirits* and he tels you he knowes none better than those of Wine, name but *Immaterial Essence*, and he shall flout at you as a dull Fop incapable of sense, and unfit for Conversation ; Nor is he ever better pleas'd than when he can here hedge in some young *raw Divine* to *Bulbait* with scurrility and all kind of profaneness.

By means of some small *scraps of learning* matcht with a far greater stock of Confidence, a voluble Tongue, and bold delivery , he has the ill-luck to be celebrated by the vulgar; for a man of *Parts*, which opinion gains credit to his Insolences, and sets him on further extravigances to maintain his Title of a *Wit* by continuing his practice of *Fooling*, whereas all his mighty parts are sum'd up in this Inventory. " Imprimis, A *pedling may of Fancy*, a *Lucky hit at Quibbling*, " now and then an *odd metaphor*, a conceited *Irony*, a ridiculous *Simile*, a wilde " *fetch*, an unexpected *Inference*, a *Minick Gesture*, a pleasing *knack* in humour- " ing a Tale, and lastly an irresistable *Resolution* to *speak last*, and never be " *dasht* out of Countenance :

By these *Arts* dexterously manag'd he engrosses a *vaste Repute*, The grave Citizen calls him shrewd man, and notable *Headpiece*, The *Ladies* (we mean the things so called of his acquaintance) vote him a most *accomplisht Gentleman*, and the Blades swear he is a *Walking Comedy*, the only *Merry Andrew* of the Age, that scatters *Wit* wherever he comes, as *Beggars* do *Lice*, or Muskcats perfumes, and that *nothing in Nature and all* that can compare with him.

You would think he had got the *Lullian Art*, for he speaks *Extempore* on all subjects , and ventures his words without the Relief of *Sense* to second them, his thoughts start from his *imagination* and he never troubles himself to Examine their decency, or solidity by Judgement. To discourse him seriously

6   *The Character of a Coffee-House.*

is to read the *Ethicks to a Monkey*, or make an Oration to *Caligula's Horse*, whence you can only expect a *weehee* or *Jadish spurn*; after the most convincing Arguments, if he can but muster up one plausible *jeque* you are routed, For he that understood not your *Logick*, apprehends his droll, and though *Syllogysms* may be answered, yet Jests and loud *laughter* can never be confuted, but have more sway to degrade things with the *unthinking croud*, than demonstrations; There being a Root of envy in too many Men, that invites them to applaud that which Exposes and villifies what they cannot comprehend, He pretends great skill in curing the *Tetters* and *Ring-worms* of State; but blowes in the sores till they Rankle with his poisonous breath, he shoots *libels* with his forked tongue at his Superiors and abuseth his dearest *Friends*, chusing to forfeit his neck to the *Gibbet*, or his shoulders to the *Batoon* rather than lose the driest of his idle *Quibbles*; In brief he is the *Jack-pudding of Society*, a jeering *Buffoon*, a better kind of *Ape* in the judgement of all *Wisemen*, but an incomparable *Wit* in his *own*.

Thus have we led you from *Board to Board*, like the fellow in the Tower, to shew you *strange Beasts* wherewith this place is sometimes frequented. To take now a *farewel view* of the House will be difficult, since tis always shifting Scenes and like *O Brasile* (the Inchanted Island) seldome appears twice in a posture; The *wax Candles* burning, and low devout whispers sometimes strike a kind of Religious Awe, whilst the modish Gallant swears so oft by *Iesu*, an Ignorant Catholick would take it for a Chappel, and think he were saying our Ladies Psalter; In some places the *Organs* speak it a Musick Room, at others a pair of *Tables and draught board*, a smal gaming house; on a sudden it turns *Exchange*, or a Warehouse for all sorts of *Commodities*, where fools are drawn in by inch of Candle, as we betray and catch *Larks* with a Glass; The Bully-*Rook* makes it his *Bubbling* pond, where he angles for *Fops*, singles out his man, insinuates an *acquaintaince*, offers the wine, and at next Tavern sets upon him with *high Fullums*, and *plucks* him: The *Ingenuist* use it for an after *Rehearsal*, where they bring *Plays* to Repetition, sift each *Scene* examine every *uncorrected Line*, and *damn* beyond the fury of the *Rota*, whilst the *incognito Poet* out of an overweening affection to his *Infant Wit*, steals in *muffled* up in his Cloake, and sliely *Evesdrops* like a *mendicant Mother* to praise the *prettyness* of the *Babe* she has newly pawm'd on the Parish.

But 'tis time to be *gone*, who knows what *Magick* may be a working, For, behold the *Coffee-Powder* settles at the bottome of our dish in form of a most terrible *Saracens Head*. For a parting blow then give us leave to *unbend* a little; and say,

A *Coffee-House* is a *Phanatique Theatre*, a *Hot-House* to flux in for a *clapt understanding*, a *Sympathetical* Cure for the *Gonorrhea* of the Tongue, or a *refin'd Baudy-House*, where *Illegitimate Reports* are got in close *Adultery* between *Lying lips* and *Itching Ears*.

                    Si quid novisti rectias Candidus Imperti

FINIS.

Coffee-houses Vindicated in answer to the late published Character of a Coffee-House asserting from Reason, Experience, and good Authours, the Excellent Use and Physical Vertues of that Liquor. With The grand Conveniency of such civil places of Resort and Ingenious Conversation (London, J. Lock for J. Clarke, 1673), 6pp.; 2°. Huntingdon Library: 133277. ESTCR1813. Hünersdorff.

A folio prose satire replying to *The Character of a Coffee-House, with the Symptomes of a Town-Wit* (see above, pp. 81–90), mimicking its physical appearance, and satirising the debased intellectual attitudes of the writer of 'Characters'. This text begins with a defence of the medicinal properties of coffee, describing the 'salutiferous' or health-giving properties of coffee using the ancient humoural theory to describe the effects of coffee on the human body. The humoural analysis of coffee offered here broadly follows that contained in a contemporary compilation of coffee scholarship, *The Vertues of Coffee* (1663; see Volume 4, pp. 75–84), which reprinted excerpts on the natural history of coffee by Bacon, Parkinson, Sandys and Howell. Building on this information, the author then develops an apology for the sociability of the coffee-house, suggesting that, contra its detractors, the coffee-house is cheap, given to sobriety, and an encouragement to trade. Furthermore, coffee-house discourse is modest, and knowledgeable, and does not deserve its reputation for sedition, gossip or 'Irreverent reflections on Affairs of State'. As the pampleteer recognises, coffee-houses had been repeatedly identified as locations for the dissemination of unofficial news and intelligence critical of the court, becoming a matter of concern for the authorities throughout the 1670s and the Succession Crisis of the early 1680s. In defending the civic and refined tone of coffee-house conversations, the pamphleteer writes an apology not only for the coffee-houses, but the new urban Restoration culture of which they are emblematic.

Nothing is known of the author, and the printer and publisher were known for their broadsides and pamphlets. John Lock was a printer active in London 1673–5 (Plomer), in the Long Walk near Christ Church Hospital, near the sign of the Drawers. John Clarke was a publisher of broadsides at the Harp and Bible in West Smithfield. Two copies are extant, one at the Huntingdon Library, California, and the James Ford Bell Library, University of Minnesota, Minneapolis, Minnesota. There were no further editions, although editions in 1674 and 1675 are sometimes erroneously noted in secondary literature, including Edward Robinson, Aytoun Ellis and Hünersdorff. Both the *Character* and the *Vindication* were guaranteed a significant afterlife by their republication in the *Harleian Miscellany* in 1745, and again in that anthology's reprints of 1808–11 and 1808–13 (see *The Harleian Miscellany*, 8 vols (London, T. Osborne, 1744–6), vol. VI, pp. 433–6). Both the *Character* and the *Vindication* were excerpted in Charles W. Colby (ed.), *Selections from the Sources of English History, B.C. 55 –A.D. 1832* (London, Longmans, Green, 1920), pp. 208–12. The *Vindication* – dated to 1675 – is noted by Thomas Babington Macaulay in his research for the coffee-house section in his *The History of England from the Accession of James the Second*, 5 vols (London, Longman, Browne, Green and Longmans, 1849), vol. I, p. 368n.).

Coffee-houſes Vindicated

I N

A N S V V E R

To the late Publiſhed

C H A R A C T E R

O F A

C O F F E E · H O U S E

Aſſerting

From *Reaſon*, *Experience*, and good *Authours*, the Excellent *Uſe*, and *Phyſical Vertues* of that *Liquor*.

With

The grand *Conveniency* of ſuch civil places of *Reſort* and Ingenious *Converſation.*

L O N D O N,
Printed by *J. Lock* for *J. Clarke.* 1675.

[1]

Coffee-Houses Vindicated.

IN

A N S W E R

To the late Published

Character of a Coffee-House.

W It of late is grown *so wanton*, and the humour of *Affecting* it, become so common, that each little *Fop* whose spungy Brain can but coyn a small drossy *Joque*, or two, presently thinks himself priviledg'd to *Asperse* every Thing that comes in his way though in it self never so *Innocent*, or *beneficial* to the Publick; To the Influence of this predominant *Folly*, we may not improperly refer the Production of those swarms of Insect *Pamphlets* which the Press weekly spawns into the World, and particularly the Nativity of that *Folio-Impertinence* which occasions our present Reflections; A Peice whose *flanting Title* raised our thoughts to an expectation of somewhat extraordinary; But finding little in it but down-right *Abuse*, The Quinteffence of *Billingsgate Rhetorick* Dreggs of *Canting*, and such *Rubbish Language*, as *Bubbling*, *Bully-Rock*, *Fluxing*, *Gonorrhea*, &c. Charity it self could not but *suspect* the Authour more conversant somewhere else then in *Coffee-houses*, and conclude those places being too *Civil* for a debaucht Humour, had given occasion for his exposing them As *Lay-Conventicles*, &c.

However we shall preserve that equal regard to *Solomons* double-fac'd advice, To *Answer* and not *Answer* such as our characterizing Authour, That we shall decline *Retorting* any thing particularly to his scurrilities; Let the *Town-wits* (whom we leave to take his own satisfaction)

A 2   Fence

(2)

Fence with him if he pleafe at thofe Weapons ; a formall *Anfwer* would be too great an Indulgence to his Vanity, and make him think too *confiderably* of himfelf ; Befides to reply in the pittyful ftile of his *pedling* Drollery is to ingage in a Game at *Pufh-pin*, And to fay any thing *ferious* will be no more to borrow his *Phrafe* than *reading a Lefture to a Monkey*; Inftead therefore of wafting our own or the Readers *time* fo Impertinently, We fhall briefly endeavour to give you an Account of the *Ufe* and *Vertues* of *Coffee*, and next confider fome of thofe many *conveniences* Coffee-houfes afford us both for *bufinefs* and *converfation*

Though the happy *Arabia*, Natures *fpicery* prodigally furnifhes the voluptuous World with all kind of *Aromaticks* and divers other Rarities, yet I fcarce know whether Mankind be not ftill as *much* obliged to it for the excellent fruit of the humble *Coffee fhr b* As for lady other of its more fpecious productions, For fince there is nothing we here enjoy next to Life valuable beyond *Health*, certainly thofe things that contribute to preferving us in good *plight*, and *encrafy* and fortifie our weak bodies againft the continual Affaults and Batteries of *Difeafes* deferve our reguards much more, than *Thofe* which only gratine a liquorifh Palat, or otherwife prove fubfervient to our delights ; As for this *falutiferous Berry*, of fo general a Ufe throrgh all the Regions of the *Eaft*, 'tis fufficiently known when prepared to be moderately *hot* and of a very *drying attenuating and cleanfing Qualiry*, whence Reafon infers That its *decoction* muft contain m ny good *Phyfical properties*, and cannot but be an Incomparable Remedy to diffolve *Crudities*, comfort the *Brain*, and dry up *Ill Humours* in the Stomach, In brief to prevent or redrefs in thofe that frequently drink it *All* cold drowzy *Rheumatick Diftempers* whatfoever that proceed from Excefs of *Moifture*, which are fo *numerous*, that but to name them would *Tire* the Tongue of a *Mountebank.*

This confideration alone fhould methinks be fufficient to Ingratiate it to our *Efteem*, fince the ufe thereof does thence appear abfolutely *neceffary*, efpecially to *us* in whom *Fhlegm* is apt to abound both by reafon of the *Northern* fcituation of our Country and the ill habit of extraordinary *drinking* grown too Epidemicall among us.

Experience proves That there is nothing more effectual than this reviving Drink to reftore their *fenfes* that have *Brutified* themfelves by immoderate Tipling heady Liquors which it performs by its *exficcant* property before-mentioned, that inftantly dries up that cloud of giddy *Fumes* which boyling up from the over-charged *Stomach*, opprefs the *Brain* ; But this being only a kindnefs to *voluntary Divels* (as my Lord Cock calls common *Drunkards*) we fhould fcarce reckon amongft *Coffee's* virtues did it not evidence its *quality* and fhew how beneficial it may prove by parity of Reafon, when defigned to more worthy and noble Ufes, Such as *expelling Wind, fertifying the Liver*, refrefhing the *Heart*, Corroborating the *Spirits* both *Vital* and *Animal*, quickning the *Appetite*, affifting Digeftion, helping the *Stone*, taking away *Rheums* and *Defluxions*, with a thoufand other kindneffes to Nature, which we might Enumerate, did we not think it a fufficient *Argument* of its Excellency only to obferve, *How Univerfally it takes in the World*, For we cannot without an Affront to our *Nature* imagine mankind fo *fottifh* As greedily to entertain a Drink that has nothing of *fweetnefs* to reccommend it to the Guft, nor any of thofe pleafant *blandifhments* wherewith Wine and other Liquors tempt and debauch our Palates, *unlefs* there were fome more then ordinary *vertue and efficacy* in it, yet we fee without any of thefe infinuating advantages, *Coffee* has fo generally prevail'd that *Bread* it felf though commonly with us voted the *ftaff of Life*) Is

fcarce

(3)

scarce of so universal use, For of that the *Tartars* and *Arabians* vast and numerous people Use little or none, whereas both they and the *Turks*, *Persians* and almost all the *Eastern World* are so devoted to *Coffee*, that besides Innumerable *Publick houses* for sale of it, There is scarce a private *Fire* without it all day long; As any that are but moderately acquainted with *Sashes and Turbants* can witness, Is it not enough to silence the Barking of our *Little Wits* against this Innocent and wholesome Drink That is so generally used by so many mighty *Nations*, and those too celebrated for the most *witty and Sagavious*.

Nor wants this Liquor the *Suffrages* of excellent Authors ; The famous *Parkinson* in his exquisite Herbal p. 1622. commends it for the strengthning weak Stomacks, Helping digestion and obstructions, and Tumours of the Liver and Spleen ; The Incomparable *Verulam* in his *Natural History fo.* 155. amongst other encomiums asserts that it comforteth the Brain, and by condensing the Spirits expelleth fear and maketh them strong and chearful ; *Sandy's* in his Travels, and the Judicious Sir *H. B.* both in his *Voyage to the Levant* and elsewhere speaks very advantagiously of it, Nor did the Ingenious Mr. *Howel* in his Life time deny it his publick testimony in Print, In a Letter to Mr. Just. *R.* before his *Organon salutis* ;

After so many worthy *Names* have given it their Votes, what have our puisne *Quiblers* to object ? Only this, Tis *black* and thereforeWith must be shown to call it *Stygian Puddle*; And besides this, Tis *bitter*, and therefore a Lye must be fram'd, That it is made of *Soot*.

For the first, were they but so well acquainted with the *Prince of Latine* Poets As our *Charracter-maker* would make us believe he is with *Ovid* by his dull *tedious* and Impertinent *Quotation*, They might remember

Alba Ligustra cadunt, vaccinia Nigra Leguntur.,

'Tis the opinion of better *Heads* than any on their *Shoulders* That this Liquor is no other than that famous *Black Broath* of the *Lacedemonians* so much *celebrated* by Antiquity.

For it's *Tast* 'tis a pittyful childish humour always to Indulge our Palates, Diseases are removed by *butter* Pills, and the most sanative Potions are oft-times very *ungrateful* to swallow, But the truth is, this Drink has nothing in it of *Nauseousness*, nor any Tast but what familiariz'd by a little use will become pleasant and delightful.

The dull Planet *Saturn* has not finished one Revolution through his Orb since *Coffee-houses* were first known amongst us, yet 'tis worth our wonder to observe how *numerous* they are already grown, not only here in our *Metropolis*, but in both *Universities* and most *Cities* and eminent *Towns* throughout the Nation ; Nor indeed have we any *Places* of entertainment of more *use* and general *conveniency* in several respects amongst us.

First, In regard of *easie expence*, being to wait for or meet a Friend: A *Tavern reckoning* soon breeds a Purse-Consumption, In an *Ale-house* you must gorge your self with Pot after Pot, sit dully *alone* or be drawn in to *club* for others reekonings, be frown'd on by your *Landlady* As one that cumbers the house and hinders better Guests, But *here* for a *penny* or two you may spend 2 or 3 hours, have the shelter of a *House*, the warmth of a *Fire*, the diversion of *Company* and conveniency if you please of taking a Pipe of *Tobacco*, And all this without any grumbling or repining.

Secondly, I or Sobriety, 'tis grown by the Ill Influences of I know not what *Hydroptick Stars*

B   al-

(4)

almost a general *custome* amongst us, That no *Bargain* can be drove, or business concluded between Man and Man, but it must be transacted at some *Publick House*, This to Persons *much* concerned in the World must needs be very Injurious, should they always run to *Taverns* or *Ale-houses*, where continual *sippings*, though never so warily would be apt to fly up into their *Brains*, and render them drowsie and indisposed for business; Whereas having now the opportunity of a *Coffee-house*, they repair thither, take each Man a dish or two (so far from *causing* that it *cures* any dizziness or disturbant Fumes) and so dispatching their business, go out more *sprightly* about their affairs then before ; The like may be said of *Mornings draughts* which taken in *Wine Ale* or *Beer*, most times either destroy or very much mayhem the business of the *whole* day, whereas if people would be perswaded to play the *Good-fellows* in this wholesome wakeful Innocent drink, They would find it do no *less* good to their bodies, and much *more* promote and advance their *business* and *Imployments*.

Lastly, For *diversion*, Tis older than *Aristotle*, and will be true when *Hobs* is forgot, that Man is a *sociable creature*, and delights in *Company*, Now *whither* shall a person wearied with hard study or the laborious turmoils of a tedious day repair to *refresh* himself, or where can young *Gentlemen* or *Shop-keepers* more Innocently and advantagiously spend an *hour* or two in the Evening then at a *Coffee-house*; where they shall be sure to meet *Company*, and by the custome of the house not *such* as at other places *stingy* and reserved to themselves, but *free* and *communicative*, where every Man may modestly begin his *story*, and *propose* to, or *Answer* another as he thinks fit ; *Discourse* Is *Pabulum Animi, cos Ingenij*, The minds best *Dyet*, and the great *Whet-stone* and Incentive of Ingenuity, By *that* we come to know Men better than by their *Physiognomy's*, *Loquire utte videam* speak that I may see thee, was the *Phylosophers* Adage, To read *Men* Is acknowledged more useful then *Books*, but where is there a better *Library* for that study generally than *Here*, amongst such a variety of *Humours* all expressing themselves on divers subjects according to their respective Abilities?

But our *Pamphlet-monger* (that sputters out sencele's *Characters* faster than any *Hocus* can vomit *Inckle*) will needs take upon him to be dictator of all Society, and confine company to sit as mute in a *Coffee-house* As a *Quaker* at a *silent meeting*, or himself with a little Wench when behind the Hangings they are playing a Game at *Whist*, To this purpose he *babbles* mightily against *Tatling*, and makes a great deal of *cold mirth* with three or four stale Humours that you may find a thousand times better described in a hundred old *Plays*, yet to collect those *excellent observables* cost the poor Soul above *half* a years time in painful Pilgrimage from one *Coffee-house* to another, where planting himself in a dark *corner* with the dexterity of *short-hand* he recorded these choice *Remarks*, whilst all the Town took him for an *Excise-man* counting the number of dishes ; the World is now obliged with the fruits of his Industry, which proves no more then that some giddy-headed Coxcombs like himself (whose Skulls instead of *Brains* are stuft with *Saw-dust*) do sometimes intrude into *Coffee-houses*, A doctrine we are easily perswaded to believe, For if their doors had been kept shut against all *Fops* 'tis more than probable *Himself* had never known so much of their Humours, We confess *In multiloquio non deest vanitas* amongst so *much* Talk there may happen *some* to very little purpose, But as we doubt not but the *Royal Proclamation* has had the good success to prevent for the future any *dangerous Intelligence* sawcy prying into *Arcana Imperij* or Irrevent reflections on *Affairs* of State, so for the little *Innocent Extravagancies* we hold them very *divertising*, Every *Fool* being a *Fiddle to the Company*, for how el'e should our

Author

(5)

Author have raised so much *laughter* through the Town ? Besides how infinitely are the *vain pra-tings* of these ridiculous Pragmaticks over-balanced by the *sage* and *solid* Reasonings Here frequently to be heard of Experienced *Gentlemen*, Judicious *Lawyers*, able *Physitians*, Ingenious *Merchants*, and understanding *Citizens*, In the abstrusest points of *Reason*, *Philosophy*, *Law* and publick *Commerce* ?

In brief 'tis undenyable That as you have here the most *civil* so 'tis generally the most *Intelligent Society*, The frequenting whose *Converse*, and observing their *Discourses* and *Deportment* cannot but *civilize* our manners, Inlarge our *understandings*, refine our *Language*, teach us a generous *confidence* and handsome *Mode of Address*; And *brush* off that *Pudor Subrusticus* (As I remember *Tully* somewhere calls it) That *clownish kind of modesty*, frequently incident to the *best* Natures, which renders them *Sheepish* and *Ridiculous* in company.

So that upon the whole matter, spight of the idle *Sarcasms* and paltry reproaches thrown upon it, we may with no less truth than plainness give this brief *Character* of a *well regulated Coffee-house* (for our Pen disdains to be *Advocate* for any *sordid holes* that assume that *Name* to cloak the *Practice* of *Debauchery*) That it is

> The *Sanctuary* of *Health*.
> The *Nursery* of *Temperance*.
> The *Delight* of *Frugality*.
> An *Accademy* of *Civility*.
> A N D
> *Free-School* of *Ingenuity*.

F I N I S.

The Grand Concern of England Explained; in Several
Proposals Offered to the Consideration of Parliament.
1. For Payment of Publick Debts. 2. For Advancement
and Encouragement of Trade. 3. For Raising the Rents
of Lands ... By a lover of his countrey, and well-wisher to
the prosperity both of the King and kingdoms (London,
n.p., 1673), [4], 62pp.; 4°. BL: 100.g.71. ESTCR23421.
Extract, pp. 21–4. Hünersdorff.

A sixty-page quarto political tract written in defence of domestic British economic interests, which, the writer argues, were threatened by the growth in
foreign imports, especially of expensive luxuries like coffee and brandy. The
unknown author identifies himself only as 'A Lover of his country and well-
wisher to the prosperity both of the King and kingdoms'. The early 1670s were
a period of growing criticism of the economic policy of Charles II's ministers,
who were accused of not having the nation's interests at heart. These critics identified themselves increasingly as a group or interest known in Parliament as the
Country Party, centred on the circles around Buckingham and Shaftesbury (see
John Spurr, *England in the 1670s: 'This Masquerading Age'* (Oxford, Blackwell,
2000), pp. 18–20, 77–9). Amongst the thirteen specific proposals the tract
advances are: a restriction on the further expansion of London; the regulation
of the booming property market; the general naturalisation of all foreign protestants; the regulation of stage coaches; the establishment of a court of Requests
(for small claims amongst poor people) in all towns, as it is in the City; and 'That
a Bound be put to the Extravagant habits, and Excesses of all sorts of Persons' (p.
5, not reproduced here).

  With regard to coffee, the tract develops an argument it first makes against
brandy, where it suggests that a prohibition on the importation of brandy
would lead to an increase in the price of domestic malt and wheat, as consumers
returned to the traditional beverages of beer and ale. 'Before Brandy ... came
over into *England* in such quantities as now it doth, we drank good Strong Beer

and Ale; and all laborious people ... did therefore every morning and evening use to drink a pot of Ale, or a flagon of strong Beer' (see below pp. 105–6). While coffee itself attracts criticism as a luxury, coffee-houses are strongly criticised as well, not only as places which promote idleness amongst tradesmen and artisans, but as centres for the dissemination of seditious news. Here the writer borrows the criticisms made in the pamphlet satires, but rewrites them in a more measured tone. The printer of the tract is unknown. Numerous copies of the tract are extant; and it was republished in volume VIII of the *Harleian Miscellany*, 8 vols (London, T. Osborne, 1744–6).

THE
Grand Concern
OF
ENGLAND
EXPLAINED;

IN SEVERAL

PROPOSALS

Offered to the Confideration of the
PARLIAMENT.

1. For Payment of *Publick Debts.*
2. For *Advancement and Encouragement of Trade.*
3. For *Raifing the Rents of Lands.*

In Order whereunto, It is proved Neceffary,

I. *That a Stop be put to further Buildings in and about* London.
II. *That the Gentry be obliged to live fome part of the Year in the Countrey.*
III. *That Regifters be fetled in every County.*
IV. *That an Act for Naturalizing all Foreign Proteftants, and Indulging them, and His Majeftie's Subjects at home, in Matters of Confcience, may be paffed.*
V. *That the Act Prohibiting the Importation of* Irifh *Cattel, may be Repealed.*
VI. *That* Brandy, Coffee. Mum., Tea, *and* Chocolata, *may be prohibited.*
VII. *That the Multitude of Stage-Coaches and Caravans may be fuppreffed.*
VIII. *That no Leather may be Exported Un-manufactured.*
IX. *That a* Court of Confcience *be fetled for* Weftminfter, *and all the Suburbs of* London, *and in every City and Corporation in* England.
X. *That the Extravagant Habits and Expence of all Perfons may be curbed; the Exceffive Wages of Servants and Handicrafts-men may be Reduced, and all Foreign Manufactures may be prohibited.*
XI. *That it may be made lawful to Affign Bills, Bonds, and other Securities; and that a Courfe be taken to prevent the Knavery of Bankrupts.*
XII. *That the* Newcaftle-*Trade for Coals may be managed by Commiffioners, to the Eafe of the Subjects, and great Advantage of the Publick.*
XIII. *That the* Fifhing-Trade *may be vigoroufly profecuted, all poor People fet at work to make* Fifhing-Tackle, *and be paid out of the Money Collected every Year for the Poor, in the feveral Parifhes in* England.

By a Lover of his Countrey, and Well-wifher to the Profperity both of the King and Kingdoms.

London, Printed in the Year, 1673.

V I.

THe Sixth thing proposed, is, the Prohibition of *Brandy*, *Mum*, *Coffee*, *Chocoletta* and *Tea*, and the suppressing *Coffe-Houses*.

Thefe greatly hinder the Confumption of *Barley*, *Malt* and *Wheat*, the Product of our Land, and thereby bring down the prices of thefe Grains, confequently the Rents of Land; to the ruine of Tenants, who cannot fell their Corn, when they have it; and of Landlords, whofe Rents Tenants are not able to pay, becaufe they have no vent for the Product of their Farms.

There is (as I am (upon ftrict Enquiry of the moft knowing p fons) informed) fo vaft a quantity of *Brandy*, *Mum*, *Coffee*, *Tea* and *Spanifh Chocoletta*, every year imported into *England*, and confumed here, that reckoning the *Brandy* to be fold at two pence the Quartern, and no more (whereas moft of it by retail is fold for three pence) the Mum at fix pence a Quart, and the *Coffee*, *Tea*, *Chocoletta*, at the rates they are ufually fold for, yet is there expended by the Subjects yearly in thefe drinks above 400000 *l.*

If thefe Liquors were prohibited, then would there be made in *England*, with our Wheat, or Malt, fuch quantities of Brandy, or a Spirit equal to it, and of Mum alfo, as would, in all probability, occafion the Confumption of at leaft two or three hundred thoufand Quarters of Wheat and Malt every year more than now is confumed; and that would raife the price of the Commodity, and thereby keep up the Rent of Lands, which every year falls for want of a Confumption of the Product thereof: And the Prohibition of Brandy would be otherwife advantageous to the Kingdom, and prevent the deftruction of His Majefties Subjects; many of whom have been kill'd by drinking thereof, it not agreeing with their Conftitutions. How many inftances have we had yearly of mens dying fuddenly, after drinking of Brandy How many after over-drinking themfelves with this Liquour, have lain languifhing till they have dyed thereof! Before Brandy (which is now become common, and fold in every little Alehoufe) came over into *England* in fuch quanties as now it doth, we drank good Strong Beer and Ale; and all laborious people (which are the far greateft part of the Kingdom) their bodies requiring, after hard labour, fome ftrong drink to refrefh them, did therefore every morning and evening ufe to

drink

(22)

drink a pot of Ale, or a flagon of strong Beer: which greatly promoted the Consumption of our own Grain, and did them no great prejudice, it hindred not their work, neither did it take away their senses, nor cost them much money. But now this sort of people, since Brandy is become so common, and sold in every little house (a small quantity costing them three pence) do sometimes spend their days wages in this sort of Liquor, before they get home in an evening, and thereby impoverish their Families, and not only so, but frequently by their drinking to excess, they are bereft of their senses for two or three days together, so that they cannot work.

In short, Brandy burns the hearts of His Majesties Subjects out; in few years it hath been the destruction and death of some thousands, who if they had kept to Beer and Ale, might have received better refreshment therefrom, and now been living to have served the King and their Countrey, and might have help'd to consume the Manufactures and Provisions of the Kingdom. And if so, then what reason can any man give for the Importation thereof? For my own part I declare, I know of none, unless it be, because it pays a great Custom or Excise to the King. And as to that, I answer and affirm, That if *Brandy* be prohibited, the Excise of the Beer and Ale that would be then consumed, more than is now, will more than answer the duty of *Brandy* that the King shall lose by such Prohibition as is desired (admitting that all the *Brandy* imported paid the duty imposed, when as not one half thereof is paid for, the same being stoln; insomuch, that when the duty to the King was four shillings *per* Gallon, Brandy was sold for three shillings, which was twelve pence less than the Kings Duty:). But admitting that if *Brandy* should be prohibited, the additional Excise of Ale and Beer would not answer the Kings lose he shall sustain thereby; and taking it for granted, that our English Constitutions are now so accustomed to *Brandy*, that it is become absolutely necessary for them to use the same, or some Liquor like it: If it be so, then from our Malt and Wheat may be extracted a Spirit equally as good, if not for our Constitutions much better than *Brandy*: And then laying a small duty (as a penny a Gallon) upon *low Wines*, will more than answer what the additional Excise shall fall short of to the King, yea, and very much exceed what he shall lose by the Prohibition desired. And in as much as nothing is so much wanting in *England* as people; Therefore all means possible, in point of Prudence and Policy, ought to be used to preserve the lives and healths of those we have: But the Importing of *Brandy* hath destroyed many, is like to destroy more; *ergo*, it ought

to

(23)

to be prohibited. And the rather, in regard that *Brandy* comes from *France*, and whatever we import from *France*, ready money is paid for the same, or for the greatest part thereof: For although we impose but between Four and Ten pound *per cent.* upon any of the Manufacturies or Commodities of the growth of *France*, except the duty upon Wine and Brandy, yet the French King either prohibites the Importation of the Manufactures of *England* into his Dominions, or the selling them there, unless they be sealed, for which Seal, a great duty is paid, or else he burns them if they are imported, and sold without such Seal) as he did the Silk Stockings) or imposeth upon the Importation thereof, a duty of 30, 40, or 50 *l. per cent.* which is double as much as was imposed, till within these few years last past, and is in effect a Prohibition. For, when we do Transport any thing thither of our Growth or Manufacturies, the French, by reason of the high duty imposed upon them, undersel us, whereby we are necessitated to keep our goods till spoiled, or bring them back. And if so, then plain it is, that whatsoever we have from *France*, ready money goes for the same: So that by a moderate computation, they have at least 400000 *l. per annum* in money from us; which is a vast prejudice to *England*, and a great enriching to *France*, who impose upon us, not only vast proportions of their Brandy and Wines, but also of their Silks, Stuffs, Ribbons, Laces, Points, and divers other things, whereby our Manufacturers in *England* are ruined, and the Treasure of the Nation exhausted. I know it will be said, that we lay far greater Impositions upon their Wines and Brandy, than they do upon any of our Manufactures, and it is true, that we do so. But consider, that whatever duty we lay upon Wines, is laid upon the King of *Englands* own Subjects, they pay it, and such duty doth not hinder the Importation thereof; for more comes in now then ever there did, when the duty was not half so high, and the French force the English to pay more for their Wines than ever they paid before. But the Impositions laid by the King of *France* upon our Manufactures, have stopt us from sending any thing considerable thither, whereas before such duties imposed, we sent great quantities: So that in a few years, if not prevented, the very Commerce with *France* is like to destroy *England*. As for *Brunswick* Mum, I am sure we brew as strong in *England* as they do there, and yet afford to sell it for half the price they sell theirs for, therefore there is no necessity of the Importation thereof, to supply any defect we have here, consequently, 'tis not fit to be encouraged, because it hinders the Consumption of the Grain of this Kingdom.

And

(24)

And for *Coffee*, *Tea* and *Chocoletta*, I know no good they do ;
only the places where they are fold are convenient for perfons to meet
in, fit half a day, and difcourfe with all Companies that come in, of
State-matters, talking of news, and broaching of lyes, arraigning the
judgements and difcretions of their Governors, cenfuring all their
Councels, and infinuating into the people a prejudice againft them ; extolling and magnifying their own parts, knowledge and wifdom, and
decrying that of their Rulers, which, if fuffered too long, may
prove pernicious and deftructive. But fay there were nothing of this in
the cafe, yet have thefe *Coffee* Houfes done great mifchiefs to the Nation,
undone many of the Kings Subjects, for they being very great Enemies to Diligence and Induftry, have been the ruine of many ferious
and hopeful young Gentlemen and Tradefmen, who before they frequented thefe places, were diligent Students or Shopkeepers, extraordinary husbands of their time, as well as money : but fince thefe
Houfes have been fet up, under pretence of good husbandry, to avoid
fpending above one peny or two pence at a time, have got to thefe Coffee
Houfes, where meeting Friends, they have fate talking three or four
hours, after which a frefh acquaintance appearing (and fo one after another all day long) hath begotten frefh difcourfe ; So that frequently they have ftaid five or fix hours together in one of them :   All which
time their Studies or Shops have been neglected, their Bufinefs left undone, their Servants been trufted, and an opportunity given them
thereby to be idle and deceitful ; the taking of money in many of thefe
mens fhops hath been hindred, and their Cuftomers gone away dif-
pleafed : How many by thefe means have received great loffes and dif-
advantages in their Trade ! and by accuftoming themfelves to thefe
houfes, have made it fo habitual to them, that they cannot forbear
them, thongh, together with their Familes, they are ruined thereby.
Thefe Houfes being very many of them profeffed Bawdy Houfes, more
expenfive than other houfes, are become fcandalous for a man to be feen
in them, which Gentlemen not knowing, do frequently fall into them
by chance, and fo their Reputation is drawn into queftion thereby.

The Women's Petition Against Coffee. Representing to Publick Consideration the Grand Inconveniences accruing to their Sex from the Excessive Use of that Drying Enfeebling Liquor. Presented to the Right Honourable Keepers of the Liberty of Venus. By a Well-willer (London, n.p., 1674), [2], 6pp. BL: 1038.i.47.(1). ESTCR11811. Hünersdorff.

The Women's Petition Against Coffee is a libertine squib on the revolution in sexual manners supposedly inaugurated by the emergence of the coffee-house. *The Women's Petition* returns to the genre of the mock petition, closely related to other mock tracts of restoration satire, especially the mock complaint and mock queries. Like these forms, the satire is directed against the authoritative and political pretensions of the original form: in this case the petition addressed to an authoritative body: here '*the Right Honourable Keepers of the Liberty of Venus*', an ironic reference to rakes and whores. Ostensibly the satiric focus is on men: the coffee-house renders them impotent and effeminate. The theory that coffee 'extinguishes the Inclination to Venery, and induces Sterility' had been reported by Olearius in his embassy to Persia in 1634, and confirmed in the Danish physician Simon Paulli's *Commentarius de abusu tabaci et herbae thee* ([Strasbourg], Argentorati, 1665), fols 37r–39r. But the satire is not directly concerned with medical theory: rather the topic is gender roles, directed against the desiring woman, whose libidinality is limitless and whose carnal appetite is insatiable (a reprise of enduring misogynist discourse). The petition begins by recalling nostalgically the days when English men were virile and lusty, and ascribes the passing of this sexual vigour to this 'Newfangled, Abominable, Heathenish Liquor' called coffee. The satire is directed against the cultural reformation that coffee-houses were understood to have introduced in London society: the men who congregate in the coffee-houses are associated with the supposedly feminine attributes of talking and gossiping. Men in the coffee-house '*out-babble* an equal number of [women] at a *Gossipping*, talking all at once in Confusion, and running from point to point ... insensibly, and ... swiftly' (below p. 116). This conceit is literalised as sexual impotence, and concatenated with complaints about the amount of time men devoted to the homosocial world of the coffee-house. The contrast between kinds and manners of drinking probably carried political connotations: the flamboyant and libertine world of wine and beer drinking was associated with Royalist politics; while the austere and discursive world of coffee-house debate was associated with radical and republican politics.

The tract is in prose amounting to six pages, and is anonymous. There is no extant evidence about the author, and no conclusions can be drawn concerning the writer's gender from internal evidence. The title has suggested to some a woman author, following the model offered by a petition on behalf of women debtors addressed to Cromwell during the Commonwealth, entitled *The Womens Petition, to the Right Honourable ... Lord Cromwell* (London, n.p., 1651). George Woodcock suggested Aphra Behn in the 1970s, but this has not been widely followed. According to Peter Brown, 'various names have been put forward as to the author', concluding that it 'was no lady who wrote this' (Peter B. Brown, *In Praise of Hot Liquors: the study of chocolate, coffee and tea-drinking 1600–1850* (York, York Civic Trust, 1995), pp. 16–17). Habermas, in *The Structural Transformation of the Public Sphere* (1962; trans. by Thomas Burger ([Cambridge], Polity Press, 1989)), makes use of this satire as evidence for women's resistance to the homosocial coffee-house public (p. 257n.). Such a conclusion might only be drawn, one suspects, without a first-hand knowledge of the text, or even its subtitle, as the tract makes its satirical purpose more than clear. The satire was reprinted in four pages in 1700 as *The City-VVifes Petition, against Coffee. Presented to the Publick Consideration, the Grand Inconviences that accrue to their Sex, from the Excessive Drinking of that Drying, and Enfeebling Liquor: to the Right Honourable, the worshipfull court of female assistants, the humble petition and address of several thousands of buxome good vvomen, languishing in extremity of want* (London, A. VV., 1700).

THE
WOMEN'S
PETITION
AGAINST
COFFEE.

REPRESENTING
TO
PUBLICK CONSIDERATION
THE
Grand INCONVENIENCIES accruing
to their SEX from the Excessive
Use of that Drying, Enfeebling
LIQUOR.

Presented to the Right Honorable the
Keepers of the Liberty of *VENUS*.

By a Well-willer ————

London, Printed 1674.

(1)

To the Right Honorable the Keepers of the Liberties of *Venus*; The Worfhipful Court of *Female Affiftants*, &c.

The Humble Petition and Addrefs of feveral Thoufands of Buxome Good-Women, Languifhing in Extremity of Want.

SHEWETH,

THat fince 'tis Reckon'd amongft the Glories of our Native Country, To be *A Paradife for Women*: The fame in our Apprehenfions can confift in nothing more than the brisk *Activity* of our men, who in former Ages were juftly efteemed the *Ableft Performers* in Chriftendome; But to our unfpeakable Grief, we find of late a very fenfible *Decay* of that true *Old Englifh Vigour*; our *Gallants* being every way fo *Frenchified*, that they are become meer Cock-fparrows, fluttering things that come on *Sols*, with a world of Fury,

A 2 but

(2)

but are not able to *ſtand* to it, and in the very firſt Charge fall down *flat* before us. Never did Men wear *greater Breeches*, or carry *leſs* in them of any *Mettle* whatſoever. There was a glorious Diſpenſation ('twas ſurely in the Golden Age) when *Luſty Ladd*, of ſ *ven* or *eight hundred* years old, *Got* Sons and Daughters; and we have read, how a Prince of *Spain* was forced to make a Law, that Men ſhould not Repeat the *Grand Kindneſs* to their Wives; above *N I N E* times in a night : But Alas ! Alas ! Thoſe forwards Days are gone, The dull *Lubbers* want a *Spur* no *w*, rather than a *Bridle* : being ſo far from doing any works of *Supererrogation* that we find them not capable of performing thoſe Devoirs which their *Duty*, and our *Expectations* Exact.

The Occaſion of which Inſufferable *Diſaſter*, after a ſerious Enquiry, and Diſcuſſion of the Point by the Learned of the *Faculty*, we can Attribute to nothing more than the Exceſſive uſe of that Newfangled, Abominable, Heatheniſh Liquor called *C O F F E E,* which Riffling Nature of her Choiceſt *Treaſures*, and *Drying* up the *Radical Moiſture*, has ſo *Eunuch*t our Husbands, and *Crippled* our more kind *Gallants*, that they are become as *Impotent*, as Age, and as unfruitful as thoſe *Deſarts* whence that unhappy *Berry* is ſaid to be brought.

For the continual ſipping of this pittiful drink is enough to *bewitch* Men of two and twenty, and tie up the *Codpicepoint* without a Charm. It renders them that uſe it as *Lean* as Famine, as Rivvel'd as *Envy*, or an old meager Hagg over-ridden by an Incubus. They come from it with nothing *moiſt* but their ſnotty Noſes, nothing *ſtiffe* but their Joints, nor *ſtanding* but their Ears : They pretend 'twill keep them *Waking*, but we find by ſcurvy Experience, they
ſleep

(3)

sl ep quietly enough after it. A Betrothed *Queen* might trust her self a bed with one of them, without the nice Caution of a *Sword* between them: nor can all the Art we use revive them from this Lethargy, so unfit they are for Action, that like young Train-band-men when called upon Duty, their *Amunition* is wanting; peradventure they *Present*, but cannot give *Fire*, or at least do but *flash in the Pan*, instead of doing Execution.

Nor let any Doating Superstitious *Cato's* shake their Goatish *Beards*, and tax us of *Immodesty* for this Declaration, since 'tis a publick Grievance, and cries aloud for Reformation. *Weight* and *Measure*, 'tis well known, should go throughout the world, and there is no torment like Famishment. Experience witnesses our Damage, and Neceffity (which easily superfedes all the Laws of Decency) justifies our complaints: For can any Woman of *Sense* or *Spirit* endure with Patience, that when priviledg'd by Legal Ceremonies, she approaches the Nuptial Bed, expecting a Man that with *Sprightly* Embraces, should Answer the Vigour of her Flames, she on the contrary should only meet *A Beaful of Bones*, and hug a meager useless Corpfe rendred as *sapless* as a *Kixe*, and *dryer* than a *Pumice-Stone*, by the perpetual Fumes of *Tobacco*, and bewitching effects of this most pernicious *C O F F E E*, whereby Nature is *Enfeebled*, the Off-spring of our Mighty Ancestors *Dwindled* into a Succefsion of *Apes* and *Pigmies*; and

——— *The Age of Man*
Now Cramp't into an Inch, that was a Span.

Nor is this (though more than enough) *All* the ground of our Complaint: For besides, we have reason to apprehend and grow *Jealous*, That Men by frequenting these *Stygian Tap-houses* will ufurp on our Prerogative of *Tatling*.

(4)

ling, and soon learn to excel us in *Talketiveness* : a Quality wherein our Sex has ever Claimed preheminence :
For here like so many *Frogs* in a *puddle*, they sup muddy
water, and murmur insignificant notes till half a dozen of
them *out-babble* an equal number of us at a *Goſſipping*, talking all at once in Confusion, and running from point to
point as insensibly, and as swiftly, as ever the Ingenious
Pole-wheel could run divisions on the Base-viol ; yet in all
their prattle every one abouuds in his own sense, as ſtiffly
as a *Quaker* at the late *Barbican* Dispute, and submits to
the Reasons of no other mortal : so that there being neither *Moderator* nor *Rules* obſerv'd, you may as soon fill a
Quart pot with *Syllogiſmes*, as profit by their Diſconrſes.

Certainly our Countrymens pallates are become as *Fanatical* as their Brains ; how elſe is't poſsible they ſhould
Apoſtatize from the good old primitive way of Ale-drink-
ing, to run a *whoreing* aſter ſuch variety of diſtructive *Forraign* Liquors, to trifle away their *time*, ſcald their *Chops*,
and ſpend their *Money*, all for a little *baſe, black, thick,
naſty bitter ſtinking, nauſeous* Puddle water: Yet (as all
Witches have their Charms) so this ugly *Turkiſh* Enchan-
treſs by certain *Inviſible VVyres* attracts both Rich and
Poor ; ſo that thoſe that have ſcarce *Twopence* to buy
their Children *Bread*, muſt ſpend a penny each evening in
this *Inſipid* Stuff : Nor can we send one of our Husbands
to *Call a Midwife*, or borrow a *Gliſter-pipe*, but he muſt ſtay
an hour by the way drinking his two *Diſhes*, & two Pipes.

At theſe Houſes (as at the Springs in *Afric*) meet all
ſorts of Animals, whence follows the production of a
thouſand Monſter Opinions and Abſurdities ; yet for being dangerous to Government, we dare be their Compur-
gaters, as well knowing them to be too tame and too tal-
kative

(5)

kative to make any desperate Polititians : For though they may now and then destroy a Fleet, or kill ten thousand of the *French*, more than all the Confederates can do, yet this is still in their politick Capacities, for by their personal valour they are scarce fit to be of the Life-guard to a Cherry tree : And therefore, though they frequently have hot Contests about most Important Subjects ; as what colour the Red Sea is of ; whether the Great Turk be a Lutheran or a Calvinist ; who *Cain's* Father in Law was, &c. yet they never fight about them with any other save our Weapon, the Tongue.

Some of our Sots pretend tippling of this boiled Soot cures them of being Drunk; but we have reason rather to conclude it makes them so, because we find them not able to stand after it : 'Tis at best but a kind of Earthing a Fox to hunt him more eagerly afterward : A rare method of good-husbandry, to enable a man to be drunk three times a day! Just such a Remedy for Drunkenness, as the Popes allowing of Stews, is a means to prevent Fornication: The Coffee-house being in truth, only a Pimp to the Tavern, a relishing soop preparative to a fresh debauch : For when people have swill'd themselves with a morning draught of more Ale than a Brewers horse can carry, hither they come for a pennyworth of Settle-brain, where they are sure to meet enow lazy pragmatical Companions, that resort here to prattle of News, that they neither understand, nor are concerned in ; and after an hours impertinent Chat, begin to consider a Bottle of Claret would do excellent well before Dinner ; whereupon to the Bush they all march together, till every one of them is as Drunk as a Drum, and then back again to the Coffe-house to drink themselves sober ; where three or four dishes a piece, and smoaking , makes their throats as *dry* as Mount *Ætna* enflam'd with Brimstone ; so that they must away to the next *Red Lattice* to quench them with a dozen or two of Ale;

(6)

Ale, which at laft growing naufeous, one of them begins to extol the blood of the Grape, what rare Langoon, and Racy Canary may be had at the *Miter* : Saift thou fo? cries another, *Let's then go and replenifh there-with our Earthen Veffels* : So once more they troop to the Sack-fhop, till they are drunker than before ; and then by a retrograde motion, ftagger back to *Soberize* themfelves with Coffee: Thus like *Tennis Balls* between two Rackets, the *Fopps our Husbands* are *bandied* to and fro all day be-tween the *Coffee-houfe* and *Tavern*, whilft we poor Souls fit *mopeing* all a-lone till *Twelve* at night, and when at laft they come to bed fmoakt like a *Weftphalia Hogs-head* we have no more comfort of them, than from a *fhotten Herring* or a dryed *Bulrufh* ; which forces us to take up this La-mentation and fing,

> *Tom Farthing, Tom Farthing, where haft thou been, Tom Farthing ?*
> *Twelve a Clock e're you come in, Two a Clock e're you begin, And*
> *then at laft can do nothing : Would make a Woman weary, weary;*
> *weary, would make a Woman weary,* &c.

Wherefore the *Premifes* confidered, and to the end that our Juft *Rights* may be reftored, and all the Antient *Priviledges* of our Sex preferv-ved inviolable ; That our Husbands may give us fome other *Teftimonies* of their being Men, befides their *Beards* and wearing of empty *Panta-loons* : That they no more run the hazard of being *Cuckol'd* by *Dildo's* : But returning to the good old ftrengthning Liquors of our Forefathers ; that Natures *Exchequer* may once again be replenifht, and a Race of Lufty Hero's begot, able by their Atchievments, to equal the Glories of our Ancefters.

We *Humbly Pray*, That you our Trufty Patrons would improve your Intereft, that henceforth the *Drinking COFFEE* may on fevere penal-ties be forbidden to all Perfons under the Age of *Threefcore* ; and that in-ftead thereof, *Lufty nappy Beer, Cock-Ale, Cordial Canaries, Reftoring Malago s,* and *Back-recruiting Chocholat* be Recommended to General Ufe, throughout the *Utopian* Territories.

In hopes of which *Glorious* Reforma-
tion, your *Petitioners* fhall readily Pro-
ftrate themfelves, and ever *Pray*, &c.

F I N I S.

The Mens Answer to the Womens Petition Against Coffee, Vindicating Their own Performances, and the Vertues of that Liquour, from the Undeserved Aspersions lately cast upon them by their Scandalous Pamphlet, (London, n.p., 1674), [2], 5pp.; 4°. BL: 1038.i.47.(2). ESTCR30522. Hünersdorff.

An anonymous prose reply to *The Women's Petition* (above pp. 109–18), which is noted on the title-page as a 'Scandalous Pamphlet'. Satires such as these reinforce their own controversial status by alerting readers to their place in a dialogue with other texts. In this case, the supplemental status of the satire is clearly indicated in the title, as an answer to particular complaints voiced by the women. The satire begins with the lament that women are ungrateful for men's efforts to please them. The male satirist, however, understands that for women pleasure is almost exclusively sexual (keying into a discourse of misogyny broadly contiguous with that which it seeks to answer). The text proceeds to a point-by-point response to observations made by the women's petitioner, revisiting, for example, both the rhetoric of cock-sparrows and dildos. Again, as with *The Women's Petition*, the satire is addressed to contemporary sexual mores as much as coffee or coffee-houses. In identifying lascivious and libertine sexual practices amongst women in contemporary London, the satirist attacks the sexual politics of the Restoration, widely identified with the cavalier culture of the court of Charles II. The political contours of this satirical landscape are reinforced when the text turns to its defence of coffee. The satirist observes that the 'Sober and Merry' drink of coffee was sent by 'Providence' during the Republic, 'at a time when Brimmers of Rebellion, and Fanatick Zeal had intoxicated the Nation' (below, p. 124). It is the sobriety of the coffee-house, the satirist observes, that confuses women: and in fact both coffee-houses and coffee encourage libidinality amongst men. Nothing is known of the author, not even their sex: Peter Brown's suggestion of John Locke has no known foundation (*In Praise of Hot Liquors: the study of Chocolate, coffee and tea-drinking 1600–1850* (York, York Civic Trust, 1995), pp. 16–17). Four copies survive, at the British Library, Harvard, Yale and the Folger.

THE

Mens Answer

TO THE

Womens Petition

AGAINST

C O F F E E:

VINDICATING

Their own Performances, and the Vertues of their
Liquor, from the Undeserved Aspersions lately Caſt
upon them, in their

SCANDALOUS PAMPHLET.

LONDON, Printed in the Year 1674.

THE
MENS ANSWER
TO THE
WOMENS PETITON, &c.

COuld it be imagined, that ungrateful Women, after so much laborious Drudgery, both by Day and Night, and the best of our Blood and Spirits spent in your Service, you should thus publickly Complain? Certain we are, that there never was Age or Nation more Indulgent to your Sex; have we not condescended to all the Methods of Debauchery? Invented more Postures than *Aretine* ever Dreamed of! Been Pimps to our own Wives, and Courted Gallants even with the hazard of our Estates, to do us the Civility of making us not only Contented, but most obliged Cuckolds: Is he thought worthy to be esteemed a Gentleman, that has not seven times pass'd the Torrid Zone of a Venerial Distemper, or does not maintain, at least, a Brace of Mistresses; Talk not to us of those doating Fumblers of seven or eight hundred yeares Old, a Larke is better than a Kite; and Cock-Sparrows, though not long liv'd, are undoubtedly preferrable for the work of Generation before dull Ravens, though some think they live three hundred yeares: that our Island is a Paradice for Women, is verified will by the brisk Activity of our Men, who with an equal Contempt scorn *Italian* Padlocks, and defie *French* Dildo's, knowing that a small Doze of Natures Quintessence, satisfier better in a Female Limbeck, than the Largest Potion infused by Art.

Let silly Cits--- complain never so much that Madam Money is Dead and Buried, we dare Appeal to all the Commissioners of *Whetstones Park*, the Suburb Runners, and *Moor-fields* Night-walkers, if ever they had better Trading; Nay, have we not forced languishing Nature by preparations of Cantharides, spiced Meats, Anchoves, Cullises, Jelly-broths, Lambstones, Diasatyrion, Bononia Sawsages, &c. All to answer the height of your Amorous Passions, and prevent the pitiful Letchery of an Artifical Tranguin. Have we not with excess of Patience born your affronts, been Sweated, Purged, Fluxed between two Feather-beds, flog'd, Jib'd, and endured all the rest of the Devils Martyrdoms, and will you still offer to Repine? Certainly experienc'd *Solomon* was in the right, when he told us that the Grave and the womb were equally Insatiable.

But why must innocent COFFEE be the object of your Spleen? That harmless and healing Liquor, which Indulgent Providence first sent amongst us, at a time when Brimmers of Rebellion, and Fanatick Zeal had intoxicated the Nation, and we wanted a Drink at once to make us Sober and Merry: 'Tis not this incomparable settle Brain than shortens Natures standard, or makes us less Active in the Sports of *Venus*, and we wonder you should take these Exceptions, since so many of the little Houses, with the Turkish Woman stradling on their Signs, are but Emblems of what is to be done within for your Conveniencies, meer Nurseries to promote the petulant Trade, and breed up a stock of hopeful Plants for the future service of the Republique, in the most thriving Mysteries of Debauchery; There being scarce a Coffee-Hut but affords a Tawdry Woman, a wanton Daughter, or a Buxome Maide, to accommodate Customers; and can you think that any which frequent such Discipline, can be wanting in their Pastures, or defective in their Arms? The News we Chat of there, you will not think it Impertinent, when you consider the fair opportunities you have thereby, of entertaining an obliging friend in our Absence, and how many of us you have dubb'd Knights of the Bull-Feather, whilst we have sate innocently sipping the Devils Holy-water; we do not call it so driving the Cace-daemon of Letchery out of us, for the truth is, it rather assists us for your Nocturnal Benevolencies, by drying up those Crude Flatulent Humours, which otherwise would make us only Flash in the Pan, without doing that Thundering Execution which your Expectations Exact, we dare Appeal to Experience in the Case. Coffee is the general Drink throughout Turky, and those *Eastern* Regions, and yet no part of the world can boast more able or eager performers, then those Circumcised Gentlemen, who, (like our modern Gallants) own no other joys of Heaven, than what consists in Veneral Titillations; the Physical qualities of this Liquor are almost Innumerable and its vertues (if you will believe *Pointing*), able to out-noise the Quack-bil of an all-healing Doctor, when your kindness at the Close Hugg has bestowed on us a virulent Gonorrhaea, this is our Catholicon, *Ens Naturae*, and *Aqua Tetrachymagogon* is an Ass to it, 'Tis base adulterate wine and surcharges of Muddy Ale that enfeeble nature, makes a man as salatious as a Goat, and yet as impotent as Age, whereas Coffee Collects and settles the Spirits, makes the erection more Vigorous, the Ejaculation more full, adds a spiritualescency to the Sperme, and renders is more firm and suitable to the Gusto of the womb, and proportionate to the ardours and expectation too, of the female Paramour.

As for our taking Tobacco you have no reason to object, since most your own Sex are so well skilled in managing a pipe; and if you find that of your Husband's to be naught, 'tis his natural infirmity, or your own perpetual Pumping him (not drinking Coffee) is the occasion of the defect, and therefore let such *Tom Farthings* be forbidden the decoction of the rare *Arabian* Berry, and condemned everlastingly with the rest of doelittles Congregation, to the carrying of Glisterpipes for the use of the well effected Sisterhood.

You may well permit us to talk abroad, for at home we have scarce time to utter a word for the insufferable Din of your ever active Tongues, the Foolish extravagancies of our lives, are infinitly out-done by the wild Frolliques of yours; 'Till Noon, you lie a Bed hatching Concupiscence, then having paid your Adorations, to the Ugly Idol in the Glass, you descend to Dinner, where you gormondiz enough at one Meal to Famish a Town Besiedg'd; after that, you are call'd out by a Cozen, and hurried out in his Honours Coach (whose jogging, serves as a preparative to your Letchery) away to the Play-house, where a Lacivious Dance, a Bawdy Song, and the Petulant Gallants Tickling of your hand, having made an Insurrection in your Blood, you go to Allay it with an evenings Exercise at the Tavern, there you ſpend freely, yet being Rob'd of nothing we can miss, home you come in a Railing humour, and at laſt give us nothing for Supper but a Butter'd Bun.

Cease then for the Future your Clamours againſt our civil Follies. Alas! alas! Dear Hearts, the Coffee house is the Citizens Accademy, where he learnes more Wit than ever his Grannum taught him, the Young-Gallants, Stage where he diſplays the Wardrope of his excellent no Parts; 'Tis the Non Cons Bull-baiting, the News-mongers Exchange, the Fools business, the Knaves Ambuscade, and the Wise mans Recreation: here it is where we have the ſparkling Cyder, the mighty Mum, and the back recruiting Chocolate; 'Tis Coffee that both keeps us Sober, or can make us so; and let all our wives that hereafter shall presume to Petition againſt it, be confined to lie alone all night, and in the Day time drink nothing but Bonny Clabber.

FINIS

A Brief Description of the Excellent Vertues of that Sober and Wholesome Drink, called Coffee, and its incomparable effects in preventing or curing most diseases incident to humane bodies (London, printed for Paul Greenwood, and are to be sold at the sign of the Coffee-Mill and Tobacco-Roll in Cloath-fair near West-Smithfield who selleth the best Arabian Coffee-Powder and Chocolate, made in Cake or in Roll, after the Spanish Fashion, &c., 1674). BL: C.20.f.2.(377). ESTCR226768. Hünersdorff.

A large half-sheet verse broadsheet handbill, perhaps printed as an advertisement for coffee, coffee-houses and the retail coffee business of Paul Greenwood. As well as two poems, adding up to 110 lines of rhymed verse couplets in rudimentary Hudibrastic pentameter, the broadside offers a naïve engraved illustration, the earliest visual record of a coffee-house outside the Levant. The engraving is a lozenge set into the title, comprising two compartments. In the upper compartment, the left side depicts a coffee shrub laden with berries, captioned with the words 'The Desarts of Arabia'; the right side a grape vine laden with grapes: both are surmounted with an ornamental crown. The contrast between coffee and wine is developed at length in the first poem (ll. 1–78). In the lower compartment is an interior view of a corner of a coffee-house, depicting a single central table with five gentlemen, one smoking, two wearing hats (perhaps Nonconformists), and three with wigs (perhaps cavaliers). The cavaliers have oversize ornamental sleeves and pockets. The variety exhibited by the men's costume may indicate the diverse interests of the clientele. A boy waiter approaches the table carrying a dish and a black jug, presumably containing coffee. On the table are three flat bowl-like coffee dishes and a pipe. The room has two windows, with small lozenge-shaped glass.

The first poem presents a quarrel of beverages, contrasting the intoxicating effects of wine and ale with the 'sober and merry' effects of coffee. The verses elaborate the medical effects of coffee described using the humoural system, including a defence of coffee's healing powers in various cases and symptoms. The verses conclude by arguing that coffee, not wine, should be the muse of poetry and music. The second set of verses, separately titled 'The Rules and Orders of the Coffee-house' are a lightly satirical account of the expected forms of behaviour in the coffee-house. These ironic 'Rules' delineate a convivial regime of equality, openness and politeness in the coffee-house, but they also reveal a considerable anxiety about the fragility of this peace: legislating against swearing, disputes and noise. Nonetheless, this poem has been widely read as a sincere statement of the regulations pertaining in the 'primitive institution' of the coffee-house (Edward Forbes Robinson, *The Early History of the Coffee-Houses in England* (London, Kegan Paul, Trench, Trübner & Co., 1893), pp. 57, 109–10). John Timbs argued in 1866 that these 'regulations, printed on large sheets of paper, were hung up in conspicuous positions on the walls' of coffee-houses (John Timbs, *Club Life of London with Anecdotes of the Clubs, Coffee-Houses and Taverns of the Metropolis During the 17th, 18th, and 19th Centuries*, 2 vols (London, Richard Bentley, 1866), vol. II, p. 109) – an idea repeated often since that time (see for example Aytoun Ellis, *Penny Universities: a history of the coffee-houses* (London, Secker & Warburg, 1956), pp. 46–7, 267–8).

The very long printer's imprint gives a precise location for Paul Greenwood, at the sign of the Coffee Mill and Tobacco-Roll in Cloath-fair, West Smithfield, who did not publish anything else. Cloth-fair was and is a lane leading off West Smithfield, parallel to Long Lane and adjacent to St Bartholomew's Church. It was generally inhabited by drapers and textile merchants, and was at the centre of the ancient and great cloth fair held annually in Smithfield, known as Bartholomew Fair. As the imprint makes clear, Paul Greenwood was in any case a retail merchant of coffee and chocolate 'who selleth the best Arabian Coffee-Powder and Chocolate, made in Cake or in Roll, after the Spanish Fashion'. Chocolate, which was widely understood as a product derived from Spain (or Spanish colonies in America), was sold in cakes or rolls. As the production of a coffee-merchant, *A Brief Description* might best be thought of as an advertising broadsheet. Two copies survive in the British Library, and another is preserved amongst the personal collection of Hünersdorff.

A BRIEF
DESCRIPTION
OF THE
EXCELLENT VERTUES
OF THAT
Sober and wholefome Drink,
CALLED
COFFEE,

AND ITS
INCOMPARABLE
EFFECTS
IN
PREVENTING or CURING
MOST
DISEASES
INCIDENT TO
HUMANE BODIES.

——Florefcat Arabica Planta.

When the fweet Poifon of the Treacherous Grape,
Had Acted on the world a General Rape;
Drowning our very Reafon and our Souls
In fuch deep Seas of large o'reflowing Bowls,
That New Philofophers Swore they could feel
The Earth to Stagger, as her Sons did Reel:
When Foggy Ale, leavying up mighty Trains
Of muddy Vapours, had befieg'd our Brains;
And Drink, Rebellion, and Religion too,
Made Men fo Mad, they knew not what to do;
Then Heaven in Pity, to Effect our Cure,
And ftop the Ragings of that Calenture,
Firft fent amongft us this *All-healing-Berry,*
At once to make us both *Sober* and *Merry.*
  Arabian Coffee, a Rich Cordial
To Purfe and Perfon Beneficial,
Which of fo many Vertues doth partake,
Its Country's called *Felix* for its fake.
  From the Rich Chambers of the Rifing Sun,
Where and all good Fafhions firft begun,
Where Earth with choiceft Rarities is bleft,
And dying *Phœnix* builds Her wondrous Neft:
COFFEE arrives, that Grave and wholefome Liquor,
That heals the Stomack, makes the Genius quicker,
Relieves the Memory, Revives the Sad,
And cheats the Spirits, without making Mad;
For bring of a Cleanfing QUALITY,
By NATURE warm, Attenuating and Dry,
Its conftant Ufe the fulleneft Griefs will Rout,
Removes the Dropfie, gives eafe to the Gout,
And foon difpatcheth wherefoever it being
Scorbutick Humours, Hypochondriack winds,
Rheums, Ptificks, Palfies, Jaundife, Coughs, Catarrhs,
And whatfoe're with Nature leavyeth Warrs;
It helps Digeftion, want of Appetite,
And quickly fets Confumptive Bodies Right;
A Friendly Entercourfe it doth Maintain,
Between the Heart, the Liver, and the Brain,
Natures three chiefeft Wheels, whofe Jars we know,
Threaten the whole Microcofme with overthrow;
In Spring, when Peccant Humours Encreafe moft,
And Summer, when the Appetite is loft,
In Autumn, when Raw Fruits Difeafes Breed,
And Winter time too cold to Purge or Bleed;
Do but this Rare *ARABIAN* Cordial Ufe,
And thou may'ft all the Doctors Slops Refufe.
Hufh then, dull QUACKS, your Mountebanking ceafe,
COFFEE's a fpeedier Cure for each Difeafe;
How great its Vertues are, we hence may think,
The Worlds third Part makes it their common Drink;
The Amourous Gallant, whofe hot Reins do fail,
Stung by Conjunction with the Dragons-Tail:
Let him but Tipple here, fhall find his Grief
Difcharg'd, without the Sweting-Tubs Relief;
Nor have the LADIES Reafon to Complain,
As fumbling Doe-littles are apt to Faign;
COFFEE's no Foe to their obliging Trade,
By it Men rather are more Active made;

'Tis ftronger Drink, and bafe adulterate Wine,
Enfeebles Vigour, and makes Nature Pine;
Loaden with which, th' Impotent Sott is Led
Like a Sowc'd Hogfhead to a Miffes Bed;
But this Rare Settle-Brain prevents thofe Harms,
Conquers Old Sherry, and brisk Clarret Charms.
Sack, I defie thee with an open Throat,
Whilft Truify COFFEE is my Antedote;
Methinks I hear Poets Repent th'have been,
So long Idolaters to that fparkling Queen;
For well they may perceive 'tis on Her fcore
APOLLO keeps them all fo Curfed Poor;
Let them avoid Her tempting Charms, and then
We hope to fee the Wits grow Aldermen;
In Breif, all you who Healths Rich Treafures Prize,
And Court not Ruby Nofes, or blear'd Eyes,
But own Sobriety be your Drift,
And Love at once good Company and Thrift;
  To Wine no more make Wit and Coyn a Trophy,
But come each Night and Frollique here in Coffee.

The RULES and ORDERS of the

COFFEE-HOUSE.

*Enter Sirs freely, But firft if you pleafe,
Perufe our Civil-Orders, which are thefe.*

Firft, Gentry, Tradefmen, all are welcome hither,
  And may without Affront fit down Together:
Pre-eminence of Place, none here fhould find,
But take the next fit Seat that he can find:
Nor need any, if Finer Perfons come,
Rife up to to affigne to them his Room;
To limit Mens Expence, we think not fair,
But let him forfeit Twelve-pence that fhall Swear:
He that fhall any Quarrel here begin,
Shall give each Man a Difh t' Atone the Sin;
And fo fhall He, whofe Complements extend
So far to drink in COFFEE to his Friend;
Let Noife of loud Difputes be quite forborn,
No Maudlin Lovers here in Corners Mourn,
But all be Brisk, and Talk, but not too much
On Sacred things, Let none prefume to touch,
Nor Profane Scripture, or fawcily wrong
Affairs of State with an Irreverent Tongue:
Let Mirth be Innocent, and each Man fee,
That all his Jefts without Reflection be;
To keep the Houfe more Quiet, and from Blame,
We Banifh hence Cards, Dice, and every Game:
Nor can allow of Wagers, that Exceed
Five fhillings, which oft-times much Trouble Breed;
Let all that's loft, or forfeited, be fpent
In fuch Good Liquor as the Houfe doth Vent,
And Cuftomers endeavour to their Powers,
For to obferve ftill feafonable Howers.
Laftly, Let each Man what he calls for Pay,
And fo you're welcome to come every Day.

London, Printed for *Paul Greenwood,* and are to be fold at the fign of the *Coffee-Mill* and *Tobacco-Roll* in *Cloath-fair* near *Weft-Smithfield,*
who felleth the beft *Arabian* Coffee-Powder and Chocolate, made in Cake or in Roll, after the *Spanifh* Fafhion, &c. 1674.

William Hicks, *Coffee-house jests. By the author of the Oxford-jests* (London, printed for Benj. Thrale at the Bible in the Poultrey near Cheapside, 1677), [2], 238pp.; 12°. BL: 12314.df.40. ESTCR11013. Extract, pp. i, 1–9. Hünersdorff.

A miscellany of 396 numbered prose comic anecdotes and jests, in a 238-page duodecimo jest book (price one shilling). The jest book was an established publishing concept, having emerged in the Tudor period as collections of bon-mots, anecdotes and classical wit (see Margaret Spufford, *Small Books and Pleasant Histories: popular fiction and its readership in seventeenth-century england* (Cambridge, Cambridge University Press, 1981)). The jest book addresses a popular audience, but it is capable of making scholarly jokes and learned puns. Nonetheless, the bulk of these jests turn on vulgar and low topics, often with a pronounced satirical edge attacking folly and pretension. The significant number of jests that ridicule the events and attitudes of the Interregnum confirm the book's allegiance to the politics of the court. The miscellany's relationship to the coffee-house is at best tenuous: it could be read as a kind of evidence of the forms of humour prevalent in coffee-house conversations. More likely, however, the coffee-house is a trope locating the comic commodity within the dominant culture of fashionable urban sociability.

Manuscript marginalia in the British Library copy of the first edition of 1677 (BL 12314.df.40) suggest that many of the anecdotes and jests are compiled from other sources. Subsequent editions are numbered, implying that they are revised versions of the same text, but in fact there is virtually no textual similarity between the first edition and the fourth other than the title. No copies are extant of the second and third editions, but the contemporary bibliography *The Term Catalogues* (ed. by Edward Arber, 3 vols (London, Arber, 1903–6)) records the third edition as 1684. After the fourth edition (1686), which has an excellent illustrated frontispiece of a coffee-house interior, the text is relatively stable. Further editions with extant volumes include the fifth ('refined and enlarged') in 1688, and the editions of 1696, 1702, 1733 and 1760.

William Hicks (fl. 1630–82), editor of miscellanies, was a tapster or tavern keeper known later in his life as Captain Hicks, a resident of Oxford. Anthony Wood described him as 'a sharking and indigent fellow while he lived in Oxon, and a great pretender to the art of dancing (which he forsooth would sometimes teach)'. A man of some education, with a limited knowledge of Latin, his first two publications were *Oxford Jests* (Oxford, Simon Miller, 1671) and *Oxford Drollery* (Oxford, J. C., 1671). Wood dismisses his writing as 'little trivial matters merely to get bread, and make the pot walk' (*Athenae Oxonienses*, ed. by P. Bliss, 4 vols (1813–20; reprinted New York, Johnson Reprint Co., 1967), vol. III, p. 490). In 1673 he published *London Drollery, or the wits academy* (London, F. Eglesfield), a miscellany of poems, songs and lampoons. *Coffee-house Jests* was followed by a comic Latin primer entitled *Grammatical Drollery* (London, Tho. Fox, 1682) (*ODNB*).

Coffee-Houſe

JESTS.

By the Author of the

OXFORD-JESTS.

This may be printed.

March 30. 1677.

Roger L'Eſtrange.

LONDON,

Printed for *Benj. Thrale* at the *Bible* in
the *Poultrey* near *Cheapſide.*
MDCLXXVII.

(1)

Coffee-House
JESTS.

1.

A Doctor of Divinity in *Oliver's* dayes that had been sufficiently perfecuted and plundered for his Loyalty to his Prince ; which made him and many others (that held his Tenents)to talk at random fometimes when they had noth'ng to lofe ; but this talking of his happened to be a benefit to him: for divers did acquaint *Oliver*, that he was often heard to fay ; that he did heartily wifh that *Oliver* and all his Army were in Hell: upon which *Oliver* fent him a Summons to appear before him; and be-

A 2   ing

Coffee-house Jests.

ing come; Why how now Doctor, says
he, I did never expect to hear such Language to have proceeded from a man of
your Coat; why Sir, says the Doctor,
what did I say, why says *Oliver*, I heard
that you should wish, that both my self
and all my Army were in Hell : Is that
all, says the Doctor , why truly Sir you
need not endeavour to procure any testimony to make this manifest; for I do
confess that I have said so a hundred
times, and do wish the same still, and I
think I have done exceedingly well in so
wishing ; and my reasons are these : For
if you and your Army have conquered
three such Kingdoms as these ; if you
were all in Hell, I think it were impos-
sible for that one Kingdom to withstand
you, and that being conquered would
it not be a great blessing to us all . which
conceit not only procured his pardon but
a restitution of his parsonage also, and
likewise a gratuity ; which made him as
loyal to him as he was before.

2.

A Scottish Minister being Chaplain to
an English Regiment of Foot , in the
time of the Rump Parliament at St. *Ed-
monds Bury* in *Suffolk*; and there as he

was

was preaching to them, ſaid, *Good Lord bleſs the grand Council above (* viz. *the Parliament) and grant they may aw hang together.* which a Country fellow that ſtood underneath hearing, ſaid, *Yes ſir with all my heart, and the ſooner the better ; and I am ſure 'tis the prayers of all good people .* But *good friends ,* ſays the Parſon, *I do not mean as that naughty man means ; but I pray that they may all hang together in Accord and Concord · Yes,* ſays the fellow again, *In any Cord ſo it be a ſtrong Cord ·* And when he had ſo ſaid, he ſlipt away from the company ; at laſt being ſearcht for by the chief Officer there, they could not find him : *How,* ſays he, *is he ſlipt away ; if he had not he ſhould have had the ſlip beſtowed upon him, for his unreverent language to the Parliament.*

3

A great Cavalier in the time of the War betwixt the King and Parliament, was taken Priſoner in the County of *Cheſter* by ſome of the Parliament Forces ; and in regard that this Gentleman was a Collonel, and had been very active in the Kings Service ; he was adjudged by the ſaid Parliament aforeſaid, not only to Priſon in *Nantwich* ; but there to

4 𝕮𝖔𝖋𝖋𝖊𝖊-𝖍𝖔𝖚𝖘𝖊 𝕵𝖊𝖘𝖙𝖘.

be put in a dark Dungeon, with nothing but Straw to lie on; which he patiently endured for two days but on Saturday night, he told the Jaylor, *That he desired that he might have liberty to go to Church on the morrow to hear their preaching; perhaps*, says he, *I may be of your Opinion then* which Sir *William* granted; and as the preacher was praising God for all their great Victories, he pray'd God that he would be a Centinel alfo, over that only Town of *Nantwich*, that had been so faithful to the Parliament; with that the Collonel started up, saying, *Pray Sir must he be a Muscatier or a Pikeman* upon which he was conveyed to his aforesaid lodging agen.

4.

In a Village in *Norfolk* where the Church stands upon a high Stony-hill; the Lady there and her family, when they went to Church, did use to load the Fool with all their Cloaks and Saveguards, for fear it should rain by the way; and always gave him a stick between is Leggs, telling him he should ride up, for 'twas a Horse; which he often did with confidence and satisfaction to himself. but being one time come

to

Coffee-house Jests.   5

to the top of the hill, and being much loaded with the aforesaid things, he began to puff and blow extreamly, saying, *D'ye call this a Horse, I am sure but for the name of a Horse, I had as good a gone a foot all the way.*

5.

A Cobler was sitting in his shop a singing merrily, his song was this; *Tamberlain was and he was, and Tamberlain was and he was;* and continued so singing, and nothing else, many times together; which a Gentleman that past by took notice of, and said to the Cobler, *Prithee friend,* says the Gentleman, *what was he? why,* says the Cobler, *as arrant a fool as your self, for ough I know:* Sirrah, says the Gentleman, *you are a rascal, come out and I'll kick you; no sir,* says he, *'tis no matter, I thank you for your love as much as if I had it, for I don't want kicking* · Sirrah, says the Gentleman again. *Come out and I'll give you a kick; No sir,* says he, *You need not trouble your self I won't come if you'd give me two.*

6.

A School-master did always dictate to his Scholars, *H non est Litera*, that is *H* is no Letter; and on a time he call'd
   A 4   one

6 𝕮𝕠𝕗𝕗𝖊-𝖍𝖔𝖚𝖘𝖊 𝕵𝖊𝖘𝖙𝖘.

one of the Scholars to him, and bid him
beat the Cawdle, and when he askt for it,
the Scholar told him, *that he had done
with the Cawdle as he bid him, What's that*,
fays his Mafter, *why Sir*, fays he, I d d
eat it : Sirrah, fays he, *I bid you heat it
with an H : Yes Sir*, fays he, *But I did eat
it with Bread.*

7.

A Gentleman defired of a covetous
Neighbour of his to lend him Ten pounds,
he profeffed he had none to fpare, but
the Gentleman having at that time very
great occafion, told him he had a Gelding that he had been offered twelve
pounds for, but for the prefent he would
take ten : *Well Sir*, fays the Mifer, *I'll
go and try a friend* (which you may be
fure was his Cheft) *and fetch the money
prefently* : which when the Gentleman
had received, and the Horfe delivered,
he faid, *Now I find that Horfes have
more credit than Men, and fo God-a-mercy
Horfe.*

8.

Two Fellows going with a prefent to
a covetous Man, one of them faid they
fhould but lofe their labour, well fays
t'other, I'll hold you a Crown that we
fhall

shall get there both Meat , Drink and
Money ; Done, says t'other : and being
come thither , one of 'them told him
that he was very dry , then he bid them
go down into the Celler; and when they
came there, he told the Butler , that he
could not drink without eating ; then
the Butler went up and told his Master
of it , who bid him set a cold Pasty before them; of which they eat plentifully: and when they had fill'd their Bellies ,
they both went to the Master to take
their leaves of him (also expecting some
gratuity) which when they saw not appearing, says one of them boldly, *Pray
Sir what shall we say to my Master if he
should ask us what you gave us :* which put
him to a stand for a while, at last he
gave them half a Crown: so the fellow won his wager of the other man.

9.

A Cavalier in *Oxford-shire* , that was
very zealous in his loyalty for his Prince,
and had suffered very much for it ; and
once meeting with some of the Rumpish
Officers at *Oxford,* says one of them to
him, *God save you Noble Squire, and you,* says
he, *if it be possible :* for he did believe that
all that were against the King could not
be saved.   A 5,   10. Some

𝔖.   𝔠𝔬𝔣𝔣𝔢𝔢-𝔥𝔬𝔲𝔰𝔢 𝔍𝔢𝔰𝔱𝔰.

10.

Some Women were making merry together at a Goſſipping at *Limus* near *Rat-cliff*, and the God-father was there among them; but òne of the Women that was an arch Jade, ſaid to him, *Sir I have ſomething to ſay to you*, well, ſays he, *ſay on : Don't you know*, ſays ſhe, *Ratcliff Market*, yes, ſays he, *very well*. Why, ſays ſhe, *if you will meet me there too morrow morning with a Tu — in your mouth, i'll give you a pint of Sack : but*, ſays he, *I muſt drink it to waſh my mouth, and if I do not do it, then you ſhall have the Sack again at ſecond hand*. Will, ſays ſhe, *I ſee that you would caſt your kindneſs upon me, if I'd accept on't : Well*, ſays ſhe. *If I do not meet you there, yet I'll come hither and tell you that I can't come*.

11.

There were two Modeſt and Civil *Whetſtons-park* Women that were ſcolding moſt comfortably in the ſtreet together, and amongſt their vertuous diſcourſe (of which there was great ſtore) to the great ſatisfaction of all the neighbourhood, that their Daughters might learn the better how to behave themſelves : One call'd the other Whore :-

Ea th.

Coffee-house Jests.

Faith, says she , *and thou wouldst fain be a Whore to , but that thou art so ugly that no body will lie with thee : What you Whore,* says she, *I can have one for a Groat a night and thank ye too.*

12.

A Gentleman was riding through a Forrest in *Oxford* Shire, where two suppofed Cripples begg'd fomething of him, then he put his hand in his pocket, and bid them give him a Groat and he would give them Six Pence , which they did ; and when he had the Groat , he rod away with it : with that one of them fwore a great Oath , faying, *Cut thy Girth Tom, cut thy Girth , you Rogue, and let us after him :* And though he gollopt a good pace away , yet they were fo nimble (and fo by confequence Cripples), that they overtook him as he was opening a Gate, and had almoft laid hold on him; that the Gentleman, for his fecurity was forc'd to throw two or three Shillings down on the ground , and whilft they were fcrabling for that he got away.

A Bridle for the Tongue: Or, A Curb to Evil discourse: Published to Regulate the great Abuses in Coffee-Houses, Taverns, Ale-Houses, &c. With Permission (London, for N. T., 1678), 5pp. BL: 12316.f.23.(3).

A religious tract attacking blasphemy and unregulated discourse in coffee-houses. In the early 1670s coffee-house debates on affairs of politics attracted the attention of the authorities, who considered these discussions seditious, and proposed various mechanisms for their control or suppression. By contrast, *A Bridle for the Tongue* argues that what was dangerous about coffee-house discussion was its licentious nature, its tendency to 'scoff at religion' and 'repeat prophane, debauch'd or scurrilous Language'. This blasphemy not only threatened to corrupt and poison the morals of young people, but was itself a kind of treason against the King of Heaven – and as such, a more serious fault than treason against Charles II. In response the writer calls for men to join together to 'reform this sinful Nation' by forming themselves into 'reforming Societies', prefiguring the societies for the reformation of manners formed by Anglicans and Nonconformists that were active in the 1690s.

The author is unknown. The title – *A Bridle for the Tongue* – enjoyed a vogue amongst Protestant divines of all colours in the second half of the seventeenth century: it was used by no less than five distinct tracts between 1654 and 1671, by authors including the Presbyterian William Bagshawe (1628–1702), the puritan John Brinsley (1600–65) and the Anglican William Gearing (fl. 1663). The text is extremely rare, surviving in one copy at the British Library, and not recorded in the established bibliographical resources (Wing, ESTC, *Term Catalogues*), nor in Hünersdorff. The printer is identified as 'N. T.'; eight tracts printed between 1678 and 1688 make use of these initials. Wing suggests he may be the same as Nathaniel Thompson, a noted printer and bookseller of Nonconformist religious tracts and seditious pamphlets, whose shop was at the entrance to the Old Spring Garden near Charing Cross (Plomer).

A
BRIDLE
FOR THE
TONGUE:

OR,

A Curb to Evil Difcourfe :

Publifhed to Regulate the great Abufes in

COFFEE-HOUSES,

Taverns, Ale-Houfes, &c.

With Permiffion,

LONDON,
Printed for *N. T.* 1678.

(1)

A

Bridle for the Tongue:

O R,

A Curb to Licentious & Exorbitant Difcourfe ;

Not only in

COFFEE-Houfes, Taverns & *Victualling-houfes,*

BUT ALSO

At our *Tables*, and in all other Societies whatfoever.

T O

Prevent that Epidemical **E V I L** of this **A G E**, Wherein Corrupt Communication doth fo abound, to the Poyfoning of the Youth; who may have juft Caufe to curfe their Predeceffors in fucceeding Ages, for giviug them no better **E X A M P L E S**.

For we owe all the Debauchery of our Youth to our our own Corrupt and Vain Converfations;

They (naturally) being apt to fuck in Evil by *Example* before they underftand a *Precept :*

And therefore as we prize, both their and our own Immortal Souls, let us ferioufly confider ;

A 2   That

(2)

*That God ordained Speech but for these Two great
Ends, (viz.)*

To Glorify God,   *And from thence let*
        &   *Us Consider ;*
To Benefit Mankind.

THat if we must give an Account of every idle Word ;
It will be most certain, whatever part of our Difcourse anfwers not of thefe two original Ends of Speech,
will not hold weight in the Ballance of the Sanctuary ;
      For :

He that is Truth himfelf hath told us, That by our
Words we fhall be Juftified; and by our Words we fhall
be Condemned : Therefore,

He that is not furnifhed with matter of Difcourfe to
anfwer thefe Ends, were far better (in the account of
God and good Men) to be filent, than to offer the Sacrifice of Fools : For that Man moft certainly hath a
very lean and empty Pate whofe Head is fo barren of
folid Knowledge, that he cannot maintain one quarter
of an hours Difcourfe ; but he muft either fcoff at Religion, or Sacred Offices, or repeat prophane, debauch'd
or fcurrilous Language, or make Reflections upon other
mens Infirmities or Misfortunes.

And to prevent any fuch barren Babblers broaching
their Folly ;

Let all fober Men then prefent be mindful of their
Duty :

Firft to God.

If God be any ways Difhonour'd, or his Name taken
in vain; let him not want a Friend to take his part :
                                        For,

(3)

For ;

If it be Treafon to conceal Affronts done to the Majefty of Earthly Princes, much more will the Great God of Heaven account all Traytors againft Himfelf, who fhall prefer the Creature before the Creator ; And are either affraid or afham'd to reprove Traytors againft Heaven, when they-bear Treafon by Oaths and Execrations breathed out by his Fellow-Subjeds, againft the great King of Heaven their Maker.

When any Perfon fhall refled upon any of what Degree or Quality foever, that are abfent, let all the hearers become Advocates for the abfent perfon, whofe Name, Infirmities or Misfortunes are ript up or call'd in queftion ; Confidering how great a kindnefs they themfelves would efteem it if fuch Friends fhould appear on their behalf, if they at the fame time were back-bited elfewhere.

Sir *Thomas Moore*, once Lord Choncellor of *England*, caufed this Diftick to be fet up over his Table of Entertainment,

Quifquis amat Dictis, abfentem radere amicum,
Hanc menfam Vetitam, noverit effe fibi.

Which may admit this Paraphrafe in Englifh.

The Lord of Truth this Sacred Rule did give,
To deal, as we would willingly receive :
If fo, let no man (abfent) want a Friend,
His Name, and Fame, from flander to defend.

This

(4)

This would be a means to purge the Land of the worst of Vermine, Slanderers, and Backbiters, the only incendiaries of all Division in Neighbourhood; as also in Church and State, when their Raileries and Detractions, should find no welcome entertainment: As Thieves and Vagabonds would have little encouragement to steal, if there were no persons ready to receive their stollen wares.

And also, this would be the most likely way to reform this sinful Nation, and prevent our approaching ruine; (which work must be begun by reforming Societies.) If God (as we may speak after the manner of men) and absent persons, might find one, or more such friends in every Society, where the Devil hath (too frequently) so many officious Agents. And lastly, this is the most likely way to make us good Christians, and consequently the only means to make Loyal Subjects.

For only they that fear the Lord, and make conscience of their words, have such inward Principles as will oblige them to Loyalty, and hatred of Treason.

But he that doth so little fear the great God, that he dares violate his Sacred Laws, by belching out execrable Oaths; and hath so little shame of sin, that he glories in his Debaucheries, and scoffs at all that is Sacred, or serious; that man has so far stifled the murmures of his Conscience, and remonstrances of his Reason (let his pretences be what they will) he will (when opportunity serves) sell his Prince, betray his Country, and his dearest friend (as he hath already done his own Soul) to gratifie his lusts, and indulge his sensual Appetite.

Our

[5]

Our Sins have been like *Pharaoh*'s, great and many; our Plagues have been like his, many and dreadful: God came down in the flesh, to be our *Moses*, and our Guide; but like *Pharaoh*, we will not let our selves to go, nor obey the voice of the Lord, calling so loud in one Judgment following another.

Let us no longer, like him, harden our hearts, left the Red-Sea of Gods wrath swallow us up, like the Egyptians or Sodomites, whom we exceed in horrid Impiety, and most filthy Abominations.

Happy is the man that puts his hand to this Plough, that he may share in the blessing whilst he lives, and be called blessed in the age to come, for assisting to begin, and carry on so blessed a Reformation.

FINIS.

A Satyr Against Coffee ([London], n.p., [1679]). BL:
Roxburghe Ballads III (831). ESTCR37203. Hünersdorff.

A brief single-sheet Royalist broadside verse satire against coffee. The poem is 27 lines in length, organised into nine three-line stanzas, rhymed in triplets. The satire is directed against coffee, which is troped as a satanic interloper into England. The third stanza places coffee as the third in a line of serious subversions against the English crown, after printed libels and the Gunpowder Plot of 1605. Against the backdrop of the feverish conspiracies and counter-conspiracies of the Popish Plots of 1678, this suggest the poem plays a role in the wider cultural factionalism of the Exclusion Crisis, although a specific allegiance is not identifiable.

The poem's title claims that it is a 'Satyr'. In Greek mythology, a satyr is a woodland demon halfway between man and beast. The term has long been confused with satire, a Roman form of poetic essay commenting on vice or folly (perhaps because in the Athenian 'satyr plays' of the 5th century BC, a chorus of satyrs commented satirically on the action). In the seventeenth century, the term 'satyr' was often used to denote a particularly biting and censorious kind of satire. John Phillips (1631–1706) started the craze when he published his 22-page Juvenalian verse satire, *A Satyr Against Hypocrites* in 1655, which was frequently reprinted over the following decades. Subsequently, satires were written against scribbling, mankind, women, virtue, and especially during the Exclusion Crisis 1679–82. The cause of this flood of satyrs may be the relaxation of press censorship in 1679, occasioned by the lapse of the Licensing Act, which allowed multitudes of scabrous libels and subversive satires to be openly printed and disseminated.

The satire has no known author or publisher. Although sometimes dated 1674, the text may be dated with some accuracy to 1 December 1679 from manuscript annotations on the copy once owned by the pamphlet collector Narcissus Luttrell (1657–1732) now in the Newberry Library, Chicago. Many copies have survived: not only in the British Library's Roxburgh Collection of Ballads, originally collected by Robert Harley, Earl of Oxford, but also in Lincoln's Inn Library; the Newberry Library, Chicago; the Huntingdon

Library, California; the Spencer Research Library, Kansas; and the university libraries at Harvard; Brown; and Austin, Texas. The satire was known to Macaulay.

A

SATYR

AGAINST

COFFEE,

Avoid, *Satanic Tipple!* Hence
Thou Murhterer of Farthings, and of Pence;
And Midwife to all *false Intelligence*!

Avoid, I say, of Hell thou art,
For God no liquor doth man impart,
But that which quenches *Thirst*, or chears the Heart.

Bak'd in a pan, *Brew'd* in a pot,
The third device of him who first begot
The Printing Libels, and the Powder-plot.

A *Swill* that needs must be accurst,
And of all sorts of Drink the very worst,
By which the *Devils Children (Lies)* are nurst.

Now if I fancy not amisse
Vespatian, who impos'd Excise on Piss,
Would for no *smell of Lucre* suffer this.

The sister of the common Sewer,
That passes theough the Reins with Stream impure;
That Robs the Vintner and undoes the Brewer.

For by this poor *Arabian* Berry,
Comes the Neglect of *Malago* and *Sherry*,
And *sooty Surges* rise to *Charon's* Ferry.

The Sweat of *Negroes*, Blood of *Moores*,
The Blot of *Sign-post*, and the Stain of *doors*,
And *the last Shift of Publicans and Whores*.

Give o're you *Whifflers* then! Enough;
Convert your *Powder* into Irish *Snuff*
And lay your *Lace* upon some richer *Stuff*.

A dialogue between Tom and Dick, over a dish of coffee, concerning matters of religion and government ([London], n.p., 1680), [2], 14, 17–35, [1]pp.; 4°. BL: E.2090.(2). ESTCR27858.

A prose dialogue between two citizens discussing political events in the form of a parody of Roger L'Estrange's *Citt and Bumpkin*, published the previous month. It presents itself as an ironic dramatic dialogue, and is arguably readable as an example of coffee-house conversation, albeit couched in a satire. In this estimation, such coffee-house discussions are colloquial yet informed; based on covert intelligence but speculative and inquiring; conspiratorial yet revelatory; knowledgeable yet vulgar.

The dialogue is an entry into a vituperative contemporary controversy known as the Popish Plot. According to an informant named Titus Oates, England was threatened by a Catholic conspiracy that intended to murder Charles II, replace him with a Catholic monarch, presumably the Duke of York, and destroy the Protestant religion. The panic occasioned by Titus Oates's allegations lasted from 1678 to 1781, despite much of his evidence being revealed as bogus. More generally, the Popish Plot episode was a continuation of the longer contest in the 1670s between the Crown and Parliament, amounting to two rival theories of government, autocratic monarchy or limited constitutional monarchy.

The specific target of *A dialogue between Tom and Dick* is Sir Roger L'Estrange's *Citt and Bumpkin. In a Dialogue over a Pot of Ale, Concerning Matters of Religion and Government* (London, Henry Brome, 1680), the first part of which, according to Narcissus Luttrell, was published on 10 February 1679/80, and the second on 31 March 1680. Luttrell described the first part as 'A piece writt by L'Estrange, to abuse ye dissenters' (in *Narcissus Luttrell's Popish Plot Catalogues*, ed. by F. C. Francis (Oxford, Luttrell Society by Basil Blackwell, 1956), inserted page opposite p. 13). *Citt and Bumpkin* satirises the conduct of political debate amongst the common people, reflecting the Court party's wider belief that discussions of 'affairs of state' should only take place between the King and his advisers and courtiers. In pursuit of this end, *Citt and Bumpkin* attacks the Petitioning movement, which sought wide and popular support for their call for the King to recall Parliament. *Citt and Bumpkin* offers evidence that the petitioners are well organised and funded: this is explained by L'Estrange as further evidence for a Protestant plot against the King. *A dialogue between Tom and Dick* presents a news-writer called Tom (or Crack-fart, modelled on L'Estrange), a hack writer of plot narratives and conspiracies, who discusses events with his disingenuous friend Dick, a fool. The tract claims that critics of the plot-narrative are evidence of a wider conspiracy hatched by secretive Catholic conspirators. The text is a long and complex parody of L'Estrange, making a sophisticated attempt to satirise his style and method, as well as his argument. The author was not identified at the time, and has not subsequently come to light. As the publication was intended to evade official scrutiny, it does not state the name of the printer or publisher. A number of copies survive.

A DIALOGUE

BETWEEN

TOM and DICK,

OVER A

𝔇𝔦𝔰𝔥 𝔬𝔣 ℭ𝔬𝔣𝔣𝔢𝔢,

Concerning MATTERS of

RELIGION

AND

GOVERNMENT

Printed in the Year; 1 6 8 o.

(1)

A

DIALOGUE

BETWEEN

TOM and DICK.

Tom. SO! we Two are got together into a Corner of this *Coffee-houſe*, where none can over-hear us; Prithee *Dick*. let us Diſcourſe like our ſelves.

Dick. Ay *Tom*. juſt like *Cit*. and *Bumpkin*; this is the place for *Dialogues*: There ſat *Cit*. where you do, and here ſat *Bumpkin* where I do; now if we could but talk ſo wiſely.

Tom. Why! What diſcourſ'd they of *Dick*?

Dick. Of matters of *Religion* and *Government*; what ſhould they talk of elſe? 'tis all the Diſcourſe now, from the *Lord* to the *Fidler*, all are grown *States-men*.

Tom. Well, and how handled they matters?

Dic. Peſtilent well; and they begun about *Petitions*, things that have made a great Buſtle, and much Diſcourſe.

A 2   *Tom.*

(2)

Tom. Let us talk a little too, very freely our minds.

Dick. Come with all my *Heart*; but first clear your Eyes with the steem of the *Coffee*, 'tis good for your *Brain*. It must be your task to *speak*, and *write*.

Tom. Write ! why I have writ my self half *purblind* already, I *write* commonly in my *sleep*, and *Dream* out politick Difcourfes:& *Farther Difcoveries*, which I have thought many a time and oft *Old Nick* Himfelf injects into my Skull, they are fuch notable *unlucky* ones ; the Government could never be at quiet for me in thofe days of Your, till I got Four or Five hundred a Year by chattering, and whilft that lafted, I was as mute as a Bell-founder, or *Will. Pryn*, when buried amongft mufty *Records* ; but now to tell you the truth, I have nothing elfe to *live on*, but my *Wits*, and yet am at my *Wits-end*, becaufe I can get no living Creature to anfwer me; that I might with a handfome colour continue the Wrangle.

Dick. Let your Bookfeller hire fome body to reply.

Tom. Hang him ; he fays he *lofes* by my works already, that I am grown a meer *Fumbler* at Scribling, and forc'd to be my own Plagiary ; but a Book's a Book, and a Bargain's a Bargain, and therefore hitherto I have done well enough with him.

Dick. Well then, All's well that ends well, but we come to *argue* matters of State, and I fay (as aforefaid) it muft be your Province to *invent* and *hold forth*.

Tom. And yours *Dick.* to *hear* and *believe*.

Dick. But I'le fpeak in my turn, though to little *purpofe*.

Tom. You fay well, for none always fpeaks to purpofe, though he fpeaks *purpofely*.

Dick.

(3)

Dick. I bar *Riddles*, for if you fpeak 'um, you muft un-riddle 'um too, and that's *Labour*, you know my *Capacity*.

Tom. Well then I'le tell thee *Dick*, to fpeak *purpofely* in our *Language*, is to fet People together by the Ears; and not to fpeak to the *purpofe* is when for all that, they won't go together by the Ears.

Dick. Very well, truly *Tom.!* very well, I fee you are an *enlightning* Man, and hath a plaguy *long fnout* of your own to fmell a Presbyterian Plot. I begin already to have my *Eyes* open, I can fee through a *Milftone* as far as another. You'l make me lofe my *Nature*, and become *Wife*.

Tom. Ne'r fear it, there be a great many *Knowing Fools*.

Dick. What at Riddles again !

Tom. How fhould we difcourfe elfe ? That is fuch as *read* much, and underftand *little*, that hear *wife men* talk, and like *Parrets* can fay after them; that have the *Languages* without the *Wit*, to make true ufe of them : That talk like *Ariftotle*, and write like *Seneca*, but live like Sir *Formal*, and act like Sir *Foplin.*

Dick. I fay thou art an *enlightning* Man; that there fhould be fuch *knowing Fools* : But moft *Fools* are knowing in their own *Conceits*, at leaft they think *themfelves wife.*

Tom. But to our purpofe, if there were not fo many *Fools*, there would be fewer *Knaves*: For if there were not a great many believing *Fools*, there would be far lefs inventing, prateing, and fcribling *Knaves*.

Dick. You are much in the right in that; we have talk'd of *Fools*, but a word or two of *Knaves*.

Tom.

(4)

Tom. Well, I will endeavour to satisfie you in that, There are a very great number of that *profeſſion*, and we have alſo our *Committees*, and *Sub-Committees*, *Clubs*, and Meeting *Houſ s*, even from *Algate* to *Temple-Bar*, in the City of *Weſtminſter*, Burrow of *Southwark*, & in the *Country*, throughout *Eugland* , and in all the Chief *Corporations* thereof ; and we go *buzing*, or rather *roreing* and *railing* up and down againſt *praying*, *deſiring*, *intreating*, *requeſting*, *ſupplicating*, and the like ; as *dangerous*, *abominable*, *prophane*, *tumultuous*, *incendarious*, *republicanical*, and *rebellious*. Nay, we have our *Gazets* too, our *Pamphlets*, our *Poems*, our *Intelligences*, our *Compendiums*, our *Coffee-tales*, and more tricks by half than *Cit.* can be imagined to have.

Dick. I ſay you talk like a fallen *Angel* , a very *Intelligence* ; What a *fool* was I, to know nothing of your *Clubs* ! but the *Righteous* call them *Jeſuitical.*

Tom. 'Tis true, they have got that Title of late, and to tell you the truth, thoſe learned Gentlemen have much *enlightned* our Eyes, and taught us how to carry things *cloſely*, and *cunningly*. and to *work* and *undermine.* They are the *Maſters* at *Supping*, and have laid down for us *Mathematical Rules.*

Dick. As how ?

Tom. As when we have a *mind* to ſet People together by the Ears. to begin vvith *Religion*, to invent *new Plots*, to raiſe *Stories*, to forge *Lies*, to Create *Relations*, to make *Dialogues* , to feign *things* that never vvere, to cauſe *Jealouſies*, to ſtir up *Feudes*, to rail at the *Presbyterians* and other *Sectaries* , and to frame them *Clubs*, *Committees*, *Officers*, *Intelligences*, nav, to tell aloud their ſecret *Whiſpers*, *Thoughts*, and *Motions* of their *Souls.*

Dick

(5)

Dick. But why is all this ? for what *end* ? Don't we live in *Peace* ? And has not *God* given us *Plenty* and *Riches* , and a good *King*, that grants us all juft *Liberties* ?

Tom. Why there's the thing *Fool:* I'le tell thee inftantly in a Word, 'its to break this *Golden Chain*, and to caufe *Commotions* and *Rebellion* if we can.

Dick. What will you get by it ?

Tom. I can't tell *Fool* what you will get : But I am fure I fhall get fufficiently. Tis good to *Fifh* in troubled *Waters* ; and there were never any *Troubles* yet, but as we had our *Fingers* in them, we knew (as they fay) how to lick 'em.

Dick. I thought all the *Knaves* had been among the *Citts* and *Sectaries.*

Tom. No *Fool.* There be *Court Knaves*, and *Jefuitical Knaves*, *Ungodly*, *Unfanctifyed*, *Irreligious* and *Prophane Knaves*, as well as *Demure*, *Religious*, and *Saintlike Knaves*, nay there be *Monarchicals*, as well as *Republican* Knaves: *Lords* and *Knights* and *Gentlemen*, as well as *Citts*.

Dick. But pray Sir, are there not alfo, as many of my *Profeffion* too, befides *Bumpkins* ?

Tom. Yes fure ; and moft commonly, the *Knave* and the *Fool* goes together, as we now do, for they love one another 𝕾𝖙𝖗𝖆𝖓𝖌𝖊𝖑𝖞.

Dick. That's 𝕾𝖙𝖗𝖆𝖓𝖌𝖊 me thinks, yet I obferve them often together.

Tom. The *Knave* knows not well how to be without the *Fool* ; this *Latter* is the *others Inftrument*, his *Tool* with which he works *Miracles* : He makes ufe of him, as the *Monkey* does of the *Catts Foot*, to pull the Nut out of the *Fire.* So *Fool*, you muft be my *Inftrument*, and I will Inftruct you, perhaps in time, you may get *Preferment* as well as *Bumpkin* ?   *Dick.*

(6)

Dick. Prethe do : I will endeavour to Learn.

I   *Tom.* Why firſt you muſt learn to *Invent*, marke me, *nvent things* that never were, nor ever like to be ; or if you are not good at *Invention*, wee'l do it for you ; then it muſt be your *work* to *believe*, and to cauſe our *Inventions* to be *believ'd*, though they be againſt *Sence* and *Reaſon*, againſt *Proofs*, *Oaths*, *Witneſſes*, and *Demonſtration* it ſelf.

Dick. What, Narratives of *Dragons*, *Prodigies*, and 𝔖𝔱𝔯𝔞𝔫𝔤𝔢 𝔖𝔦𝔤𝔥𝔱𝔰 ? That's the way *Citt* takes.

Tom. No, no, 𝔖𝔱𝔯𝔞𝔫𝔤𝔢𝔯 Relations; though the *Sun* ſhine, you muſt ſay and believe it is *Night* : Though the *Land* be *Embroyl'd*, and in great *trouble*, you muſt think it is in *Peace* : Though the *Wind* Blow, you muſt ſay 'tis *Calm*, though it be *Sultry weather*, you muſt cry it is damn'd *Cold*, and blow your Fingers. Though you ſee *Popery* ſpread, you muſt ſay the *Presbyterians*, and *Sectaries* bring it in under hand. Though you feel the *Shoe ring* the *Foot*, you muſt ſay 'tis an *eaſy ſhoe* : You muſt endeavour to turn *Plots* into *Ridicule*, and to make *Sectaries Jeſuits*, *Knaves* to ſeem *Honeſt Men*, and *Honeſt Men Knaves*.

Dick. But you muſt give me the *means* to do it.

Tom. Oh ! You muſt be diligent, when we *Write*, *Speak* , *Exclaim* , *Rail* , *Huff*, *Roar*, *Swear*, *Rant*, and *Lampoon*, to run every where, and publiſh them in all *Companies*, and *Places*, eſpecially among the *Fools*, the *Royſters*, the *God-dam-mees*, the *Jeſters*, the *Fidlers*, the *Careleſs*, the *Prophane*, the *Tyranical*, the *Rapacious*, the *Cheats*, the *Hectors*, the *Bullies*, and the *Shirks* in the *Bawdy-houſes*, *Play-houſes*, *Gaming Ordinaries*, the Court of *Requeſts*, and *Weſtminſter-hall*, and every where, and in all Companies, to gain Credit, and Eſpecially among the *Papiſts*, and the *Mungril Papiſts*, who are neither *Fleſh*,

(7)

Flesh, nor *Fish*, nor good *Red Herring*:

Dick. I fee a man may live and Learn, I think I have the Advantage of *Bumpkin* in this.

Tom. That thou haft, for you may do it with eafe, and neither fear *Pillory* nor *Imprifonment*. We have many great *Men* will take your part, the *Jefuits* underhand will incourage you, and we have a *Party too*, that rather than you fhall want, know how to part with *Money* to Promote a *good defign*, and that out of pure *Charity*, can releafe perfons out of *Prifon*, to do their *Stabbing jobs*. Don't think all the *Policy* lies in the *Cits* Lords.

Dick. And I muft fpeak againft *Petitioning* too, and *Parliaments*.

Tom. Ay againft the *firft*, with full mouth, *Authority* will back you; but againft the *latter* Cautiously, like a very *Presbyterian*. And though we could heartily wifh, there might never be any more *Parliaments* (unlefs it were to make an *Act* that fome of us might *Supervife the Prefs*) we muft not fay fo, becaufe of the damn'd *Priviledges*, and *Old Mufty Records*, *Magna Charta*'s and many *Moldy Statutes*, which the *Common People* are fond of, and will draw an *Odium* upon us.

Dick. But what was that true that *Cit* and *Bumkin* faid tother Night, about getting of *Hands* and *Subfcriptions* to *Petitions*, and putting in falfe, and Invented *Names*?

Tom. 'Tis no matter whither it were he or not, thefe New-fafhioned Court-made *Citts* are often given to Lying and *Bragging*, however though we don't believe it our felves 'twill make much for us, if the *People* will believe it.

B   *Tom.*

(8)

Dick. I am affraid truly, they have the greateſt *Party* on their ſide.

Tom. Thou talk'ſt now right Fool, but if they had, we are the *Wiſeſt*, and know how to be even with them : We know how to Chop and Change *Perſons* in Buſineſs, till we have Molded them to our Humour, and till we are ſure we have got ſuch, as will at leaſt *Connive* at our *Politicks*.

Dick. I know not how it came about, that the *Petitions* fell ſo ſoon, both in *City* and *Country*, till *Cit* Inform'd me.

Tom. I tell thee, thou muſt not believe all *Citt* ſays, he is a very *Lying Fellow*, the truth on't was, many of us made uſe of their Wits in that Affair, we ſpake *fair* to ſome, we *Threatned* others, we *Flatter'd* many, and us'd no ſmall *Diligence* and *Policy* to put a Stop to *Petitioning*, which like an *Itch* had ſpread over the *Land*, but indeed under the Roſe, many were affraid, but *more* had ſome *Conſcience*, and loved the *King*, and *Peace* of their *Country*, and ſo were extream unwilling to diſpleaſe His *Majeſty*, ſince he had ſhew'd his diſlike, and this was the *true Reaſon*, that broke the *Heart* of the *City* and *Country Petitions*, and put a ſtop to the *inundation* of *Hands*, that were coming up.

Dick. Then I perceive, theſe Men had ſome *Conſcience*, 'tis true indeed, *Citt* ſaid, they had got all *ſorts* of *Conſciences.*

Tom: No, no, they have not all the *Conſciences* neither, for they have left ſome for us.   There is a *Fools Conſcience*, and a *Knaves Conſcience*, a *Little Conſcience*, a *Large Conſcience*, and no *Conſcience* at all ;

Dick.

(9)

Dick. I thought 'twas impoffible for *Citts* to have left any *Confcience,* but that they had ingroffed all to themfelves. But I pray; what do you mean by thefe *Confciences?* Explain your felf a little.

Tom. That I will for your *Edification* ! Know then that a *Little* or *Small Confcience* is no bigger than the *Bag* of a *Bumble Bee* ; and this may be call'd the *Fools Confcience*: 'Tis ufual to fay, a Man has *Little Confcience,* and fuch an one is he, that will take ones *Money* for nothing, that will ftrain at every *Gnat, Kicks* at the very mention of any *Papifts* having a hand in the Late Kings Murder, or that is poffible for a *Proteftant* that cannot Swallow every little Ceremony to be a good *Subject.* He is one that Promifes *much,* and performs *Little,* Receives *all,* and pays *none,* keeps his *Whore,* and breaks his Word with her, runs in *Debt,* and then to the *Fryers,* or a Protection, fets his *Inftruments* a work, and leaves them in the *Lurch* ; Ruins the *poor,* to inrich *himfelf,* Fires *Houfes,* and Robs by the *light* of them, and endeavours to fet the *World* together by the *Ears* to get a *Reward,* or a *Petty Place* to Domineer in.

Dick. Who would think there was fo much in a *Little Confcience* ! What is then your *Large Confcience?*

Tom. 'Tis much bigger than the *Tun* at *Helderburgh,* and that may be called the *Knaves Confcience. Ten Thoufand* pound will lie in one *Crevice* of it, and not be feen at all. He that has it, can Swallow whole *Lordfhips,* and an *Hundred Thoufand Pound* will not fill one little *Corner* of it? 'Tis big enough to drain the *French Kings Finances,* and our *Kings Exchequer.* 'Tis fo wide, the *Devil* may

B 2   run

(10)

run a Race in't, and be out of Breath before he reaches the end of it. They that have this *Confcience* Swear a-bove half as many Oaths as they fpeak words, fpend all on their *Whores*, and leave their *Wives* in want. And, the *Whores* have this *Confcience*, that for a little fport, require *Thoufand's*, large *Setlements*, great *Gifts*, and, if they could get it a *Kingdoms Revenew*.

Dick. Very good, but what is it to have *no Confcience at all?*

Tom. That's a *Jefuitical Confcience*, fuch as can *Swear* all *Oathes* Glibly, take all *Tefts*, Profefs all *Religions* and be of *none*, *Lye*, *Swear*, *Forfwear*, *Imprecate*, *Atteft*, *Blaf-pheme*, *Fire Houfes*, *Confpire the Death of Princes*, *Lay Plots*, and *Defigns* for *Maffacre*, and *Rebellion*, and yet ftoutly deny their *Guilt*, even at the *Gallows*, and at the *Laft Gafp* fay, they are as *Innocent* as the *Child Unborn*.

Dick. But have we no *fimple*, *true*, *Religious Confci-ence*, that loves *God* for *Gods fake?* That Submits to *Laws* Peacably, becaufe *Chrift commands* it? Obeys *Magiftrates*, Loves *Peace*, both in *Church* and *State*, becaufe 'tis the *Do-ctrine* of *Jefus*, and of his *Apoftles?*

Tom. This fort of *Confcience* is not among us.

Dick. I heard *Cit* fay, 'twas only to be found indeed in the *Goal*, or in the *Hofpital*, in Men in *Adverfity*, or in *Sicknefs*.

Tom. 'Tis a *Jewel* indeed, the *Elixir of the States Man*, that would convert all *Evil Politicks* to *Gold*: The *Phi-lofophers Stone* of a *Divine*, that would enrich all his *Thoughts* with *Celeftial Treafure*. But let us ne're feek after it, 'tis as hard to be got as the *Univerfal Medicine*,
or

(11)

or to be found as *ò Brazell*. Hang it 'tis a *Chymara*, to be look't for only among *Roficratians*, or in *Fairy Land*.

Dick. But I heard *Cit* fay, that *Confciencious Men*, might be known by their *Looks, Giftures,* and *Pulpit Actings*.

Tom. True enough, we have of thefe fort of *Confcientious Men*, they are not all among the *Citts:* Who more *Demure* than a *Reverend Father Fefuite?* That fhall give you *words* like *Sugar*, which are in the mean time *Rank Poyfon?* That can *Equivocate* and *Diffemble*, and *Smile* in your *Face*, and if an *opportunity* be given, Cut your *Throat*, or Fire your *Houfes?* That can *drink* with you, and take the *Sacrament* with you, and then wipe their *Mouths* and *Plot* the *death* of their *Soveraign*, the *Subverfion* of *Religion*, and *Sub-plot*, to put all off their own *Backs* upon that of the *Hereticks?* What think you, are not thefe *Demure, Grave, Holy look'd, Confciencious* Men? Then as for their *Activity* in the *Pulpit*, I defy er'e a *Presbyterian* of them all, to come near a *Seraphick Francifcan*, or a *Mouthing Dominican*. I once heard one of the former at *York Houfe*, and never *Fugler, Tumbler*, or *Fack-Pudding*, had more Poftures than he had; therefore let not *Cit* Brag of his *Pulpit Activity.*

Dick. But what fay you to thofe *Moving Metaphors* that fome of them have? There they out do all others.

Tom. Neither, for we have enough *Ship Stocking* Priefts who have many more *delicious Similies*, and pretty

(12)

ty Metaphors, that would make a Man draw his Mouth of one fide: And that Learned grave *Dulman* in the *Univerfity* is not to be forgotten, who praying for the young *Students* in that place, Cry'd, *O Lord make thefe* Young Willows *to grow up to be* Old Oakes, *that they may become* Timber, *fit to* Wanfcote *thy* New Jerufalem.

Dick. So much for *Confcience*, and *Confciencious* Men: Let me now ask you what *Religion* I fhould be of, or which is moft *convenient* for my *Capacity?*

Tom. Don't you know what *David* the *King* fays; *The fool hath faid in his heart there is no God.* He has pointed forth thy *Religion Fool*; that is to fay no *Religion*, an *Atheift* in thy *Heart*, but what thou wilt in *fhew.*

Dick. I thought that had been your *Religion*; there be a very great number of this *Religion*, who plainly teftifie it, both in their *words* and *actions*:

Tom. As for my *Religion*, tho' that fhall never much trouble me, and 'tis *fafhonable* to *fcoff* and *jear* at all *Religions*; and is a mark of *wit* and gentile *breeding* fo to do; yet I having fome little belief, that there may be a *God* and a *Heaven*, and an *Hell*, I think good to be of that *Religion*, wherein I may purchafe *Heaven* with my *mony*, and buy it as men do Land: take my full wing of *Pleafure*, commit all manner of *Sins* and *Debaucheries*; care not how I live, or what I *fay* or *do* all the *week*, and on *Sunday Morning* be made as clean as a Houfe that's new wafh'd; and fo as foon as all my filthy *fins* are carried away by *abfolution*, return again frefh and hungry to new *Commons*; and thus *toties quoties*, from one *weeks* end to another, as long as I *live.*

O!

(13)

O! This is a brave *Religion* ; and a *world* fuch as I have lately embrac'd it ; and all the brave *Whores* have followed our fteps ; It gives *authority* to our *Pleafures*.

Tom. I think very well of this *Religion* , and I am refolved to believe this, and profefs the other for a time, for I find this to be in *vogue* , and to *fpread* mightily.

Dick. Yes, 'tis to promote this *Religion* that all this *Puther* is made ; but we moft *fafely* and *cunningly* do it, under a fecure and dreadful notion , by railing at the *Prefbyterians*, and pretending burning zeal for reformed *Catholicks* ; whilft indeed we intend to pull down the reformed *Bifhops*, and to fet up the *Romifh*

Tom. But one thing *Dick*, I muft mind you of, that you come fhort of *Cit* in.

Dick. What's that ?

Tom. You have not the *Knack* of getting by *Imprifonment*, or ftanding *ftifly* and *ftoutly* for the caufe.

Dick. That's your miftake *Jack*, for I tell you, they learnt that *Trick* of us ; for we have feveral , that weekly and daily fearch all the *Prifons* in Town, for *working Tools* , that is, out of thefe *Colleges* do pick Perfons fit for *defperate defigns*. Alas ! in that *Cit* is a *Fool* to us ; for we have thofe, that have lain years, like *Fies* in the *Inquifition* in *Newgate*, the Kings *Bench Fleet*, *Gate-houfe* and other *Prifons*, only to pick and chufe *Inftruments* fit for our purpofe, and to *infinuate* into them, and to *indoctrinate* them ; and having made and moulded them fit for purpofe, paid their *Debts*, tho' of a confiderable *value* ; or if in for other wicked *Actions* and flagitious *Crimes*, get their *Reprieves*, and then their *Pardons*, or fome way work their *efcape*, and

(14)

and then thefe are eternally obliged to us, being ftill
Feed with *mony*, and kept at the *publick charge*. Don't
you fee then *Jack*, that the way to *Preferment* is by
being *clapt up* ? And we have *Lords* and *great men* too,
that with their *Purfes* and their *Guinees* fpare for
no coft to *bolfter* up the *Caufe*.

Tom. But what if any of thefe fhould *betray* you, and
confefs all this at laft ?

Dick. We have befides the *Impudence* of *Denying* (for
we work with out *witneffes*, the way of *Godfrying* fuch
a one prefently, or of fending him beyond *Seas*, as
foon as we have done with him, or before he has any
opportunity, and then he is paft *telling Tales*.

Tom. But won't your *great men* deceive them at
laft ?

Dick. Not till they have fully done with them, and
then are not fo *generous* as *Cits great Men:* before they
dare not for their own *Intereft*; and befides, they have
always *Spies* upon their *actions* and *behaviour*; and if
fuch a one *fpits* but awry, he's gone; he's then like a
Crackt Tool, to be flung afide, and when he has done
what he was intended for; he becomes like a *Worn-
out-Tool*, fit only for the *Fire*, or to take a *Dance* with
CO L E M A N at *Tyburn*.

Tom. I am well fatisfied as to this *point*, and thank
you that you are fo *free* with me, for I fhould be much
troubled. if you fhould come behind *Cit* in any thing;
well, I think I am fitted now for your fervice, I pray
you get me fome place or other, and let me be a perpetual working-Tool.

Dick.

[17]

Dick. As moft of your *Capacity* are ; for our *Fools* are fuch incorrigible *Tools* they never *wear out:* therefore you need not be afraid of being laid a-fide.

Tom. But have you as much *Chriftian Liberty* as *Citt ?* And *Freedom* from all *Humane Laws*, and only fubject to the immediate *Commands* of God, and the Spirit, though againft the Written Laws, *Divine* and *Humane*, and the Commmands of *Kings* and *Gover-nours ?*

Dick. Yes fure, more than *Citt* has: For we have a better way by half, than to pore in the *Scriptures,* or to hearken to the Motions of the *Spirit*, which may be irregular; therefore we have our *Infallibility* at *Rome*, who, like the *Sun*, difperfes his Beams, that is, the *Priefts*,who carry his *Infallibility* all the World over: And fo inftead of waiting on the *Spirit*, that fometimes is fullen, and won't fpeak, we go but to the next *Prieft*,and he givesall the *Chriftian Liberty* that *Citt* fo much brags of. And having his *Prieftly* and *In-fallible Licence*, overthrowing the *Government* is no *Treafon*, taking up Arms againft the King no *Rebelli-on*, robbing the Reformed Bifhops, or the Heretical Prefbyterian Churches no *Sacrilege*, taking away *Ab-by* and *Church-Lands* fo long fetled on *Lay* men, by Authority of *Parliaments* no Oppreffion,taking away Eftates no *Robbery*, Imprifoning, Racking, Burning, and *Tormenting* perfons no *Tyranny*; and all this un-der the Name and Notion of Religion, no *Hypocra-fie* : forcing Oaths contrary to ones Confcience, *Per-jury* and *Blafphemy*, no *Impiety*; and the blowing up of the King, Houfe of Lords and Commons, Com-

C   paffing

[18]

paffing,and Contriving the Death of their Sovereign, or Stabbing and Shedding the Sacred Blood of Princes no *Murther*.

Tom. Very good, *live* and *learn* I fay; before you inform'd me, I thought *Citt* had been the moſt *Pub-lick Man* in the World; and had been beſt furniſhed with *Principles*, to Act and bring about his *De-figns* of any other; but I fee you are even with him, though he bragged he had more Villanies than the *Jefuites*.

Dick. I tell thee he is a very *Bragadocio* : For all' thoſe things he takes upon himſelf, and which perhaps ſome of them have made uſe of, he had from the *Jefuites School*. I tell thee man, they are in all *Shapes*, and *become all to all* to promote the *Caufe*.

Tom. But a word as to *Oaths* ; *Citt* fays, they are excellent at *Swearing*.

Dick. Nay then, if they furpafs us at *Swearing* or at *Forfwearing* either, I'le be *bak'd* : For look you, they fwore but once in a Year or two, and they were only bare *Oaths* ; now we fwear our people once a Week, and feal it with the *Sacrament* (a *Knack Citt* hath not) when ever we have a Defign on Foot; befides the *Chriſtian Liberty* that is granted ours, to to take all *Oaths* befides our own, and to reckon them none : For to fwear by a *Proteſtant Bible* is no more obliging than if one had fwore by the *Al-coran*.

Tom. I think now I am fully *inſtructed*, and fit for your *purpofe*.

Dick.

[19]

Dick. Stay, I heard you repeat a *Golden Sentence* of *Citts.* I will alſo furniſh you with one or two that you ought ſtill to have in *mind.*

Tom. O I love *Sentences, pithy ſhort Memorials,* and fit to be wrote down in my *Common-place* Book.

Dick. They are theſe, Firſt, Aſperſe boldly, ſome-thing will ſtick. To dye for *Treaſon* at *Tyborn,* is the ready way to be *Sainted* at *Rome.* To commit *Murther,* and to dye for it, is the beſt way to become a *Martyr.* To deny the Guilt of *Crimes,* at the laſt *Gaſp,* and to profeſs *Innocency,* is a Sign of *Grace* and *Jeſuitical Fortitude.* That the *Pope* exerciſes more Authority than *God,* who pardons not *Sinners* without *Repentance*; whilſt the *Pope* gives *Indulgence* for Sins to be committed for Mony for a 1000 years to come. To commit *Murder, Adultery, Theft, Drunkenneſs,* and the like, are great Sins, unleſs adviſed or conſented to, by the Prieſt; and for the *Good* of the *Cauſe.* To murther an *Heretick,* is no more Sin, than to kill a *Dog*: To ſtab an *Excommu-nicated Prince* or other *Magiſtrate,* is the beſt way to become a *Romiſh Heroe,* and to have *Elegies* wrote in his *Praiſe.* To have any *Trouble* or *Remorſe* of *Conſcience* before or after the *Commitment* of ſuch *ſanctified Murders,* is to fall from *Grace,* and to mer-rit *Pennance.*

Tom. Very Good, I ſee *Citt* has not all the *Golden Sentences,* theſe will I put down in my *Book.*

Dick. You muſt believe theſe as your *Creed,* have them by *Heart,* and as perfect as your *Pater-noſter* or *Ave-Maria.*

C 2   *Tom.*

[20]

Tom. But what *Employment* have you now ?

Dick. I am a *Knave* by *Profeſſion*, and therefore cannot want *Employment*, but the *chiefeſt* thing that I get *Money* now by, is *Scribling* all ſorts of *Pamphlets*, that may make for *Our Cauſe*; Damning the *Presbyterians* to the *loweſt* Pit of *Hell*, *Lampooning* and *Dialoguing*, and *Lettering* the *Plot* into *Ridicule*.

Tom. But are you *well paid* for it ?

Dick. Better paid than you think for, and I have a Bag by me, to pay you too, if you go about your *Buſineſs* handſomly. We have already almoſt brought it about, to make the *People* believe, there is no *Plot:* Be ſure you be *diligent* in promoting that *Belief*, and *beſpatter* the *Evidence* all you can: call them *Rogues*, *Vagabonds*, *Debauch'd* Fellows, *Perjur'd*, *Lying*, *Inventive Knaves* and *Raſcals*. Fellows kept out of *Charity*, and releaſed from Goals; any thing that may beget an *Odium* of *Them*, and the *Common Enemy*.

Tom. But whom mean you, by the *Common Enemy* ?

Dick. You are a B*lind Fool*, if thou ſee'ſt not that; why all that oppoſe ſetting up of P*opery*, whether *Church of England*-men, *Presbyterians*, and the reſt of the *Heretical Fry*, by what *Titles* or *Denominations* ſoever; for they are all *Hereticks*, and alike to us.

Tom.

[21]

Tom. Then 'tis not only the *Presbyterian Proteftants* that you *aim* to overthrow.

Dick. No, No, though we pretend *That,* yet we *aim* alfo at *Root* and *Branch.*

Tom. What is that?

Dick. A thorow *Reformation* of the *Whole.* A fetting up the *Mafs* in its *Splendor,* and the retrieving all our *Church Lands,* as fully and wholly as they were before that *Fat-Gut Harry* the *8th.* took them from us. Come I tell thee, we hope *once more* to Reign, and to *pufh* on the *Plot,* in fpite of thofe pittiful *Rogues, Oates, Bedloe, Dangerfield,* and the reft of them.

Tom. Bravely refolved. I think now, I am pretty well *inftructed* in the *Methods,* and *Fundamentals* of the *Holy Caufe.*

Dick. I have yet fome *neceffary Hints* to *qualifie* you the better for our *Defign.* Firft, as to your *Behaviour,* you are to *transform* your felf into *all Shapes;* but you may for the prefent appear, *Huffing, Ranting,* and *Hectoring* in the *Coffee-Houfes,* and rail extreamly at *Oates* and *Bedloe;* *laugh* aloud at the *Plot,* and do all you can, to make it be unbelieved. Sometimes put it upon the *Presbyterians,* and *Commonwealths-men,* and rather than fail, on the *Earl* of *Danby,* or any Body *elfe,* but our *felves:* you muft feem a very *Hector,* and make a *fneaking Citt* afraid of you.

Tom. Very good, I *underftand* you.

Dick.

[22]

Dick. Then you muſt get the *Art of Memory*, mark me, the *Art of Memory*, to call to *Mind*, *Relate*, *Print* and often *talk of* (notwithſtanding the *Acts of Obli-vion*) all the *Evils* of our late *Rebellion*, the *Murther* of his Sacred Majeſty *Charles* the Firſt; the *Baniſhment* of our *King*, the *Suppreſſion* of the *Cavaliers*, the *De-cimation* and *Confiſcation* of the *Eſtates* of the *Royal Party*. You muſt *renew* all theſe things again daily, and *paint* them as *ugly*, and in the *worſt Shapes* you can. Here will be work for *Tropes*, *Figures*, and *Metaphors*. You muſt rake in old *Soars*, and *ſtink-ing Dunghills*, to make the *Stench* come freſh into the Noſtrils of the *Royal Party*, to *Incenſe* them anew, and to cauſe *Fears* and *Jealouſies* both in the *King*, and in thoſe who are *zealous* for him againſt *this Par-ty*; and though all that *Wickedneſs*, was acted by a *few*, the *baſe* and *diſowned Company* of *Olivarians*, yet put it upon the whole *Presbyterian Party*, and men-tion not for your Ears, any *Service* they ſince did to his *Majeſty*. And though the *King* has *forgiven*, and paſt *Acts* of *Grace* and *Oblivion*, and *command-ed* that all ſhould be *forgot*; yet I ſay, you muſt now *revive all*, and put it upon the *Citts*.

Tom. Ay, theſe *Citts* are *terrible* Fellows, they have *Pike* and *Gun* too, and they are *able* they ſay to do *Service*, if need be, if *Monſieur* ſhould come to aid us.

Dick. 'Tis true, if it were not for theſe *Cits*, we ſhould do our *Buſineſs*, for all the *Bumpkins*; but they are much *agreed*: yet if we could but find ſome *Trick* to wreſt *Musket* and *Pike* out of their *Hands*, we ſhould do the Feat *eaſily*.

Tom.

[23]

Tom. You say well, we might then *fire Houses,* and *cut Throats* at our Pleasure: pick and choose as we please, the *Fat* from the *Lean.* But I doubt *we* are *too weak,* our *Party* is *too few.*

Dick. Not so *few* as you think for neither; indeed the *bare-fac'd* Papists, are not so very *numerous,* but we have an *Army* in *Masquerade.*

Tom. Who are they?

Dick. Church Papists, and a many both *Lay* and *Clergical,* that do not much care which *End* goes formost. Some are down right *Papists* in their Hearts, others are but *Popishly inclined,* but *lean* so much, that the left *Push* of *Advantage* flings them to *Mass;* and others are so *absolutely Regardless,* so they may get either Money or Promotion, that they *care* not much, which sort of *Bishops* sets in the *Chair.* And let me tell you, we have of all these, that will never *dye Martyrs* for *Protestantism* no small *Company,* that when once the *Scale* begins to *turn,* will bring it *down* on our side *amain.*

Tom. I am glad to hear on't. But I understand by *Citt,* that all the *Sectaries* are *unanimous,* nay, and seem to *close* now, with all the moderate *Church of England*-men in the main Points, for a joynt Opposition of Popery.

Dick. And that I must ingenuously *confess* to thee, is no *small Trouble* to us, and I have *wondred* at it, and *scratch'd my Head* for *Vexation.*

Tom.

[24]

Tom. 'Tis their *common Intereſt* ſure enough to be ſo, you know *Intereſt won't lye.* They ſee the *Deluge* coming, and if they go into *Parties*, and ſtand not *cloſely* and *roundly* together now, they will be *overborne.*

Dick. It muſt be therefore our *Maſter-piece* to *break* 'um : That is an other Advice I am to give you : make 'um *jealous* one of another if you can ; and ſay, why if the *Papiſts* are overthrown, and rooted out of the *Land*, you *Presbyterians* will be never the near, the *Church of England* will ſtill *Reign* and *Tyranize* over you, ſo that you had as good have the *Popiſh Rocket*, as the *Reformed Lawn-Sleeves*. Then to the *Church of England*-men, you muſt ſay, If you *root* out all the *Papiſts* out of the *Land*, the *Presbyterians* will be too hard for you, and turn you a *grazing* again. The *Papiſts* are inconſiderable, and ſerve but to *Ballance* the *Scales*, and to make the *Sectaries* a little afraid of their *Party*, therefore be *wiſe* and not *ſevere* againſt them.

Tom. This is as good as the *Citts Canting*, I like it well, 'tis *politickly* ſaid by my Troth. But another thing, the *Citts* are very *credulous*, and believe their *Printed Domeſticks* more than their *Creed*, though the things are never ſo improbable.

Dick. That's but one Doctors Opinion, however, we love our Domeſticks too, and ſwarms of other *Pamphlets*, that have *private Marks*, which are *credited* by our *Party*, though the thing be *impoſſible.* And we have *Legends* of *Lying Miracles*, which ſurpaſs the *Domeſticks* many a *League*, yet are no more *doubted*, than that 'tis *Day* when the *Sun ſhines*. Beſides, our *Arts of inſinuating*, what ever a *Prieſt ſays*,

is

[25]

is believ'd by the *Vulgar* of our fide, *ipfo facto*. Nay, they are *bound* to *believe* it, and that the *Citts* are not their *Domefticks*.

Tom. Then I *fancy*, many of thefe *Idle Reports*, are *cunningly* fpread by our *Party*, and put upon the *Citts*.

Dick. 'Troth fo they are, more than you are aware of; we are *excellent* at *fpreading falfe News*, and *raifing Slanders*, 'tis one of our *Mafter-pieces*.

Tom. O Heaven's ! I *thought* moft of thofe had been *Citts Inventions*.

Dick. There's our *Skill*, firft to *raife them*, and then to put it upon the *Citts*; for it feems very *unlikely*, that they fhould *come* from us, becaufe we feem by many of them to *bewray* our own *Neft*. But 'tis no matter for that, if we *befhit* it ten *times* over, we'l make the *Citts clean* it.

Tom. But one *Virtue Bumpkin excells* you in, and that is *Ignorance*, for he thought the *Ten Commandments* were made by *Henry the Eighth*, and call'd them the *Ten Tables*.

Dick. Don't let that *trouble* you at all, for it is a *Maxim* among us, *Ignorance is the Mother of Devotion*; and therefore we make it our *Work*, to keep the *Vulgar* in *Ignorance*, and let them neither read *Bible*, or any other *Book* that may adminifter to 'um the leaft ray of *Light* or *Knowledg* ; fo that many of our people never fo much as heard of *Mofes*, and fcarce any of them ever faw or heard the Ten *Com-*

D   *mand-*

[26]

mandements : For we have ſtifled one of them, and when any of the reſt is broken , can preſently ſodder it up again with a Confeſſion. And as for God Almighty, they take him to be as they have ſeen him *pictur'd*, an Old Man ſomewhat like the *Pope*, ſitting in a *Chair*, with a Rabble of Hee and Shee *Saints* kneeling before him. Therefore let not *Bumpkin* think he has got the ſtart of us in that Vertue.

Tom. You have much rectified my *Underſtanding* : But one thing more before we part. What if there ſhould be an *Hell* now, and I ſhould go thither at *laſt* for all my pains ? This Queſtion *Bumpkin* asked *Citt.*

Dick. And how did *Citt* anſwer it?

Tom. By a pretty *Simily* of the Seven *Deadly Sins*, and Seven *Vials* ; but the *Application* was, that Men were ſeen ſtill to thrive by all theſe *Evil Ways*, and that they were not *poyſon*, as ſome would make them believe, but as ſweet and wholeſome as *Muskadine*, and none ſeemed the worſe for them ; therefore there was no danger in committing thoſe Seven *deadly Sins*, or drinking out of the Seven *Vials*.

Dick. 'Twas well ſaid , and the *Application* will hold good alſo on our ſide ; but we have a trick that *Citt* has not, to cheat the *Devil.*

Tom. I pray what's that ? I ſhall ſay then you are *cunning* indeed.

Dick. Why ? We have a *Purgatory* to go to, when we die acting and rolling in the Seven *deadly Sins* ;
and

[37]

and if they are so profitable as *Citt* says they are, we may then be able to leave a little Money behind us for a *Welch Priest* (or any other *Priest* will do it as well) who by the muttering of a few *Masses*, relea-ses a *Soul* out of *Purgatory*, and sends him immediate-ly to *Paradise*. I think then the *Devil* is cheated for all his Baits of Seven *deadly Sins*,

Tom. Indeed, indeed we have here the advantage of *Citt*, and as I take it, *Encouragement* enough to drink stoutly of *Citt's* Seven *Vials* of *Deadly Sins*.

But what think you of the *Appeal*? *Citt* braggs he knows who wrote it,

Dick. 'Tis no matter whoever wrote it, he was one of my *profession*; and I'le tell you his name too under the Rose,

Tom. Prethee do, for I long to know.

Dick. It was one Mr. *Turbulent*, let him be *Citt* or otherwise; but more of such I say, we fare the bet-ter for them: I know one got Fifty pound by that Job.

Tom. But what if *Truman* should come now, and having overheard our *Discourse*, fall into *Dispute* with us?

Dick. Ne'r fear; he rarely *intermixes* in our Com-pany: but if he should, I know how to handle *Citt's* Arguments, and they would damnably puzzle him.

D 2   *Tom.*

[28]

Tom Heblew all away with a puff, and fell **Tooth**
and Nail to vindicate one *L'Eſtrange*, prethee.

Dick. Who's he? Do'ſt know him? Know him,
Ay almoſt as well as Madam *B*. he's a Wit, a plaguy
Fellow at the Gooſ-quil, a very *Lucian* at Dia-
logues.

Tom. Well, but is he a Friend?

Dick. Hold thy prating, what a rude Fool art thou
to queſtion a *Gentlemans Religion*; he that is not a-
gainſt us, is with us, and I never heard he ever wrote
againſt Catholicks, (except it were a *Proteſtant Catholick*, and that, he ſays, is a *Soleciſm*) but he has pepper'd the *Presbyterians*. A Proteſtant he ſays is a *Lutheran*, and *Catholick* the *Charaċteriſtical* Note of a
Chriſtian; and it ſeems he would have the Church of
England ſtick up her Briſtles, and diſown all *Fellow-
ſhip* with Proteſtants abroad, and knock out all *Non-
conformiſts* Brains at home, as the only way to prevent *Popery*. And in particular he has ſerenaded
Dr. *Oats* of late moſt notably; and careſs'd him juſt as
Joab did *Abner*, and would father that Baſtardly
projeċt on him, with ſeveral other happy Jobbs. Ah
Jack! thou canſt not Fadome the Talents and neceſ-
ſary Abilities of this mighty Bully of the Juck-pot.
Let him go on and proſper, receive the Applauſes of
Man's *Coffe-Houſe*, and the Acclamations of St. *Ome-
rian* Companions; but let thee and I go on with our
Chat.

Tom. But ſtill I am afraid of ſome *Eveſ-dropping
True-man*: For we live in a damnable Informing
Age.

Enter

[29]

Enter Goodman.

Goodm. Tho' *Truman* be not here, I am one that
has as honeſt an Heart, perhaps, and deſires to
ſpeak a word or two with you : For I have overheard all the *Rogueries*.

Tom. Why, who are you? We know you not.

Goodm. My Name is *Goodman,* and I aſſure you
I am no Knave, and have not over much of the
Fool in me neither. I am no *Papiſt,* either *bare-
fac'd* or *Vizard-maſqu'd*; I am no *Citt* or *Factious
Bumpkin*; no *Republican,* nor yet *Fanatick*; but
ſince you ask the Queſtion, I ſhall tell you, that
I am a true Lover of my King and Countrey, and
one that perfectly hates all your *Wicked Villanies,*
that both you two, and *Citt* and *Bumpkin* diſcour-
ſed of. It is ſuch as you that endeavour to ſet true
Engliſh-men by the Ears: You are the Envenomed
Ferment of the *Nation,* that will neverleave working,
till you have put it into a *Malignant Fever*: You are
a *plague* that infects the Blood, and Humours of this
political Body : You are *Dogs* that have lick'd up
the *Old Vomits,* and are now ſpewing all up again:
You are the very *Gaderine Swine* the Devils entred
into, and are ſent from the *Bottomleſs pit,* to roule
your ſelves in all the *Filthy ſinks* and *Standing-
puddles* of the Nation, to raiſe up a *Stench* enough
to bring a new Plague of *War* upon Three Kingdoms.

Tom. This is a very wrathful Fellow.

Dick.

[30]

Dick. Come Sir, we care not a Fart for you, nor your *Similies* neither; whatever you are, or whatever you make *us to be*, wee'l go on in our Business.

Goodm. You will so? I question it not; for ye are the *Catterpillars* of the *Nation*, the *Locusts* that would *devour every thing:* but yet, notwithstanding both *yours* and *Citts Politicks*, there will come an *East Wind* call'd *Gods Providence*, that will *sweep* the *Nation clean*, from such *Vermine.*

Dick. In the *mean time*, dare you *dispute* with me about *Government?* and I'le hold *Citts* Arguments against you.

Goodm. This is no *Place* for *Disputes*, and I desire not to *meddle* with *Governours*, nor *Governments.* I have already told you what *I am*, and by that you might believe, I am no *Medler*, nor *troubled* with the *Itch* of *disputing.*

Tom. What makes you meddle with us then, could not you let us alone?

Goodm. Because I am a *Good-man* in a *Moral Sense*, and cannot hear such *wicked*, *leud*, and *abominable Discourses* as have past between you, without a *Reproof* for your *Villanies.* Therefore think of it, both of you, and be *ashamed*; (if you are not quite past all *Shame* and *Grace*) and do not thus study worse than *Magical Arts* to *embroyl a Nation*, to cause *Fear* and *Jealousies* in the *People*, *Anger* and *Suspicion* in the *King*, and *Magistrates*

to

[31]

to break the *Bleſſed Unity* of the *King* and his People, to talk of *Government* and *Priviledges* after your Rate, to *invent Lyes* and *forge falſe Reports*, and in fine, to bring all into a *Flame* and *Combuſtion*.

Dick. Then you dare not *Diſpute* with us?

Tom. No, No, he's *affraid* you'l be too *hard* for him.

Goodm. What is your *Argument*?

Dick. Firſt, That 'tis better to *obey God* than Man.

Goodm. I ſay ſo too, 'tis *literally* true, and if it were not abſurd, to name the *Scriptures* to ſuch as *ſcoff* at them, I might tell you that *God* has ſaid it in them; Though you would from this, draw a falſe Inference, and ſet up an *Infallible Spirit*, like the *Quakers Light* within you, and that ſhould be accounted the *Commands* of *God*, which ſhould be *dictated* by this *Spirit*, though contrary to *thoſe* he has already laid down in his *Written Word*, for a *Rule* of our *Faith* and *Life*. But, Sir, this I am ſure is not your *true* Belief, though it be *Citts Argument*, and you look on it as a *two Edg'd Sword*, that *cuts* every way ; for let me tell you, that you hold it *better*, and more *lawful*, to obey *Man* than *God*, or your *Earthly* God (as ſome of you call him) than the *heavenly* God. Don't you hold the Pope *Infallible*, and that he cannot Err ? and therefore, what ever he *commands*, though it be againſt the very *Letter* of the *Sriptures*, tho'

[32]

tho' againſt the *Ten Commandements*, tho' againſt the Expreſs Commands of Chriſt, and the *Doctrine* of the Apoſtles, and the Fathers of the Church of Chriſt, for ſeveral *Centuries* immediately following: Nay, though againſt *Nature*, *Reaſon*, and *Senſe* it ſelf, you do, (and are ſo bound to) both Believe and Act : And therefore I think you may let *Citts* Argument alone, and hold your own.

Tom. Why, this is ſhamming, he runs from the point. ----- To him with another of *Citts* Arguments.

Dick. Well, what ſay you to the *Sovereign Power* being in the people ?

Goodm. I ſay to you I am no *Commonwealths-man*, and I know there was a King, and Sovereign power before there was a people. Thoſe are not Arguments for either you or me to meddle with : We are happy in our *Monarch* who cannot wrong us ; But ſuch as you, by your Evil Councels and bad *Deſigns* may, when you try by all evil ways to turn the *Soevereignty* to *Tyranny*, and the *Imperial Crown* to a *Deſpotical*, which will never be: For the King loves his *People* too well to deſire it ; and as long as he has the Love and Hearts of his People (which only ſuch as you ſtrive to rob him of) he is a moſt abſolute *Prince*, and may command both their *Lives* and their *Fortunes* without Force or Compulſion. We may cry out, *O Fortunate Engliſh-men*, *if truly ſenſible of their own Happineſs.*

Dick.

[33]

Dick. But is not the King one of the Three
Eſtates ?

Goodm. Yes, ſure he is, or elſe there were not
Three Eſtates ; but he is as the Head of the Body, and if the Hands ſhould not adminiſter Food
to the Head, I am of the Opinion, that the Body
would ſoon become a *Skeliton.* I ſay again, of
all the Nations of the World, we are the moſt
happy in the *Conſtitution* of our *Government* ;
where the King and his People are ſo united
and incorporated, as the Head and Body of a Living Creature, that one cannot do Injury to the
other, without making both ſuffer, and endan-
gering the ruine of the whole. And therefore
they ill adviſe, to break the Ancient Conſtituti-
ons, Cuſtoms, Priviledges, and known Rights
and Liberties of the people ; and they as wicked-
ly endeavour, who would any way go about
Sacrilegiouſly to rob the King of the leaſt Ray
of *Prerogative,* which is the *Halus* or *Glory* that
ſurrounds the *Head* of *Majeſty.*

Tom. Methinks the Gentleman ſpeaks Reaſon.

Goodm. As on the one ſide, no Laws can be im-
poſed on us, but by the Conſent of the people
in their Repreſentatives, and the Nobility and
Clergy in theirs : So on the other ſide, none can
be made, that ſhall prejudice the Sovereignty, or
infringe the King's Prerogative, without his Conſent and Sanction ; which Kings are wiſe enough,
not to grant in prejudice to themſelves, as the
People likewiſe are careful not to frame any to
E   their

[34]

their own *Hurt*: fo that we certainly have a moft happy *Conftitution* of *Government*, and a better cannot be *defired*, when the *King* cannot do *Injury* to his People, nor they any ways hurt him, without *Rebellion* on the one fide, and *Tyranny* on the other.

Tom. But is not a *Commonwealth*, a better Government?

Goodm. We are a *Commonwealth*, though not in your *Senfe*; and it is my *Opinion*, that no *better Government* can be found in the *Effence* or *Being*, than what we have; though as to the *outward Branches*, they may be better prun'd perhaps, and we fee them in *every Age*, rectified by new and wholefome Laws; for fome, like decayed Limbs, become *obfolete* and without *Life*, fuch are cut off, and new *fpring* up in their *Places*, with new *Sap* and *Vigour*. I judge it much againft the *Humour* and *Conftitution* of this People, to become fuch a *Commonwealth* as you mean; for it will not be poffible, but that in a little *Time*, he that can get *Power* will be our *Tyrant*, as we faw by Example in the late *Tryal* was made thereof. And therefore you *wicked Emiffaries*, leave off creating thefe *Jealoufies* and *Fears* of a *Commonwealth*; for the only way that I know to make one, is that which you now take, to bring us out of *Love* with *Monarchy*, fo into *Rebellion*, *Confufion* and *Anarchy*, and to raife up the like *Combuftion* this *Land* too lately felt; which I pray *God* of his *Mercy* avert, and fo I'le leave you.

Tom.

[35]

Tom. This is a peſtilent Fellow.

Dick. Ay, Ay, Let him prate: don't you be afraid of his *Eaſt-Wind* of *Providence*: go about your *Buſineſs*, and obſerve my *Rules* and *Maxims*. Let Good men talk as long as they will; *Words* are but *Wind*, but if the *Turn comes*, we two ſhall be *Rich* : And ſo Farewel.

FINIS.

At Amsterdamnable-Coffee-House On the 5th of November next, will be Exposed to publick Sale these Goods following, in several parcels ([London], n.p., [1682]), 2pp. BL: 8138.h.1.(113). ESTCR9812. Hünersdorff.

A two-page Tory folio pamphlet satire in the form of a mock auction cata-logue. Printed catalogues advertising goods for sale were commonly distrib-uted in advance of the sale during the Restoration period. Coffee-houses had served as locations for auctions from the early 1660s, and by the late 1670s some had developed dedicated rooms for auction sales. Political parodies of the auc-tion catalogue form emerged in 1679: in the Sloane Manuscripts in the British Library there is a manuscript satire attacking the Court party entitled 'A Paper of Sale left by Mr Karr. On Thursday May 29th is to be sold at a publicke sale by an intch of Candle at ye Royall Coffy house, neer Charing Cross' (BL Sloane MSS 647, fol. 122r–v). The satire presents 35 lots supposedly revealing uncom-plimentary intelligence of bastards, mistresses and the sale of places and seats in parliament, mapping the private immorality of the court onto the public corrup-tion of the ministry. Scribal satires remained unprinted to evade prosecution for libel, but still enjoyed considerable influence through circulation in manuscript (see Harold Love, *Scribal Publication in Seventeenth-Century England* (Oxford, Clarendon Press, 1993)). Uncensored manuscript news-letters and satires were widely disseminated through coffee-houses. For example on 26 June 1680, Roger L'Estrange took a deposition from an informant named Thomas Adamson con-cerning a letter found on his person, 'he says he found it yesterday under a table at the Amsterdam coffee-house, and put it in his pocket, but that he never read it' (*CSPD 1679–1680*, p. 528).

Scandalous satires or libels such as *At Amsterdamnable-Coffee-House* were proscribed, and prosecutions were brought against authors and publishers when they could be identified. In the fevered political atmosphere of the Popish Plot and Exclusion Crisis, satire was an important weapon in defining faction. Two coffee-houses in particular stood as emblems for each side: the Amsterdam and Sam's. The Amsterdam was associated with the Country party or Whigs, the faction associated with the two great opposition lords, Shaftesbury and Buckingham.

The *Amsterdamnable-Coffee-House* satire attacks the political probity and motives of the leaders of the Whig party, suggesting that their actions are motivated by hypocrisy, venality and covert republicanism. The satire can be dated by internal evidence to 1682 (specifically the period between 28 September to 5 November, see note to p. 199, ll. 10–11). This tract also circulated in manuscript before it was printed. In the Sloane Manuscripts in the British Library (BL Sloane MSS 1009, fols 142r–143v) a scribal copy of the satire can be found among the collection of the Huguenot scientist Gedeon Bonnivert. The manuscript version is a sheet folded to make four folio pages, written in neat secretary hand, and entitled 'A New Bill of Sale, at Peter's Coffee-house in Covent garden On the 20th instant October will be exposed to Publick Sale by Inch of Candle These Goods following in severall Parcells'. It describes thirty lots: nine are not included in the printed version, and lots 22 and 23 in the printed version are new. Moreover many of the abbreviated names give more detail, allowing satirical subjects to be identified. Numerous copies of the printed edition survive.

AT

Amsterdamnable-
COFFEE-HOUSE

On the 5th. of *November* next, will be Exposed
to pulick Sale these *Goods* following, in several parcels.

Lot. 1. **T**Hree large Volumes of the D. of *Ms*. Politiques, valued at three Crowns to advance 3d. each bidding.

2. Two Bundles of the faid D. Behaviour, Loyalty and Obedience, in 5 parcels, of small value to advance nothing.

3. One *Hobbs Leviathan* with large additions, much studied by the late E of S. in his Retirements, Teaching the reasonableness of Seperation, and laying the foundation of Government in the people, valued above all the Fathers, to advance Atheists and Republicans.

4. Several Noblemens cast Suits Fac'd with Loyalty, and Lined with Honesty, not much the worse for the wearing, which because they are not in fashion will be sold at half the value to advance 6 d. each bidding.

5. Two span new Maidenheads sold by their own mother, for 100 Guinneys, now valued at half the value to advance 2 s. 6 d. each bidding.

6. One large invisible Ring of Sir *Tho. Armstrongs* Engraven with Crownes and Scepters, with a large Chain of the Mobile to lead a fooll by the Nose, valued at a Kingdome, as they shall find occasion.

7. Six brace of Winding Hornes that were sent from the K. of *Poland* to his Principal Secretaryes of State, *M. Gray, Russel*, and to raise the Beagles of the old game, valued at a Generals pay to advance 2000 dogs a piece.

8. Two large Waggons of the fame to be distributed among *Armstrong* and the rest of the inferiour Mungrels to raise the blood scented Rabble, to advance a Rebbel each bidding.

9. Six Whiggs Sheriff Chains with as many Aldermens of the fame value to advance the fame rate.

10. Two Cabinets of rich Jewels, Beads and Necklaces taken by Sir W. W. for Popish Reliques Valued at two thousand pound, to advance the spawn of the Old Rump.

11. The Noble Peers Speech, the Appeal, the Raree show, with a large bundle of Seditious Libels, by C. C. and the rest of the true Protestant-Pamphleteers not worth the hanging, to advance the Pillory.

12. Three Loyal Votes pipeing hot from the house of Commons, One to exclude the lawful Heir, and set up a Lawles one, 2. To make the King great by giving him

no money, The third for Establishing the Church and Monarchy, by fetting up Presbyttery, valued at the publick good, to advance the Good Old Cause.

13. Two narrative Sham-plots of *Tapskies* own invention, as true as Gospel, valued at a Polish Crown, to advance the Salamanca Dr.

14. Twic as many Presbyterian Plots, proved as clear as the Sun, valued at nothing to advance proportionably.

15. 6 Brace of Irish Mastiff Evidences in Pension to carry on the Presbyterian Plott against the Papists.

16. Ten thousand spick and span new Protestant Flails, besides Swan Quills, Goose Quills and Crow Quills to settle the Protestant Religion, by knocking Monarchy on the Head valued at the Authors necks, to advance the Protestant Joyners.

17. Two models of the Association, from the Cabal, under the pretence of Running Races, to raise the Countrey in Arms, valued at half a Crown to advance a Coxcomb.

18. Two Ells of the Association, valued above six Ells of the Covenant, to advance a new Common Wealth.

19. Two Sucking Bottles for the Babes of Grace, taken from the Tap head of Reformation, by turning the Church into a Conventicle, to advance the Protestant Religion.

20. An Epidemical Elixir in three Doses, Protestant Religion, Liberty, and Property, as an infallible Antidote against Popery and Arbitrary Power, fresh from the same Tap, valued at the price of a Scaffold to advance a Traytors head.

21. Six pots of round and sound Protestants of the Church of *England*, among whom are *Be.* Dr. *B.* Author of *Julian* the Apostate, the Ignoramus Dr. all valued at so many Halters to advance thirteen pence half penny.

22. A new Experiment teaching how to avoid the stroakes of Justice, by cutting ones own throat, valued at the Authors life.

23. A Magazeen of *Blunderbusses*, *Musquets*, *Pistols*, and designed by a Crow of damned *Rebels*, to make a sacrifice of Royal Blood, valued at the purchase of a Sledge to advance them to *Tyburne*, to be drawn, hang'd and quartered 𝔊𝔬𝔬𝔡𝔢𝔫𝔬𝔲𝔤𝔥 for such Hellish Traytors.

ADVERTISEMENT.

At the same place you may be furnished with a Treatise called, *The true Protestant Ttranslator*, teaching how to translate *Rome* to *Geneva*, Jesuits into Phanatiques, Pharisees into Dissenters, Monarchy into Parity, Order into Confusion, Unity into Schisme, Gospel into Sedition, Light into Darkness, Truth into falshood, Subjects into Soveraigns, Churches into Stables, Pallaces into Sayles, and Kings from a temporal Crown to an eternal: Published by a late Assembly of Pharisaical, Hipocritical and seditious Whiggs and Covenanters.

FINIS.

J. C. B. [Aphra Behn?], *Rebellions antidote: or A Dialogue between coffee and tea* (London, printed by George Croom, at the sign of the Blue-Ball in Thames-street, over against Baynard's-Castle, 1685), 1/2°. BL: C.20.f.2(378). ESTCR35140. Hünersdorff.

A broadsheet verse satire of 73 lines, mostly in heroic couplets, but including a concluding acrostic on coffee. The verses offer a Tory commentary on the succession in 1685, calling for national unity in the new reign. Despite the predictions of some Whig controvertialists, the accession of James II passed without protest. A contemporary witness remarked 'Everything is very happy here. Never king was proclaimed with more applause than he that raignes under the name of James the Second' (Earl of Peterbrough, quoted in W. A. Speck, *Reluctant Revolutionaries: Englishmen and the revolution of 1688* (Oxford, Clarendon Press, 1988), p. 42). The peace was disturbed by the rebellion of the Duke of Monmouth in June and early July. The dialogue of this text chimes with the Tory viewpoint that this was a time for moderation and unity.

The dialogue between coffee and tea in *Rebellions antidote* offers a political allegory, albeit of some obscurity. The commodities themselves speak in their own defence (a common poetical device of the period, as seen in numerous equestrian statue poems), and each is made to represent a kind of political sociability or faction. Tea – the 'dear sister' of coffee – was comparatively expensive in London, and as such was associated with a high status clientele, with women, and with domestic consumption. Coffee retained its associations with the culture of news, debate and controversy in the coffee-house – in effect, with Whig dissent. In the dialogue, the poem proposes a moderate course of action, repudiating both the Caroline practice of immoderate toasting in ale and wine, and the 'rage and madness' described by coffee. The emblem of this political moderation is twist, a drink composed of a medley of drinks, especially tea and coffee.

A number of controvertialist works made use of the trope of 'the antidote' in the 1680s, using the term to mean a reply to an incendiary pamphlet designed not only to answer particular points, but also stifle further debate on the topic.

The poem is signed '*J, C, B.* A.B.', and Janet Todd and Virginia Crompton ('Rebellions Antidote: a new attribution to Aphra Behn', *Notes and Queries*, n.s. 38 (June 1991), pp. 175–7) argue that the dialogue is co-authored by Aphra Behn (A.B.) and an unknown male writer (J.C.B.), either Jeffrey Boys or John Bowman. Todd includes the poem in *The Works of Aphra Behn* (7 vols (London, Pickering & Chatto, 1990), vol. I, No. 54, pp. 163–5). There is no other evidence internal or otherwise suggesting that the poem is the work of two writers, and the signature '*J, C, B.* A.B.' could equally suggest that the writer J.C.B. has a bachelor of arts degree. The printer George Croom kept shop at the Blue Ball in Thames Street, near Addle Hill by Baynards Castle. John Dunton said that 'Some would insinuate as though he favoured the Jacobites, but I take him for a man of more sense' (*Life and Errors of John Dunton* (1705), ed. by J. Nichols (London, J. Nichols, Son, and Bentley, 1818), p. 252). During the early 1680s, however, in the period of the Exclusion Crisis and Monmouth's Rebellion of 1685, he printed a great many works defending Tory causes, including the Jacobite succession. In 1685 he also printed many loyalist verses and elegies.

Rebellions Antidote:
OR A
DIALOGUE

Between *COFFEE* and *TEA*.

Tea. **A**LL hail kind Friend fweet Balfom of our Age,
What mean'ft thou by fuch tragick Equipage?
Coff. Welcome dear Sifter, Bafis of my Life,
Better than Goodnefs, dearer than a Wife;
Forbear inquiring, left thou force to rife
Tears to a Deluge from my doleful Eyes,
Such are my Plaints, and fuch my cruel Fate
Tongue can't exprefs their too to Ridged State.

Tea. A Curfe all Curfes elfe below
On thofe who do produce thy Woe;
Death, Helland Vengeance on him fall
Who makes thy Fate fo Tragical.

Coffee. Merit on Merit, loe now I fee
A Life throu mayeft command of me,
Command thy Pleafure, I'll not Decline,
Thy Goodnefs has oblieg'd me thine;
And fince as *Dido* thou command'ft my Grief,
I'll with *Æneas* fum up all in Brief.

Tea. All that I beg is but the Reafon
What makes thy Vifage out of Seafon.

Coffee. The Rage and Madnefs of the Nation
Moves both my Heart and eke Compaffion,
Unto that height I cannot Force
My Horrour to a mean Divorce;
Since all the World does now rely
On Madnefs and Debauchery,
Lewd and Diftract to fuch a Strain
As if invoking back again.
Grim Chaos of accurft Confufion,
The product of our grand Delufion.

Tea. Truth without Error needs no Oath,
All thou haft faid is Naked Truth;
Thus far th'art gone, but prethy tell,
What 'tis occafions Death and *Hell?*
Whence fprings our Dolour, what's the fourfe
That Operates this Hellifh Curfe.

Coffee. 'Tis *Wine* and *Ale* and eke the *Grape*
Has fpawn'd this fpurious beftial Rape;
What is't but thofe produce, what horrid Fact
But *Wine* and *Ale* and *Beer* will act;
Death *Hell* and Judgment Hand in Hand
With them and theirs do always ftand;

Rapes, Murders, Thefts, and thoufand Crimes
Are gender'd by foul *Ale* and *Wines*;
Thefe are but Trifles to the Woe
That *Wine* and *Ale*, and *Beer* can do;
From whence unlefs from thefe do daily fpring
Rebellion, Treafon, and Sham-ploting Sin;
Thefe Storm the Fort and let the Devil in.
Judge you th' Effect where *Satan* Rules as Chief,
'Tis then too late to cry ftop Thief, ftop Thief.

Tea. In thefe Extreams there's but one way I find,
My Life for yours and that will Undermine
The *Devil* himfelf, and give you all a Laughter,
T' expell his Vengeance by an holy Water,
Allay the Billows of the flowing Rout,
One Difh of *Twift* will force the *Devil* out.   (Portic

Coffee. Tho' haft hit the Pin, and *Twift*'s the Sovereign
To turn the Tide, reverfe the *Alewives* Oacen,
Difgorge, God, *Bacchus*, and prepare a Stage
Once more to entertain a Golden Age.

Tea. Thanks noble Sir for this Relation
In order to Retaliation,
I'll force my Mufe to fuch an height
I'll thy deferv'd *Acroftick* Write.

C ome frantick Fools leave off your Drunke:. fits,
O bfequiens be and i'll recall your Wits,
F rom perfect Madnefs to a modeft Strain,
F or Farthings four I'll fetch you back again.
E nable all your mene with tricks of State,
E nter and Sip and then attend your Fate;

Come Drunk or Sober for a gentle Fee,
Come ne'r fo Mad i'll your Phyfician be.

F, C, B.   *A B.*

This may be Printed, *R. L. S.* 1685

LONDON,
Printed by *George Croom*, at the Sign of the *Blue Ball
Thames-ftreet*, over againft *Barnard's Caftle* 1685.

The School of Politicks: or, The Humours of a Coffee-House. A Poem. Licensed, Apr. 15. 1690 (London, R. Baldwin, 1690), [4], 24pp.; 4°. BL: 11626.e.52. ESTCR4030.

An extended Hudibrastic satirical poem on the variety of coffee-house discussion, comprising approximately 564 lines in 16 stanzas. The poem describes these stanzas as odes, recalling the method of the Anacreontic ode. Named after Anacreon of Teos (6th century BC), the *Anacreontea* comprise 60 short, lyrical poems on wine, love and song. *The School of Politicks* is clearly one poem, however, and the influence of the Anacreontics perhaps does not extend beyond the felicity of the theme. In the poem, the speaker, having time on his hands, visits a coffee-house by himself, and after describing the general buzz of conversation there, moves around the room to overhear the discussion at each table. Using the conceit of the invisible spectator, the poem is able to satirically describe both the variety of topics in coffee-house conversation, but also something of the diverse sociabilities encountered therein. The spectator witnesses conversations between a politically radical leveller, a disgruntled soldier, a group discussing the great storm of 1689, another discussing prodigies and prophecies, some country bumpkins discussing politics in ludicrous rural accents, some silent conspirators, and finally a group discussing affairs of state, such as the legacy of the republic, the war in Ireland and the election of 1690. The general tendency of the satire is to attack radical voices (both commonwealthmen and Tories) and celebrate the Williamite succession. A second edition, 'Corrected and much Enlarged', was published in September 1690, and for this, the poem was extended by another eight stanzas, to something over 700 lines. The additions make much of William's successes in Ireland in the campaign of 1690, including a portrait of a drunkard who demonstrates the battle of the Boyne using a tankard of ale and some tobacco pipes (pp. 14–15).

The School of Politicks is frequently but erroneously attributed to Ned Ward. Both Wing and the ESTC accept the attribution, as do many library catalogues (but not the British Library). Ward's first publication, also Hudibrastic verses, were published in 1691. Ward was the author of two unconnected later works of similar title: a periodical satire called *The Humours of a Coffee-House: A Comedy*, which ran for seven numbers between June and August 1707 (see below, pp. 259–88); and 'The Humours of a Coffee-House' in *The Diverting Muse, or, the Universal Medly* (London, S. Bragge, 1707), pp. 41–56. However the authorities on Ward – Howard Troyer's biography and James Sambrook in the *ODNB* – do not accept the attribution. The key evidence is that neither Ward, nor his contemporaries, claimed the work as his, even though this would have been his first publication, and in later life Ward was zealous in defining his *oeuvre*. The question as to who the author was remains unanswered. However, in 1692, the same poet published *The Miracles Perform'd by Money; a Poem. By the Author of the Humours of a Coffee-house* (London, printed, and sold by the Booksellers of London and Westminster, 1692), a twenty page Hudibrastic satire (also erroneously attributed to Ward, and never acknowledged by him).

The School of Politicks is listed in the *Term Catalogues* as being published in May 1690 (Edward Arber (ed.), *The Term Catalogues, 1668–1709 A.D.* (London, privately printed, 1903–6), vol. II, p. 313). The copy of the second edition in the British Library (BL 163.l.68) states that it was published on 18 September 1690, although dated 1691, and that the first edition appeared on 16 May 1690. The book was published by Richard Baldwin (*c.* 1653–98), a bookbinder who kept shop next to the Black-Bull tavern in Ball Court, on Great Old Bailey (which ran between Ludgate and Newgate). Baldwin had emerged as a major Whig publisher in the early 1680s, printing a large amount of incendiary Whig propaganda. After the accession of William III, his published a number of works championing the Whig cause. The anti-French and anti-papist nature of some of these works attracted the attention of the authorities more than once. After moving his shop to Warwick Lane in late 1690, Baldwin finally entered the Stationer's Company in 1692.

THE

School of Politicks:

OR, THE

HUMOURS

OF A

COFFEE-HOUSE.

A

POEM.

Tantúmne ab re tua otii eſt, aliena ut cures? Terent.

Licenſed, *Apr.* 15. 1690.

LONDON,

Printed for *Richard Baldwin,* next the *Black-Bull* in the *Old-Baily.* 1690.

(1)

THE

School of Politicks:

OR, THE

H U M O U R S

OF A

COFFEE-HOUSE.

ODES.

I.

'TWAS *Claret* that we drank, and 'twas as fine,
 As ever yet deferv'd the name of *Wine*;
Each Man his *Flask* we thought a mod'rate Dofe,
When juft as we were giving o'er,
Comes in our honeft *Landlord* in the Clofe,
Protefting we fhould drink his *Bottle* more:
 Which done, and all our *Reck'ning* paid,
 Each did a fev'ral way repair ;
 Some went *to walk,* and fome *to bed:*
 But I, who had an hour to fpare,
Went to a nighb'ring *Coffee-houfe,* and there
With fober Liquor to refine my Head.

B   H.

(2)

II.

What e'er th'occafion was I cannot tell,
Whether the *Wine* had difcompos'd my *Mind*,
Or fome falfe *Medium* did my *Reafon* blind,
But fo it was, I took the *Place* for *Hell*;
The *Mafter* of the Houfe, with *fiery Face*,
　　Did like infulting *Pluto* feem,
　　Whilft all his *Guefts* he did condemn
To drink a *Liquor* of infernal Race,
Black, fcalding, and of moft offenfive fmell:
Trembling and pale, I crofs'd my felf all o'er,
And mumbled *Ave-Maries* by the fcore.
At length, by ftrange infenfible degrees,
My fears all vanifh'd, and my Mind found eafe,
My fcatter'd Reafon re-affum'd its place,
And I perceiv'd with *whom*, and *where* I was.

III.

The murmuring *Buzz* which through the Room was
Did *Bee-hives* noife exactly reprefent;　　　(fent,
And like a *Bee-hive* too 'twas fill'd, and thick,
All tafting of the *Honey Politick*,
Call'd *News*, which they as greedily fuck'd in,
As Nurfes Milk young Babes were ever feen.
The various *Tones* and different noife of *Tongues*,
From lofty founding *Dutch* and *German* Lungs,
　　　　　　　　　　　　　　　　Toge-

(3)

Together with the soft melodious Notes,
Of *Spaniards*, *Frenchmen*, and *Italian* Throats,
Who met in this *State-Conventicle*,
    Compos'd a kind of *Harmony*,
Which did in Concord disagree;
Nay, even *Babel's* fatal Overthrow,
More sorts of *Languages* did never know,
Nor were they half so various, and so fickle.

IV.

The place no manner of distinction knew,
'Twixt *Christian*, *Heathen*, *Turk*, or *Jew*,
    The *Fool* and the *Philosopher*
    Sate close by one another here,
And Quality no more was understood
Than *Mathematicks* were before the Floud.
Here sate a *Knight*, by him a *rugged Sailer*;
    Next him a Son of *Mars*,
    Adorn'd with honourable Scars;
By them a *Courtier*, and a *Woman's Taylor*:
    A *Tradesman* and a *grave Divine*,
Sate talking of affairs beyond the *Line*;
Whilst in a Corner of the Room
Sate a fat *Quack*, the fam'd *Poetick Tom*,
Pleas'd to hear *Advertisements* read,
Where 'mongst lost Dogs, and other fav'rite Breed,
His famous *Pills* were chronicled:

                                                The

(4)

The half Box eighteen Pills for eighteen Pence,
Though 'tis too cheap in any Man's own Sense.
Lawyers and *Clients*, *Sharpers* and their *Cullies*,
Quakers, Pimps, Atheists, Mountebanks and *Bullies*,
　　　Clean or unclean, if here they call,
The place, like *Noah*'s Ark, receives 'em all.

V.

　　　Had *Lilbourn* been alive to see
　　　This *Hotch-potch* of *Society*,
　　　Some other *measures* he had ta'en,
When he the Work of *Levelling* began;
　　　For *All* here stand on equal ground.
　　　As I have seen in *Storms* at *Sea*,
For common safety all are willing found,
　　　To hawl a *Cable*, guide an *Oar*,
To stem the *Tide*, and bring the *Ship* to Shoar;
　　　So in this *School* of *Polity*,
Each thinks *himself* as much concern'd as *they*
Who sit in *Council Chamber* ev'ry day;
　　　And all their *Maxims* have a share
Of the *Professions* which their *Masters* are.
The *quick-eye'd Sectary* pretends to see
Under *Lawn Sleeves* the growth of *Popery*.
The *Smith* upon the Anvil of his Brain
　　　Forms a new *Commonwealth* again.

The

(5)

The *Carpenter* in his projecting Pate
Makes Props t'uphold the *tott'ring State:*
  The *Quack* too, with his *Close-stool Face,*
  Does with his senseless Reasons urge,
  The *British Islands* want a *Purge* :
And *Ah!* —— Were he but once in Place,
He'd------ but there stops, and thinks the Age not fit
 To know the Wonders of his mighty Wit.

V I.

  But the *chief Scene* was yet to come,
Which was to hear the various Argument
  Which fill'd all corners of the Room,
Concerning the Affairs of *Christendom.*
  I being seated to content
Lift'ned with most profound attention to
  One of the loudest of the *prating Crew,*
  Who after spitting thrice began,
Stroaking his Beard,-------Quoth he, *Here sits the Man*
 Who Thirty *several* Campaigns *has seen,*
  At five *and* forty Sieges *been,*
And in both foreign *and* domestick *Wars*
  Receiv'd as many Scars,
 As I upon my Head have Hairs.
You prate, continued he, *to make you merry,*
 Of Sligo, *and of* Bellishannon,
 Of Carrickfergus *and* Dundalk,

        And

(6)

And of the thund'ring Bombs *and* Cannon,
Were us'd at Siege *of* London-derry;
Mere ftuff, *and nothing elfe but* Talk.
Now if the Wars *you would delight in,*
And fee the very Soul *of* Fighting,
   Go *but this Spring to* Flanders,
  Flanders *the Scene of Action, where*
  Death *keeps his* Revels *all the Year:*
There are no Petticoat Commanders,
Things clad in red, *which have no braver* Souls
    Than Parrots, Apes, *or* Owls;
  But hardy Youths,------ fo us'd to ruff,
That their own Skins *become a nat'ral Buff:*
Thefe are the Lads,----- *and I was* one,
Although I fay't my felf, ------ have often gone,
    Through thickeft Squadrons of the Horfe,
    And with my fingle force,
  Made a whole Troop *retire in hafte:*
This good old Blade *which by my Side I wear,*
   Affifted by my Arm, *I fwear,*
Has kill'd a dozen Men *before I broke my faft,*
  Nor living is that daring He,
  Who but provokes this trufty Sword,
But fhall-------
      ----- At fpeaking of which *word,*
   Two *Serjeants* came and laid
  Their *Paws* upon this *daring Blade;*

                                      But

(7)

But fo fubmiffive, and fo tame,
  Was this courageous *Son of Fame!*----
The Company with Laughter let him pafs
To *Prifon,* for a moft *vainglorious Afs.*

VII.

Scarce was this *Son of Thunder* gone,
Who tir'd the Ears of every one,
Yet with his *bluft'ring Language* warm,
  But new Difcourfe began,
Talk underftood by every one
Concerning the late *dreadfull Storm.*
Lord! Nighbour, did you ever hear
(Says one) *fo terrible a* Wind?
I that have liv'd this threefcore Years,
  The like could never find,
How Sir, (replied his Friend,) ------*have you forgot*
That bluft'ring Night that Noll th'Ufurper *died?*
  When all the Winds *in order tried,*
  Who jhould blow hardeft on the Spot,
  A Storm *fo dreadfull that 'twas thought*
    About by Witchcraft *brought;*
  When trembling Atheifts *went to Prayer,*
  Thinking the Day *of* Judgment *near;*
  And Fear *appear'd in ev'ry* Face.
Pifh, (cries his Friend,) ----- *what that time was,*
I well remember, but, alafs!

To

(8)

To the late Wind *it was no more,*
Than farting *of a* Cloud, *or* ſhrieking *of a* Door.
I'll tell you: There was lately ſent
To me a Letter out of Kent,
Which ſays, it blew the Devil's Drop
(A Rock *by* Dover *ſeen*)
Along the Shoar, *as if 't had been*
A School-boy's Gig *or* Top,
And plac'd it on this ſide the Hope,
And that was ſtrange.———
        ——— But not by half,
So wonderfull (another ſpeaks,) *as that*
I now am going to relate :
Grazing it took an Eſſex *Calf,*
Near to the Shoar, *and blew him croſs the* River,
Quite into Kent, *where the* poor thing *remains*
As found *and* well *as ever.*
This cauſ'd the *Company* to laugh out-right:
Which *Mirth* t'increaſe a jolly *Sailer* ſwore,
That on that ne'er to be forgotten Night,
(Though to preſerve her they had ſpar'd no pains,)
Their goodly Ship *was ſtranded near the Shoar,*
Laden with Claret *from* Bourdeaux *ſhe came;*
The Veſſel *dáſh'd to pieces, every* Man
Nimbly to ſave himſelf began;
I, for my part, ſeeing a Hogſhead *float,*
Quickly aſtride upon it got,

Where

(9)

And, Faith, I think I was not much to blame,
My drunken Friend *and* I *got safe to Land,*
　　Where in requital of the good
　　He did me, caus'd his deareft Bloud
　　To iffue *from him upon my* command,
My Friends *and* I *were merry at his* death,
And I *fhall ne'er forget* him *while I've* breath.
Finding this *dull Romantick* ftrain,
Amongft that *Company* to reign,
Whofe *Talk* was nothing elfe but *Fable*,
I, leaving *them,* went to another Table.

VIII.

At which by accident (no doubt) were got
Demurely *grave* of *Citizens* a knot,
　　With fhaking *Heads* and lift up *Eyes,*
　　Difcourfing upon *Prodigies.*
Ah Friends! the Times (fays one) *are very* fad,
Although the Wicked *ftill remain as* bad
As if all things were fettled -----*T'other Night,*
As very late by Weftminfter *I came,*
Methought the Element *was all on flame,*
*And one of th'*Heads *upon the* Iron Spire
Over the Hall, *diftinctly cried out* Fire:
Nay, I a while ago was told,
That, at Noon-day, *the* Horfe *which ftands*

　　　　　　　C　　　　　　　　　　　　*In*

(10)

In the Stocks-Market *neigh'd aloud*
For Provender, *while the affrighted Croud*
Stood shivering both with Fear and Cold:
Now when Vice *grows so* strong, *and* Faith *so* weak,
No wonder 'tis the very Stones *should* speak :
What these unlucky Signs *portend*
I must confess I cannot comprehend;
Let God (and then he d'offt his Hat)
In his good time discover that.
Why, Nighbour, (says his Elbow-Friend,)
   For certain 'tis, you cannot be
     So blind as not to see,
The Head *which cried out* Fire *denotes*
A disagreement in the Senate's *Votes*;
   But Heav'n *avert the* Prodigy;
*And th'*Horses Neighing *speaks as plain*
 This Summer's *scarcity of* Grain:
But I'm no Prophet, *if I were,*
   Events more wonderfull I'd shew,
Than ever Gadbury *or* Lilly *knew,*
   Events *should make the* Nation *stare*;
What pity 'tis that Prophecy *is ceas'd!*
What pity 'tis, (thought I) thou are not plac'd
   In *Bedlam,* where there cannot be
     One half so *Lunatick* as thee:
Darkness, fresh Straw, and *slender Diet,*
   And *shaving* th'Hair from thy *thick Skull,*

May

(11)

May make thy *Brains* and *Tongue* more *quiet:*
   But leaving this fo very *dull,*
   Moft *whimfical,* and *fenfelefs* Crew,
   I foftly to another place withdrew.

IX.

Where *fix* raw *Countrey Fellows* fate
To hear an *empty Wittal* prate:
They to no Sermon in their Lives
Did ever fuch attention lend,
And each one by his *grinning* ftrives
Who moft fhall his *Difcourfe* commend:
One whifp'ring t'other in the Ear,
   E'fack, Ned, *did you ever hear*
(Says he) *fuch Stories from our* filly Vicar,
O'er Whitfon Ale, *or* Chriftmafs Liquor?
No, Vaith, Tom, (anfwers he,) *in all my born*
I ne'er heard like an ean, who does not fcorn
To tell us all the News; he fhould, I'm zhure,
By's head-piece, be a Countfeller.
   By this time our *admired Wit*
Had drank his Difh of *Tea,* and then
   Begins with——
      —— *Look ye, Gentlemen,*
'Tis plain, the Emperour intends
To make a ftrict Alliance *with his* Friends,

                                              To

(12)

To pull down Chriftian *and* Unchriftian *Turk;*
   E'gad, you'll fee fome curious Summers Work,
     And if things do but hit,
     (And I may live to fee it,)
Thofe two proud Tyrants *tumble from their* Thrones,
     And on their humble Marrow-bones,
Beg to b'admitted Grooms *of th'Stable,*
And eat Scraps *from the Servants Table:*
When this is done, they will, I hope,
     Have at his Holinefs *the* Pope,
     With all his red-faced Cardinals,
   Who wait upon St. Peter's Chair;
A Chair *has held this Sixteen hundred Year*
     Without being mended, as I hear.
The great Mogul *next to their Fury falls,*
     And when they've overcome the Cannibals
The Work is done, and we may live at peace,
   Enjoy our Friends, and always be at eafe.
Boy, *bring the* Gazette.----Sir, 'tis not come in.
Pox take you, fetch it, for it has been feen
At Jonathan's *two hours ago.-----*But, Sir,-----
     But, Puppy, *What do I come hither for,*
To fpend my time in this dull fmoaky Room?
Pray be not angry, Sir, the *Gazette's* come.
Here, Lad, *let's fee't-----So, fo, here's tickling News,*
     Loft Dogs, *loft* Horfes, Soldiers *run away*
     Without their Wits, *and to avoid their* Pay.

                             Books

(13)

Books *fold at* Tom's *by* Auction------ *once, twice, thrice,*
The Hammer's down----- he has you in a trice.
But, Sir, (fays one,) *what kind of News is this?*
For let me dye if I know what it is.
Oh, Sir, (replies the Spark) *I always read*
Gazettes *as Witches pray; for they, 'tis faid,*
Do backwards mumble out their Pater Nofter;
But now for News, *i'th' twinkling of an Oyfter.*

    Reads.

    '*Francfort, March* 29. Several Boats arrive daily with
' Provifions that are ordered to be laid up here for
' the ufe of the Imperial Forces, which will now very
' quickly be in motion. The late Flouds have broke
' the Bridge of Boats at *Philipsburg.*

    ' *Bruffels, April.* 2.------
Hold, *Sir,* (fays one,) *e'er farther you go on*
Pray tells us where abouts does ftand that Town
Call'd Francfort.-------
        ------- *Why, Sir,* (anfwers he,) *it lies*
Upon the barb'rous Coaft of Africa,
Snatch'd from the Moors *by mere furprize;*
     For on a very memorable day,
     Or rather Night, as they were all employ'd
     In gazing on the then Eclipfed Moon,
The Emp'rours Veffels, cruifing near the Shoar,
     Took the advantage of their bufied fenfe,
And gain'd the Town:---not many were deftroy'd;

                             Fear.

(14)

Fear bound the Hands of many, Wonder more ;
So with small Bloudshed they were Captives soon.
The City's neatly built, and 'twas from thence
The German Balls, *so fam'd for cleaning Shoes,*
First came.------ I'd read some other News,
          But I'm oblig'd by such an hour
To be at------ Gentlemen, I am your
Most humble Servant.------Boy, here's for my Tea.
Then leaves the Room.----But, Lord! to hear the Praise
These Blockheads did to his bold Nonsense raise,
Would almost make a witty Man forswear
          All Claim to Modesty and Sense,
          Since the Accomplishments which bear
A Man through Life, are Ignorance and Impudence.

X..

In *close Caball* were in a Corner met
          A Knot of Men, whose Faces wore
          The *Livery* of *Discontent,*
Sighs from their *Breasts* incessantly were sent,
One by their *Looks* might see their *Hearts* did fret,
          Like murm'ring *Israelites* of yore,
They *frown'd,* they *stamp'd,* they *bit* their *Thumbs,*
They *wink'd,* they *nodded,* nay, would sometimes *smile,*
When something did their airy hopes beguile,
Yet not a *Word* between their *Lips* there comes.
                                        What

(15)

What this *dumb Scene* did reprefent,
Or what by *Signs* and *Nods* was meant,
Conjecture only gives us leave to guefs:
They were no *Friends* to th'*Government*,
But there they met their *Thoughts* to eafe,
Which *Thoughts* by *Words* if they fhould dare t'exprefs,
Their *Necks*, or Purfes at the leaft,
Might pay for th'*Tongue's* untimely *Jeft*.
Self Prefervation's firft of Nature's Laws:
To be *Well-wifhers* they're content,
But care not to be *Martyrs* for the *Caufe*.

XI.

From this moft *unintelligible Crew*
I went, another *Scene* to view,
If the forementioned were *referv'd* and *clofe*,
Thefe were more *open*, and more *free*,
For *Wine* no fecret ever knows,
And that thefe *Sparks* had drank t'a large degree.
You Sirrah *Boy*, (fays one,) *go fetch m'a* Whore,
A lufty ftrapping Bona Roba,
E'gad, I fhall fo jerk *her* Toby,
I'd make her——but I ll fay no more
At prefent.——*Pox this* Coffee *fcalds my* Throat,
(Another cries,) *'tis in all Senfe too hot*;
Prethee go fetch a Pair of Bellows *hither,*
And make my Difh *know cooler weather:*

That

(16)

That ever Man *ſhould be ſo great an* Aſs,
To ſuffer Wine (*that plaguy Thief*) *to paſs*
Between his Lips, *that ſily did convey*
His Senſe, *his* Reaſon, *and his* Brains *away:*
    How happy thoſe dull Nations *are,*
      That know no other Liquor *but* ſmall Beer!
You, Harry, (then there bawls a third,)
If of Sobriety *you ſpeak one word,*
By Jupiter, *and all the* Heathen Gods,
Your Sword *and mine ſhall be at mortal odds;*
I for my part, without Reflexions,
Againſt Small Beer *have forty* Actions;
They're to be tried next Term, *and if I caſt it,*
I'll make't High Treaſon *for my Friends to taſte it:*
    Boy, bring m'a Glaſs of Uſquebaugh,
    By People nicknam'd Lill' bullero,
    'Tis good againſt the Gripes, *they ſay,*
    *My Humour's this-----*Dum ſpiro ſpero:
Come here's a Health *to th'King of* Poland;
Well, here ſit I, who though I've no Land,
Suppoſe my ſelf as great as he,
Nay, as th'great Cham *of* Tartary;
My Crown's *a fuddling* Cap, *a* Pipe *my* Sceptre;
    My Bottle *repreſents my* Globe,
And any Cloaths *ſerve for a Regal* Robe;
My Queen *my* Miſtreſs, *when I kept her;*

Drawers

(17)

Drawers *(or elſe 'tis very hard)*
Will ſerve me for my Corps du Guard ;
But when Incognito *I reel,*
A Link-boy *ſerves the turn as well ;*
And, Gentlemen, *to ſhew I'm yours,*
Know you're my Privy Counſellours.
Well, we adviſe thee to go home,
(Says one,) *and try by* Sleep *to overcome*
This Humour.-------

         -------- *Well, for once it ſhall be ſaid,*
(Says he,) *That Counſel I obey'd ;*
Here, Boy, *your Money,------ Gentlemen let's go,*
Egad methinks I tread on Wool, *or* Snow,
My head's ſo light,------- well, when I come again
I'll make new Orders in my drinking Reign.

XII.

This *merry Farce* diverted all the Room :
Theſe you may know had no deſign
The *Quiet* of the *State* to undermine,
He thinks no *Treaſon* that's top-full of *Wine* ;
Men that ſit *brooding* o'er their *Fears* at home,
Or elſe abroad in private Corners meet,
     And there with *ſecret Whiſpers* ſit,
Are thoſe diſturb the *Peace* of *Chriſtendom* ;
The *Juice o'th'Grape* may nurſe an ill deſign,
But certain 't never was begot by *Wine*.
         D   XIII.

(18)

XIII.

Hearing loud *Talk* and warm *Dispute*,
I sate me down to listen to't:
A *Cluster* were ingag'd, but chiefly *Two*
Unsheath'd their *Arguments*, and drew
In *Controversie's* open Field;
He who did the *defensive Weapon* wield
    Was both to *Wit* and *Sense* allied,
      Nay, more, the *Truth* was on his side;
His *Habit* rich, but modest,----t'other,
    Yea plainly, a *dissenting Brother*,
    Who confidently would maintain,
    The *Papists* first the *War* began,
In those sad Times *when Jealousies and Fears*
    Set Folks together by the Ears;
    Nay, more, that they the Persons were
    Who brought the King into the *Snare*,
    And when they had him safely there,
    Did, in the sight of all *Beholders*,
    Take off his *Head* from off his *Shoulders*.
    (A *Lye* so very gross like this,
    What Hearer would not take amiss?)
    This caus'd the *Gentleman* to storm,
    Already with his *Canting* warm;
How, Sir, (says he,) *can you with any Face*
    Transfer the Guilt, *most justly* yours,

(I

(19)

(I mean your Party's,*)* *on the* Papists ? *They,*
'*Tis own'd, are bad enough*; *but can you,* '*pray,*
Inform us who amongſt thoſe ruling Powers
That ſate at Weſtminſter *that fatal Day,*
When Charles *(the Good, the Pious, and the Juſt,*
Being from Kingdoms three *moſt baſely thruſt,)*
Was tried, which of them all e'er went to Maſs ?
What Roman Catholick *to ſign was known*
The Warrant *for his* Execution ?
Hold, Sir, (replies the other,) *not too faſt:*
Upon *the* Stage *they did not much appear,*
'*Tis own'd, but they behind the* Curtain *ſtood, and what*
Was ordered to be done was then effected.
Good Counſel *ought not, Sir, to be rejected,*
(Replies the other,) *but 'tis plain and clear,*
The Guilt *ſhould only at your Doors be caſt.------*
At mine, Sir, pray excuſe me, I comply
With ev'ry Government.------*That's uppermoſt you mean.*

    But, Sir, ſince you and I have been
Diſputing thus, let me one Secret *tell.------*
A Secret, (ſaid I;) *no, 'tis known too well,*
No Government *your* Party *ever pleas'd*;
And if that Miracles *had not been ceas'd,*

    Should Heaven *to humour you create*
  A Kingdom, Commonwealth, *or* State,
Together with ſuch wiſe and wholeſome Laws,
Wherein ſharp Criticks *could diſcern no flaws,*

        D 2   *Yet*

(20)

Yet you'd be still uneasie.------

------Sir, too far

You stretch your Argument, *for are*
We not as quiet *in the present* Reign,
As those who stiffly Monarchy *maintain?*
Yes, doubtless, you (replies the other) *can*
Conform to all the Modes *which e'er*
The Government *are ready to prepare*;
But your Compliance *is but* Masquerade,
Your Loyalty *is forc'd, your* Faith *a Trade*;
T'enjoy your Liberty *the* State *thinks fit,*
Pray Heav'n *you make good use of it*;
Forbear your Canting, Whining, idle Style,
With no amusements see you do beguile
Your Hearers; *strive but to be true*;
Against the Laws *do you forget to rail,*
And let but Sense *'gainst* Bigotry *prevail*;
And then------

------Oh! Sir, we know what best to doe,
We come not here to be inform'd by you.------
But Counsel's *cheap, Sir, I demand no* Fees.------
But you may counsel others if you please.------
Nay, if you're angry, Sir, I'm gone;
This 'tis when good advice is thrown
Away on Men; but e'er your Company I leave,
Remember this, while vainly you believe
Others to cheat, you don't your selves deceive.

XIV.

(21)

XIV.

Great News from Ireland, is heard at Door,
Which puts the *Audience* to a ſtand,
To fetch it in there is command,
    And one attempts to read it o'er
But interrupted by a *prating Fop*.
You talk, (ſays he,) *I mean you hope*
That Ireland *will this* Summer *be reduc'd*;
    You may as well ſuppoſe
    The Bay *of* Biſcay *will be froze*;
No, no, with Stories *you're amus'd*,
K. J----*'s Men and Money's not ſo poor*,
    And I pronounce him Son of ' Whore,
Who wiſhes Him *or's* Army *were confus'd*.
    This made the Company to ſtare:
At laſt one takes him up with----*Sir, I dare*,
    Though not to's Perſon, *yet to's* Cauſe
    Wiſh ruin, *and if any here*
    Do not the ſelf-ſame thing aver,
He is without much Complement an Aſs.
An Aſs, *Sir*, (cries the other,) *Faith, I don't*
Much uſe to pocket up ſuch an Affront;
You wear no Sword, I ſee, and 'twould be baſe
    To draw upon a naked Man,
But here's my Diſh of Coffee *in your Face*.

                          T'other

(22)

T'other, though fcalded, would not be
Behind hand with him in Civility,
But flung a Glafs of *Mum* fo pat,
It fpoild both *Perriwig* and Point *Cravat*:
  On this a Quarrel foon began,
Till *Conftable*, with pacifying Staff,
  Appeas'd the Fray, and the *Contenders* have
  Some refpite, one his *Face* to cure,
And t'other to refrefh his *Garniture*.

XV.

The *Votes* are come----- Ay, there's fome *News* indeed,
  And one does all diftinctly read;
  Which finifh'd, every one began
  To make remarks.-----With fhaking Head,
Cries one, *I think the* Parliament *are mad*
  To tax us thus ; we fhall e'er long
  Not know to whom our Souls *belong ;*
  Nay 'tis reported they prepare
  A Bill to regulate our Fare;
  And none without accuftom'd Fees
  Shall eat of Licens'd Bread *and* Cheefe;
  For------
  ------*Hold, Sir, cries another Man,*
E'er farther in your Nonfenfe *you go on;*
  What to the Taxes *have you paid,*
  Or given to the Royal Aid?

If

(**23**)

If I miſtake not, you're no more
Than Journeyman t'a Shoe-maker,
And yet your Little Worſhip muſt complain,
  But 'twould, alaſs! be but in vain
  To preach Senſe to thy cloudy Brain;
  Or elſe, 't might be evinc'd that none
In Europe's *large Dominions are ſo free*
From griping Taxes *of the Purſe as we;*
  Beſides, what in that nature's done,
 Is the effect of mere Neceſſity,
*Shall th'*King *his Perſon for our ſakes expoſe,*
  And we our little Aids refuſe?
  They're woiſe than Infidels *and* Jews,
  Who out of Complaiſance to Purſe,
  Their future Happineſs will loſe,
And on Poſterity *entail a Curſe.*

XVI.

More various Scenes of Humour I might tell,
    Which in my little ſtay befell;
Such as grave *Citts*, who ſpending Farthings four,
Sit, ſmoke, and warm themſelves an hour,
    Of modiſh Town-ſparks, drinking *Chocolate*,
      With *Bevir* cockt, and laughing loud,
      To be thought Wits amongſt the Crowd,
      Or ſipping *Tea*, while they relate

                                        Their

(24)

Their Ev'ning's Frolick at the *Rofe*.
But now I think 'tis time to clofe,
Left to my *Reader* I fhould give offence,
And he be tir'd with mine,
As I was with their dull *Impertinence*.
My Reck'ning paid, I left the Room,
And in my paffage Home,
Reflected thus——Is this the much defir'd
Bleffing of Life, which moft unjuftly we
Call *Regular Society?*
Well, to my Clofet I'll repair,
Paft Times with prefent to compare,
My felf to ftricteft Study I'll condemn,
And 'mongft fome Authours wife and good,
Who Mankind beft have underftood,
My Weeks, Months, Years, endeavour to redeem,
Which vainly foolifh, and unthinking I
Have fpent in what we falfely call *Good Company*.

T H E E N D.

The Art of Getting Money by Double-Fac'd Wagers: or, Cross and pile whether Mons be taken, or no? A dialogue between a courtier, a citizen, and a sharper of the town. The scene, Jonathan's coffe-house (London, n.p., 1691), 4pp.; 4°. Huntington Library, California: 33273. ESTCR9408.

A four-page prose satirical dialogue on gambling in coffee-houses, directed generally at the confusion of values in contemporary society for which, again, coffee-house sociability is deemed emblematic. The particular focus of the satire is gambling on the outcome of military campaigns, set in the context of the War of the League of Augsburg. Betting on such events, where the outcome depended on the lives of soldiers, and the national interest was at stake, was widely considered morally questionable. A newspaper, *The Weekly Remarks* (No. 2, 8 April 1691), commented that some were 'more *surprized* and *dejected*' at the fall of Mons than becomes 'brave *Men*'. Others, 'who are *deep in Wagers* [...] may be more concerned at the *Loss* of their *Money* than the *Garrison*'. Such gambling, then, was perceived as part of a wider set of concerns about the Whig financial revolution of the 1690s.

The War of the League of Augsburg, also known as the Nine Years' War, was a major war fought between 1688 and 1697 between France and the League of Augsburg. Also known as the Grand Alliance, the League of Augsburg was formed by a group of small German states, including the Holy Roman Empire, the Palatinate, Bavaria, Brandenburg, Hanover and Liege, who were joined by Portugal, Spain, Sweden and the United Provinces (the Netherlands). After the English revolution of 1688, the alliance added Britain to its forces. The campaign discussed in the satire is the siege of Mons, a notable French victory in March 1691. The city was invested on 5 March by French forces under Lieutenant-General Louis François de Boufflers (1644–1711), and the first shot was fired on 17 March. On 29 March the town, led by the Prince de Berghes, capitulated. According the French, this was the result of a hard won military victory: the Allies attributed it to the townspeople, who were unwilling to see their city destroyed, and were mindful that the town was to be heavily fined for every day the siege continued. The capture of Mons was strategically important for the French, and the news of the defeat was greeted with dismay in London. For the best account of the siege of Mons, and the war as a whole, see John Childs's *The Nine Years' War and the British Army 1688–1697: the operations in the Low Countries* (Manchester, Manchester University Press, 1991), pp. 156–78.

The satire is in the form of a prose dialogue, and the anonymous writer makes some attempts to develop the three characters; a courtier (expressing opinions associated with the royal court), a citizen (associated with the City, who has been betting on the outcome of the siege) and a sharper or rogue (one of those setting out to profit from the situation). The printer and publisher are unknown. Internal dating suggests it was published in April 1691. Only two copies are extant, one at the Huntington Library, California and the other at the University of Chicago Regenstein Library, Chicago, Illinois.

THE

𝕬𝖗𝖙 𝖔𝖋 𝖌𝖊𝖙𝖙𝖎𝖓𝖌 𝕸𝖔𝖓𝖊𝖕

B Y

Double-Fac'd WAGERS;

O R,

Cross and Pile whether *MONS* be Taken, or no?

A *DIALOGUE* Between a *Courtier*, a *Citizen*, and a
Sharper of the Town.

The SCENE *Jonathan's* COFFE-HOUSE.

Parturiunt MONTES *Nafcitur ridiculus Mus.*

Court. **H**Ere Sirrah——*A Dish of Tea*, and defire that
Gentleman in the *Band* to fpeak with me——*Oh,
Sir, your Servant,* (to the *Citizen*) 'faith I lately
came from the *Prefence*, and 'tis faid, the *Queen*
receiv'd an *Exprefs* juft now, that *Mons* was taken; Pray what
News have you in the *City?*

Citiz. *Mons taken, Sir?* Ay, fo is *Venice*, Sir! *Lord*, you *Gentlemen* of the t'other end of the Town have the ftrangeft Intelligence!
why, nothing but *Pacolet's Flying Horfe* could bring over the News
fo fuddenly.

Courti. Why do you doubt the Truth of it, Sir?

Cit. I know no Reafon I fhould let any Mans Opinion be the
Standard of my Faith, for——

Courti. Perhaps 'tis your Intereft, Sir, to disbelieve it, you have
laid fome *Wagers* upon that occafion, and I muft confefs, the Hopes
of Winning, and the fear of Lofing, will make any man fufpend his
belief for fome time.

Citiz. The Truth on't is, Sir, I am a *little dipt*, fome five or fix
A

Hundred

Hundred Pounds to several Persons, and unless the Prince *De Bergue*, the Governour of the *Town*, sends me a Letter from his own hand, shall hardly believe the Affirmation of any *Offender* that comes by the way of *Plimouth*. Meer Shams, Sir, meer Shams.

Courti. (*Turning aside*) Well, now have I a Roguish Inclination to bite this *Opus & Usus*, and tho' I my self am a little doubtful of the matter, yet the fingring of some *City Gold*, will be more pleasant to me, than a little Estate won at the *Groom Porters*. (*Turning to him*) Well, Sir, have you a few *Dormant Guineas* in your Closet, you are indifferent whether you Win or Lose upon this Occasion ?

Citiz. Truly, Sir, Mony was never reckon'd by me amongst things indifferent ; but I have *Fifty Pound*, I will venture to odds with any Person, that *Mons* will not be in the *French King*'s Hands by the first of *May*———

Courti. No more words, Sir, I am your Man, here's ten hard pieces of *Old Barbary Gold*, with the *Royal Effigies* upon them——— which said Sum shall be yours, if in a little time I do not convince you the *Town* is in the *French* hands; the Counterpart of which Obligation is, you are to give me Fifty Guineas, when you are undeniably convinc'd the Town is taken.

Citiz. With all my Heart, Sir ; in Token whereof, here's my hand, Sir, and so good Luck attend me.

Enter a Sharper.

Sharp. Boy———the *Gazett*———quickly, here's such a doe with a little *Netherlandish Town*, not so big as *Rumford*, as if all *Europe* lay at stake, and the Peace of *Christendome* depended upon the Relief of that single place———(*softly to himself*) Well, Money is my aim, and if 'tis any where, 'tis in the *City* ; these Grave out-of-Fashion Sparks command the Gold, and 'faith, *Good Men and True*, it shall go hard, but I'le rid you of some on't in a very civil way. So, so, I see a kind of malicious Pleasure in a Gentleman's Face yonder, discoursing with Mr. *Get-all* the Merchant, I'le go a little nearer, and observe their motions, some *Wager* going forward, my Life to a Pepper Corn ; (*comes up to 'em*) What News, Gentlemen, from *Flanders* : Is *Mons* taken yet :

Citizen. Sir, You ask a very hard Question, I am no Privy-Counsellor, Sir.

Sharp. (*Aside*) No, I dare swear it——— Come here's twenty Guineas with any man, that *Mons* is not now under the *French* power.

Cour. What odds d'ye allow, Sir, and what d'ye mean by the word *Now* :

Sharp. D'ye take one form of suit, Sir ? By *Now*, I understand th'
Numerical

[3]

Numerical Hour of One in the Afternoon, *April* the 11th. 1691. And for the Wager, I am upon the square.

Court. I take you up, Sir——here's the Money; and by reason we are both Strangers to one another, we will deposit our Money in this civil *Gentleman's* hands, he is a substantial man, and his Word will pass where a *Nobleman's* Bond will signifie nothing.

Sharp. With all my Heart, Sir——(*Speaking to the Citizen*) And now to you, 'Mr. *Treasurer*, I will lay the contrary Wager, that *Mons* has been in the *French* power ever since *Tuesday* the 31st. of *March* last.

Citiz. Why, Sir, do you lay cross Wagers?

Sharp. No matter for that, Sir, if you accept me, there's your money; for yours you are your own Cash-keeper.

Citiz. Come, Sir, 'tis done——' *strike hands.*)

Sharp. Gentlemen, there's a Sea-Captain gone down the Ally, I must needs speak with him. Your pardon, Gent.   [*Exit.*

Court. This is one of the pleasantest Sparks I ever met with; why this is like playing at Cards for nothing——However, tho he gains little he is sure to be no loser by the bargain.

Citiz. For my part, I wish no better Estate to befall me, than the Wagers laid, *pro* and *con*, about this business: Complaints are made of the want of money, when you can hardly go into any Tavern or Coffee-House, but the *Guinea's* are tumbling about with *Mons* is taken, and *Mons* is not taken; when upon the whole matter I cannot, with my political Spectacles, discern what mighty matter can be in it—— But Interest swears all men to be true to their Principles.

Court. But if the *French* King pushes on his Fortune, all *Flanders* will be his in a little time, and then *Myn heer Van Pickleberring* look to your self; for if he goes on at this rate, he may dine in *Amsterdam* by *Michaelmas* day, for any thing I can guess.

Cit. Yes, and at *Christmas* in *Northampton*! not too fast, Sir, not too fast; the *Spaniards* are a People slow in Action; but we have a *Prince of our own*, whom I hope will stop his Progress, and make him slacken his pace a little.

Court. If your Faith be great, I wonder it does not attempt to remove Mountains; were your Charity but half as large, you would certainly go to Heaven.

Cit. So I shall, I hope, tho' I call the *Pope* the *Whore of Babylon.*

Courti. A little more Civility tho', as he is a *Temporal Prince*, 'twould not beamiss. But, Sir, what News have you of the *Bilboa Fleet*, they say the *French* have taken it, and sunk the *Man of War*, who was its Convoy?

Citiz. You may as well believe, the *Peke* of *Tenariff* is sunk; no, no——Heaven be Praised, they past by *Plimouth* a few days since.

Couri.

[4]

Courti. Why, a Mafter of the *Infurance Office,* offered Twenty Thoufand Pound to any one, who would bear their Bank harmlefs; upon the firft Rumours of the *Veffels* being loft.

Citiz. Had any one had the Gift of Prophecy, and taken his Money, he might have fhook hands with an *Alderman.*

Courti. But, Sir, does the *News* hold good, that the *Pacquet Boat* wherein the Bifhop of *L*—— Dr. *Scot,* Dr. *Grove,* &c. were fuppos'd to be, is ftill miffing?

Citiz. Meer Lyes, Shams, Tricks, Amufements; well, thefe Inventing Lying Sons of Caterpillers, were I a Magiftrate, fhould fuffer the Law moft feverely, and Dance from *Algate* to *Newgate,* and from thence to *Tyburn,* to the Tune of Dr. *O*——*tes* his *Jig.*

Courti. The Truth muft be confeft, there are a fort of defigning People, who having no bufinefs of their own, make it their Imployment to invent Lyes, Stories, and Contradictions, to difturb the minds of the unthinking Vulgar——but I hope, Sir, Men of your refin'd Thoughts give no Credit to 'em.

Courti. Thanks for the Complement, Sir.

Enter the Sharper *in another Drefs.*

Sharp. Gentlemen, fet your Hearts at reft, *Mons* is as certainly gone as *Luxemburgh.*

Courti. (To the Citizen) D'ye hear that, Sir, D'ye hear that?

Citiz. Why I am not Deaf. But d'ye think I credit every flying idle Report?

Sharp. Sir, I came from a Gentleman juft now, who had it from the Secretary's Office, who heard my Lord——affirm it, and I prefume you Read the *Gazette* yefterday, Sir.

Citiz. Yes, but I don't believe a word on't; and to affure you I do not, give me *Ten Guineas,* Sir, and I'le enter into Bond to pay you Twenty Shillings a week, every week while you live, during the time (the fuppofed taken) *Mons* remains in the *French* Cuftody.

Charp. (Afide.) This is what I would have. Come, Sir, there's your Money. Now I think I have bit him finely, the *French* don't ufe to part with their Conquefts fo eafily; this is as good as an Annuity for Life, come, Sir, if you pleafe we'll to the Scriveners.

Citiz. Not too hafty, Sir——well, Sir, let me fee you here to morrow. *(Speaking to the* Courtier.)

Courtier. I'le not fail to wait on you, Sir.

Sharp. Nor I neither.

Let Scraping Mifers *hoard up fordid Gains,*
The beft Eftate is a large ftock of Brains.

LONDON: Printed in the Year, 1691.

The City Cheat discovered: or, A New Coffe-house Song. Perswading all civil and sober Men not to frequent the Coffee-houses so much, whether in London, Wapping, Westminster, or Common-Garden (London, printed and sold by J. W. between the Two Gateways going into White-Fryers, 1691), [1]p.; 1°. Pepysian Library, Magdalene College, Cambridge University. ESTCR174065.

A broadside folio ballad song, in sixty-four lines organized in eight numbered stanzas of eight lines each, with a four-line evolving refrain. The ballad was intended to be sung 'To the tune of Lilli-burlero', the enormously popular melody that was the signature song of the Williamite Protestants after 1688. Bishop Burnet's *History of his own time* (1724–34) said of 'Lilli-burlero' that it was 'a foolish ballad ... treating the papists, and chiefly the Irish, in a very ridiculous manner ... The whole army, and at last all the people both in city and country, were singing it perpetually' (6 vols (Oxford, Clarendon Press, 1823), vol. III, p. 319). The tune was composed as early as 1686, and some early manuscript copies are attributed to Henry Purcell, albeit doubtfully. A great many ballads and songs were set to 'Lilli-burlero' in the 1690s and thereafter: each retains its implicit allegiance to the Williamite cause (see Claude Simpson, *The British Broadside Ballad and its Music* (New Brunswick, NJ, Rutgers University Press, 1966), pp. 449–55).

In *The City Cheat discovered*, the satire is directed against the corrupting effect of coffee-houses, which are here associated with sexual license and excessive drinking of alcoholic beverages, and by extension, to the wider moral corruption in the city occasioned by the financial revolution of the 1690s. By contrast, the tavern or ale-house is depicted as a place of restraint and probity: a neat reversal of the topography of such connotations during the Restoration. The repeated tumbling word play of the ballad's refrain mimics the doggerel of the original's chorus.

Nothing is known of the ballad's author. The ballad was licensed, and published by 'J. W.' or John Wallis, a printer of numerous broadsides and news-sheets who kept shop in Whitefriars from 1682–1700 (Plomer). The only extant copy of *The City Cheat discovered* is held in the Pepysian Library of Magdalene College, Cambridge. The poem is reprinted in facsimile in the *Catalogue of the Pepys Library at Magdalene College, Vol. 5: The Pepys Ballads*, ed. by W. G. Day (Cambridge, Brewer, 1987), p. 102. In Pepys's categorization, this ballad was included in 'State and Times', a collection of political ballads associated with the Williamite cause.

The City Cheat difcovered:

O R,

A New Coffe-houfe Song.

Perfwading all civil and fober Men not to frequent the *Coffe-houfes* fo much, whether in *London, Wapping, Weftminfter,* or *Common-Garden.*

Licenfed according to Order,   Tune of *Lilli-bulero.*

(1)

THE *Coffe-houfe* Trade is the beft in the Town;
Young fparks that have money they thither repair:
The Affairs of the Nation they have written down,
To blow up their Noddles as light as the Air.
Stories, Stories, Lies and Stories;
There's nothing but Stories when they begin.
Pox on your News-Letters, they lye bomb and flatters;
They are but a Trap to wheedle Men in.

(2)

At *Coffe houfe* chat, I heard a Dear Joy,
Proteft that King *James* was lately made Pope:
Who the Ifle of *Great Britain* would quickly deftroy,
And hang all the Hereticks up in a Roap.
Stories, Stories, Impudent Stories,
Such foolifh Stories make my Brains full.
In fuch fenflefs Stories a Jacobite glories,
Tho' they all be but Tales of a Cock and a Bull.

(3)

Fire-fhips and Friggots, with Top mafts and Sails,
At Coffe-houfe-Bay they caft Anchor at Night;
The Miftrils falutes them in nafty Night-rails,
Come in hanfome Women, I know you are right.
Kiffing, Kiffing, nothing but Kiffing;
Kiffing and Billing is all that they doe;
There's Kiffing and Wooing, and fomething els doing.
And this is the Ruin of Jack and Tom too.

(4)

Some honeft Houfe-keepers, that ne'er went aftray,
They go to the Coffe-houfe with good Intent:
But when they begin with fweet Madam to play,
There's nothing their paffion of Love can prevent.
With painting and Patches, they make up the Matches;
With kiffing and wheuling, and tickling her Womb.
And then comes the tugging, the jugging, the hugging,
Whilft the honeft good Woman fits dreeping at home.

(5)

To Tavern or Ale-houfe no fober Men come,
But all to the Coffe-houfe now they moft go.
Yet Mifs with her delicate Syder and Mum,
Can pick all their Pockets before they well know.
Yes Sir, pray Sir, do Sir, ftay Sir;
What ye call, that ye fhall, welcome Sir.
Tho' after his billing, he has not a Shilling,
Which when he comes home makes a horrible Stir.

(6)

The Cook-wench that lately efcaped the Cart,
A Thorn-back Maid that lives by her Wits,
She flily has learn'd the Coffe-houfe Art;
And now, like a Madam, the Confidence fits.
Dear Mifs, rare Mifs, prithee Mifs, fair Mifs,
That ne'er has been troubled with the Scurvey nor Itch.
With a humbling and fumbling, with tumbling & jumbling,
With a roaring Gold-watch, that hangs at her Breech.

(7)

My Dear and my Honey, pray lend me fome money;
And thus with her Charmes fhe bewitcheth the Fool.
Sometimes fhe wants Rings, with other fuch things
And makes the poor fellow as blind as an Owl.
Wheedling, Wheedling, nothing but wheedling;
Lying and wheedling all the Night o'er.
But a Pox on her Placket, fhe pays off his Jacket,
And makes him give Money for paying the Score.

(8)

Then honeft good Fellows go, when you are dry,
And joyn for a Pottle, your two pence a piece;
You'll have more Content at an Ale-houfe hard by,
Then you'll have at the Sign of the *Shepherd* and *Flute.*
Roger, Roger, Richard and Roger,
Drink off a Health to William our King.
The Baftard King Lewis, that fwears to undo us,
He ne'er to Subjection this Nation fhall bring.

Printed and Sold by *J.W.* between the *Two Gateways* going into *White-Fryars.* 1691

*The complaint of all the she-traders in Rosemary-lane,
Black-Mary's-Hole, Ratcliff, Dog-and-Bitch-Yard, Moor-
fields, and Petticoat-lane, against the city cheats, or the
new coffee-houses, about Charing-Cross, Westminster,
Covent-garden, Fleet-street, and those parts of the town.
To the tune of an Orange* ([London], printed by J. Wallis,
between the Two Gateways going into White-Friars,
[between 1682 and 1693]), [1]p.; 1°. Pepysian Library,
Magdalene College, Cambridge University: P5 405.
ESTCR174202.

A satirical broadside ballad of seventy lines, in fourteen five-line stanzas, with
an evolving four-syllable refrain. The verses are written as a complaint from the
whores of the East End of London – who work in the areas long associated with
vice – addressed to a new kind of prostitute who they claim is working in coffee-houses of the West End. These new prostitutes, they claim, counterfeit their
trade by appearing in the dress and demeanour of honest women working as
maid servants and coffee-women. In this way, the ballad is a satire on the chang-
ing moral and cultural climate of the city following the Glorious Revolution,
for which coffee-houses are again emblematic. The title alludes to the complaint
form well known in coffee-house satires, although the conceit is not pursued at
great length. The tune to which the *The complaint of all the she-traders* is sung
was noted for its associations with William III (William of Orange), but the
specific political dimension of this ballad is obscure, if it exists at all. The implicit
contrast between the East End and West End of London was also at this time a
relatively new phenomenon, as the East End had only in recent decades lost its
historically enduring associations as a place where wealthy merchants resided.

Nothing is known of the author, and the publisher, John Wallis, was a noted
publisher of ballads (see headnote to *The City Cheat discovered* above, pp. 239–
40). The only extant copy of *The complaint of all the she-traders* is held in the

243

Pepysian Library of Magdalene College, Cambridge. The poem is reprinted in facsimile in the *Catalogue of the Pepys Library at Magdalene College, Vol. 5: The Pepys Ballads*, ed. by W. G. Day (Cambridge, Brewer, 1987) p. 102. In Pepys's categorization, this ballad was included in a group he called 'Various Subjects Mixt. viz.t Romantick Feats, Cheats, Frollicks, Fashions &c.'

THE
COMPLAINT
OF
All the She-Traders
IN

Rofemary-lane, *Black-Mary's-Hole*, *Ratcliff*, *Dog-and-Bitch-Yard*, *Moor-fields*, and *Petticoat-lane*, againft the *City Cheats*, or the *New Coffee-houfes*, about *Charing-Crofs*, *Weftminfter*, *Covent-garden*, *Fleet-ftreet*, and thofe parts of the Town.

To the Tune of an Orange.

A Curfe of your Shams, ye Coffee-houfe Dames,
Who, infted of extinguifhing, cherifh mens Flames;
How finely you draw the poor Genleman in,
With your Devil's Commander, Wine, to the Sin
Fornication.

Sobriety cloaks your Luft, with a Pox,
While we deal more plainly, like honefter Fokes,
Altho' we can hardly keep open our Dores,
For all we maintain the perfecteft Whores
In the Nation.

When Mifs is with Kid, that fhame may be hid,
For a Coffee-houfe for her ftrait Money is bid,
Where Bantling comes out, and then fhe's as pure
As a Girl of fifteen, that ne'r play'd the Whore
But in Fancy.

At Night to the *Star* the Bullies repair,
Where *Robin* has fix'd a Planet more fair;
Whofe Afpect alone portends more annoy
Than the glitt'ring Flames that devour'd old *Troy* :
O brave *Nancy.*

Strait *Nancy* comes down in her flowr'd Sattin Gown,
And in fcoring ten Shillings fhe cheats but a Crown,
Too little ('alas! to maintain the Jade's pride,
And the lavifh Expence of her Bully befide,
I muft tell ye.

Chocolat, Syder, Mum, flows all o're the Room,
Of which ('tis believ'd) Madam *Nancy* drinks fome;
But to *Robin* this Drinking is but a meer Task,
For he fwears he can't fleep without t'other Flask
In his Belly.

The Flasks go round, and Glaffes are crown'd,
Till fome fall o' fighting, and then to the ground;
When *Robin* and *Nancy* th' advantage do take
Of picking their Pockets before they do wake,
Of their Silver.

If Gold was there, you boldly may fwear,
They got it by means not honeft or fair;
For whatever they cram into Fob or to Gut,
You may be all confident is nothing but
What they Pilfer.

Then from *Rofemary-lane*, we all do complain,
From *Black-mary's Hole*, from *Ratcliff* again,
From *Dog-and-Bitch-Yard*, and from famous *Moor-fields*,
To the Sparks of this End of the Town, of the Ills
We lye under.

In time then appeafe our harfh Miferies,
Or the cruel Affli&ion you Gallants will feize,
Elfe we fhall be forced e'r many a day
To turn honeft Women all; which you will fay,
Is a Wonder.

O *Petticoat-lane* ! that long did'ft maintain
The Quack, that pretends to cure the Rein,
How low art thou fall'n from thy Trade in a trice,
What before for a *George*, may now for a *Sice*
Be procured.

Then let us All a Council call,
And cry out amain, A Hall! a Hall!
For fuch damn'd Impofitions were ne're before known,
Since *Damaris Page*, here, and can be by none
Here endured.

Let's mufter our Force, both our Foot and our Horfe,
Thofe who ride on Crutches and thofe who hak worfe,
And let us proclaim it Expulfion by Law,
To thofe who from our Affiftance withdraw,
Or lye Skulkers.

For 'ti'n't worth our while to Buttock and File,
And to Clap is both our own Pain and our Toil;
Then either offord us in Vifits relief,
Or fome of the Traders may find to their grief,
We'll turn Bulkers.

Printed by I. Wallis, *between the Two Gateways going into* White-Friars.

'Letter from a French gentleman in London to his friend in Paris ... Containing an Account of Will's Coffeehouse, and of the Toasting and Kit-Kat-Clubs. Made English', in *Letters of Wit, Politicks, and Morality. Written originally in Italian, by the famous Cardinal Bentivoglio; in Spanish by Signior Don Guevara; ... Done into English, by the Honourable H— H— Esq; Tho. Cheek, Esq; Mr. Savage. Mr. Boyer &c. To which is added a large collection of original letters of Love and Friendship*, ed. by Abel Boyer (London, J. Hartley, W. Turner, and Tho. Hodgson, 1701), 437pp. BL: 93.c.5. ESTCT102964. Extract, pp. 215–24.

A descriptive epistle supposedly written by a French gentleman travelling in London to his 'Friend in Paris', describing the role of coffee-house sociability in the literary culture of London at the turn of the eighteenth century. In the first section, the letter-writer offers subtle and sophisticated critical judgements about the literary writings of the 'wits', a self-defined group of writers of the period who assemble at Will's Coffee house. The French correspondent writes here as a critic, naming individuals and making remarks about particular texts. In the second half, the letter moves into a more satirical mode to discuss the 'would-be-wits', an un-named group of hacks and aspirant writers whose writing and critical judgements are dismissed as shallow and ill-considered. Such distinctions were important in defining the nature of criticism in the early eighteenth century.

Will's Coffee-house was, from the Restoration to the reign of Queen Anne, the most celebrated coffee-house for poets and wits. William Urwin opened his eponymous coffee-house shortly after the Restoration, in Russell Street, close to Covent Garden and the theatres. From an early date the coffee-room attracted a group of writers in the circle of the poet and critic John Dryden. Samuel Pepys recorded meeting with this literary society in his diary in February 1664, when he 'stopped at the great Coffee-house there' in Covent Garden, 'where I never was before'. There, he says, he found 'Draydon [Dryden] the poet (I knew at Cambridge) and all the wits of the town, and [Henry] Harris the player and Mr. Hoole [William Howell] of our college; and had I time then, or could at other times, it will be good coming thither, for there I perceive is very witty and pleasant discours' (Pepys, *Diary*, vol. V, p. 37). Curiously, the dominance of Will's in the literary world was being challenged for the first time when this letter was written, by the rising success of Tom's Coffee-house across the road.

The compilation and editing of the *Letters of Wit, Politicks, and Morality* has been attributed to Abel Boyer (*c.* 1667–1729), a Huguenot hack writer who arrived in England in 1689. Boyer first made his name with a series of pedagogical text-books, compendiums, histories and dictionaries: his *Royal Dictionary*, first published in 1699, established his reputation and, running through twenty editions, was a standard work of reference throughout the eighteenth century. The letter extracted here, and the opinions about poets that it offers, has been ascribed to Boyer in numerous works of criticism. The extract is a section entitled 'Original letters on Divers Subjects by Several Hands' (pp. 203–307). Many of these are attributed in the text, but not the present letter. There is no extant manuscript original. The volume was published by a tripartite of successful booksellers: John Hartley next door the King's Head Tavern in Holborn, William Turner in Lincoln's Inn Fields and Thomas Hodgson near Grays-Inn-Gate in Holborn.

LETTER III.

The same to the same. Containing an Account of Will's *Coffeehouse, and of the* Toasting, *and* Kit-Cat-Clubs.

Made *English.*

Dear Sir,

SInce my last, wherein I gave you a view *en passant,* of the Court of *England,* I have endeavour'd to gather an Account of the ingenious

O 4   Men

Men of this Country, which, confidering how referv'd the *Englifh* naturally are to Strangers, has been no fmall difficulty.

The *Englifh* have no fettled *Academies de Beaux-Efprits*, as we have in *Paris*, but inftead of fuch Affemblies, the moft ingenious Perfons of their Nation, meet either in Places of promifcuous Company, as *Coffee-houfes*, or in *Private Clubs*, in *Taverns*. Among the firft *Will's* Coffee-houfe in *Covent-Garden*, holds the firft Rank, as being confecrated to the Honour of *Apollo*, by the firft-rate Wits that flourifh'd in King *Charles* II's Reign, fuch as the late Earl of *Rochefter*, the Marquis of *Normanby*, the Earl of *Dorfet*, Sir *Charles Sidley*, the Earl of *Rofcommon*, Sir *George Etherege*, Mr. *Dryden*, Mr. *Wycherly*, and fome few others; and tho' this Place has loft moft of its illuftrious Founders, yet it has ever fince been fupported by Men of great Worth; but its being accounted the Temple of the *Mufes*, where all *Poets* and *Wits* are to be initiated, has given occafion to its being pefter'd with abundance of falfe Pretenders, who rather darken, than heighten its former Splendor.

The Company which now generally meets at *Will's*, may be divided into two Claffes; the firft of which contains the *Wits*, juftly fo call'd, and the other the *Would-be-Wits*.

Among the firft are Men of diftinguifh'd Merit and Abilities, fuch as Mr. *Wicherley*, Dr. *Garth*, Mr. *Congreve*, the Honorable Mr. *Boyle*, Colonel *Stanhope*, Mr. *Vanbruk*, Mr. *Cheek*, Mr. *Walfh*, Mr. *Burnaby*, Mr. *Rowe*, and fome few others whofe names at prefent do not occur to my memory.

                                                    Mr.

on various Subjects.

Mr. *Wycherly* is univerſally allow'd the firſt place among the *Engliſh* Comick-Poets, who have writ ſince *Ben. Johnſon*. His *Plain-Dealer*, (of which he took the firſt hint from *Moliere's Miſanthrope*) is the beſt Comedy that ever was compos'd in any Language. The only Fault that has been found in it, is its being too full of *Wit*; a Fault which few Authors can be guilty of. He has alſo writ three other Plays, the beſt of which is the *Country Wife.* Mr. *Wycherly* is one of the politeſt Gentlemen in *England*, and the moſt civil and affable to Strangers, eſpecially to thoſe of our Nation, for whom he has an Eſteem; he is a little ſhy and reſerv'd in Converſation, but when a Man can be ſo happy as once to engage him in Diſcourſe, he cannot but admire his profound Senſe, Maſculine Wit, vaſt Knowledge of Mankind, and noble but eaſie Expreſſions. Theſe qualities gain'd Mr. *Wycherly* the Love and Eſteem of his Maſter King *Charles* II. and of his Succeſſor the like King of *Britain*, as the Comelineſs and Gracefulneſs of his Perſon did the Hearts of ſeveral Ladies of their Amorous Courts.

Dr. *Garth* is an eminent Phyſician, of univerſal Learning and polite Literature; his Looks is ſmiling and cheerful; his Converſation free and entertaining; he admires the *Ancients* no farther than they are to be admired; and underſtands and values our beſt *French* writers, eſpecially Monſ. *Deſpreaux*. He has writ a Poem in *Engliſh*, call'd the *Diſpenſary*; wherein he has equall'd, if not exceeded the *Lutrin*, which he had propos'd to himſelf as a Model. His *Diction* is pure and correct; his *Verſes* numerous; his *Satyr* genteel and nice; and his

his *Praises* delicate and natural; in a word, this little Piece is worth an Epick Poem. The only difference I find between him and *Boileau* is, that our *French* Poet got a good Penſion for commending his King, whereas Dr. *Garth* has got nothing for the juſt Praiſes he has beſtow'd on his.

Mr. *Congreve* is a Gentleman whoſe Poetry has been in vogue for 6 or 7 years paſt, but whoſe late Performances have not met with ſo favourable a Reception; not ſo much, as I am told, thro' the defeſt of his Muſe, as the fickleneſs of the Town, in their Taſtes and Opinions. He has writ two Comedies, *viz.* the *Old Batchelour*, and *Love for Love*, and a Tragedy call'd, *The Mourning Bride*, which have been aſted with an univerſal Applauſe. His Maſter-piece is an Elegy, by way of Paſtoral, on the Death of the late Queen of *England*, which comes up to the beſt performances of that kind of *Theocritus* and *Virgil*. Mr. *Congreve* it a polite, well-bred Perſon, but ſomewhat cold and referv'd, unleſs he be among his intimate Friends. He is particularly belov'd by my Lord *Dorſet*, and my Lord *Hallifax*, the *Mæcenas's* of the *Engliſh* Muſes.

The Honourable Mr. *Boyle*, tho' Grandſon to the famous Earl of *Orrery*, is yet more diſtinguiſhed by his Learning, Politeneſs, and Affability, than by his illuſtrious Birth. He underſtands *Greek* and *Latin* like an Vniverſity Profeſſor of thoſe Languages; and writes *Engliſh* as well, as if he never had ſtudied any thing but his Mother-Tongue. He has, like his Grandfather, a happy Vein in Poetry. To this Gentleman we owe a very Correſt Edition, with a *Latin* Verſion, of

the

on various Subjects.

the Epiſtles of *Phalaris,* and a very learned *Diſ-ſertation* on the ſame Epiſtles, occaſion'd by Dr. *Bentley*'s the King's Library Keeper, refuſing to lend him the *Greek* M S.

Colonel *Stanhope* (Nephew to my Lord *Cheſterfield*, and Son to the famous *Nego-tiator* Mr. *Stanhope*, at preſent King *Wil-liam*'s Envoy at the *Hague*) is a Gentleman of great Literature and Judgment; he underſtands *Spaniſh* and *Italian*, and is acquainted with the Beauties of our Language to a greater Perfection, than any *Engliſh* Gentleman that ever I had the op-portunity to diſcourſe with. Beſides theſe Qua-lifications, he is well Read both in ancient and modern Hiſtory, which gives him a clear in-ſight into the preſent Intereſt of Princes.

Mr. *Vanbruk* is a Gentleman of great natural Parts which he has ſtill improv'd by Travel, and Converſation, more than by Books; he has writ three Comedies, *viz.* the *Relapſe*, *Æſop*, and the *Provok'd Wife*; wherein he diſcovers a great knowledge of Men and Manners, and a wonder-ful Happineſs in expreſſing his Thoughts, and which ſhews him to have always convers'd a-mong the Good.

Mr. *Cheek* is a Gentleman who both by his Education, and his converſe with the beſt Authors, and moſt ingenious Men of the Age, has ac-quir'd a true Taſte of Poetry, and Proſaick Wri-ting. He is alſo famous for writing a great ma-ny Songs, full of Wit and inimitable Graces.

Mr. *Walſh*, a Member of the Parliament of *England*, is a Gentleman of univerſal Literature and juſt Diſcernment. He underſtands and re-liſhes our beſt *French* Authors, eſpecially *Voiture*, and *Boileau*; and is ſaid to be the Author of a
very

very learned and judicious Differtation prefix'd to *Virgil's* Paftorals, tranflated by Mr. *Dryden.*

Mr. *Burnaby*, is a gentleman of a very happy Genius in Comedy; of which he has given us the firft Effay in a Play call'd *The Reform'd Wife*, which for the Excellency of the Plot, and the fhining Charaêter of a fick Lady, has met with the general Approbation.

Mr. *Rowe* is a Gentleman that promifes very much, he hath given us a Tragedy call'd the *Ambitious Step Mother*, which has been univerfally applauded.

Befides the foremention'd Gentlemen, there are many others that frequent *Will's* Coffeehoufe, who have great skill in the Liberal Arts and Sciences, as Mathematicks, Architeêture, Mufick, Painting, *&c.* and who diftinguifh themfelves from the impertinent *Writings*, by their Polite, ingenious, and Regular Converfation; for here, as indeed every where elfe, the moft foolifh are always the loudeft, and thofe fpeak moft who have the leaft to fay.

Now to give you the Names and Charaêters of all the *Would-be-Wits*, that refort to *Will's*, would be as tedious and impertinent, as their Converfation is to Men of Senfe; however 'tis but fit I fhould defcribe them to you in general Terms, that you may avoid their Company, if ever your curiofity fhould bring you to the place.

Some of thefe *Wittlings* diftinguifh themfelves by Railing both at the *French* Writers, whom they don't underftand, and at thofe *Englifh* Authors, whofe Excellencies they cannot reach with them *Voiture* is flat and dull; *Corneille* a

ftranger

on various Subjects.

ftranger to the Paffions; *Racine* ftarch'd and affected; *Moliere, Jejune*; *La Fontaine*, a poor Tel-
ler of Tales; and even our Divine *Boileau*, no
more than a Plagiary from the Ancients.   As
for the *Englifh* Poets, they treat 'em almoft with
the fame freedom: *Shakefpear*, with them, has
neither Language nor Manners; *Ben. Johnfon* is
a Pedant; *Dryden* little more than a good Verfi-
fier; *Congreve* a laborious unnatural Writer; and
Garth a Copier.   Some of thefe *Criticks* are great
admirers of the Ancients, but their ill, lame
Tranflations of them, ridicule thofe they would
commend; Others are ftrenuous fticklers for the
Moderns, but their own ill Compofures deftroy
the force of their Arguments, and do the Ancients fufficient Juftice, Others, in a fond imitation of the incomparable *Milton*, miftake *Bombaft*
and *puffy Expreffions* for *Sublime*; and having had
their fuftian Plays damn'd upon the Stage, ran-
fack *Boffu* and *Dacier*, to arräign the ill Tafte of the
Town.   Others having met with the fame misfortune, hope to preferve their unlawful Title
to Wit, by bringing all that write, down to
their own level.   Thefe Men are indefatigably
Induftrious in enquiring what Plays are upon
the Stocks, what ready to be launch'd forth;
and if they can be inform'd of any remarkable
Fault in them, they never fail to whifper it a-
bout, to fecure the Damnation of the Play, before its Reprefentation.   Others have got a Reputation by their undigefted Medleys of *Comedy* and
Farce.   For, Sir, you muft know, upon the
Englifh Stage, any thing that is eminently Ill, has
almoft the fame fuccefs with what is excellently
Good.   Others ferve the Town in the double
                                        Capacity

Capacity, of Poets and Players; and what by reviving, altering, and travesting old Plays; fathering other Peoples Productions, and filching Plots from some Authors, who trust their writings to their perusal, make a shift to get more Money than the true Poets. *All these Would-be-Wits*, are never so busie as on the first night of a new Play, for then 'tis that their Grand-Jury sits, and the boldest of the Company having read the Charge against the Poet at the Bar, the most Eloquent opens the Indictment, learnedly explains the three Unities, the Fable, Manners, and Language which are requisite in the *Drama*, and having prov'd the Criminal to have Trespass'd on most of the fore-mention'd Heads, the grave Fore-man finds the *Bill*, and they all unanimously conclude, that *the Play will not run;* but then it generally happens, that the Town, who certainly is the best Critick, reverses the Verdict of those unwarranted Judges, and with loud Applauses acquit the Prisoner.

Among the other Pretenders to Wit, that repair to *Will's*, some have nothing to depend on but *Quibbling* and *Punning*; and these are the sport of the true Wits, who laugh (at least simper) at the cold Jester, whilst they seem to Laugh at the Jest. Others are only Conspicuous, by disturbing ingenious Company with their accounts of *Bear-Garden* Entertainments, and Bawdy-Stories, which they often repeat, till they are left by themselves. Others retail the *Politicks* they had at *Tom's* (a Coffeehouse adjoining to *Will's*) by wholesale; and in return they carry away whole Bales of *scraps of Wit*, which they vend at *Tom's*. In general, most People here, that frequent Coffee-houses,

on various Subjects.

fee-houfes, fet up for *Politicians*; it being the Prerogative of an *Englifh-man* to fettle the Nation, altho he be not worth a Groat. There come alfo to *Will's* fome Gentlemenn of nice Drefs, which the *Englifh* call *Beaux*, let them be never fo ugly ; and thefe frequent the place only the better to gain the Favour of fome Ladies in this Town, who are mighty fond of Intrieguing with a Wit ; and care not what becomes of their *Honour*, fo they may fecure the Reputation of their *Senfe*. Some Poets have of late ridicul'd thefe *Beaux* upon the Stage, which I much wonder at, they being a fort of inoffenfive, well-bred People, that never quarrel with any Body, except their Taylors, and Perriwig-makers.

Befides the Company at *Will's*, there are in *London* two famous Clubs of Gentlemen, that meet at fet times in Taverns, for the pleafure of Converfation; the firft and ancienteft is that of the *Knights of the Toaft*, whofe number is never to exceed Thirteen; the other is the *Kit-cat-club*, whofe number is about 36, but yet unlimited. Thefe Clubs are compos'd of felect Perfons, eminent as well by their Birth and Titles, as by their Wit and Senfe. To give you an account of the particular Characters of the Members of thefe illuftrious Clubs, and of the Rules they obferve, would fwell this Letter to a large Volume; nay, the very Derivation of the Names of *Toaft* and *Kit-cat* is fo dubious, and controverted, that it would require a Differtation to trace it to its true Original. You muft therefore excufe me, if I fay no more upon that matter at prefent.

Befides

224   *Original Letters.*

Befides the *Wits* that refort to *Will's*, there are
a great many *Englifh* Gentlemen, (and even Peers
of the Realm) who are famous for their ingenious Compofitions and good Literature ; but
having already trangreft the compafs of a Letter, I refer to fpeak of all thefe in a particular
Account of the *Englifh* Poets, which you may expect in a little time.

   I am,

     S I R,

         &c.   &c.

Edward Ward, *The Humours of a Coffee-House: a Comedy* (London, for Bohee the Coffee-Man, and sold at the publishing-office, in Bearbinder-Lane, 1707), 28pp. BL: Cup.401.K.11. ESTCP225. Hünersdorff.

A weekly satirical newspaper in which each issue is a four-page prose dialogue between small groups of men who meet in Bohee's coffee-house, a fictional location in London (bohea is a quality of China tea). Each man represents an interest or profession. Ward uses this format as an opportunity to stage discussions between these various characters about affairs of state and other matters of public concern, such as the conduct of the War of the Spanish Succession in Europe, the stock-market, astrology, charitable fund-raising and quack remedies – and especially how these diverse discourses are mutually informative. As Ward remarks: 'All men own *News* and *Coffee-House Conversation* is the very Life of London' (p. 283). The purpose of the paper is not to impart news of events, which were covered with much greater accuracy and detail by others, nor to criticise the conduct of the war, although many critical remarks are voiced. Rather, the coffee-house comedy is exploited to show how the same events are understood, discussed, and reflected upon by different kinds of people. In Ward's world, each man reacts to events according to how they impact upon his own interest. Unlike *The Tatler* and *Spectator* of Steele and Addison, which borrowed the coffee-house conceit from publications like Ward's, there is no figure like Mr Spectator who expresses a middle way and a reformative project. In Ward's coffee-house satire, man is ineluctably selfish, ready to sacrifice everything – nation, religion, monarchy – to his own personal prosperity.

Edward, or Ned, Ward (1667–1731) was one of the pre-eminent satirists of the early eighteenth century. His first Hudibrastic verses, *The Poet's Ramble after Riches*, were published in 1691 (London, printed by J. Millet). After publishing several prose satires, he found great success with *The London Spy*, a monthly periodical prose satire that took the form of a guided tour of the seamy side of London life, including several scenes located in coffee-houses. *The London Spy* had more than five editions in Ward's lifetime, and has had several modern editions (*The*

London Spy, ed. by Paul Hyland (East Lansing, Colleagues Press, 1993)). While publishing the London Spy, Ward also published *The Weekly Comedy, as it is dayly acted at most Coffee-Houses in London, etc.* (London, J. How, 1699), which ran for ten issues between 10 May and 10 July 1699, and which prefigured the structure and approach of the 1707 venture. *The Humours of a Coffee House* was published in weekly parts, coming out on Wednesday mornings in penny numbers. It was published by the bookseller Samuel Bunchley, who kept shop at the Publishing-Office in Dove-Court, near Bearbinder-Lane, near the Stocks Market in the City. The paper came to an end after seven issues on 6 August 1707. After the interval of a week, the paper was continued for another twenty-four issues (Wednesday 13 August 1707–Thursday 22 January 1708) by William Oldisworth under the revised title *The Weekly Comedy: or, The Humours of a Coffee-House*, published by John Morphew. See Howard Troyer, *Ned Ward of Grub Street* (Cambridge, MA, Harvard University Press, 1946), p. 222.

(1)

THE
Humours of a *Coffee-House* :
A
COMEDY.

As it is Dayly Acted by

Levy, *a Recruiting Officer.*
Hazard, *a Gamester.*
Bite, *a Sharper.*
Nice, *a Beau.*
Blunt, *a Plain Dealer.*
Whim, *a Projector.*

Venture, *a Merchant.*
Talley, *a Stock-Jobber.*
Querpo, *a Quack.*
Trick, *a Lawyer.*
Horoscope, *an Astrologer.*

Shuffle, *a Time-server.*
Bays, *a Poet.*
Compass, *a Sailor.*
Harlem, *a News-writer.*
Bohee, *the Coffee-man.*

Note, These Persons are introduc'd only as occasion serves.

Wednesday, June 25th, 1707.

The PROLOGUE.

THE *various Humours that Divert the Age,*
  In Pomp appear on This *frequented Stage:*
  Soldier and Priest, each in their different ways,
Prophanely Curses, or Devoutly Prays:
The Doctor *here, cries up his Cordial Pills,*
Which some for Gain, but few for Conscience *Sells.*
The Parson, *Gravely proves, from Writ Divine,*
Coffee's *a Christian Liquor, —— after Wine ;*
Yet in his warmer Hours his Soul Unmasks,
And Bans the Heritick's *Averse to Flasks,*
But would more willingly a Turkish *Faith approve,*
Did but their Mufties Drink as well as Love.

The

The Soldier *talks of* Hockftedt's *Fatal Plain,*
Of Cities *Storm'd, and* Gallick *Heroes Slain ;*
But the Fair Sex, *who well his Valour knew,*
Says, He more Soldiers *Got than e'er he Slew:*
And when Inftructing Time the Truth unfolds,
His Dead appear,———————— but on the Mufter-Rolls.
The Painted Fop, *who Graceful Carriage Apes,*
And to his Artful Taylor owes his Shapes :
Pleas'd-with the Fictious Tale of Foreign Wounds,
Protefts he'll leave the Tender Sex, *Gad Z——;*
And meet the French Gens d' Arms *on* Banftead Downs.
The Merchant *here, of Lofs complains in Trade,*
But never tells you what his Miftrefs *had ;*
Tradefmen, *in Aprons, moft profoundly Wife,*
Turn Statefmen; *and the* Government *Advife.*
Officious Fame *a Thoufand Stories tells,*
Improves the Thoughts, and fo to Falfehood fwells ;
From hence the Prattler *takes her fudden Rife,*
Pleas'd with her Toil, *grows ftronger as fhe flies.*

Enter Blunt, Harlem, Nice, Whim, Venture *and* Talley.

Blunt. POUGH——, pcugh---, for Heaven's fake, a little Air! Here, you Boy, what have you got to drink befides your damn'd Mahometan and Heathenifh Liquors of *Coffee* and *Tea ?* O, Mr. *Harlem,* your Humble Servant ; Mr. *Nice* yours ; Gentlemen I'm all your Humfervants.   *(Going out.)*

Harlem. Dear Mr. *Blunt,* whither are you going fo hiftily ?

Blunt. Going ! with a P——, I have more reafon to afk why you ftay. Pray, Gentlemen, tell me your Satfsfaction here ; for if you love *Fire* and *Smoke,* why don't you Lift your felves in the Army ? If *Noife* and *Nonfenfe,* why don't you go to Sea ? If you wou'd learn *Politicks,* why not go to the *Meeting-Houfe ?* But if you have a mind to Sleep, why con t you go to *Church ?* As I hope to be a Member of Parliament, this is not a piace fit for Human Society, for I neither Hear, Speak, See, or Breath what I wou'd do.

Nice. As I hope for the Ladies Graces, Mr. *Blunt,* you are the moft miftaken Man in the whole World ; for a *Coffee-Houfe* is the perfect Epitome of Mankind. You have furely loft your tafte of every thing that is Curious aud Delicate.

Blunt. And you wou'd have me lo e my Underftanding too. I thank you heartily, Gentle-men, the Weather is not hot anough yet for *Bedlam ;* but 'tis abundanily too warm to live in a *Coffee-Houfe-Stove* all Day, while the Air blows cool refrefhing Breezes in St. *James's* *Park,* Spring-Garden, &c. But what *News* have you got among you to invite my ftay ?

Harlem. Indeed, Sir, the Town is very Barren at prefent, but we are big with great Expectations ; and I am fure to have the firft and beft Account of any ; for I will not ftick to fay,—— but I believe I have Intelligence as quick, and mine is as good too as fome People that ought to have better ; you know, Gentlemen, what I mean, but Talking is dangerous in thefe Times, when Matters don't go fo well. However, you know the Duke of *Savoy* is a Brave Ally. Well, I cou'd fay fomething on that Head, very Great and Noble, but a little time will fhow it all. In fhort, Gentlemen, he will certainly penetrate *Dauphine.* I have an Agent, or, as I may call him, a *Minifter* of mine, that will attend the Army all this *Campaign.* I am fure of an exact Journal of all their Proceedings ; not a Horfe or a Man wil be Loft, or Taken, but what I fhall have an Account of.

Nice. What fay you to that, Mr. *Blunt ;* is not this worth two or three hours Santring in a *Coffee-Houfe ?* For my part, I think it the Life

of

(3)

of Converſation. For this way of Prognoſtica-ting of Affairs, as I may call it, has ſuch a tick-ling Satisfaction in it, I cou'd be pleas'd with it all Day ; 'tis out of the Common Road ; I hate ev'ry thing that is Vulgar. Here have we now this Morning, with Mr. *Harlem*'s aſſiſtance, March'd the Army, and Settled the Quarters of all the Forces in *Spain, Savoy, Flanders,* and *Germany,* for a Week together ; and I dare lay you a Bottle of *Burgundy,* Mr. *Blunt,* that none of 'em March an *Italian* Mile wide of the places we have appointed them.

Whim. Nay, I can aſſure you, Mr. *Harlem* is always pretty well aſſured of what will happen before he ſays it ; for if I find it in his Paper, that the Allies are near the Enemy, that their Troops are in good Order, and deſire an Engage-ment, tho' there be a Superiority on the other ſide, what do I do ? But whip to the *Change,* take a Thouſand Pounds, or more, to give three, if a Battle does not happen in ſo many Days, and we beat the Army ; I durſt, almoſt, venture upon the number of Slain and Priſoners, but that you know wou'd be a little too much, and might be reckon'd Preſumption. And this way, I can aſſure you, Mr. *Blunt,* I have won at leaſt Twenty Battles of thoſe that have been Fought this laſt War.

Blunt. Twenty Battles ! Ha--, ha--, ha--. Pray how many, do you reckon, have been Fought this laſt War ?

Whim. At leaſt a Hundred. I'm ſure Prince *Eugene* has Fought above Thirty of 'em, that are freſh in my Memory ; and the Duke of *Marlborough* cannot but have Fought twice as many. Hold, let me ſee, if we look into the *German* Journal, we ſhall find a great many more. Come, Mr. *Blunt,* I'll lay you a hundred Guineas of what I ſay.

Venture. Pray, Mr. *Whim,* let me go Twenty with you.

Talley. And me Twenty more, here is the Money.   (*Pulling out Gold.*)

Blunt. Put up your Moneys, Gentlemen, I am no Wagerer ; but ſince you are ſo particular in your Account of Battles Fought, pray what had you upon the like Battle of *Almanza ?*

Whim. I thank Mr. *Harlem* for it, not one doit. But you muſt know, I never approv'd of our Affairs there after my Lord *Peterborough* went away : How he bang'd 'em about from *Pillar* to *Poſt.* 'Tis true, my Lord *Galway* is a Brave General, and a Man of Excellent Conduct ; but what then, if Luck is not on his ſide ? Give me a Fortunate Man to Lead an Army. A Man that will Fight 2 or 1000 with 500, and beat 'em when he has done.

Nice. I think, with ſubmiſſion to the Company, Mr. *Whim,* tho' he is ſeldom miſtaken, is now

beſide the matter ; for if a Lucky General ſhou'd engage againſt ſo great a Superiority, and be bea-ten, his Conduct wou'd be call'd in queſtion.

Whim. I have nothing to do with Conduct ; but I tell you, if he's beaten, he's an *Unlucky Man,* and I am for a *Fortunate General,* that was ne-ver beaten.

Nice. But how ſhall a General tell whether he ſhall be beaten or no before he Engages, only from the Goodneſs of his Troops, or the Equal-lity of his Numbers?

Whim. Mr. *Nice,* that is not the Point I am upon ; but if a Man is a *Fortunate Man,* he can-not be an *Unfortunate Man* ; and I'll put that to the Company, if I am not in the right on't.

Blunt. Moſt undoubtedly. I wonder any Body ſhou'd diſpute it with you. And now we are in for *Politicks,* pray, Mr. *Harlem,* what Intelligence from the *North* ?

Nice. Did not I tell you this was the moſt Diverting Converſation in the World. Oh the Felicities of *Coffee-Houſe* Chit Chat ! I'll warrant you'll have no power to ſtir this Evening now : The Varieties of this place are not to be Paral-rel'd in the Vniverſe again.

Harlem. Pray, Sir, excuſe me, Mr. *Blunt* was aſking after the Affairs of the *North* ; and, I be-lieve, I am capable of giving him an Inſight in-to thoſe Tranſactions farther than any Body, tho' they are Dark, and ſomething Myſterious, that I muſt own, but the Golden-Key unlocks the Cabinet of Princes. I pay Dear for my In-telligence ; but the Town conſiders it, and va-lues my Papers beyond the *State-News* ; I have Letters ſometimes that every one wonders from whence they ſhou'd come ; but let 'em wonder on, that's a Secret I ſhall not diſcloſe, I give an Account of things done in *Spain,* and the *Mediterranean,* before any Mails can arrive.

Blunt. How's that poſſible, good Mr. *Harlem ?* Methinks you put the Matter a little too far ; Do you keep a *Pegaſus* on purpoſe for your own Diſpatches, that will ſerve no Body elſe ?

Harlem. I hope you will excuſe me, Sir, I told you it was a Secret. I won't be Pumpt, Sir, you miſtake your Man.

Blunt. (*Aſide.*) If you had your Deſerts, you ought to be Pumpt, but I'll humour the Fool a little for my own Diverſion. You are Paſſionate, Mr. *Harlem,* and have quite forgot my Queſtion. I aſk'd you what Intelligence from the *North* ?

Whim. A Word in your Ear, Sir, upon my Credit he has ſome things from the *North,* will make you ſtand upon your Head. But, as you are a Gentleman, let it go no further ; there is Money to be got. You know the Lands of *Sile-ſia,* whoſe they are, to whom they are aſſign'd, and for what ? But who's going there think you, and to what End ? God knows ! Things go ve-ry oddly !   *Harlem.*

(4)

Harlem. You are a ftrange Man, Mr. *Whim,* to make fuch a Fool of a Queftion, when you know, I know all that Matter, and I think I can tell my Story as well as Mr. *Whim.*

Blunt. Pray, Gentlemen, don't Quarrel about fuch a Trifle; but let me have the Account from either of you.

Harlem. A Trifle! Do you call i ? I think it was very Impertinent in Mr. *Whim* to take upon him the telling of a Secret I had juft communicated to him without my Privity. I have nothing to fay againft Mr. *Whim's* Capacity in his own Affairs; but this was peculiar to my Province; and he ought, in Civility and Good Manners, to have left it to me. I own he's a Notable Man in his own Bufinefs; but what's that to *State-Affairs?* It requires a *Head*; it requires *Secrecy*, and *Difpatch* to be a Man of my Bufinefs; and I muft tell you, Mr. *Blunt*, every little Fellow is not fit to tell *News* ; there is more in it than every one is aware of : It requires *Thought* to *Digeft*; *Memory* to *Recollect*; and *Eloquence* to *Exprefs* it aptly and agreeably to the Tafte of the Town.

Blunt. But what's all this to the *North* ?

Harlem. I think it a great Matter both to *Eaft, Weft, North,* and *South,* Sir, to have a Story told as it fhou'd be, and therefore defire to be excus'd. But to the Matter, you know the King of *Sweden* has a Powerful Army; but you do not know what he defigns 'em for; 'tis a Myftery to many, but not to me. I had Letters from *Saxony* the laft Mail, he is there yet, and may continue fo fome time, but——— Well, Mr. *Blunt*, you feem to be a clear Headed Gentleman, I need not explain things fo openly as a Man would be oblig'd to do to fome fort of People. Have you a mind to Buy or Sell *Stocks,* I'll put you in a way. There's Mr. *Talley* now, one of us, he'll ufe you like a Friend. There's Money to be got, Mr. *Whim* knows it. Some People are frighted with the *Swedes* Marching thro' *Silefia;* I can tell the Secret of that; *Stocks* muft fall; but I fay Buy.

Whim. You may depend upon Mr. *Harlem,* as I faid before, he's feldom or never miftaken in thefe matters. If you wont Buy, come, now, I'll be your Chapman; will you Sell?

Blunt. I fhall neither Sell nor Buy, indeed, Mr. *Whim.* But where's the News all this while ?

Whim. You don't take it. I'll whifper a Word in your Ear: The *Swedes* only ftay in *Germany* till they have made *Stocks* fall. The *Stock-Jobbers* on the *Change* of *London* will raife them 100000*l.* Contribution, that they may have the Advantages they are capable of

making of fuch an Expedition; and then they'll order them to March back again.

Blunt. Pray communicate this Affair to Mr. *Venture* there, for I'm an Abfolute Stranger to the Myftery of *Stock-Jobbing.*

Venture. And I defire to continue fo, fo long as I live. But if Mr. *Harlem* could fatisfie me when I fhall have fuch a fafe Convoy as I may venture my Ships out of Harbour without danger from the Enemy, I fhou'd be infinitely oblig'd to him.

Whim. Yours are bound for the *Weft-Indies,* I think, Mr. *Venture* ; I'll *Enfure* you upon that Head, for 12 *per Cent,* which is very Modeft at this time of day.

Venture. And pray, Mr. *Whim,* whom will you get to *Enfure* that a *Projector* fhall ftand till my Venture returns?

Whim. If you are fo unreafonable to require it, I dare engage my Neighbour *Tally* and Mr. *Harlem* will enter into Bonds with me.

Venture. Truly, Mr. *Whim,* I fhall not be fo reafonable as to accept of all the *Projectors, Stock-Jobbers,* and *News-Writers* in *Great Britain* for my Security.

Whim. And why, Mr. *Venture,* are not we as good as e'er a *Merchant* of you all ? It you go to that, I believe you'll find two of you fail for one of us.

Venture. The Reafon of that's plain, we are moft *Honeft Men,* and you are *all Knaves.*

Talley. Come, come, Mr. *Venture,* we are not talking now, *who are the Honefter Men,* but, according to the General Acceptation of the Word in way of Trade, *who are the Beft Men;* and then pray tell me what you have to Object againft any of us? There's Mr. *Harlem;* take him fingly, his very *Poftfcripts* are worth a Thoufand Pounds a Year, befide his *Poft-Man,* his *Poft-Boy, Flying-Poft, Englifh-Poft,* and *Daily Courant.* And do you think the Bufinefs that paffes thro' my Hands is not double and treble the value? I thought Mr. *Venture* had underftood Bufinefs better.

Blunt. Let me defire you, Gentlemen, to lay afide Difputes of this Nature ; but it is high time to be moving now; however, If you will promife to be good Company, I will venture into a Coffee-Houfe with you now and then for an Hours Diverfion, and oblige you with what Occurrences fall in my way.

Nice. I hope the next time we meet we may have fome good News to entertain our felves withal, in the mean time I am, Gentlemen, your very Humble Servant.

All. Adieu.

London, Printed for the Benefit of *Bohee,* the *Coffee-Man*; and Sold at the **Publifhing-Office,** in *Bearbinder-Lane,* 1 7 0 7.

(5)   Numb. II.

THE

Humours of a *Coffee-House*:

A

COMEDY.

As it is Dayly Acted by

Levy, *a Recruiting Officer.*	Venture, *a Merchant.*	Shuffle, *a Time-server.*
Hazard, *a Gamester.*	Talley, *a Stock-Jobber.*	Bays, *a Poet.*
Bite, *a Sharper.*	Querpo, *a Quack.*	Compass, *a Sailor.*
Nice, *a Beau.*	Trick, *a Lawyer.*	Harlem, *a News-writer.*
Blunt, *a Plain Dealer.*	Horoscope, *an Astrologer.*	Bohee, *the Coffee-man.*
Whim, *a Projector.*		

Note, These Persons are introduc'd only as occasion serves.

From **Wednesday**, June 25th, to **Wednesday** July the 2d, 1 7 0 7.

Shuffle. MR. *Hazard*, your Humble Servant. How go Matters at the *Groom-Porters*, and at *Marrow-bone?* What, down in the Mouth? I wish I had not spoke to him: A Thousand Pounds to a Penny but the Rogue Borrows Money of me. *(Aside.)*

Hazard. Nothing can be worse than Ill-Luck, that Damn'd Jilt *Fortune* has turn'd her Tail upon me; and suffer'd me to be strip'd to a single *Guinea.* ——The Bowling-Green stands just where it did, and those that have least occasion for it are always the greatest Winners.

Horoscope. How! *Fortune* a Jilt? Take care of offending a *Goddess* whom all the World makes Application to. *Fortune* is always in the right, and those that blame her in the wrong. You should have consulted your Stars, Man, that they might have Pointed you out a Lucky Minute.

Hazard. Consulted my Stars! That was the way to be Poorer by a couple of Shillings, or half a Crown, than I am. A Murrain take all *Astrologers.* They were Born under Three-penny Planets themselves, and the whole Fraternity joyn'd together can't furnish a Man with Fifty Pieces upon occasion; but here's Honest *Ned Shuffle*, is the Man for my Money.

Shuffle. And for his own too, for he designs to keep it. *(Aside)* Hang all Sorrow, or rather Drown it I say, *The worse Luck now the better another time.* I wish it was in my Power to serve you, but I must away this Moment to wait upon a certain Great Man, and so Adieu to you.

Bohee. Coffee or *Tea* Gentlemen?

B   *Bohee.*

(6)

Hazard. The way of the World to a Hair's breadth: All he has to do is to *Serve himself*, and be of the fame Complection with the *Prevailing Party.* In King *Charles* the Second's time, who more eager than him for putting the *Penal Laws* in Execution ; in King *James's*, who a greater Stickler for abolishing them ; in King *William's*, who more violent for fending home the *Dutch* Blew-Guards in the *English* Service ; in Queen *Anne's* who more Complaifant to our *Dutch* Allies.

Bohee. Had you play'd your Game half fo well as he has, you would have been a better Man than you are by fome Thoufands. But to the purpofe, what *News* ftirring among the Great Ones? For that's all they give thofe for their Money that Play with 'em ?

Hazard. Good again ! As if I came to a *Coffee-Houfe* to tell News inftead of hearing it. Come, I know you long to be difcharg'd of all you know, what fay the Wagerers about *Thoulon ?*

Bohee. Thofe that lay 'twill be Taken, are almoft certain that it will not, and thofe that hope it will not be Taken, Wager that it will.

Hazard. This is meer putting the *Doctor* upon my Underftanding; be pleas'd to explain your felf Sweet Mr. *Milk and Water.*

Bohee. That is eafily done without an *Oedipus.* Becaufe they that lay it will be Taken, only do it in order to draw in others to Stake that *it will not*; and thofe that hope it *will not* be Taken, Wager that it *will*, in order to difguife their *Principles*.

Hazard. All Trick and meer Artifice. Thofe *Stock Jobbers* and *we Gamefters* are Brother-Sterlings, that they may take four to one on One Side, that they may take four to one on the Other. But a Fig for the *French* King and all his Fortreffes. What Domeftick News have you ? For this Town is fo Fruitful you can't be without fome, fo long as *Knaves, Fools*, and *Madmen* Refort to't.

Bohee. Why, that's true ; and for fear we fhould not have enough at Home, we have a frefh Supply from *France.*

Hazard. Mercy upon us ! As if we had not *Madmen* enough of our own Growth, but muft be furnifh'd with thofe of a Foreign Extraction. Prithee what fort of *Lunaticks ?*

Bohee. Such a fort as never came under *Tyfon's* Hands ; you have heard of the *French Prophets ?*

Hazard. The Town rings of 'em, Pray what of them ?

Bohee. Nothing, but that they are come to reveal wonderful things, as the down'al of *Po-*

-pery, and five Hundred other Occurrences that will tend to the Benefit of this Famous City.

Hazard. I doubt they will fearce be as big as their Words ; fince, what with Briefs for the Support of thefe pretended *French Proteftants*, and what with underworking the Natives of that Country which gives 'em Bread, they have reduc'd many to *Poverty*, for want of what they Rob them of.

Bohee. Sir, if you pleafe to give me leave to tell out my Story, well and good, if not, I'll go and tell it to fome-Body elfe. ——— You muft know that thefe *Camifars* were taken Up, and admitted to Bail.

Hazard. Great News indeed ! As if our Ears had not been Deafen'd with them, and their Proceedings at a *Half Penny a piece.*

Bohee. But my Neighbour *Tea and Nay*, the *Quaker*, was here juft now, and has given fuch a Relation of 'em as is altogether *New*. They were no fooner got out of the *Juftice of Peace* his Hands, by being Bail'd, but they took a Shop of *Infpiration*; (as they call it) in *Barbican*, which, by their way of managing themfelves, might be called the *Club-Room of Ugly Faces.* And here they whin'd and fcrew'd themfelves into fuch Poftures, that feveral People, I won't fay as *Great Knaves*, but as *Wife as themfelves*, became their *Profelites* ; among the reft, a Man of *WORSHIP* and *AUTHORITY*, that fhall be Namelefs, becaufe he writes himfelf an *Efquire*, made his Appearance, who, no longer fince then *Thurfday* laft was Sevennight, open'd their Affembly with a *Pathetick Difcourfe* in Praife of their *Sanctity* and *Pious Revelations* for the *Good and Advantage of this Ancient and Honourable City.* This Puny *COUNSEL* had no fooner made his Harrangue, but who but a *Camifar* of his *Infpir'd Tribe* to fecond him, and enters into the Merits of the *Caufe*, which was done in the Language of the *Dumb-Man*, by abundance of *Yawns, Miferable Howls, Diftortions*, and *Grimaces. Yet at laft he fpake with his Tongue* ; but fo little to the Purpofe, that the People, who came out of Curiofity to fee the Refult of their great *Sanctity*, Emphatically declar'd 'em *Impoftors*, by breaking their *Windows*, defacing their *Pews*, and many other Indignities.

Hazard. Moft certainly thefe Fellows will be Profecuted, and found Guilty of the Statute of Queen *Elizabeth.*

Bohee. As fure as Eggs are Eggs ; but the Cream of the Jeft lies in the worthy Gentleman above-mentioned, who muft needs be a *Dreamer of Dreams*, forfooth, and run away with a Detail of them to a certain Great Man. He was no fooner afk'd his Errand, but his Anfwer was

the

(7)

the Lord had sent him to reveal a Matter of the highest Importance, which was, That he was Commanded from Above to Order a Noli Prosequi for these Righteous Offenders. The Great Man, for he was no Less, heard him with a wonderful Attention, and often ask'd him if he was sure The Lord had sent him to him, and was always answer'd in the Affirmative. Hold, said the Magistrate, very Gravely, Sir, you are undoubtedly mistaken, for had the Lord sent you, he had certainly sent you to the Attorney-General, and not to me, for it is altogether his Business: Which was no small Mortification to the Mad-Messenger, who had Modesty enough amidst his Impudence, to Blush at so unexpected a Reply.

Hazard. Notably well said my Friend Bobee.

——— Prithee, Bays, an Extempore Line or two upon these Enthusiasts.

Bays. Have at them by Guess, then, as the Saying is.

    Is England's Bedlam grown so thin
      Of Folks without their Senses,
    That we must Foreigners call in
      To Cheat us with Pretences?
    O Fair Augusta! Suffer none
      On Britain to Impose,
    But such as you for Natives own,
      And are from Britain's Rose.
    Else I, that am no Prophet, swear
      By all that's Just and Holy,
    Your Madness may with their's compare,
      As you exceed in Fol'y.

Whim. Well said, Bays, thou'rt a Merry Mortal; but Horoscope looks as Dull as a broken Gamester, and as Sneaking as a Captain broke for Cowardice: I'll warrant Constellation's afraid these Prophets will beat him at his own Weapons, and get the Whip-Hand of him with the Stars.

Horoscope. Don't tell me of your Journeymen-Jesuits, your Enthusiastical Sedition-Mongers, come, or rather sent over to Distract us, as Jo. J———bs, that Raking Draper-Trooper, and now Whisking Tubster has already done: I fear them not. I have a Wonderful Scheme in my Head: You must understand I design a Reformation in Astrology and Astronomy too: For it is a Shame that in a Country call'd Christian, we shou'd not endeavour to remove Paganism out of the Heavens where those Heathenish Astrologers, like the Antient Ægyptian Idolaters, Worship'd Rams, Bulls, Bears and Horses. Certainly this is a great Oversight in our Modern Astrologers, not to Banish these Heathenish Rubbish out of the Firmament, and place in their room some Good Christian Saints; for what right had Perseus more to be Constellated for Killing

a Whale, than St. George for Killing a Dragon?
Blunt. But then, Sweet Mr. Horoscope, supposing it to be as you say, we must then argue after this manner, instead of saying Mars or Jupiter are in Conjunction with Venus or Saturn, we must say, St. George, or St. Denis is in Conjunction with St. Mary or St. Agatha.

Horoscope. Right, Sir, upon my Life you understand the Cœlestial Sciences; and I admire your profound Capacity.

Blunt. Then again, Sir, instead of saying the Sun is so many Degrees Eclips'd in Cauda Draconis, we must say, St. George's Nose is enter'd so many Degrees into St. Winifreds Tail; and then 'tis easie to conceive that St. George's Face must of necessity suffer a total Eclipse for that time.

Horoscope. Hold, worthy Sir, you are too Prophane now, and wou'd bring a Scandal upon the Saints at this rate. A strong Fancy will soon rectifie all this, and it wou'd Immortalize our Names after so Glorious an Union; at the beginning of a new Æra, to pull down those old Cobweb Hangings of Heathenism and Superstition, and hang up in their room true fresh Mortlock Workmanship: Who knows but that such a Change in the Spheres above, might procure a Reformation of Manners below? The Influence of those Saints wou'd undoubtedly be more kind and civil, than the Operations of a Company of Pagan Deities.

Blunt. For Example, I say, suppose we fancy St. Francis in the room of the Dog, we need not fear them, but that the Zeal of that Saint will be altogether as sufficient to enflame the heat of the Dog-Days, as the Breath of a pityful Drover's Cur. Fancy St. Dominick in the room of the Bull, and then we shall hit the Nail on the head; for they say there never was such a Town Bull as St. Dominick was in the World.

Horoscope. Indeed, Sir, I must not permit you to scant upon the Saints at this rate, for that will spoil the whole design of this Reformation, wherein I do suppose the Saints wou'd be more Serene and Calm, the Weather less Tempestuous, less Uncertain, we shou'd not have so much Blust'ring upon the Ocean, fewer Shipwrecks, when the Government of the Heavens were once at the disposal of the Moderation Principles.

Blunt. And, perhaps, you wou'd have better luck in erecting of Schemes, if it was not for the Malevolence of a parcel of Pagan Deities, that run Retrograde on purpose to thwart your Designs; for can any Good Man think it fair that Diana shou'd prefer Orion, one of her old Deer-Stealers, to the Cœlestial Globe, as some of our Noblemen recommend their worn out Pumps to the Charter-House ?   Horos.

(8)

Horoscope. By *Jupiter*, Sir, you are the moſt Ingenious Perſon on this ſide the *Equinoctial*, and I beg you wou'd oblige me ſome other time with an Hours further Conference on this Subject ; for I am now engag'd to finiſh this *Scheme* I was telling you of, for a Great Miniſter, who is to Tranſmit it to the Court of *Savoy*, with Deſign that they ſhou'd take their Meaſures according to the Directions I have given. Gentlemen I am yours, *ad Piſces*. [*Exit* Horoſcope.]

Blunt. Ha! ha! ha! The Court of *Savoy* take Directions from a *Figure-Caſter*; and ſo Prince *Eugene* March according to the motion of the *Planets*, in the Twelve Houſes *in his Aſtrological Tables*. A very pleaſant Fellow this is on my Soul ; I have not had better Diverſion this many a Day. But to me it ſeems the grandeſt Riddle in the World, that ſuch a Fellow as this ſhou'd pick up Money by the meereſt *Folly* and *Buffoonry* imaginable, while there are ſo many Men of *Learning* about this Town are ready to Starve with all their *Ingenuity*.

Bays. You are very much in the right on't, Mr. *Blunt* ; for as I hope for a good Dinner to Morrow, and it wou'd be hard, you know, that a Man ſhould want one on Sunday. The World are ſtrangely Juggled out of their Money ; let a Man take pains to pleaſe, the World calls it *Stiff* and *Dull* ; if we are *Witty*, twenty to one but we are Puniſh'd for it ; and if we are not, 'tis the ſame thing, we may Starve. Upon my Word Gentlemen, I think ours is the hardeſt Caſe in the World. There's Honeſt *Bohee*, for entertaining you now and then with ſome ſcraps of *Wit* he gleans from us, in a few Years gets Three or Four Thouſand Pounds, and whip he retires ; Mr. *Harlem*, with the Tenth part of the Slavery of a *Poet*, picks more Money out of a dull *Dutch Gazette*, than we can do out of all your *Pockets* for a Labour'd *Play* of three Years, a *Dedication* half as long as the *Play*, or a *Panegyrick*, that has as many Compliments in it as wou'd make a *Cook-Maid* believe ſhe was a *Dutcheſs*, a *Cinder-Wench* a *Beauty*, or an *Oyſter-Woman* an *Empreſs*.

Bohee. Well, Mr. *Bays*, you cannot complain of me, for when I was Married to this laſt Wife, I gave you a Guinea, you know, for an *Epithalamium*, as you call'd it, which I found afterwards Printed in Mr. —— Works.

Bays. Not a Word more of that, *Bohee*, I ſhall tell what you Remark'd upon the *Gazette* th' other Day ; you muſt turn *Critick*, indeed, we ſhall have fine times when *Coffee-men* muſt be made *Judges* ; nay, if you ſay another Word,

I'll tell Mr. *Harlem* what you ſaid of his News-Papers too.

Blunt. O pray, Mr. *Bays*, let us have *Bohee's Criticiſm* by all means ; the Dog has *Wit*, we ſhall have him *Hunted* one of theſe Days.

Bays. Theſe are the Words : *Our Publick Hiſtories tell us of the old Invaſions of the* Scots *upon* England, *and their often opening a Door to the* French *to Aſſault us that way ; but the Happy Union of* England *and* Scotland, *never till now perfected, by Your Majeſties Care and Wiſdom, hath ſtopt that Poſtern Paſſage, and will turn the ſharp Thiſtles of that Kingdom INTO the Faces of our* French *Enemies, who formerly kept the ſame cloſe to our Backs.* The Rogue had a mind to be Waggiſh, I believe ; that was all. *Well*, ſays he, *when Doctor* Querpo *comes, I'll tell him, he may aſk his Patient whether he's Bound or Looſe after a nicer manner than uſual, and he may do it from Authority too ; he may ſay to a Lady very Modeſtly, Madam, is your Poſtern Paſſage ſhut or open ?*

Blunt. Aye, and 'tis twenty to one ſhe may never underſtand him : But hark-ye, *Bohee*, what ſaid you to the *Thiſtles* being turn'd *into* the Face of our *French* Enemies ? Shou'd not they have been turn'd *againſt* them ?

Bohee. No, no, Sir, I'll have nothing to do with the *Scotch Thiſtles*, I remember they are *Prickly* ; and ſome Body or another in my Houſe Tranſlated the *Motto* to the *Thiſtle*, *Nemo me impune laceſſit*. *Let no Man think to go unpuniſh'd that meddles with me. Old Birds are not to be caught with Chaff.* I hope you'll excuſe me, Gentlemen.

Advertiſement.

THE Britiſh Court: A Poem. Deſcribing the moſt Celebrated Beauties at St. James's, the Park, and the Mall. The Ladies Characteriz'd. 1. Dutcheſs of Marlborough. 2. Dutcheſs of Ormond. 3. Dutcheſs of Bolton. 4. Counteſs of Ranelaugh. 5. Lady Ryalton. 6. Mrs. Collier, Maid of Honour. 7. Mrs Foreſter, Maid of Honour. 8. Counteſs of Sunderland. 9. Counteſs of Bridgewater. 10. Mrs. Cludde. 11. Mrs. Spanheim. 12. Lady Hyde, Lady o' the Bed Chamber. 13. Mrs. Dunch and Digby. 14. Lady Cowper. 15. Counteſs of Mancheſter. 16. Lady Colvert. 17. Lady Harper. 18. Mrs. Price. 19 Marchioneſs of Monthermer. 20. Mrs. Gibbons. 21. Dutcheſs of Somerſet. 22. Counteſs of Orrery. 23. Mrs. Wortley. 24. Mrs. Long. 25. Dutcheſs of Beauford. 26 Mrs. Newington. 27. Dutcheſs of St. Albans. 28. Dutcheſs of Eſſex. 29. Lady Woodſtock. 30. Mrs. Wyndham 31. Counteſs of Wharton. 32. Lady Elizabeth Seymour. 33. Dutcheſs of Bucks. And Normandy. The Second Edition, with Additions. Price 6 d. Sold at the Publiſhing Office, in Bearbinder-Lane.

London, Printed for the Benefit of *Bohee*, the *Coffee-Man* ; and Sold at the Publiſhing-Office, in *Bearbinder-Lane*, 1 7 0 7.

(9)   Numb. III.

THE

Humours of a *Coffee-House* :

A

C O M E D Y.

As it is Dayly Acted by

Levy, *a Recruiting Officer.*	Venture, *a Merchant.*	Shuffle, *a Time-ferver.*
Hazard, *a Gamefter.*	Talley, *a Stock-Jobber.*	Bays, *a Poet.*
Bite, *a Sharper.*	Querpo, *a Quack.*	Compafs, *a Sailor.*
Nice, *a Beau.*	Trick, *a Lawyer.*	Harlem, *a News-writer.*
Blunt, *a Plain Dealer.*	Horofcope, *an Aftrologer.*	Bohee, *the Coffee-man.*
Whim, *a Projector.*		

Note, Thefe Perfons are introduc'd only as occafion ferves.

From **Wednesday,** July the 2d, to **Wednesday** July the 9th, 1707.

Enter *Blunt, Whim, Venture, Talley, Shuffle.*

Blunt. WHAT, *Hippifh, Hippifh,* Mr. *Whim?* How goes your Twenty Guineas up- on *Thoulon?* I think you gave them to have a Hundred : I wifh you had your Money again.

Whim. I don't value it, Mr. *Blunt,* of a *Fillup* ; but was drawn into it by my Lord ————'s. Advice, that I muft needs fay : However, I dare venture twice as much more on Prince *Eugene's* Head : He's one of your Fortunate Generals, he can do Wonders.

Blunt. Nay, nay, Mr. *Whim,* he muft perform Miracles too, if he can Take *Thoulon* before he comes at it. You and I will reafon now like Sober Men, fince Mr. *Harlem* is not here with his Nonfenfical Rattle to interrupt us. Do you confider where Prince *Eugene* is, and the di- ftance he has to go, and the difficulty of his Paf- fage? *Firft,* He is not in the plain Country : but, *Secondly,* is Barracaded by Inacceffible Hills, and Fortified Avenues ; and then, again, the *French* have fome Forces there, and you may de- pend upon it no Induftry is wanting to keep fuch a Powerful Enemy out of the Heart of their Country. Have you confider'd all thefe things now?

Whim. I confider'd them ! 'Tis none of my Bufinefs to confider them ; but I take the News as I find it.

Blunt. And do you part with your Money without confideration too ? There's Mr. *Venture* there,

C

(10)

there, I believe wou'd not lay out his Money in way of Trade at that rate.

Venture. Not I, upon my Word, Mr. *Blunt*, for by the same reason I might as well pretend to Engross a Commodity upon a Flying report, That such a Fleet, or such a Number of Ships was Taken by the Enemy, and if it shou'd happen to be false, as a thousand to one it is, if I never examine into the reasonableness or probability of the thing, I'm undone.

Whim. You don't consider, Gentlemen, I never Venture my Moneys but on the Government side; *Safe's the Word there :* I'll stand or fall by the Government.

Blunt. And so must we too, Mr. *Whim*; but you don't take it right; for at this rate you may be ruin'd, and neither do the *Government*-Good, nor the *Government* all this while receive any Damage. For if you believe every groundless Rumour of the Town, and upon that are drawn into a Wager, if the Report be false you are injured, not the *Government*, because it might be of something that was never concerted or design'd to be done. I speak not this of *Thoulon* directly, but of any other Affair in general, where there is the greatest improbability to expect it, and Men must be oblig'd to renounce their Reason, and quit their Understanding to embrace a vain Faith, that has no manner of Foundation in it, purely to be Complisant to a sort of Men who are very Angry that others won't believe every Report that they do.

Whim. Odso ! Mr. *Blunt*, I think you are in the right on't; I won't believe all the News I hear, again this good while. But here's my Neighbour *Trick*; we'll know [*He Enters.*] what's become of the *French Prophets*. You have been in Court I hear, what's done?

Trick. Why, your *French Prophets*, as you call them, are undone; They are found Guilty of Publishing their *Cry from the Desart*; but the *Jury* had more Sense than to find them Guilty of Composing it, *Poor Shatter-Brain'd Fellows*, some Cunning Rascal or another did that Job of Work for 'em: You know we have several *Refugees* that are *Scribblers* about Town. Don't you remember the other Day *Tom Harlem* had like to have come into a *Scrape* about them ?

Whim My Friend, Mr. *Harlem*, do you say; I am heartily sorry for it; but I know this well enough of him, if they are got into Trouble, he'll be their humble Servant —— another way.

Trick. Here, a Dish of *Bohee*.

Bohee. Quickly, Sir; for I have a fresh Pot a making.

Trick. I am just overcome : Mr. *Talley*, I wish

I cou'd have seen you in Court : I have been just spent in packing a *Jury :* I cou'd not find an Old Acquaintance in all *Guild-Hall*, I was forc'd at last to get a parcel of *Serjeants* and their *Followers* but the Dogs were so squeamish I had like to have got no Damages. The Cause was *Counsellor Squabble's*, in an Action for *Scandal*, for saying he Kiss'd the *Pope's* Great Toe. We lay'd our Action for a Thousand Pounds, and these *Conscientious Sons* of a *Compter*, gave us but Fifty : For my own part I'll forswear Packing *Serjeants* and *Bailiffs* in a *Writ of Enquiry* again, unless the Dogs will learn to do as they shou'd do.

Talley. Pray Mr. *Trick*, was this *Counsellor Squabble* of Norfolk, or *Essex ?* For I think they are both of the same Family.

Trick. I cannot tell that, I never rip up Families; but this I know, he's a great *Essex-Calf*, Nothing in the World vexes me, but after all this we have as good as lost the *Cause*, for we proved not a Farthing Damages, tho' we got Fifty Pounds. My *Client* insisted it was Damages enough to have it said, That a *Counsellor at Law* shou'd be so great a Fool as to go as far as *Rome* to Kiss the *Popes* Toe. But the *Court* were of another Opinion; The *Defendant* mov'd in *Arrest of Judgment*, and has thrown us quite of our Backs. For my part I'll Renounce the *Law*, there's nothing now to be got by it ; I have had but three *Causes* this *Term*, and lost every one of them; whereas I use to have fifteen and twenty a *Term* for these twenty Years together.

Blunt. We are much oblig'd to our Wife *Law-makers* for that ; I hope, Mr. *Trick*, by the next *Term* you may have never a *Cause*, and then you'll do like all old Sinners, leave the Practice of the *Lawyers*, as they do their *Vices*, when their *Vices* have left them.

Trick. But, Sir, as a Man of Sense, you ought to Consider every one is to live by Business, Sir, by my Soul, as the *Law* stands now, I cannot live by mine.

Blunt. Not Honestly I dare Swear, nor ne'er cou'd. (*Aside.*)

Trick. This taking away of *Sham-Pleas*, *Mis Nom's*, and not half so many *Errors* remaining, has quite destroy'd the Practice of the *Law*. An Old *Practitioner* cannot get his Bread, Sir, he is quite out of his Rode now ; the *Law* runs in another Chanel.

Blunt. So much the better, you may therefore take another Course, and in time find the right Rode to *Heaven*.

Shuffle. That's a hard thing for any Man to do

(11)

io. fince our Guides themfelves differ fo much about it. We are Puzzled even in things that every Body wou'd think were plain enough on *Earth*, therefore we fhall find the way difficulter than we imagine to *Heaven*.

Blunt. Not without you *Occafionalifts*, that ne'er defign to go thither your felves, block it up. We are all poffitively agreed in the Rode to *Heaven*, but we are not of your Opinion to go the *Shorteft way* : There is an excellent old Proverb, oppofite to that, that truly fays, *The fartheft way about is the nearett way Home*.

Shuffle. Come, come, Mr. *Blunt*, I know you are Vers'd in the Controverfies of the Times, what fay you to that betwixt the *Archbifhop* and the Lower Houfe of *Convocation*?

Blunt. I fay they are both in the wrong ; the one in extending his Power beyond its due limits, and the other in denying the Power of a *Metropolitan*, becaufe the *Metropolitan* has affum'd the Power of a *Legate*.

Shuffle. But the matter in Difpute is as plain as the Nofe on your Face, that the *Archbifhop* has Power to *Adjourn* or *Prorogue*.

Blunt. And that's what the *Convocation* never difputed. But what makes the Argument fo Clear and Evident on their Side, is, you know the *Prolocutor* was *Sufpended* for *Non-Attendance*, and immediately the *Convocation* was *Prorogu'd*; after which the *Arch-Bifhop* proceeds againft him for his *Contempt*, notwithftanding the *Prorogation*. Now let me afk you, Mr. *Shuffle*, If the *Commons* commit a Member for any Offence againft the *Houfe*, you will grant nothing is fo well known as that the Acts of that Seffion *Terminate* in the *Prorogation*, and the Member fo committed is difcharg'd of Courfe. This is the Method of *Parliamentary Proceedings*, and according to all their *Precedents*, it has been the fame Cuftom in the *Convocation* as in *Parliament*, and from whence do you think fhou'd rife the Difpute?

Shuffle. If the Matter is as you State it, Mr. *Blunt*, I can conceive no Reafon why they fhou'd not fubmit to their *Spiritual Governour*, as they expect others fhou'd fubmit to them upon the fame Account. Befides, every Body will own that His Grace of *Canterbury* is a Perfon of thofe *Moderate* and *Reafonable Principles*, not to make a wrong ufe of any *Priviledge* that they fhou'd give up to him, tho' it was not ftrictly and legally due.

Blunt. But pray Mr. *Shuffle*, do you confider all this while that the *Supremacy* of Her *Majefty* is concern'd in this Controverfie ; that the *Inferior Clergy* are maintain'd by Her *Preroga-*

tive againft any Invafions of it, either on one Hand or the other ; for tho' it fhou'd, at this time, be put into the Hands of an Honeft Man, we are not affur'd it fhall always continue fo. Befides, how fhall they be able to anfwer to their Succeffors the Breach of Truft committed to their Charge, which they muft commit if they admit of a Violation of their *Immunities*, and not do their utmoft to Record that it was not done by their Confent, and if they are Invaded without that, it amounts to no more than an *Ufurpation* ; which can never be admitted as a *Precedent* againft them. Have you confider'd the Act of *Premunire* of *Henry* the 8th, againft the *Clergy* if they acknowledged any *Supremacy* but that of the Crown of *England*, *Independant* or *Legative-Power*, as that lately attempted by the *Metropolitan*.

Shuffle. Indeed, Sir, you amaze me ; I did not confider that Her Majefties *Prerogative* was fo nearly concern'd, which if it be as you fay, I'll affure you, Mr. *Blunt*, I'll think again before I engage in this Argument any more.

Enter Harlem *in bafte*.

Harlem. A Mail, a Mail, Gentlemen ; Extraordinary News I can affure you : I beg you wou'd do me the Favour to take no Notice of it till the *Poft-Man* comes out ; you know of what Importance it is to me, and I know you are Gentlemen, and fcorn to prejudice me.

Whim. Mr. *Blunt*, what will you give me for my 20 Guineas on *Thoulon* now ? You fee what it is to be on the *Government*'s fide now.

Blunt. I neither fee nor hear any thing to alter my Opinion yet. Pray, Mr. *Harlem*, what Intelligence have you got that may be acceptable ? For I can affure you, from the bottom of my Heart, no Body will rejoyce more Cordially than I fhall do upon any Succefs to my Country : I believe all the Gentlemen prefent are fatisfied I have fomething to lofe with the reft, and therefore I muft be a *Mad-Man* not to be pleas'd with the Advantages that muft accrue to it from its Profperity.

Harlem. Why, Gentlemen, I'll tell you, *Thoulon* will be ours; Prince *Eugene* is March'd; the Duke of *Savoy* will follow; our Fleet is in the *Mediterranean* ; in fhort, the Bufinefs is done.

Blunt. I believe the Bufinefs will be done if we will but have Patience. But, pray Mr. *Harlem*, don't run before your Accounts, produce your News, and we fhall be the better able to Judge. Don't fay a Place is Befieg'd before an Army is before it ; and don't fay it is Taken before it is Befieg'd; by this means, inftead of ferving the *Government*, you injure

it,

(12)

it, and render their Accounts Ridiculous. Be pleas'd only to read your News.

Harlem. Letters from *Milan*, *Savoy*, and *Province* say, *First*, That the Duke of *Savoy* and Prince *Eugene* are to take the Field directly, and then design to March towards *Province* in order for *Thoulon* or *Marseilles*, for Expedition a considerable Train of *Artillery* is prepared from *Savoy* : They say Prince *Eugene* is actually on his March, and the Duke of *Savoy* will follow. But from *Province* they advise, That the Enemy's Fleet has Alarm'd the Coast, whereupon the *Militia* of *Province* has taken up Arms, and March'd towards the *Sea-Coast* to Oppose them. That the Garison of *Thoulon* is well provided, and consists of 3000 Men, and has above 200.pieces of Cannon ready mounted on the Works of the Place : That all the Men of War are laid up, and secured behind the *Royal-Fort* : That they have plac'd at the Entrance of the Harbour 12 *Fire-Ships*, 10 *Bomb-Ketches*, and 3 Flat Vessels with a Battery of 25 pieces of Cannon on each of them, for the Security of their Men of War. But the *Confederate* Fleet from *Oneglia* to *Leghorn*, to above 40 Men of War, besides 60 Transports, are preparing to Land, as is suppos'd, on the Coast of *Province*.

Blunt. And, pray Mr. *Harlem*, what's all this to the Security you express of *Thoulon* being ours ? 200 Great Guns are mounted you say, 3000 Men in the Town, and 3. Batteries of 25 Guns each; besides the Regular Fortifications to the Sea; and how do you think this will be so easily ours ? I only wish it was, upon Condition I paid the 20 Guineas Mr. *Whim* has laid, and that's the worst Wish I have for *Great Britain*.

(*Going.*

Harlem. Well, Mr. *Blunt*, I find you're in haste now ; the next time I meet you, I doubt not but to convince you *Thoulon* will be ours.

Advertisements.

THE Present State of Great Britain, under the Auspicious Government of Her most Sacred Majesty Queen Anne. Containing, 1. A General Description of *England*, *Scotland*, and *Wales*, through their several Cities, Counties, Districts, Principalities, &c. 2. Of the Present Genius, Language, Trade, Laws, and Religion of the Britains. 3. Of the several Ranks and Orders of Men ; the Nobility, Gentry, Clergy, and Commonalty. With a Particular Ac-

count of Precedency, from the First Peer to the Meanest Peasant. Taken from the Authorities of the best Lawyers, both Common and Civil, as well as Antiquaries, Heralds, &c. such as Cambden, Selden, Segar, Ferne, and many others. 4. Of the Present Monarchy of Great Britain ; its Greatness and Power ; the Sovereign's Prerogative, Dignity, Title, and Arms ; Her Court, Forces, and Revenues of the present Princes and Princesses of the Blood Royal, and the Succession of the Crown, as settled by Act of Parliament. 5. Of the High-Court of Parliament, Privy-Council, and all Courts of Judicature. With the Newest and most Perfect List of Her Majesty's Officers in Church and State, and of the present Parliament and Convocation of Great Britain.

THE British Court: A Poem. Describing the most Celebrated Beauties at St. James's, the Park, and the Mall. The Ladies Characteriz'd. 1. Dutchess of Marlborough. 2. Dutchess of Ormond. 3. Dutchess of Bolton. 4. Countess of Ranelaugh. 5. Lady Ryalton. 6. Mrs. Collier, Maid of Honour. 7. Mrs Forester, Maid of Honour. 8. Countess of Sunderland. 9. Countess of Bridgewater. 10. Mrs. Cludde. 11. Mrs. Spanheim. 12. Lady Hyde, Lady of the Bed-Chamber. 13. Mrs. Dunch and Digby. 14. Lady Cowper. 15. Countess of Manchester. 16. Lady Colvert. 17. Lady Harper. 18. Mrs. Price. 19 Marchioness of Monthermer. 20. Mrs. Gibbons. 21. Dutchess of Somerset. 22. Countess of Orrery. 23. Mrs. Wortley. 24. Mrs. Long. 25. Dutchess of Beauford. 26 Mrs. Newington. 27 Dutchess of St. Albans. 28. Dutchess of Essex. 29. Lady Woodstock. 30. Mrs. Wyndham. 31. Countess of Wharton. 32. Lady Elizabeth Seymour. 33. Dutchess of Bucks. And Normandy The Second Edition, with Additions. Price 6 d.

THE London Bell's: Or, a Description of the most Celebrated Beauties in the Metropolis of Great Britain. The Ladies Names. 1. Mrs. Goulston's. 3. Mrs. Ward. 4. Mrs. Dashwood. 5. Mrs. Ellick. 6. Mrs. Maddocks. 7. Mrs. Richmond. 8. Mrs. Leuton. 9. Mrs. Furnesse. 11. Mrs. Bull's. 12. Mrs. Vernon. 14. Mrs. Stringer. 15. Mrs. hompson. 18. Mrs. Crafford's. 19. Mrs. Duport. 20. Mrs. Buckle. 22. Mrs. Lawrence 23. Lady Child, Widow. 26. Mrs. Rawlinson. 27. Mrs. Houblon. 29. Mrs. Chill. 30. Mrs. Gore. 31. Mrs. Shepherd. 32. Mrs. Ashurst. 33. Mrs. Beckford. 34. Mrs. Benson. 35. Mrs. Crawley. 36. Mrs. Newland. 37. Mrs. Way. 38. Mrs. Eyre. 39. Mrs. Dodwell. 40. Mrs. Davis. 41. Mrs. Jackson. Price 6 d.

AN Alphabetical List of the Names of all those Persons who have surrendered themselves to, or have been Summon'd in to be Examined by the Commissioners, in the several Commissions of Bankrupt awarded against them. According to the late Act of Parliament, Anno Quarto & Quinto Annæ Reginæ, Intituled, *An Act to prevent Frauds frequently committed by Bankrupts.* Price 6 d.

All Four Sold at the Publishing Office, in Bearbinder-Lane.

《 13 》 Numb. IV.

THE

Humours of a *Coffee-Houſe* :

A

C O M E D Y.

As it is Dayly Acted by

Levy, *a Recruiting Officer.*	Venture, *a Merchant.*	Shuffle, *a Time-ſerver.*
Hazard, *a Gameſter.*	Talley, *a Stock-Jobber.*	Bays, *a Poet.*
Bite, *a Sharper.*	Querpo, *a Quack.*	Compaſs, *a Sailor.*
Nice, *a Beau.*	Trick, *a Lawyer.*	Harlem, *a News-writer.*
Blunt, *a Plain-Dealer.*	Horoſcope, *an Aſtrologer.*	Bohee, *the Coffee-man.*
Whim, *a Projector.*		

Note, Theſe Perſons are introduc'd only as occaſion ſerves.

From **Wednesday** July the 9th, to **Wednesday** July the 16th, 1707.

Enter *Whim, Bite, Talley,* and *Trick.*

Whim. Gentlemen, I have a *Thought* to communicate to you; it may be worth while to give me your Attention, and your Advice upon the Matter.

Bite. Well, Mr. *Whim,* what is it? Any thing from you, I dare Swear, will be acceptable to the Company.

Whim. It is a very great Deſign, Sir, and if you, Mr. *Bite,* and the reſt of you here wou'd aſſiſt me, I dare ſay, I could compaſs it.

Bite. You need not doubt of our Aſſiſtance, If the thing appears to be feaſible; and, I believe, Mr. *Talley,* Mr. *Trick* and I, are as capable of ſerving you as any Men in the Kingdom again.

Whim. Laird, Sir, there's no-Body diſputes that; but this *Projection* of mine is ſo Plain, and ſelf-Evident, I know you'll be ſatisfied it will take, as ſoon as you hear it, if it be but well manag'd.

Trick. Why do you keep us in Suſpence then? Pray let us hear it, and we'll give you our Opinions preſently.

Whim. I have had a Scheme for Building an *Hoſpital.*

Trick. I'll have nothing to do with Building *Churches* and *Hoſpitals*; a *Lawyer* and trouble himſelf about *Charitable Undertaking*. I ſhall loſe my Buſineſs to be I am'd in't, and be laugh'd at by the *Profeſſion* into the Bargain.

Whim. Why, Sir, you wont hear me; I

D don't

(14)

don't mean a *Charitable Hospital*, but a *Project-ing Hospital*; an *Hospital* to get Money by. It shall be call'd, *The* British *Invalides: Or, an* Hospital *for* Superanuated *and* Disabled Dogs *and* Horses. Do you take me right now?

Talley. Upon my Honest Word, Gentlemen, 'tis a Notable Thought, I like it well; we have Scope enough to draw in half the Kingdom. Mr. *Nice* was speaking to me about a *Running-Horse* of his, the other Day, he values mightily, tho' he's past all Service; I'm sure he'll come into the *Project.*

Whim. You mistake me mightily, Mr. *Talley*, I wou'd let no Body into the *Project*, that is, the Secret of the *Project*, but our selves. I design we four shou'd set about *Subscriptions*, and when we have got what we expect, then divide it into shares, and then—— Mr. *Bite,* you know what I mean.

Bite. Know; any Body may know. —— Adso, Mr. *Whim's* an Ingenious Man, 'tis the prettiest Contrivance in the World: There's Mr. *Hazard*, now I'll have him in for a *Subscriber* presently, I know *Nice* won't stick out, he *Subscribes* to all the *Opera's* and *Nonsense* that comes out about the Town: I can draw in *Shuffle* too, he's a great Admirer of *New-Market,* you know that it is the highest Compliment to my Lord—— *T——*, a Man cannot be a *Courtier* without being a *Jockey* now. 'Tis the luckiest time Mr. *Whim* cou'd have thought upon such thing; I am sure 'twill do.

Trick. Do; I'll Pawn my *Green-Bag* on't, and you all know I don't use to be drawn into *Projections* easily. I'll set about drawing the Proposals instantly: I have half a Dozen *Clients* of mine that want a *Nursery* for their *Superanuated Lap-Dogs*; my Lady *Fiddle-Faddle* was asking me Yesterday, if I did not know of ever a Careful *Nurse* that wou'd take Care of her *Strephon*, for, poor Rogue, he was troubled with *Gouty Eyes*, and it had cost her a great deal of Money on *Doctors*, and she was resolv'd now to see what a *Good Air* and *Wholesome Diet* would do for him. She offer'd Five Pounds a Year to have him out towards the *Gravel-Pits.* You must mind that hint, Mr. *Whim*, that we propose to Build our *Hospital* some where about *High-Park*, for by that means both the *Ladies* and the *Gentlemen* will have the Opportunity of paying a Civil Visit to their *Dogs* and *Horses*

Bite. Well, this is pure, I Swear; we shall hook in all the *Country Fox-Hunters* Bravely. I know Squire *Chase*, of *Hogs-Norton*, in our Country, has always 10 or 20 Old *Dogs* on his

Hands; we shall have a pure *Chap* of him; I'll warrant he would not Hang one of 'em for to save his Wife's *Longing*, or his Eldest Son from the *Gallows*.

Talley. Our Friend *Venture* dotes mightily on his worn-out *Horses*, he is never without two or three in his *Stables*, which he visits as daily as he does the *Change* ; I'll engage him for a *Subscriber:* Besides, he's an intimate Acquaintance of Sir *Jo——nt*, in the City, who keeps several Topping *Racers*, I'll warrant now, if his *Bay-Colt* should Graul, be *Shoulder-slip'd*, or the like; *Whip Sir*, we have him, he wou'd not value 100 a Year to have particular Care taken of him.

Whim. O Dear Sir, we must not pretend to such Extravagant Rates, they'll be mightily eas'd by their first *Subscriptions*, and we hope in time to manage the matter so that we will maintain all that are brought to us for nothing. For *First*, I propose to raise 10000 *l.* by *Subscriptions*, 10000 of which shall be Employ'd in Building *Stables*, *Dog-Kennels*, &c. 10000 more in Offices for *Grooms*, *Dog-Keepers*, &c. and the rest to be laid out in Land, which shall be in the Management of the *Governour*, or *Governours*, who shall keep Servants on purpose to *Till* it and *Pasture* it, as most Profitable for the use of the *Hospital*; and by this means they will be enabled to keep double the Number than the bare Profits of the Land wou'd do.

Enter Hazard, Nice, Blunt.

Bite. There are Mr. *Nice*, and Mr. *Hazard* come in, shall I communicate something of the Design to them?

Whim. You cannot tell it perfectly yet, for I have not settled the whole Business as I would have it; besides, there's Mr. *Blunt* with them, I don't like he should hear of it, and I am a little busie my self, and cannot stay to explain the thing to 'em as I would have it done.

Bite. O let me alone for that; I know how to Humour 'em to a *T——*. Besides, here are *Talley* and *Trick* to back me.

Whim. Be sure you manage wisely, I must be gone.

[*Exit* Whim.

Nice. Your Servant, Gentlemen, what busie? I find Mr. *Whim* has got Business in his Head, he's posted away so quickly.

Blunt. I believe quite otherwise now, that he has no Business in his Head at all; he has left it with those Gentlemen there: Come, come, pray

(15)

pray let us have, I know you are full of it: What new *Whims* are on Foot? 'Tis impoſſible ſo many Days ſhould have paſs'd, and no new *Project* ſprung from ſo Fertile a *Brain:* I ſee Mr. *Talley* looks ſo big with it he's ready to burſt.

Nice. 'Tis with *Laughing* then, I fancy, he looks ſo *Merry* about the *Mouth:* Pray, Mr. *Talley,* tell us what *Merry Conceit* you have got?

Talley. Something that will pleaſe you very well, Mr. *Nice,* I can aſſure you: For I know you are a Lover of fine *Horſes,* which often-times get Accidents, and become very Trouble-ſome and Chargeable to you, upon Account that you Love 'em, and cannot bear to think of having 'em *Sold* and put to *Drudgery:* Now I have heard of a *Project* on Foot, for an *Hoſpi-tal* to entertain all Diſabled and Superanuated *Horſes* and *Dogs,* upon reaſonable Terms.

Nice. I like the Deſign mighty well; how is it Propos'd?

Bite. By *Subſcription,* Sir; you know there are abundance of Gentlemen that will be very fond of ſuch a Propoſal, conſidering what a great Charge they are at now to maintain their Old *Dogs* and *Horſes,* that are of no uſe to them.

Nice. Right; very right, Mr. *Bite:* You have nick'd the very thing we all wanted; I'll be my Twenty Guineas towards the *Subſcription,* beſides a good Benefactor to the *Hoſpital;* I know my Lord D———, and my Lord K———, will *Subſcribe* at the firſt Word: What do I talk of them, every Body will do't, take my Word for-it; 'tis a *Happy Thought.*

Trick. O Lard, Sir! But, I hope, you'll be more than Twenty Guineas, your Honour *Sub-ſcrib'd* 100 to the Building the New *Play-Houſe* in the *Hay-Market,* and, I hope, you dont think there's any Compariſon betwixt the uſefulneſs of that and this Deſign.

Nice. I don't think ſo by any means, but we are wearied out with *Subſcriptions,* the Damn'd Article of *Muſick* has pick'd my Pocket of Fifty Guineas the laſt *Winter.* Come, I will be Forty. 'Tis a Noble Project.

Hazard. I'm of your Opinion, Mr. *Nice,* in-deed, I like it better than all the *Hoſpitals* that has been Built this Hundred Years, and wonder that we have not had ſuch a thing on Foot be-fore now; the *Turks* have an *Hoſpital* for *Dogs,* but this will exceed 'em much for *Horſes* and *Dogs* too. Well, a *Horſe* is a *Noble Creature:* I'll have my *Bald Nag* in, he's a little tender of one Foot, the *Dear Creature* ſhall have all the Happineſs this World can afford him. I'll

Subſcribe Forty, as Mr. *Nice* has ſaid; but Hark-ye, Gentlemen, is this *Hoſpital* to be Sci-tuated where the *Horſes* can have good *Airing,* I wou'd not give a Farthing if they cannot enjoy the Satisfaction of Living Comfortably.

Bite. There's effectual care taken about that; the *Hoſpital* is to be Built about the *Gravel-Pits,* and leave is by this time obtain'd for the Privilege of *High-Park;* nay, ſuch Meaſures are Projected, that the *Dogs* are to run down a *Buck,* once a Fortnight, to get 'em a Stomach to their Victuals, when their Appetites fail them:

Hazard. The Thoughts of this will Raviſh all the Country Gentlemen when they hear on't: I'm ſure my Couſin *Acre-man* will take Poſt, and to Town about it on the firſt News. Hark-ye, *Tom Nice,* this is one of the moſt Charming Deſigns to pleaſe us *Sports-men* in the whole World. For my part, I ſhall now riſe in a Morning early to go and ſee my *Bald Nag,* have an Airing in *High-Park,* it will give me freſh Pleaſure; every time he *Strokes* it along the *Ley,* I ſhall ſay, *There goes Bald for the Plate.*

Blunt. Gentlemen, don't part with [*Pulling Nice and Hazard by the Sleeve, Whiſpers.*] your Money, let me talk with you a little firſt. I ſuppoſe this is one of Mr. *Whim's* Projects; you know whoſe 'tis Mr. *Bite,* don't I gueſs right?

Bite. And what then, Sir, Mr. *Whim's* an Ingenious Man, all the World knows that. Theſe Gentlemen know Mr. *Whim* as well as we, I hope if the Thought's a good Thought it's ne'er the worſe for being his.

Blunt. Not a whit the worſe nor the better for being his, or any Bodies elſe as long as 'tis a *Cheat;* but, I doubt, theſe Gentlemen don't know Mr. *Whim* ſo well as you do. Mr. *Trick* can give you an Account, if he pleaſes, of his drawing People into Snares about Projections, and then Sueing them at *Law;* did you not ſee Advertiſments againſt ſome Pranks of his he play'd the other Day at ———*Houſe?* Well, 'tis no matter for the Name, you know well enough what I mean, I dare Swear he let's ſome of you into the Secret ſometimes.

Nice. This is very Rude, Mr. *Blunt,* firſt to interrupt us when we were Talking about a Matter of ſuch Importance, and then to abuſe theſe Gentlemen without any Reaſon, or Pro-vocation.

Bite. No matter, Sir, for that, let him alone, we know Mr. *Blunt* well enough, we take no Notice of what he ſays; but had it been another Man, you wou'd have ſeen us exert our-ſelves.

Blunt. Yes, as you did t'other Day at *Tom's,*

run

(16)

run away when Colonel *Bilboe* Can'd you out of the Room.

Bite. You fee, Gentlemen, I'm a *Philofopher,* a perfect *Stoick,* his Talk makes no more Impreffion on me———

Blunt. Than a *Dun* from a *Tavern,* or an *Ale-Houfe-Score;* or a Young *Cully* that comes the next Morning to beg you'd refund fome of the Money back you Cheated him of the Night before.

Trick. This is infufferable, Mr. *Bite,* I'd have you bring your Action of *Law* againft Mr. *Blunt,* a *Jury* wou'd give you whifking Damages, efpecially when fpoke againft a Man in his Bufinefs, *Gaming's* your Employ, and if you are Defam'd, your Livelihood is taken from you.

Blunt. Yes, I muft confefs, I have Scandaliz'd him with a Matter of *Truth,* and fo I fhall do you: What, you have a mind to turn *Barrettor,* and fo be turn'd over the *Bar* again, as you was laft *Michaelmas-Term,* for fetting two *Whores* together by the Ears, and being *Attorney* underhand on both Sides, till the poor Jades, having no more Money left, grew Friends, and difcover'd the *Rogue* that fet them at Variance?

Hazard. We may chufe, I hope, whether we'll believe all this or no; for my part I think there's too much *Malice* in what you fay, for any of it to be true. As to Mr. *Trick* and Mr. *Talley,* I have known them fome time; indeed Mr. *Bite's* a Stranger to me.

Blunt. I find, Gentlemen, you're difpos'd to be ———.

Trick. Not *Trick'd* I hope, Sir; I'll make you prove it if you fay fo.

Blunt. I fay nothing but *Si Populus vult defipi Decipiatur.*   [*Exit* Blunt.

Nice. Now to the Propofals you were talking of; I long to have 'em, that I might Communicate them; do you hear, Mr. *Bite,* let me have 'em the firft of any Body, before they are made Publick.

Bite. We'll befure to oblige you; but I cannot talk of this Affair now, *Blunt* has dafh'd it quite out of my Head at prefent; Mr. *Whim,* the next time we meet, fhall do himfelf the Honour to tell it you all himfelf.

Advertifements.

(17)   Numb. V.

THE
Humours of a *Coffee-Houſe* :
A
COMEDY.

As it is Dayly Acted by

Levy, *a Recruiting Officer.*	Venture, *a Merchant.*	Shuffle, *a Time-ſerver.*
Hazard, *a Gameſter.*	Talley, *a Stock Jobber.*	Bays, *a Poet.*
Bite, *a Sharper.*	Querpo, *a Quack.*	Compaſs, *a Sailor.*
Nice, *a Beau.*	Trick, *a Lawyer.*	Harlem, *a News-writer.*
Blunt, *a Plain Dealer.*	Horoſcope, *an Aſtrologer.*	Bohee, *the Coffee man.*
Whim, *a Projector.*		

Note, Theſe Perſons are introduc'd only as occaſion ſerves.

From **Wedneſday** July th 16 h, to **Wedneſday** July the 23d, 1707.

Enter *Whim, Nice,* and *Hazard.*

Nice. MR. *Whim*, I am very glad to meet with you thus Opportunely. Mr. *Hazard* and I were wiſhing to find you without Company; that we might have a little Talk with you about your *Propoſal.*

Hazard. Upon my word, Sir, I have been mightily pleas'd with the thing ever ſince I heard of it.

Whim. Heard of What? Pray, Gentlemen, what do you mean? For I don't underſtand you.

Nice. We mean your *Project*; the *Hoſpital* for *Superanuated Dogs* and *Horſes:* Mr. *Bite* and Mr. *Trick* told us of it; and we reſolv'd to Subſcribe, only we deſire a clear Account of it from your ſelf.

Whim. Gentlemen, You muſt know, I deſign'd this as a Secret, till I had compleated my Thoughts about it, which are but yet in *Embrio*. I am really heartily concern'd any Body ſhou'd expoſe me thus; but I am glad it was only communicated to two ſuch worthy Gentlemen; and ſince you do know of it, I'll tell you. ——

Hazard. Aye, Pray, Mr. *Whim*, tell me one thing that has run much in my Head ; what *Phyſick, Diet,* and *Food* have you taken care of in your *Hoſpital* for *Broken-Winded Horſes,* &c. My *Snip* has never Eat any dry Meat theſe two Years? I allow him a Quart of *Sack* every day to moiſten his *Oats* ; and he Drinks nothing but *warm Ale* to his *Hay*, beſides two *Maſhes* a week, and a *Cordial Draught* of freſh *Oyl Olive,* Dia

E   *pente*

(18)

pente and *Sack* every third day, becaufe I cannot endure to hear the poor Creature Cough, as if he wou'd throw his *Lungs* out.

Nice. Dear Mr. *Hazard*, don't interrupt Mr. *Whim* from letting us into this Affair before it become Publickly talk'd of ; for I am fure the thing will do, and I fhall hate to Difcourfe of it when every Body knows the Bufinefs. There is a great deal of Pleafure in talking of things un-known to the *Vulgar* ; I hate their common Capacities.

Whim. I wou'd willingly oblige you ; but, to be plain, I am under Articles not to Divulge the Defign to any Perfons but the Parties engag'd, till we have obtain'd a Grant for it, which is now paffing the *Seals*, and only wants a fmall matter of about 100 *l.* or fome fuch Trifle to carry it on.

Nice. But how came Mr. *Talley* and Mr. *Trick*, then, to tell us of it? They did not make fuch a mighty fecret of it as you do.

Whim. That is nothing to me, Mr. *Nice*, if they will be fo Imprudent to expofe themfelves and Bufinefs in which they are concern'd; they are much to blame Mr. *Trick* drew the *Wri-tings*, and fo was let into the *Secret* ; but he is an ill Man to Betray his *Client*. It wou'd be a breach of Articles in me to do it, I fay, before the *Grant* is pafs'd; and I believe about Sixty Pounds wou'd fetch it out of the Office.

Hazard. Mr *Whim*, you fhall not want that; here's a Bill for the Money. It fhall ftand for your Subfcription and mine Mr. *Nice*; and we'll give him Twenty more, when we fee the *Grant*.

Nice. Withal my Heart: Come now, Mr. *Whim*, you need not be fo fqueamifh in the mat-ter : Let us have an Account of the whole *Pro-ject*, that we may be able to give a fatisfactory relation to others.

Whim. I brought this thought out of *Ruffia*, where they are fo Compaffionate to their Beafts that they chufe to walk a Foot Ten Miles ra-ther than abufe the poor Brute to Ride him Five. I was pleas'd with their Tendernefs for their Fellow Creatures, and fo —— Hift, hift, —— not a word more: Here's *Blunt*, *Harlem*, and God knows how many coming towards us ; I muft take another Opportunity to tell you the Story.

Enter Blunt, Harlem, Talley, Venture, Querpo, *and* Horofcope.

Talley. What News Mr. *Harlem* ?
Blunt. O Extraordinary News ! Mr. *Harlem*

can tell you more than all the reft of the World ever heard of. Pray read his Article from the *Hague* of *July* 19. N. S.

Harlem. Aye, Gentlemen, as Mr. *Blunt* fays, have you feen that in my *Poft-Boy?*

Talley. I have never obferv'd it yet.

Harlem. Then you have heard nothing, Sir; I'll read it to you ; *Private Letters from* Paris *advife, That* Mr. Beauvilliers, *Duke of St. Aig-nan, a Perfon of* Solid Vertue *and* Great Parts, *who, for many Years paft, has oppos'd the Coun-cils of the Court of* France, *and in particular the Acceptation of the late King of* Spain's *Will, being defired by* Madam Maintenon *to ac-quaint the King with the fudden March of Prince* Eugene *into* Provence, *he comply'd with her Re-queft, and told withal to His Majefty, that* Tou-lon *was threatened with a Siege.* Toulon ! Toulon ! *Exclaim'd the* French *Monarch, in a great Surprize* ; What's the reafon *Chamillard* has told me nothing of it ? This is what every little *News-Writer* is not capable of giving you.

Blunt. That I dare Swear, Mr. *Harlem* ; nor had we had it now from any Body but a great *Blockhead:* Play fhow us this Article any where from the *Hague*, and I'll fairly afk your Pardon. *Harlem.* Sir, I'm above all that : I wou'd have you to know my Papers are as good Au-thority themfelves as e'er a *Dutch Gazette* of 'em all ; I don't tye my felf down to the Words from the *Hague*, or any where elfe, in my. *Poft Boy*, any more than my *Poft-Man*, where I take the Liberty to fay what I pleafe.

Blunt. But you ought to mind how you take the Liberty of writing *Nonfenfe*, and making *Coxcombs* of all the People to Eftablifh your *News-Paper* ; for don't you think it would be very Ridiculous for us to believe the King of *France* fo great a *Fool* as to know nothing but what Mr. *Chamillard* is pleas'd to tell him, and efpecially fince it happens in a thing all *Europe* has talk'd of thefe two Months. This is juft oppofing the Common Notions of the World, who have blam'd the King of *France* for Go-verning his People *Arbitrarily* ; and now you are making a *Fool* of him, that knows nothing of his Affairs but what his People are pleas'd to Inform him of, and fo they ride him at this rate, not he them. A very pretty Jeft, truly.

Talley. I think you are in the wrong now, to blame Mr. *Harlem*, for he does not write for fuch Gentlemen as you that can read the *Foreign Papers*, and difcant upon them ; but he writes for the Common People, who generally believe every thing in a *News-Paper*.

Blunt, And why muft the Common People be

(19)

be *Bamboosled* out of their *Senses*, and made believe *Inconsistencies* and *Contradictions*, to support Mr. *Harlem*, who has not *Senfe* enough to diftinguifh betwixt *Truth* and *Falfehood*, *Probability* and *Improbability*.

Harlem. And perhaps fuch *Criticks* as you will blame me for that piece of Serviceable News I gave you on *Thursday* laft, tho' I don't Impofe it for *Truth*, but leave every Body at Liberty to believe what they pleafe.

Blunt. Serviceable piece of News do you call it? I think it the greateft Difservice you can do the Nation, to *Amufe* and *Flatter* the People with *Ridiculous Shams*, and *Incoherent Stuff*. For tho' you know not that a thing is abfolutely falfe, yet, if by all probable Circumftances it has the Face of a *Lye*, you ought not to offer this, tho' you do not impofe it for *Truth*, becaufe it is generally known People are more fond to believe a *Lye*, than to be convinc'd of *Truth*.

Nice. Come, Mr. *Harlem*, if it was *Good News* let us hear it, whether *True* or *Falfe*.

Blunt. Fie, fie, Mr. *Nice*, you betray your Ignorance ftrangely; there is nothing can be *Good* that is *Falfe*.

Nice. I don't mind your *Quibbles*, nor your *Philofophy*: But if the *News* was on the Government's fide I fay that's *Good*, and we'll hear it.

Blunt. But if it is a *Lye*, it's neither on the Government's fide, nor againft it, but a *non Entity*, and confequently *Good* for nothing.

Nice. If it will neither do *Good* nor *Harm*, we'll have it to pleafe the Company.

Blunt. The Fools in the Company, you mean.

Whim. 'Tis about *Toulon* being Taken. I have given Money upon't. Come, Gentlemen, we'll hear it. Pray, Mr. *Harlem* Read it to us.

Harlem Reads. *An exchang'd Prifoner that came lately from* Calais *Reports, That the laft Accounts from* Paris *fay, That the* French King *had call'd in the Plate of his Kingdom in order to be Coin'd; and that an Account was come to that City, That the Duke of* Savoy *and Prince* Eugene *were come before* Toulon, *by Land; and Sir* Cloudfley Shovel, *with the Confederate Fleet, by Sea.*

Blunt. That's very notable, Mr. *Harlem*, to put it down exprefly, That the Duke of *Savoy* and Prince *Eugene* came thither by Land; for elfe every Body wou'd have Sworn they had Flown, and got thither by the *Air*; as they were forc'd to Convey their Heavy Cannon by a Stratagem, which was, by placing all their largeft at the Bottom of the Mountain, and fhoot-

ing all their Balls over the Hill firft, and fending the Great Guns after them. As to Sir *Cloudfley*'s coming before the Town by *Sea*, that's difputed; for fome Advices confirm his paffing the *Iron-Gate*, and fo Sailing, by a fhorter cut, over the *Alps*.

Harlem. For all your Bantring Raillery, Mr. *Blunt*, I had this News from a Perfon of Good Character and Reputation.

Blunt. I wou'd not Banter you by any means; but you have Banter'd the *Publick* with a Witnefs.

Nice. For fhame, Sir, let Mr. *Harlem* proceed. 'Tis ill Manners to interrupt him thus.

Harlem. After Nine Hundred Bombs was thrown into the Town————

Blunt. Pray who threw in the *Bombs*, the Army or the Fleet?

Harlem. That my Account takes no Notice of; but as foon as they had done that, the Governour fent out a *Trumpeter*, Offering to Surrender the Place on Honourable Terms: But the Duke of *Savoy* and Prince *Eugene* told him, *That they cou'd not conclude any thing without* Sir Cloudfley Shovel. And his Royal Highnefs having fent out one of his *Aid-de-Camps* to Confer with that Admiral, 'twas agreed to fend the Governour this Meffage, viz. *That be fhou'd Surrender the Place, and the Garifon Prifoners of War, or elfe expect no Quarter.*

Blunt. This is wonderful News, truly Gentlemen; and we are much oblig'd to His Royal Highnefs, and the Prince, for the great Compliment they made our *Admiral*, in advifing with him on fuch an Affair; but it is much the *Dutch Admiral* was not confulted too. And I think we ought to refent the matter, that there was no Confideration made whether or no we were able to bring away all the *Naval Stores* from *Toulon* and *Marfeilles* too, for that muft fall of Courfe; I don't like their Silence about that Bufinefs.

Nice. We have done well enough at prefent to bring 'em to a *Capitulation*; the next Mails will give us an Account of our being Mafters of the Key of *France*.

Venture. Have but Patience till then, and you fhall have my Opinion of the Matter.

Bobee. Pray, Gentlemen, excufe me, I have one Curious Queftion to afk Dr. *Querpo*, or Mr. *Horofcope*: You have all heard, I fuppofe, of the great Shower of *Flies* that fell laft *Saturday* in moft parts of the City; now I defire to know what may be the Reafon of them, or what they Portend?

Querpo. As to the *Portent* of 'em I leave
that

(20)

that to Mr. *Horofcope* ; but the *Natural Reafon*
I take to be this, That during the Heat of the
Weather, the Multiplicity of *Eggs*, fuch as we
call *Fly-Blows*, that proceed from the Markets
of the Town, for 'tis obfervable the greateft
quantities fell about thofe places, being exhal'd
into the *Atmofphere*, and hatch'd there when the
Air was cool'd by the laft Rains, and condens'd
fo as to be capable of fuftaining their weight,
they were fufpended like a Cloud, but afterwards
growing too thin by the *Rarefaction* of the
fucceeding Heat, they drop'd down during the
Heat of the Day. The fame reafon is given
for the Raining of *Frogs*, which have been
very frequent in feveral parts of the Kingdom.

Horofcope. You are too Prophane, Doctor,
to affign all things of this kind to *Natural
Caufes :* The City of late has been very Wicked, and thefe *Flies* are fent down amongft them
to Preach *Repentance :* They Portend fome General Judgments, if they refufe to obferve fuch
Signs and Tokens as are fent to them to warn
'em from fome *Crying Sins.*

Blunt. I am clearly of Mr. *Horofcope's*
Opinion, that it is fome fuch like thing : For
the fame *Flies* are undoubtedly *Hieroglyphicks*
of *High-Church* , and portend the downfall
of our *Babylonifh High-Flyers* ; befides, The
City has been very *Maggotty* of late, and fo it
is not unreafonable to fuppofe their *Spawn* according to Dr. *Querpo's* Notion may be exhal'd
into the Air, and fo Engender'd into *Flies.*

Horofcope. I fhall make it my Bufinefs to
enquire into this Affair *Meteorologically* and
Mythologically, and fo give you my Opinion
at large.

Querpo. And I fhall make a curious Dif-
quifition of it *Phylofophically, Phyfickally*, and
Anatomically, that the *Publick* may reap the
Benefit of my Labours.

Advertifements.

THE Britifh Court: A Poem. Defcribing the
moft Celebrated Beauties at St. James's, the
Park, and the Mall. The Ladies Characteriz'd. 1.
Dut hefs of Marlborough. 2. Dutchefs of Ormond.
3. Dutchefs of Bolton 4 Countefs of Ranelaugh.
5 Lady Ryalton. 6. Mrs. Collier, Maid of Honour.
7. Mrs Forefter, Maid of Honour. 8. Countefs of
Sunderland. 9. Countefs of Bridgewater. 10. Mrs.
Cludde. 11. Mrs. Spanheim. 12. Lady Hyde, Lady of the Bed-Chamber. 13. Mrs. Dunch and Digby 14. Lady Cowper. 15. Countefs of Manche-
fter. 16. Lady Colvert. 17. Lady Harper. 18.
Mrs. Price. 19 Marchionefs of Monthermer. 20
Mrs Gibbons. 21. Dutchefs of Somerfet. 22. Countefs of Orrery. 23. Mrs. Wortley. 24. Mrs. Long.

25. Dutchefs of Beauford. 26 Mrs Newington. 27.
Duchefs of St. Albans. 28. Dutchefs of Effex. 29.
Lady Woodftock. 30. Mrs. Wyndham 31. Coun-
tefs of Wharton. 32. Lady Elizabeth Seymour. 33.
Dutchefs of Bucks. And Normandy The Second
Edition, with Additions. Price 6 d.

AN Account of the Wonderful Cures perform'd by
the Cold Baths. With Advice to the Water-
Drinkers at Tunbidge, Hampftead, Aftrope, Nasborough, and all the other Chalbeate Spaws :
Wherein the ufefulnefs of Cold Bathing is farther
recommended to the Lovers of Coffee, Tea, Chocolate, Brandy, &c. Pre erring the ufe of Bathing in
thofe Springs before the Drinking of their Waters.
With a Table of the Difeafes in which Cold Baths
are proper, or dangerous. To which is prefix'd a
Letter from Sir John Floyer, in anfwer to one of the
Author's to him, about the further ufe of Cold Baths.
By Doctor Browne. Price 1 s.

Both Sold at the Publifhing Office, in Bearbinder-Lane.

THE Travels of an *Englifh* Gentleman from *London* to *Rome*, on Foot, Containing a Comical Defcription of what he met with Remarkable in every City, Town, and Religious Houfe
in his whole Journey. Alfo an Account of their
Ridiculous Religious Proceffions and Ceremonies, in their Churches, thro' their Streets, and
in the Woods. Likewife the Debauch'd Lives,
and Amorous Intrigues of the Luftful Priefts
and Letcherous Nuns. With a Pleafant Account of the Opening the Holy Gate of St. *Pe-
ters* Church : Alfo Reflections upon the Super-
ftition and Foppifh Pageantry of the whole
Ceremony of the laft Grand Jubilee at *Rome.*
The Third Edition. Now Publifhed for the Diverfion and Information of the Proteftants of
England. Price 1 s.

THE Reformer. Expofing the Vices of the Age
in feveral Characters, *viz.* 1. The Vittous
Courtier. 2. The Debauch'd Parfon. 3. The
Factious Hypocrite. 4. The Precife Quaker.
5. The Covetous Mifer. 6. The Prodigal Son.
7. The City Letcher. 8. The Infatiate Wife.
9. The Amorous Maid. 10. The Beau Ap
prentice. 11. The City Mob. 12. The Country 'Squire. 13. A Jacobite. To which is
added, The Rambling Rakes: Or, *London* Libertines, Defcovering many Mad Frolicks, committed by the Debauchees of the Town. Together with Three Knights Adventure. Containing, feveral Amazing and Diverting Accidental
Intrigues. Alfo a Step to the *Bath :* With an
Account of the Comical Paffages on the Road
And a Character of the Place. *The Second Edition.* Price 1 s. Both Sold by *J. How*, at the
Stars in *Talbot Court* in *Grace Church-Street.*

London, Printed for the Benefit of *Bohee*, the *Coffee-Man*, and Sold at the
Publifhing-Office, in *Bearbinder-Lane*, 1707.

(21)   Numb. VI.

THE
Humours of a *Coffee-House* :
A
COMEDY.

As it is Dayly Acted by

Levy, *a Recruiting Officer.*	Venture, *a Merchant.*	Shuffle, *a Time-ferver.*
Hazard, *a Gamefter.*	Talley, *a Stock-Jobber.*	Bays, *a Poet.*
Bite, *a Sharper.*	Querpo, *a Quack.*	Compafs, *a Sailor.*
Nice, *a Beau.*	Trick, *a Lawyer.*	Harlem, *a News-writer.*
Blunt, *a Plain Dealer.*	Horofcope, *an Aftrologer.*	Bohee, *the Coffee man.*
Whim, *a Projector.*		

Note, Thefe Perfons are introduc'd only as occafion ferves.

From **Wednesday** July the 23d, to **Wednesday** July the 30th, 1707.

Enter *Querpo, Horofcope, Blunt, Shuffle, Venture, Talley,* and *Harlem.*

Blunt. WELL, Mr. *Horofcope*; and what do you Prognofticate of thefe *Flies?*

Horofcope. After my Brother *Querpo*, which I muft call fo, becaufe I Study *Phyfick* as well as *Aftrology*, I fhall declare my Sentiments of the Matter, but I don't love to Affront my Betters; Doctor *Querpo*, Sir, is a *Leyden Doctor.*

Blunt. Odfo! as you fay, that's right: There's a great deal of Efteem due to a *Leyden Doctor*, for I think they have the Pre-heminence all over the Town; my Lord Duke of *M——nce*, and my Lady Dutchefs of *M——h*, will meddle with no Body, forfooth, but your *Leyden Doctors.* The Countefs of *B——*, and the Countefs of *C——*, declar'd, There were none other fit to make *Phyficians* of, they were fuch neceffary Men about a Woman. My Lady *R——* difcharg'd her *Nurfe*, t'other Day, as foon as ever the *Doctor* came. *Laird*, fays fhe, *Doctor Littlegood, you're the pureft Man in the World to let one Eat and Drink juft what one will: I fancy my felf perfectly well when I fee you.*

Querpo. Indeed, Sir, we Gentlemen of the *Faculty* are much oblig'd to you for fuch a kind Character,

Blunt. By no means, Doctor; I meant this of no Body but you *Leaden Doctors*; who, I can affure you, run away with all the Lady's Favours.   F   *Horofcope.*

(32)

Horoscope. But, pray Mr. *Blunt*, let my Brother *Querpo* tell us his Opinion of these *Fore-boding Flies*, as I may call them ; for the *Maggot* has run strangely in my Head ever since I heard of them.

Querpo. There's nothing in 'em, Gentlemen, after all ; for when we *Virtuoso's*, for you must know I am a Member of the *Royal Society*, and expect shortly to be *Secretary*, for some new Discoveries I have made of Toasting *Cheese* by a *Candle*, without burning ones Fingers ; but as I was saying, we *Virtuoso's*, as soon as the News came, and we had some *Materials* brought us, what does half a Dozen of us do, but away we scoure into *Ludgate-Street* directly, and tried all the *Microscopes, Macroscope Telescopes*, and *Magnifying-Scopes* we could meet with ; I thought, Sincerely, I should have lost my Eyes, and run peeping about the Streets for the Failure, like my Brother *Formal*, who is one of us, and the very *Cockle-Shell* of the Society : Well, but what do you think, after all, this mighty *Prodigy* was? But *Flying Ants*, tho' they were of different Sorts and Sizes.

Blunt. But, Doctor, this wont do by any means ; for you promis'd us in your last an *Anatomical, Philosophical,* and *Physical* Account of them.

Querpo. I look'd into the *Learned* on that Subject, and find that Business is done to my Hand, for *Hippocrate* and *Galen* treat at large of them ; which will please the Curious Reader wonderfully in the *Greek*, I pity'd to Translate it, because of losing all the Beauties of the Original when any thing of that Kind comes to be put into *Paultry Englsh*, it loses all its Fineness. Besides, Gentlemen, I have got a *Manuscript* that Discourses of these very kind of *Flies* ; it is a very Great Man's, I think 'tis *Æsculapius*, I'm sure 'tis one of the greatest *Physicians* we have had of late Years.

Blunt. Why, how long ago do you think 'tis since *Æsculapius* liv'd ?

Querpo. Poh —— every Body knows that ; 'tis since the *Circulation of the Blood* was discover'd he and *Avicenna* both oppos'd it at first, but were forc'd to come in afterwards, for fear of losing their *Practice.*

Blunt. You have Read so much, Doctor, I doubt you have forgot your self. *Æsculapius* was the first Founder of *Physick* ; had a *Temple* Dedicated to him ; and was Worship'd by the *Greeks* as a *God* ; and *Avicenna* liv'd some Hundred Years ago.

Querpo. You must not tell me that ; I know

better things, Sir ; I know they write in *Greek*, by several Disputes I have of theirs with *Culpepper* ; who, tho' dispis'd by some *Criticks*, was as Great a Man as any of them, as you will own, when I shall tell you what a Noble Medicine I have gain'd from him.

Blunt. O pray let us have it, if it be for the *Publick Good* ?

Querpo. That it is, I'll promise you ; I call it by an odd sort of a Name, because it is an odd sort of a Pill, that works all Ways, upwards and downwards ; backwards and forwards : The Name of it is, *Pilula ex Pillosio: Or, a Salve for every Sore.* This same *Arcanum* is *Diuretick* and *Diuletick* ; *Cathartick* and *Sudorifick* ; *Hypnotick* and *Hepatick* ; *Illisick* and *Icterick* ; *Histerick* and *Emmenagogick.* It may be safely given downwards, from a *Secretary* —— to a *Cinder-Wench* ; and upwards to a *Metropolitan* ; but take care of the *Brain* ; 'tis *Churlish Physick* ; for which reason forbear all *Ministers of State*, because, their *Heads* are full of ——, every Body knows what I mean ; and their *Bellies* are empty, inasmuch that it *Stipulates* the *Guts.*

Blunt. Stimulates, Dear Doctor, you mean.

Querpo. Sir, I mean any thing what you please. We *Physicians* don't stand upon those things. To talk Intelligibly belongs to the *Mob* : But as I was saying concerning the use of this *Wonderful Pill*, it has, Infallibly Cur'd many of an *Epidemical Distemper*, called by some, *Scribendi κακοέθες, Anglia,* the *Itch*. Mistake me not, I do not mean the *North British Itch*, to speak with the *Moderns*, but the *Scaibblers Itch*, which has the very same Symptoms, and lies betwixt the *Fingers.*

Blunt. Very Learned truly ; there is a great deal of Reason in what you say ; I believe I know the very Person from whom you took this hint : 'Tis a little Gentleman with an odd *Awkward Phiz* ; small *Ferret Eyes* ; *Carbuncled Nose* ; a *Fiery Visage* ; and who being troubled, not with a *Camerouian*, but a *Cambrian Itch* ; continually squirts out these *Pills* for the Good of the Publick, being prepossess'd with an Imagination that all Men are as *Costive* in their *Bowels* as he is in his *Brain.*

Querpo. You mistake, indeed, Mr. *Blunt*, I was the very Man that communicated this *Pill* to him first, by which means he Cur'd Sixteen *Peers*, besides an *Arch-Bishop*, of a strange Distemper call'd, *Turnitus : Or, a Tumultary Noise in the Head* ; call'd, by the Vulgar, a Din in their Ears.

Horoscope. Good lack-a-day, Gentlemen ; but

(23)

but what is all this to the *Flies?* I own my Brother *Quirpo* a Learned *Physician* as any we have; but what then? I think this *Prodigy* rather belongs to my Province to explain. In the first Place, I confulted *Albumazar* and *Ptolomy*, and then *Cardan*, who are Unanimoufly of Opinion, That when fuch unufual Accidents happen, tho' they may be accounted for in Nature, it is a certain Sign, and never fails, That there are fome Crying Iniquities of the People that deferve heavy Judgments; and thefe Wonders are fent to forwarn them, That, unlefs they Repent, greater Calamities will enfue.

Blunt. And have you confider'd what thefe Notorious Sins are with which the City is fo Univerfally Tainted?

Horofcope. I have confider'd them, and find they are ——

Talley. Not *Stock-Jobbing*, I hope?

Horofcope. The very *Second Rate Vice* of the City; for from it flow, like a *Deluge*, a thoufand others, very Scandalous ones; that, in a fhort time will go near. to over-whelm the very Foundation of this Great and Populous Place. But there are many others of as Fatal Confequence, as ——

Venture. *Wagering*, I hope.

Horofcope. You guefs right, Mr. *Venture.* *Wagering* is the very Bane of *Trade* and *Commerce*; it turns the *Heads* and *Genius* of the People another way; and all this proceeds from another Evil, that muft be deftroy'd, Root and *Branch*, before this can be Remedy'd; that is—

Harlem. Not *News* I hope? Mr. *Horofcope.*

Horofcope. Yes, yes, Sir; the Vanity and Intollerable *Itch* of Hunting after *News* has almoft Ruin'd the City of *London.*

Blunt. Wonderfully well Obferv'd, indeed; this is a Truth all Mankind muft agree to; and tho' it may be to your Prejudice, Sweet Mr. *Harlem*, I muft fay the *Little Traders* of the *City* and *Suburbs* of *London* lofe more time, and fpend more Money, in Reading and Talking of *News*, than wou'd keep them and their Families. So Impatient and Greedy after Novelty are thefe People, that you fhall fee a *Cobler* in his *Stall* Reading one of the *News-Papers* in a Morning, with one Stocking on, and another off; others again Running to the *Coffee-Houfes* half-Naked, as they were before half-Witted: And this is the way, in a fhort time, to lofe their Senfes too; as by this means they lofe their Time and Bufinefs.

Bohee. For God-fake, Sir, don't Rail againft *Coffee-Houfes*; we have much ado to Live

as we do; and at this rate you'll Break us, quite.

Harlem. Prithee, *Bohee*, don't mind Mr. *Blunt*; he's got into his fit of Railing. But all Men own *News* and *Coffee-Houfe* Converfation is the very Life of *London.* I know a Hundred Gentlemen that wou'd never fee the Town as long as they Live, were it not for that Satisfaction. The *Pleafures* they meet with there, over-Ballance all the Noife and Hurry of a City Life. Befides, Intelligence is that which keeps up the Spirits of the *People*, and Strengthens the *Government.* In this they find the Fruits of *Happy Liberty.* The *French* fhow to all the World their *Slavery* and *Oppreffion*, in having nothing but the *State-News*; fo that the *People* can know nothing but what the *Government* is pleas'd to inform 'em of.

Blunt. By which means they are a *Happier People.* Their *Minds* are lefs Difquieted; they lefs Diverted from their *Private Bufinefs*; and fo lefs given to *Faction* and *Sedition.* What you call *Liberty*, is really otherwife; a moft *Pernicious Weapon*; which being in the Hands of *Unthinking Men*, is the ready way to Deftroy themfelves.

Harlem. If Mr. *Horofcope* Rail againft *Stock-Jobbing*, *Wagering*, and *News*, as fuch Crying Sins; what does he think of *Whoring*, *Swearing*, *Lying*? &c.

Horofcope. I think *Whoring* is but a *Puny Vice* in refpect to the others, which are all Practiced in *Stock-Jobbing*, *Wagering*, and *News*; from whence Naturally proceed *Lying*, *Swearing*, and *Fore-Swearing*, and all the Immoralities of the Times.

Talley. And dare you pretend, in a *Reform'd City*, to Juftifie *Whoring?*

Horofcope. Hark'ye, Brother *Doctor*, by the By, I muft fay fomething for it; you and I Live by it. This is one of the Sins of the People, for which they fall into the Hands of the *Phyfician.* Look'ye, Gentlemen, tho' I don't downright Juftifie *Whoring*, yet I muft fay this, That in refpect of all *Unnatural Lufts*, it is but a very *little Sin*; and the *Romanifts* might well call it *Venial*; for had they known half the Wickednefs of *London*, they wou'd have made it one of the *Cardinal Virtues.*

Harlem. *Monftrum Horrendum!*

Horofcope. No, no, the *Monftrum Horrendum* is not come yet: But you fhall hear it, and then you will have a better Opinion of *Whoring*, and a worfe of fomething elfe. Some

Days

(24)

Days ago an Intimate Acquaintance of mine being Invited by his Friend to go along with him, and he wou'd fhow him a Rarity, he Confented ; and accordingly they went. When they came at the Place appointed, they were both defired to go into a *Clofet* , in order to be Witneffes to the following *Scene.* As foon as they were Conveniently Seated comes in a Grave Gentleman of about Fifty Five, with a Bundle under his Arm, and accofts the two Ladies, of the Town I mean, which were appointed to be his Executioners. As foon as his Equipage was made ready, the two Females were defired to Drefs him in Womens Cloaths, to *Patch* and *Paint* him after fuch a manner as he directed, which was liker a *Devil* than any thing in Human Shape. As foon as that was done, he *Patches* and *Paints* his *Doxies,* in the fame manner with himfelf, and then they Vifit in Form for half an Hour ; all which time our *Hermophrodite*, for fo I muft call him, affumes the Language, as well as the Shape, of a Woman: By this time all the fatal Inftruments are prepar'd for this mighty Sacrifice to the God *Priapus.* His Converfation then begins thus, *For God fake, Ladies, what do you mean to ufe a Tender Woman, as I am, with fuch Barbarity? I came to make you a Civil Vifit, and here you have prepared Cords and Cruel Bands to bind me. I beg of you to ufe me kindly. You find me a Woman like your felves.* All this time they have Orders from him to bind his *Fingers* down with *Incle,* to *Pinion* his *Arms,* and Wind his *Neck* with Twenty Rounds of *Cord* ; and after this they Crouper up his *Nofe* and under *Lip,* and Stitch up his *Ears* with a *Needle* and *Silk,* then tye his *Feet* ; and laft of all, they Sufpend him, by the *Ropes* from his *Middle* and *Neck,* a Foot from the Ground, where he hangs in the midft of the Room, half Strangled, and Black in the Face, when they take two Lufty *Rods,* and, with all their Force and Vigour, *Whip* this *Leacher,* till the Blood flows Plentifully, and Nature has every way difcharg'd herfelf. This and fuch like are the *Crying Sins* of London.

Blunt. But is it poffible that fuch a Monfter can be Living? How did your Friends Behave themfelves at fuch a Horrid Sight?

Horofcope. He and his Comrade bolted into the Room, and inftantly they cut the Villain down. *Ladies,* faid they, *what Murder have you here Committed ? And what's this Strange*

Difguifed Monfter ? The Brute unable then to fpeak or hear, lay bound upon the Ground ; a Horrid Spectacle you may believe, endeavouring to unloofe himfelf, and get his Mouth at liberty to afk for Quarter. The Women, frighted for fear of Punifhment, Confefs'd their Wicked *Accompliey*; and told how long, and after what manner, they had been his *Evil Agents*; at laft they Unbound this Devil Incarnate, who inftantly, upon his Knees, implor'd for Pity that they wou'd keep his Name a Secret ; however they expos'd his Crime, which he, with feeming Sorrow, own'd was Monftrous, and that he had been many Years a Studying and Practicing before he cou'd bring it to this Perfection ; and faid, *He believ'd that what was done to him won'd have Kill'd any other Perfon that had nor, by degrees, accuftom'd himfelf to fuch Severity.*

All. This is Incredible !

Horofcope. Gentlemen, I have all the Proof for it a Man can have in this World ; I am affured ir is a Serious Truth ; and was it not late now, I wou'd oblige you with a Story more *Heinous* and *Idolatrous* than this, which was Tranfacted in your Neighbourhood ; and which I ll tell you the next Time we meet.

Advertifement.

London, Printed for th Benefit of Bohee, the *Coffee-Man* ; and Sold at the Publifhing-Office, in *Bearbinder-Lane,* 1707.

(25).   Numb. VII.

THE
Humours of a *Coffee-House* :
A
COMEDY.

As it is Dayly Acted by

Levy, *a Recruiting Officer.*	Venture, *a Merchant.*	Shuffle, *a Time-ferver.*
Hazard, *a Gamefter.*	Talley, *a Stock-Jobber.*	Bays, *a Poet.*
Pite, *a Sharper.*	Querpo, *a Quack.*	Compafs, *a Sailor.*
Nice, *a Beau.*	Trick, *a Lawyer.*	Harlem, *a News-writer.*
Blunt, *a Plain Dealer.*	Horofcope, *an Aftrologer.*	Bohee, *the Coffee-man.*
Whim, *a Projector.*		

Note, Thefe Perfons are introduc'd only as occafion ferves.

From **Wednesday** July the 30th, to **Wednesday** Auguft the 6th, 1707.

Enter *Whim, Nice, Blunt, Venture, Talley,* and *Harlem.*

Whim. WHAT fay you now, Mr. *Blunt,* to my Moneys on *Toulon ?*

Blunt. I fay it's good Moneys when *Toulon's* Taken.

Whim. And do you fuppofe, Sir, that it is not as good as Taken by this time ?

Blunt. I don't Deal in *Suppofitions* at all, Mr. *Whim ;* but it's very plain, that if the *French* do not Fight, but Run away as foon as they fee the Faces of their Enemy, *Toulon* muft Fall, and All *France* after it ; but if it fhou'd chance that they are in a Fighting Humour, as now and then they happen to be, we fhall be kept out of that Place this Fortnight yet.

Nice. You cannot think fo ferioufly, Mr. *Blunt ;* but you have a mind to Teaze Mr. *Whim* and me; for I have laid a Wager *Toulon* is actually in our Hands on the Firft of *Auguft, Old-Stile ;* and I dare Swear I have won my Money. What think you, Gentlemen?

All. Indeed we are of that Opinion.

Harlem. I queftion not but to have it confirm'd by the next: For my Private Intelligence tells me in the laft, how the *French* quitted the *Hills* and all the *Avenues* that lead to *Toulon,* upon the firft approach of the Duke of *Savoy* and Prince *Fugene ;* and the Confternation was fo great in the Town, that it was thought they wou'd throw open

G   the

(26)

the Gates as foon as ever the Enemy came near 'em.

Blunt. I believe what you fay to be very true, Mr. *Harlem*, That the *Hills* and *Avenues* were quitted at the Sight of the Duke of *Savoy*, becaufe it was impoffible, when your Intelligence came, for him to be near the Place, unlefs you have provided him and all his Forces-Wings, to be as Expeditious in Taking *Towns*, as your *Pegafus* is in Conveying you the Intelligence of 'em. Pray, Mr. *Harlem*, let me Advife you to think a little cooly on things, before you Write 'em down, and are Angry afterwards that the World won't Believe as faft as you Invent. What think you of Sir *Cloudfley Shovel*'s Sailing up the *Var*, and then Landing Six Thoufand Men within three Miles of *Toulon*.

Harlem. Ha, ha, ha! —— Why don't you think that Fact?

Blunt. It may be fo. Becaufe I don't know but that we have found out a New Invention of *Scating* our Ships where they cannot *Sail*; for the *Var*, where we Landed 600 Men the other Day from our Fleet, won't bear a Boat of Sixty Tun Burthen: And as for approaching within three Miles of *Toulon*, I fuppofe they Slided two or three Leagues upon the Sand to come fo near it; and at this rate I don't find *Toulon* will be *Teneable*. If this be Fact I muft concede with you, Gentlemen, that the Town is ours by this.

Nice. Ho, ho; Mr. *Blunt*, I am glad any Reafon will bring you over: I thought we fhou'd convince you at laft.

Enter Bays.

Bays. Your Servant, Gentlemen. Gentlemen your very humble Servant. What always Talking *Politicks*?

Nice. I am heartily glad to fee you, Mr. *Bays*, withal my Heart. Dear Sir, how have you done this Age? And where have you been?

Bays. Out of Town. I have been in *North Britain*.

Nice. Pray oblige us with the Difcourfe in thofe Parts. I hope they are pleas'd with the Moneys return'd 'em the other Day.

Bays. Pleas'd: Yes, yes; they are pleas'd well enough: The *Scotchmen* Tofs up their *Bonnets* at *Edinburgh*, and cry *God Blefs the Onion*: But they Grumble terribly in *York-fhire*, and the *Northern Countries*, to fee the Money pafs by them, while they ftand fo

much in Need of it themfelves: It makes them lick their Lips at it, and yet, at the fame time they grind their Teeth, and Curfe fome Body for turning *Old England* into *New*. ——

Nice. What have they any *High-Flyers* in thofe Parts?

Bays. I don't know what you call *High-Flyers*; but they are all highly Angry to fee the Money pafs by their Doors, and none of it call in by the way. They refolve now to be All and One for the Ch——

Nice. Are you of that Opinion, too?

Bays. Good, indeed; Pray what Ch—— wou'd you have a Poet of? But now you are talking of that, I remember I have got a Copy of Verfes a good honeft Country Parfon gave me, which he had Compos'd by way of Advice to a New-Marry'd Friend.

Reads.

Tom, *when the heat of Battle's over,*
Man grows a-Tame and Quiet Lover ;
When Honey-Moon is in the Wain,
Its Joys cannot return again :
When Kiffes Cold and Saplefs grow,
And tir'd we are with what we do ;
We Toil and Sweat with Endlefs Pain,
Imaginary Blifs to gain.
Lock'd to the Oar, like Galley-Slaves,
Sometimes we Tug 'gainft Wind and Waves;
And when we've Tow'd the beft we may do,
We're recompenc'd with Tongue-Strappado.
My Deareft Friend, this is thy Fate,
I fee thee fcratch thy Thoughtful Pate ;
Cares and Troubles Cloud thy Brow,
And bending Hams thy Weaknefs fhow ;
Unwonted Pains thy Back hath feiz'd,
And thou'rt grown tir'd with what has pleas'd.
Come, flip thy Matrimonial Fetter,
Unbolt thy Shackles, haften hither ;
Thy Priftine Freedom now regain
Laugh at thy Folly and thy Pain:
With Mirth and Wine let us repair
The Penfive Troubles which we wear.
'Tis Claret only can create
The Freeft, Eafieft, Beft Eftate ;

Can

(27)

Can Sorrows quaſh, and give Relief,
In Preſſures both of Pain and Grief?
'Tis Claret only can defie
All the Nuptial Slavery;
Make the Marriage-Halter eaſie,
And with a Thouſand Joys can pleaſe ye.
The Soldier tir'd with Wounds and Blows,
To Quarters of Refreſhment goes;
Relieves each Want, removes each Pain,
And fits him for the next Campaign.
The Talleſt Frigot muſt Careen,
Tallow, and Waſh e'er Sail again;
Tackle reſit, Sheathing renew,
Victual afreſh, and ſo muſt you.
To ſome ſnug private Creek repair,
Where Storms are huſh'd, and Heav'ns fair;
Where Angry Blaſts cannot moleſt thee,
Or Frowning Billows e'er infeſt thee;
There may you Trim, Refit, and Tallow;
For Lands get Strength by lying Fallow.
The Galloppers, of Yorkſhire Breed,
Renown'd for Lovely Shape and Speed;
Seldom above three Heats will run,
And yet rub down at ev'ry one.
And when theſe Feeble Racers tire,
And Sinews ſtretch'd, ſome Reſt require:
A Winter's Running will reſtore
The Speed and Strength they had before.

Remember, Friend, thou art no Horſe,
Yet Doom'd to ride an Endleſs Courſe;
Marriage a tedious Race will prove,
It Ends with Care, and Starts with Love:
The Rider ſuffers in the Courſe,
Whilſt the Race-Jade is ne'er the worſe.

Hard Whip'd and Spurr'd from Night to Morn,
Like Poſts we ride, ſometimes with Horn.
And when the very beſt we've done,
We ſeldom win the Race we've run;
Whilſt we beſtride the Fiddle-Faddle,
We're often Jockey'd out o'th' Saddle;

Or if we are New-Market Switch,
We tumble into Devils-Ditch.
Thro' Thick and Thin the Bridegroom Rides,
But all the odds are on the Brides.

Conſider, Friend, thy Courſe is long,
Keep up thy Back with Swaddles ſtrong;
Chear up thy Soul with Noble Claret,
Or right good Nantz, if thou comes near it.
Reſume thy Pipe, and wonted Freedom,
If Women Frown, Friend, never heed 'em.
When once they get the upper Hand,
And Female Monarch gives Command, }
Nothing can that great Pow'r withſtand.
Keep up thy Soul, thy Courage ſhow,
Let Rib its Place and Diſtance know;
The Woman wears that Crooked Part,
Much good may't do her with all my Heart.
Our Ribs, by Nature, were deſign'd
To guard the Heart, and not the Mind;
From Head they're in due diſtance plac'd,
Their true Poſition near the Waſte.
Ah! Wou'd they their Submiſſion know,
Why Nature rangeth them below:
That Crooked Part, which downward reaches,
Durſt never ſtruggle for the Breeches.

Thy Birth-Right Breeches, Lad, maintain,
The proper Garnoture of Men;
The Hen-peck'd Fool, raiſes my Paſſion,
He is a Scandal to the whole Creation: }
A Scorn to Angels, Man's Reverſe,
A Woman's Slave, a Diſmal Curſe;
A Scavenger for Satan's A——.
Marriage was not by God deſign'd,
To Enſlave the Freedom of Mankind;
To Cramp our Liberties and Pow'rs,
And hamper us, like Evil-doers.

Man

(28)

Man *Rules, and ſhou'd the* Scepter *ſway,*
Whilſt the Meet-help *ought to Obey;*
What if a Croſs-grain'd, Peeviſh Wife
Becomes the Settlement of Life ;
Or if it be thy Fate to Wed
A Whore, *Unconſtant to thy* Bed,
A Remedy may ſoon be had.
Send her to Briſtol, *to* Ned Granger,
For Beſt Virginia *he'll Exchange her ;*
Two Hogſheads for a Luſty Jade,
And thus Ned *drives an* Honeſt Trade:
Our Chains and Bondage does remove,
And all the Incumbrances of Love;
Takes off theſe heavy Clogs of Life,
The Whore, the Slut, the Imperious Wife ;
And for thoſe diſmal Pains which grieve us,
Gives us Tobacco *to relieve us.*

Divine Tobacco ! *which gives Eaſe*
To all our Pains *and* Miſeries;
Compoſes Thought, *makes* Minds *Sedate,*
Adds Gravity *to* Church *and* State ;
Courted by Kings, *and* Men *of* Conſcience,
The Throne's *Perfume, the* Alter's Incenſe:
Arch-Biſhops, Biſhops, Prieſts, *and* Deacons,
Moſt Reverently can Fire *their* Beacons.
When Rheums, Catarrhs, *and* Colds *moleſt us,*
Doctor Tobacco *muſt aſſiſt us.*
Divine Tobacco ! Indian God !
The Courtier's Feaſt, *the* Poor-Man's Food ;
In Summer *cool, in* Winter *warm,*
Julap *and* Cordial *for each Harm.*
The mighty Sums thou doſt advance,
Will one Day help to Conquer France ;
And Import Claret *and True* Nantz.

And now, my Friend, all Joys *attend you,*
Pardon this Trouble which I ſend you.

Keep up thy Courage, Chear *thy* Soul,
Love Moll, *and let her not Controul :*
What if ſhe Whine, Shed Tears, *and Frown*
Laugh at her Folly, ſhe'll have done.
Never dry up her Tears with Kiſſes,
The more ſhe Cries, *the leſs ſhe P——.*

Friend, when you have a little leiſure,
And wou'd enjoy true Solid Pleaſure,
Shake off thy Collar, *and thy* Fetters,
None lye in Goal *but* Thieves *and* Debtors.
Come, take a Bottle, *never fear,*
I'll eaſe thy Thoughts, *remove thy* Care ;
I'll Lectures *give of* Mirth *and* Freedom,
Shall do thee Good, *if thou wilt* Read *them.*

London, Printed for the Benefit of *Bobee,* the *Coffee-Man* ; and Sold at the Publiſhing-Office, in *Bearbinder-Lane,* 1707.

Edward Arwaker, 'Fable XXIX: The Coffee-House: Or, A Man's Credit, is his Cash', in *Truth in Fiction: Or, Morality in Masquerade. A Collection of Two hundred twenty five Select Fables of Aesop, and other authors* (London, J. Churchill, 1708), [8], xvi, 326pp.; 8°. BL: 12304.d.17. ESTCT84697. Extract, Book III, pp. 234–6.

A verse fable in imitation of one of *Aesop's Fables*, satirising the reception of news in the coffee-house. In the poem, news of an allied military victory is brought to the coffee-house first by a soldier, who is not believed on account of his dirty and poor appearance. When the same news is received from a fashionably dressed fop, it is credible. The moral draws the conclusion. As well as an attack on luxury in dress, Fable XXIX reverses the moral of 'The Boy who cried Wolf': in this fable, sound news is rejected because the messenger has low status.

Arwaker's fable is extracted from *Truth in Fiction*, a collection of satirical verse fables written in loose imitation of the fables of Aesop, designed to impart moral lessons. Little is known about Aesop (580–500 BC), conventionally credited with writing the *Fables*: he may have been an African and a slave. His *Fables* were reprinted frequently through the seventeenth century, and were the subject of some controversy after Richard Bentley's *Dissertation upon the Epistles of Phalaris and the Fables of Aesop* (London, Peter Buck, 1697). The sentiment of Arwaker's fable is drawn from Juvenal's *Satires*, as advertised in the three epigraphs.

The author was Edmund Arwaker (*c.* 1654–1730), a Church of Ireland clergyman, Rector of Donaghmore, Co. Tyrone. Arwaker was chaplain to James Butler, Duke of Ormond (1665–1745), an army officer, Tory, and Jacobite who was lord lieutenant of Ireland from 1703–7 and 1710–13, one of many positions he held which gave him great powers of patronage. Arwaker wrote panegyric poems addressed to, variously, Charles II, James II, Queen Mary and William III, as well as diverse translations from Latin. The publisher was John Churchill of the Black Swan in Paternoster Row, who often operated in partnership with his brother Awnsham Churchill, recognised as the greatest bookseller and stationer of his day. Together the Churchills published Roger L'Estrange's *Fables of Aesop* in 1691.

FABLE XXIX.

The Coffee-House :

Or,

A Man's Credit, is his Cash.

AT *Will's*, where Troops of flutt'ring, gaudy
[Beaus
Parade, to pick up scraps of Wit and News ;
When a whole Swarm in the full House was hiv'd,
On the Report of an Exprefs arriv'd :   810
While there they, big with Expectation, fate,
The firft that enter'd was an old Soldate :
His Boots, with Dirt not dry, were fpatter'd o'er ;
His Coat a Brufhing 'fcap'd fome Weeks before ;
His Hat ill cock'd, his Cravat as ill ty'd ;
His Wig and Face were a right Pifs-burn dy'd ;
His Rufty-hilted Sword, that feem'd a Load,
Was hung on *mal-adroit*, not *a-la-mode* :
In fine, in this odd Drefs, he did appear
Some very mean or broken Officer.   820
The Sparks his Equipage divertive thought ;
Ask'd, whence he came, and what ftrange News he
[brought.
He told them, He from *Flanders* newly came,
And wonder'd how he had out-pofted Fame ;
Since they feem'd Strangers to the glorious Work
Perform'd by *Marlborough* and *Auverquerke* :
How they had giv'n Old *Lewis* a fatal Blow,
And his beft Troops a total Overthrow :

And

Book III.   *Morality in Masquerade.*   235

And *Flanders*, which he had by Craft obtain'd,
Their Courage, in as short a Time, regain'd.   830
  With Patience they the Story let him tell,
But not a Man believ'd a Syllable:
One, with an Oath, says, I'll not heed a Word
He speaks; he can't tell how to wear his Sword.
Another (of his Friend's Persuasion) cries,
'Tis such a shabby Curr, I'm sure he Lyes.
Fogh! says a third, If ever he was there,
He smells as if he ran away for Fear.
Hang him, concludes a fourth, 'Tis all a Jest,
He has not Din'd, and wou'd be some one's Guest.   840
Thus they, by a wrong Estimate befool'd,
The Story and the Author ridicul'd:
Yet with such Caution manag'd all their Chat,
That he shou'd hear no Noise, nor smell a Rat.
Amidst their Sport, comes in a little Prig,
Powder'd to th' Eyes, and almost drown'd in Wig:
A Golden Snush-Box, with right *Vigo* fill'd,
He, in due Form, between his Fingers held;
Whence when he had three graceful Pinches took,
With screw'd Grimace, thus the starch'd Coxcomb
                                    [spoke: 850
Great News at Court, the *French* are soundly beat,
Marlb'rough has giv'n the Dogs a clear Defeat:
Flanders is now possess'd by the Allies,
And, for its Sov'reign, *Charles* do's Recognize.
This said, without more Scruple, they believe,
And all for Gospel from his Mouth receive:
Wealth more persuades, than Probability;
And One so Rigg'd, they fancy'd cou'd not Lye.

The MORAL.

  ' Thus, when a Poor-Man, in a Thread-bare Coat,
  ' Speaks Truth, his Credit is not worth a Groat; 860
                                    ' While

236   *Truth in Fiction* : Or,   Book III.

' While ev'ry Flutt'ring Gaudy Fop's believ'd,
' And all his Words for Oracles receiv'd.
' The thoughtlefs Mob, whom pompous Outfides
          ' fway,
' To Fools well Drefs'd a mighty Def'rence pay ;
' To the Credentials of their Habit truft,
' But think none meanly Clad are True or Juft.
' Poor Men, they fancy, do the Gods contemn,
' And are as unregarded pafs'd by them ;
' But judge, the Rich their Deities revere,
' And ftill to them muft equally be dear : 870
' Thus they believe too little, or too much,
' Where only Wealth for Honefty muft vouch.

Quantum quifque fua nummorum fervat in arca,
Tantum habet & fidei ————————
        Juven. Sat. 3.

————————— *contemnere fulmina pauper*
Creditur, atque deos, Diis ignofcentibus ipfis. Ibid.

———————— *plurima funt, quæ*
Non audent homines pertufa dicere læna.
        .Sat. 5.

Edward Ward, *Vulgus Britannicus: or, the British Hudibrass* (London, James Woodward and John Morphew, 1710), 180pp.; 8°. BL: Sach.119/2 ESTC175779. Extract, pp. 117–47.

An extract of two cantos from a fifteen-book Hudibrastic satire on coffee-house politics during the Sacheverell Crisis of 1710. Written by the Tory satirist Ned Ward (see above, pp. 259–60), the poem satirises the close allegiance between the culture of print, the coffee-houses and the Whig political interest. The crisis began when the Church of England clergyman Henry Sacheverell (1674–724) preached and published two sermons in November 1709 attacking the Whig ministry for neglecting the interests of the Anglican church. When he was prosecuted for 'high crimes and misdemeanours', Tory politicians detected that political mileage could be gained. His trial, between 27 February and 23 March 1710, was a grand spectacle in Westminster Hall, and although he was found guilty, his sentence was very slight (he was banned from preaching for three years, and the two sermons were burned by the hangman). Throughout the crisis and trial, celebrations by the mob were enthusiastic and destructive, particularly of Dissenting chapels and residences. The Sacheverell Riots were unusual in that the mob was rioting against Parliament and the Whigs in defence of ideals defined and elaborated by High-Church Tories. The irony of such a church mob was that it reversed the conventional Whig rhetoric that their political authority came from the people. Coffee-houses, in Ward's estimation, are the natural home of Low-Church Whigs, whom he portrays as plotting over books by Benjamin Hoadley, Daniel Defoe and others. The best account of the Sacheverell crisis is Geoffrey Holmes, *The Trial of Doctor Sacheverell* (London, Eyre Methuen, 1973).

Vulgus Britannicus: or, the British Hudibrass is a five-book imitation of Samuel Butler *Hudibras* (London, Richard Marriot, 1662–3), extending over fifteen cantos. The poem was published in five parts with continuous pagination, beginning in April 1710, and continuing over the coming months. As Troyer observes, the serial parts offer 'an eyewitness account of the mob's activities', depending on observation and characterisation 'rather than any analysis of the issues involved' (Howard Troyer, *Ned Ward of Grub Street* (Cambridge, MA, Harvard University Press, 1946). Part Four was published between 6 June and 5 August, and presumably in July (see F. F. Madan, *A Critical Bibliography of Dr. Henry Sacheverell*, ed. by W. A. Speck (Lawrence, KS, University of Kansas Press, 1978), pp. 112–14). A second edition, comprising all fifteen cantos, was published on 14 August, and a third on 23 November, 1710. Each book was adorned with cuts. The illustrated title-page to Book Four (see p. 298 below) depicts an obscure violent altercation in a coffee-house, not described in the poem. The image depicts two long tables in the coffee-room, spread with tracts and papers, around which diverse gentlemen are assembled. In the background the coffee-woman sits in her bar, a kettle of coffee sits over a roaring fire, while in the foreground a coffee-boy pours coffee. Meanwhile a fight has broken out. The gentleman receiving a face full of coffee bears an uncanny resemblance to Titus Oates, the great Protestant champion during the Exclusion Crisis. In 1683 he was attacked in this way, when a cup of coffee was thrown in his face. The plate may be making an obscure allusion to this earlier Whig coffee-house humiliation.

Vulgus Britannicus:

OR, THE

Britiſh HUDIBRASS.

Altera jam ſeritur multis Factionibus ætas :
Suis & ſua Sacra manibus ruunt.

L O N D O N:

Printed for *James Woodward,* in St. *Chriſtopher's*
Church-Yard, near the *Royal Exchange;* and
John Morphew, near *Stationers-Hall,* 1710.

Price One Shilling.

The Fourth Part of

Vulgus Britannicus:

OR, THE

Britiſh HUDIBRAS.

In Two *C A N T O S:*

On the Coffee-Houſe Mob, or Debates *Pro,* and *Con,* on the Times.

A Character of ſeveral Sorts of *Whigs,* and *Falſe Brethren,* that are Enemies to the *Church.*

On the *Paper-War* betwixt *High* and *Low-Church.*

The *Loyal Engliſhman's* Prayer for the *Queen* and *Church.*

Written by the Author of the *London Spy.*

L O N D O N

Printed : and Sold by J A M E S W O O D W A R D, in St. *Chriſtopher's* Church-Yard, near the *Royal Exchange* ; and J O H N M O R P H E W, near *Stationers-Hall.* M DCCX.

Where may be had the Firſt, Second, and Third Parts.

(117)

Vulgus Britannicus:

OR, THE

Britifh HUDIBRASS.

PART IV.

C A N T O XI.

Of Libels, Authors, *and the feveral forts of* Perfons *who are the heightners of our Divifions.*

THE *Fleetſtreet* Preſſes now grow bold,
And num'rous *Lies* in *Print* were told;
One *Libel* gave another chafe,
And *Paper Wars* came on a pace;

R   Hawkers

118   *CANTO* XI.

Hawkers, like *Wild-geese* flew along
In *Trains*, and cackl'd to the Throng;
Stretch'd wide their *Throats*, and ftrain'd their *Vitals*,
To tempt both *Parties* with their *Titles*;
Adding to all their fenfelefs *Stuff*,
S . . . . . *l*'s Name to pufh it off;
That *Fame* unfully'd might difguife,
And give a Sanction to their *Lies*;
So he that at a publick *Table*,
For Truth reports fome monftrous *Fable*,
Fathers th' incredible *Narration*,
On fome Great Man of *Reputation*;
That his own wild and fenfelefs *Fiction*,
May pafs more free from *Contradiction*.

Some wand'ring *Scriblers* for the *Caufe*,
Skreen'd from the Danger of the *Laws*;
Now took the *Low-Church* Cudgel up,
To give their *High-Church* Foes a Wrap;
And brandifh'd it Hand over Head,
Not caring what they did or faid;

Per-

CANTO XI. 119

Perhaps " *No Drunkards or Vain Swearers,*
Yet given to more sinful Errors;
Fraud, Malice, Lying, Defamation,
Revengeful false *Infinuation*;
And Crimes to their Eternal *Shame,*
Too black and scandalous to Name:
Thus Villains of the deepest Blot,
May freely tell us what they're not;
But they are only Just that dare,
To truly shew us what they are.

Thefe arm'd with *Impudence* and *Spite,*
Began to *Rail,* that is, to *Write;*
For no Fanatick *Riming Brother*
Can well do one without the other;
Since Scandal is to *Low-Church* Wit,
The very fame as *Salt* to *Meat;*
Therefore no *Reader* ought to wonder,
If the Goofe *Saufe* fhould ferve the Gander.

But now, as I before was faying,
The fpiteful Affes would be braying;

And

120,   *C A N T O* XI.

And e'ery *Low-Church* Scribe to Mall,
The *Doctor*, dip his *Pen* in Gall ;
That with Ignoble *Heat* and *Paſſion*,
They might lay hold of this Occaſion,
To ſpit their Venom and their Hate
At him, beneath the Frowns of *State*,
So the brave *Stag* that ſtands at *Bay*,
Unwilling to become a Prey ;
When once the ſtanch old Dogs have thrown him,
The Puppies then fall in upon him.

The *Coffee Tables* now were ſpread,
With all the worſt that could be ſaid ;
And the two Good old *Cauſe Aſſerters*,
Read moſt by *Coblers* and by *Porters* ;
Were by the Saints kind *Interceſſion*,
Receiv'd again on this Occaſion,
By Houſes here and there from whence,
They had been Kick'd and Spew'd long ſince ;
Hoping their *Talents* might prevail,
At ſuch a time to turn the Scale ;

And

CANTO XI. 121

And that their Mutual *Forces* Join'd,

Harnafs'd with *Wit* fo much refin'd;

And fo adorn'd inftead of Senfe,

With Trappings of *Falfiloquence,*

Might draw misjudging *Fools* to be,

In Love with their *Sincerity;*

That they might fend a *Hand* to fave,

A Caufe that would themfelves enflave;

Which Pious Work as carry'd on,

Might foon effectually be done;

Would we for *Scripture* read Reviews,

Con *H...y's* Works inftead of *News,*

And Pin our *Faith* in all State Matters,

On Wife *North Brittifh* Obfervators;

But thofe who once have got a Name,

For trading with *Fallacious Fame;*

When they fpeak Truth, 'tis thrown away,

'Caufe none will Credit what they fay.

However, num'rous *Lies* like Weeds,

Sprang up from Old *Fanatick Seeds;*

And

122   *C A N T O* XI.

And tho' they little Rooting had,
The thriving *Cockle* spread like mad;
Audacious *Scandals* now were thrown,
By Atheists, at the *Rev'rend Gown*,
Who basely Labour'd to revile
The *Priests* with Craft the *Church* with Guile;
And rav'd and rattled in their Heat,
As if they really did conceit,
Religion but an *Ancient Cheat*;
So he that is to *Vice* resign'd,
And does no *Law* Eternal mind;
Would fain believe to mend the *Matter*,
There is no *Punishment* herea'ter.

Each *Coffeehouse* where the *Saints* were wont
To read dull News, and Preach upon't;
Was now into a *Bedlam* turn'd,
Where one side Laugh'd, and t'other Mourn'd;
As if the sober plodding *Knave*
That look'd disconsolately Grave,
Was grown quite Melancholly Mad,
To see his *Opposites* so glad;

Who

CANTO XI. 123

Who in return were laughing wild,

To fee the *Saints* fo tame and mild;

After they'd been fo crowing fure

Of winning *All* fome Weeks before;

So he that does at *Hazard* play,

And ftakes his all at beft oth' lay;

If *Fortune* treats him with Difdain,

And fends the *Chance* before the Main;

The Purblind *Gipfy* he reviles,

Scratches his *Ears*, and bites his *Nails*;

Whilft he that Wins with *Pleafure* Smiles.

Some *Saints*, whofe mod'rate Zeal extended,

Before the *Tryal* quite was ended,

To *Hanging*, *Gelding*, fo untow'rd

A Doom, their very *Wives* abhor'd;

Or *Banifhment*, the Lord knows whither,

And that to be at leaft for ever;

When all was over were again,

Become fuch foothing mod'rate Men;

That now they tun'd their *Tongues* and *Throats*

Another way, and chang'd their *Notes*;

As

124   *C A N T O* XI.

As if the *Ventholes* of their *Paſſion*,
Were double *Cruits* on occaſion ;
That as they pleas'd to *Frown* or *Smile*,
Could pour out Vinegar or Oyl ;
So *Eſop*'s *Satyr* we are told,
With the ſame Breath, *blew Hot and Cold.*

Others as Reſolute and fierce,
As *Bull-dogs* ſcorn'd to hang an *Arſe* ;
And ſince they'd ſhewn themſelves ſo violent,
Would neither Modeſt prove or *Silent* ;
But even rend their *Spiteful Jaws*,
To rail at thoſe that try'd the *Cauſe* ;
Becauſe they would not be ſeverer,
In puniſhing ſo great an *Error* ;
And ſhew themſelves more raſh than they
That hop'd to make the *Church* their Prey ;
And by triumphing o'er the *Prieſt*,
Turn *Sacred Truths* into a *Jeſt* ;
Becauſe not model'd to the ſpite,
Of each *Fanatick-Hypocrite* ;

Who

CANTO XI. 125

Who always were too Warm to hear,

Their Failings with a Patient Ear;

So he that knows himfelf a Knave,

If call'd fo, will in Paffion Rave,

And in his Vindication Cry;

Tho' true, 'tis a Nororious ly,

And to preferve, when vex'd and mad,

His good Name, which he never had;

Will Sue the Man with all his might,

For only faying what is Right.

Another fort of Men there are,

Who neither Love or Malice bear

To any Side; but dull as Brutes,

Without Concern hear all difputes:

And void of thought as Lifelefs Clay,

Sit and fay nothing either way,

Becaufe they nothing have to fay;

Paffive in e'ery thing they feem,

Their Lives are one Continu'd Dream,

As if their Parents drunk or fick,

And Natures forces very weak;

S   Had

126   *C A N T O* XI.

Had in their Sleep begot 'em a'ter,

A Droufie dofe of *Poppy Water* ;

And that they'd never truly been

Awak'd, fince firft Conceiv'd in Sin ;

Thefe never any diff'rence knew,

Betwixt the *Chriftian* or the *Jew*;

But would be equally Content,

With any *Church* or *Government* ;

Yet for their harmlefs Temper pafs,

With e'ery mild unthinking Afs ;

For Prudent Men of *Peace* that Hate

Contention, *Squabble* and *Debate* ;

When all their Calm indifference,

Afcrib'd to *Modefty* and *Senfe*,

A Man of *Brains* may plainly fee,

Is but profound Stupidity ;

So he that Padlocks up his *Chaps*,

May pafs for a Wife Man perhaps,

Who if Examin'd would be found,

An *Empty Veffel* full of *Sound.*

Others

C A N T O XI. 127

Others there are *Nurs'd* up in *Craft*,
Of all that's truly Good *Bereft*,
Who guess *Religion* but a *Mode*,
Ordain'd by Man and not by *God*;
And therefore think that they may Chuse,
Or Change their *Faith* as Men their *Shoes*;
And that it is most safe to trust,
In what so e'er Climbs uppermost;
Believing Int'rest is the *Root*,
Of all Opinions now on *Foot*;
And that the Man that does but say,
His *Pray'rs* to her, can never Stray,
Or be a *Sinner* in the Main,
That measures *Godliness* by gain;
These with the *Stream* in Consort Glide,
And humour each Revolving *Tide*:
Appear in *Puritannick Dresses*,
And Cheat the *World* with Holy *Faces*;
The *Saints* in full *Communion* join
Not thro' *Devotion* but design;

And

128   *C A N T O* XI.

And in their looks and mean difplay,

Full as much *Sanctity* as they ;

Yet darling Int'reft ftill perfue,

In er'e thing they fay or do,

Ne'er talk with heat to give Offence,

But Coax all fides to gain the *Pence* ;

That fhould fome unexpected *Blow*,

Reftore the *High* and crufh the *Low* ;

They might forfake when Int'reft calls,

Their *Modifh* meeting for St. *Pauls*,

Yet by their timely knocking under,

Give us no mighty Caufe of Wonder ;

So the Sharp *Blade* that falls in *League*,

With a Rich *Lady* of Intrigue ;

And only does pretend to Love her,

To make the moft he can do of her,

Ne'er binds himfelf with *Oaths* and *Vows*,

So clofe but that he may Efpoufe,

The Woman that he likes much better,

Whofe Fortune or whofe *Charms* are greater.

Next

C A N T O XI. 129

Next to this wav'ring wick'd Race,
In no Part *Chriftian* but in *Face*,
Who taft *Religion* like Falfe *Zealots*,
With Vitious *Atheiftick Pallats* ;
There are a fworded *Whigifh* Train,
That hold all *Vertue* in difdain ;
Hector like *Ruffins Swear* and *Rattle*,
And damn the *High-Church* o'er the *Bottle*,
Whore on like *Bullies*, drink like *Dragons*,
Call themfelves *Whigs*, but talk like *Pagans* ;
Toaft Healths to this and that great Lord,
And caufe he's *High-Church* damn the Third ;
By Raving turn the Houfe or Room,
T'a *Bedlam* where fo e'er they come ;
In *Tavern* Kitchens roar and Bellow,
And Spit their *Poyfon* when they're Mellow ;
Fright Modeft Men with bluftring Words,
And awe the Tim'rous with their *Swords* ;
Pick Shameful *Quarrells* o're the Quart,
With thofe that do their Nonfenfe Thwart ;

Make

130 *C A N T O* XI.

Make Sport with all that's good and *Holy*,
And bear down truth with Noify Folly;
Worry o're *Wine* Superiour Senfe,
With Partial Heat and Impudence,
And broach a Thoufand *Bugbear* lies,
That greater Fools may think 'em Wife;
At Random talk what would have been,
High *Treafon* in another *Reign* :
And he that hears and won't Submit
Muft be at leaft a *Jacobite.*
And all becaufe he can't Comply,
To pin his *Faith* upon a ly ;
Thefe for the *Low-Church* too declare,
All tho' they to no *Church* repair ;
Or do they ever take their fitting,
In any but a *Tavern* meeting :
Yet *Tooth* and *Nail* they will defend,
That *Church* to which they do pretend ;
Tho' 'tis believ'd they ne'er could fay,
Their *Creed* or know they how to pray ;
Except Witch like the Backward way ;

So

C A N T O XI. 131.

So worthlefs Mungrils that are bred,
Among the Hounds and with them Fed;
All tho' the Puppies have no Nofes,
They'l with them Hunt thro' Woods and Clofes;
Perfue the Game the felf fame way,
And fpend and Yelp as well as they.

But ftill there are a far worfe Sort,
Of *Whigs* who do the *Church* more hurt
Than thefe; and by their reftlefs Tongues,
And bufy Pens do greater wrongs,
To true *Religion* than the Reft,
Becaufe of Keener Parts poffeft,
Thefe with a double meaning Write,
To fhew their Wit and next their *Spite*
That betwixt Tickling and their Teafing,
Their Malice may be render'd Pleafing;
And that the Calumny and *Satyr*,
With which they do the *Church* befpatter;
May ftick the Clofer, Wound the deeper,
And in a low Condition keep her;

The

132 CANTO XI.

The Cheif of thefe whofe *Books* of late,

Were Juftly Cenfur'd by the *State* ;

Enrag'd by the provoking *Flame*,

The *Hangman* Kindled for the fame,

Has fince by new Invectives Shown

How much he Values *Church* or *Throne* ;

In laying at the *Roots* of both,

The *Ax* of Malice and untruth,

That by Perverting Solid Senfe;

With artfull querks and Impudence,

And by oppofing Real Fact,

With Study'd lies together Pack'd ;

He might Infinuate to the *Nation*,

The *Church* in *Law* has no Foundation,

And that Exemption's *Tolleration*.

So Strenoufly infer from thence

To *Couzen Fools* and pleafe the *Saints* ;

That they 're on fuch a Legal Footing,

As gives their Worfhip, better Rooting ;

Than the Eftablifh'd *Church* Divine,

That's Built upon the *Thirty Nine* ;

The

CANTO XI.   133

The Stuborn *Turk* or faith lefs *Jew*;
May fay their own Opinion's True,
And *Scribble*, *Wrangle*, *Lie*, and *Blufter*,
To make the *Alcoran* pafs *Mufter*;
Or ufe a *Crafty* Strenuous Plea,
In Right of *Infidelity*:
But fhall we to our wick'd Shame,
For fake our *Faith* to Humour them
Give up Chriftianity to pleafe,
Such *Heathenifh* Mifcreants as thefe;
No, to the *Church* let's ftick the clofer,
When fuch bold *Enemies* oppofe her:
And never heed what 'tis they Write,
Or fay againft her in their *Spite*;
Nay, tho' fome *Pharifees* that join her,
To only *Rob* and undermine her;
Who praife her *Worfhip* but in Part,
And hug her but with half a *Heart*;
Should Scruples raife and be offended,
At this or that to have it mended;

T   We

134   *C A N T O*   XI.

We fhould diftinguifh 'em the fame
With thofe, who at her Ruin aim :
And look on each *Fanatick Cavil*,
To be fome bafe infectious evil ;
Rais'd by her greateft *Foe* the *Devil:*
Church Enemies are ne'er at reft,
And when they Solemnly proteft,
They mean, alas, no Harm unto her,
Moft Mifcheif they're about to do her ;
Like *Subtile Jilts* they play their Parts,
And *Skreen* their *Ills* by private *Arts* :
Seem moft devout when 'tis to hide,
Their *Plots* their *Malice* and their *Pride* ;
And when they have moft hurt defign'd :
Give out a quite Contrary *Blind*,
Adrefs the *Prince* they would betray,
And Fawn the moft to clear the Way ;
That by pretence of being *Friends*,
They may the better gain their *Ends*,
Cry out for *Liberty* aloud ;
To gull the *poor* unthinking *Croud*,

When

CANTO XI. 135

When 'tis their hidden bafe intent,
T' enflave 'em by their own Confent,
Difguife all *Ills* in agitation
Againft the *Church*, with *Reformation* :
And always feem the moft devout,
When they've the worft defigns on *Foot* ;
Juft fo the Subtile *Crocadile*,
That lurks upon the *Banks* of *Nile* ;
Does by diffembl'd Tears betray,
Poor harmlefs *Creatures* in his way ;
And weeping takes his Heedlefs prey.
Who then would fuch a *Brood* believe,
That Fawn and *Whine* when they deceive ;
And charge on others thofe defignes,
Themfelves drive on in hidden *Mines*.

The *Church-men* tho' fincerely true,
To God their *Queen* and *Country* too;
Becaufe they wont *Submit* to be,
Enflav'd by *Factious Tyranny* ;
Muft be call'd *Perkenites* and *Traytors*,
And made moft wick'd Odious *Creatures* ;

Be

136 *C A N T O* XI.

Be Charg'd with *Plots* againſt the *State*,

And all thoſe *Ills* they truly hate;

Be ſtil'd rank *Papiſts* by their *Scriblers*,

And bear the dirt of all their *Libelers*;

Tho' they're fix'd Enemies to *Pop'ry*,

As well as to *Fanatick Fop'ry*;

And are the *Nations* only Friends,

That have prevented both their *Ends*;

And ſtop'd we hope by Countermining,

The Miſcheifs both have been deſigning.

But in return of all their heat,

And flagrant Malice they have Spit;

Should the ſame *Church* the Truth diſcloſe,

And tell their undermining *Foes*;

What Wiſe Men think, they'd rave and *Huff*,

And *Swear* 'twas only *Popiſh Stuff*,

That notwithſtanding all their thin,

Pretences which they uſe to *Skreen*;

Their dark *Intrigues* that 'tis too plain,

The Game of old's begun again;

And

C A N T O XI. 137

And that they shew themselves to be,
Rank Enemies to *Monarchy*;
Republicans who aim by stealth,
To change us to a *Common Wealth*:
That when the *Nations* thus betray'd,
Their own dull *Teachers* may invade
The *Church*, and in her *Pulpits Preach*
Such *Tenets* up that sute therewith,
Whilst leading *Knaves*, as once before,
By Craft *Usurp* the Regal *Power*,
Kill, *Hang*, *Sequester* and Oppress,
To glut their *Pride* and Avarice,
This is their aim and their persuit;
Altho' they want the *Pow'r* to do't,
But should we still Sleep on in *Silence*,
They plainly shew us by their *Violence*,
That they'l be *Vigilant* to gain,
Those ends they're lab'ring to obtain;
We therefore equal care should take,
To *Baffle* the Efforts they make;

And

138   *C A N T O* XI.

And not thro' too much *Confidence*

In them, neglect our own defence ;

For Slothful *Negligence*, we fee,

Th' effect of Vain Security,

Oft makes the ftranger Fortune's fport,

And gives the Weaker *Pow'r* to hurt ;

What *People* then when once allarm'd,

Would quit their *Sheilds* and *Sleep* unarm'd.

C A N T O   XII.

Of Mens Deportment in the Coffee-Houfes, *of the* Mine-Adventure, *The* African-*Company, of thofe who defire* War, *and others* Peace, *with a Prayer for the* Queen *and* Church.

NO w Warm debates were carry'd on,
        In e'ery *Coffee-Houfe* Pro and Con;

Where

C A N T O XI. 139

Where *Whigs* of e'ery fort and fize,

Began aloud to *Tyrannize* ;

Some *Grave* old *Cits* Nurs'd up in Trade,

Betwixt the *Church* and *Meeting* bred ;

Amphibeous Chriftians who can run

To either, but be true to none ;

Whofe *Dealings* long have prov'd too plain,

They fcarce know any *God* but Gain ;

That Gold's the *Standard* of their *Faith* ;

And Int'reft their *Celeftial Path* ;

Yet thefe will o'er their *Jewifh* Liquor,

About *Religion* Jar and *Bicker* ;

And rave till grown as *Piping Hot*,

As the dull *Grout* o'er which they fot,

But ftill they take all *Modifh Care*

To tell what Sorts of *Saints* they are ;

And by their *Loud* Revilings *Show*,

They're true *Blew Proteftants*, but *Low* ;

Affirm they Love with all their *Souls*,

The *Church*, but yet like *Knaves* or *Fools* ;

Reproach all *Goodmen* that defend her,

And fain would make her bad to mend her ;

Thus

140   *C A N T O* XI.

Thus thofe who've neither *Will* or *Grace*,

To mend themfelves but ftill are *Bafe* ;

We fee cannot forbear pretending,

To reform that which needs no mending :

Tho' they're attended with the *Curfe*,

Of allwayes making better *Worfe* ;

One by the *Mine adventure* Bit,

Will o'er their *Coffee* Railing fit;

Againft the canting cunning *Knight*,

Who tho' a *Rank* old *Jacobite* ;

Found out a lucky way to fhew 'em,

In their own *Art* he could out do 'em :

And unfufpe&ted *Pitkinife*,

The *Crafty Saints Fanatick*-wife,

Altho' they knew no *Mortal* fitter,

Than Good Sir *Mac* to *Bite* the *Biter* :

But fure thofe *Saints* had quite forgot,

Themfelves who were fo Wondrous hot ;

To truft their *Money* in the *Pow'r*,

Of one who'd flown fo high before,

And

C A N T O XII.   141

And oft Oppos'd in *Books* and *Speeches*,

Their fly Intrigues and Cunning Fetches;

But 'tis no Wonder fince we find,

That Int'reft often makes Men blind;

And Tempts 'em by a *Golden Bait*,

To truft and *Flatter* thofe they *Hate*:

Others with Equal *Warmth Arraign*,

The Company call'd *Affrican*,

And with the *World* ill Temper'd grow;

To See their *Stock* fo very low,

Charge on the *Managers* the *Blame*;

Sip, Frown, and as they *Smoak Exclaim*,

Becaufe they find the *Junto Bleft*

With Wit enough to *Fool* the *Reft*,

Thus among thofe that turn the *Penny*,

One Thrives upon the Lofs of many,

And fome *Mens Folly* 'tis that makes,

Others prove *Knaves* that hold the *Stakes*.

Some who are in *Accounts Exact*,

Demonftrate plainly that the *Act*,

U   which

142   *C A N T O* XII.

Which was of Late fo timely made,
To Regulate the Size of *Bread*;
Has left it ftill i' th' *Bakers Pow'r*,
To *Cheat* their *Cuftomers* much more,
Then e'er they us'd to do before;
Which fhews how hard 'tis to Reftrain,
The *Knavifh Practice* of fuch Men;
Who will in *Spite* of *Law* perfue it,
Becaufe theyv'e been Accuftom'd to it;
So the *Sly Lafs* that has been *Beded*,
Before She's to her *Lover Wedded*;
Will alwayes after ready be
T' Improve an opportunity.

Some full of *News* Collected from,
The *Prints Abroad* and lies at *Home*;
Sit *Gravely* fetting forth the whole,
That's faid and done 'twixt *Pole* and *Pole*;
Tell you the very *Day* and *Hour*,
When we fhall all our *Foes* o'erpow'r
What lucky *Steps* we wifely take,
And e'ery *Progrefs* that we make;

When

CANTO XII. 143

When we fhall give the *French* a *Shock*,
And at the *Gates* of *Paris Knock* ;
What *Wonders* will at laft *befal*,
And be the great *Event* of all ;
Thus fome in *Earneft* fome in *Jeft*,
With *Groundlefs Whims Amufe* the reft ;
And what the *Bufy Knaves Invent*,
The *Foolifh* take upon *Content*.

Others come *Puffing* in to tell
The *Tidings* of the laft *New Mail* ;
That *Peace* is frefh again on *Foot*,
And all Sides are Inclining To't ;
That *France* is forward to *Comply*,
And does no *Terms* we ask *deny*;
This vexes fome who long have made
Advantage of a *Secret Trade* ;
And Startles others who are for
No *Peace*, becaufe they gain by *War*;
But highly pleafes all the Reft,
Who truly wifh the *Nation* Bleft

U2

And

144   *C A N T O* XII.

And that *Britanina's* aweful *Queen*,
Who has in *War* fo profp'rous been ;
May long enjoy in *Downy Peace*,
A fweet and *unmolefted Eafe* ;
And thofe *Calm Bleffings* that arife,
From all her *Glorious Victories* ;
That then or fooner may She fee,
Her *Subjects* from *Contention free* ;
And all thofe *Quarrels*, *Fewds* and *Heats*,
That now *Perplex* her *Throne* by *Fits* ;
And e'ery *Breach* our *Foes* improve,
Unite in *Frindfhip* and in *Love* ;
May both the *Names* of *High* and *Low*,
To e'ery *Party Odious* grow ;
Till by all *Sides* they're given o'er,
And ever Ceafe to be no more ;
May we from *Anna's* Vertues *Learn*,
That good we no where elfe Difcern ;
And *Labour* to return the *Throne*,
Thofe *Bleffings* She has made our own ;

May

CANTO XII.   145

May thofe who would invade or *Lower*,
The Lawful *Rights* of *Sov'raign Pow'r* ;
And Struggle by defignes *Nefarious*,
To make the *Royal-Throne*, *Precarious* ;
Whether they're *Jacobites* or *Whigs*,
Be made as *Black* as their *Intrigues* ;
Render'd unquailifi'd to be,
Entrufted with *Authority* ;
And by the *Reins* of Human *Law*
Be alwayes *Curb'd* and kept in *Awe.*

May all good Men who ever lov'd
Their *Queen* and *Country* ftand unmov'd ;
And alwayes truly be agreed
To defend both in time of need,
Againft all ill defignes began
By *Papift* or *Republican* ;
That no *Attempt* 'gainft *Church* or *State*,
May ever be oppos'd too late ;
But in *its* Early *Progrefs* meet,
A timely and Intire *Defeat* ;

That

146   *C A N T O*   XII.

That *Pride* and *Avarice* may fee,
In *Spite* of Man *God* ftill will be ;
Th' all Powerful *Guardian* of the *Throne*,
He only makes the *Monarch's* own.

Since Bountious *Heav'n*, we muft agree,
Knows no Impoffibility ;
Within this *Realm* may all Mankind,
In Rules of *Faith* be of one *Mind* ;
That none may need within this *Nation*,
The Tender grant of *Tolleration* ;
Nor any grumbling *Party Vex*,
The *Throne*, or human *Peace* Perplex ;
No Vile *Sedicious Seeds* be fown,
No Name but *Brother Chriftian* known ;
But all beneath Bright *Anna* prove
As happy to us as her *Love*,
And we to fhew how much we are,
Indebted to her *Nurfing* Care,
Do all thar in a *People* lies,
To make her *Throne* a *Paradife*.

May

C A N T O XII.   147

May the *True Church* her safety owe,
To *God* above, the *Queen* below;
And *Flourish* in *Eternal Peace*,
In Spite of all her *Enemies* ;
Subdue by *Preaching* and by *Pray'r*,
All those who with her *Doctrines* jar ;
Use no *Severity* to those,
Who bred awry, her *Rites oppose* ;
Nor may she ever find the same,
From such who Spite her to their shame
Or Bow her Everlasting *Head*,
To those by *Crafty Guides* misled ;
But still preserve from *Errour Free*,
Her *Apostolick Purity* ;
That the *True Christian Church*, no other,
Beneath the *Queen* her *Nursing Mother* ;
May *Flourish* to the last degree,
And stand up with *Eternity*.

John Macky, *A Journey Through England. In Familiar Letters. From a Gentleman Here, to his Friend Abroad* (London, J. Roberts for T. Caldecott, 1714), BL: 797.f.16. ESTCT57747. Extract, pp. 107–14. Hünersdorff.

An extract from an epistolary travel narrative describing a tour through England. This letter describes the coffee-houses, and theatres, of London. The narrator adopts the conceit that the traveller is describing his subject for the first time to a correspondent generally ignorant of the city and its manners. This is fictional, as Macky had considerable experience of the city, but not satirical, by contrast with the same device in Ward's hands. Macky organises the coffee-houses according to two methods: the first geographical, and the second an assessment of their characteristic social and political allegiance. In this way he begins with coffee-houses in Westminster, moves on to Covent Garden, and ends up in Exchange Alley in the City. These three locations are then codified, so that the first group is analysed by political loyalty, the second as the home of the critics, and the third for commerce. Historical evidence suggests that this typology is neat and convenient, but not as unambiguous as Macky suggests.

Macky's travel writing at times seems to be based on careful observation and personal experience, as when he describes the gamblers and stock-jobbers of Jonathan's Coffee-house. Elsewhere, however, he repeats guide-book information, or makes haphazard guesses, as when he later states that '*Taverns* and *Coffee-Houses* are innumerable; and what is almost incredible, you can hardly enter into a *Coffee-House* in an Evening, but you find Company, although there be above Eight Thousand of them, by a modest Computation in and about *London*' (p. 208, not reprinted here). A more measured estimate was closer to 500.

John Macky (d. 1726) was a government spy and post-office contractor who played a role in the discovery of several important plots, invasion conspiracies and assassination plans by Jacobites. In 1713, Macky lost his post office contract and was forced to flee from his debtors to Holland. When he returned to London he turned to travel writing, producing the first volume of his *A Journey Through England* in 1714, a second in 1722 (both of which went through many editions), and further volumes on Scotland and the Austrian Netherlands. The travels were published by J. Roberts for T. Caldecott at the Sun by St Dunstan's Church in Fleetstreet.

I A M Lodged in the Street called *Pall-mall*, the ordinary Refidence of all Strangers, becaufe of its Vicinity to the *Queen*'s Palace, the *Park*, the *Parliament-Houfe*, the *Theatres*, and the *Chocolate* and *Coffee-Houfes*, where the beft Company frequents. If you would know our manner of Living, 'tis thus ; we rife by Nine, and thofe that frequent great Mens Levees find Entertainment at them till Eleven, or as in *Holland* go to *Tea-Tables* ; about Twelve the *Beau-Monde* affembles in feveral *Coffee* or *Chocolate-Houfes* : The beft of which are the *Cocoa-Tree* and *White*'s Chocolate-Houfes, St. *James*'s, the *Smirna*, Mrs *Rochford*'s, and the *Britifh* Coffee-Houfes, and all thefe fo near one another, that in lefs than an Hour you fee the Company of them all. We are carryed to thefe Places in *Chairs* (or *Sedans*) which are here very cheap, a Guinea

108 *A Journey through* England.

a Guinea a Week, or a Shilling per Hour, and your Chair-men ſerve you for Porters to run on Errands as your *Gondaliers* do at *Venice*.

IF it is fine Weather we take a turn in the *Park* till Two, when we go to Dinner ; and if it be dirty you are entertained at *Picket* or *Baſ-ſet* at *White's*, or you may talk Politicks at the *Smyrna* and St. *James's*. I muſt not forget to tell you,that the Parties have their different Pla-ces, where however a Stranger is always well received ; but a *Whig* will no more go to the *Cocoa-Tree* or *Oſinda's*, than a *Tory* will be ſeen at the Coffee-Houſe of St. *James's*.

THE *Scots* go generally to the *Britiſh*, and a Mixture of all Sorts to the *Smyrna*. There are other little *Coffee-Houſes* much frequented in this Neighbourhood, *Young-Man's* for *Officers*, *Old-Man's* for *Stock-Jobbers*, *Pay-Maſters* and *Courtiers*, and *Little Man's* for *Sharpers*. I ne-ver was ſo confounded in my Life as when I entred into this laſt : I ſaw Two or Three Ta-bles full at *Faro*, heard the Box and Dice rat-ling in the Room above Stairs,and was ſurround-ed by a Sett of ſharp Faces, that I was afraid would have devoured me with their Eyes. I was glad to drop Two or Three Half Crowns at *Faro* to get off with a clear Skin, and was over-joyed I was ſo got rid of them.

AT Two we generally go to Dinner : Ordi-naries are not ſo common here as abroad, yet the *French* have ſet up Two or Three pretty good ones for the conveniency of *Foreigners* in
Suffolk-

A Journey through England. 109

Suffolk-Street, where one is tolerably well ferved; but the general way here is to make a Party at the *Coffee-Houfe* to go Dine at the *Tavern*, where we fit till fix that we go to the Play, except you are invited to the Table of fome Great Man, which Strangers are always courted to, and nobly entertained.

I KNOW Abundance of *French*, that by keeping a Pocket-Lift of Tables, live fo almoft all the Year round, and yet never appear at the fame Place above once in a Fortnight; by looking into their Pocket Book in the Morning they fix their Place of Dining, as on *Monday* with my Lord ———, and fo for Two Weeks, Fourteen Lords, Foreign Minifters, or Men of Quality; and fo they run their Round all the Year long, without notice being taken of them.

THERE are Two very Noble *Theatres* here, and a Third for a *Comedy* which is rebuilding. That for *Opera's* at the End of the *Pall-Mall*, or *Hay-Market*, is the fineft I ever faw, and where we are entertained in *Italian* Mufick generally twice a Week; that for *Hiftory*, *Tragedy*, and *Comedy*, is in *Covent-Garden*, (a *Piazza* I fhall defcribe to you in the Sequel of this Letter) and the other that's rebuilding is by *Lincolns-Inn-Fields*, at a fmall diftance from the other.

THE *Theatres* here differ from thofe abroad; in that thofe at *Venice*, *Paris*, *Bruffels*, *Genoa*, and other Parts, you know are compofed of Rows of fmall *Shut-Boxes*, Three or Four Stories
ries

110   *A Journey through* England.

ries in a Semi-Circle with a *Parterre* below ; whereas here, the *Parterre* (commonly called the *Pit*) contains the Gentlemen on Benches ; and on the firſt Row of *Boxes* fit all the Ladies of Quality ; in the Second the Citizens Wives and Daughters ; and in the Third the Common People and Footmen ; ſo that between the Acts you are as much diverted by viewing the Beauties of the Audience, as while they act with the Subject of the Play ; and the Whole is illuminated to the greateſt Advantage : Whereas abroad, the Stage being only illuminated, and the *Lodge* or *Boxes* cloſe, you loſe the Pleaſure of ſeeing the Company ; and indeed the *Engliſh* have reaſon in this, for no Nation in the World can ſhew ſuch an Aſſembly of ſhining Beauties as here.

T H E *Engliſh* affect more the *Italian* than the *French* Muſick ; and their own Compoſitions are between the *Gravity* of the firſt and the *Levity* of the other. They have had ſeveral great Maſters of their own : *Henry Purcell*'s Works in that Kind are eſteemed beyond *Lully*'s every where ; and they have now a good many very Eminent Maſters ; but the Taſte of the Town being at this Day all *Italian,* it is a great diſcouragement to them.

No Nation repreſents Hiſtory ſo *naturally,* ſo much to the *Life,* and ſo cloſe to *Truth* as the *Engliſh* ; they have moſt of the Occurrences of their own Hiſtory, and all thoſe of the *Roman* Empire nobly Acted. One *Shakeſpear* who
2   lived

A Journey through England. 109

lived in the laſt Century, laid down a Maſterly Foundation for this in his excellent Plays ; and Mr. *Addiſon* hath improved that Taſte by his admirable *Cato.*

THEIR Comedies are deſigned to laſh the growing Follies in every Age ; and ſcarce a *Fool* or a *Coxcomb* appears in Town, but his Folly is repreſented. And moſt of their *Comedians,* in Imitation of *Molliere,* have taken that Province ; in which Mr. *Cibber,* an extream good Player, hath ſuccceeded very well.

THEY ſeldom degenerate into *Farce* as the *Italians,* nor do they confine their *Tragedies* to Rhyme and Whining as the *French.* In ſhort, if you would ſee the greateſt Actions of paſt Ages played over again, and the preſent Follies of Mankind expoſed, you muſt come here.

AFTER the Play, the beſt Company generally go to *Tom's* and *Will's Coffee-Houſes* near adjoining, where there is playing at *Picket,* and the beſt of Converſation till Midnight. Here you will ſee *Blue* and *Green Ribbons* and *Stars,* ſitting familiarly, and talking with the ſame freedom, as if they had left their Quality and Degrees of Diſtance at Home ; and a Stranger taſtes with Pleaſure the univerſal Liberty of Speech of the *Engliſh* Nation. Or if you like rather the Company of Ladies, there are *Aſſemblies* at moſt People of Qualities Houſes. And in all the *Coffee-Houſes* you have not only the *Foreign* Prints, but ſeveral *Engliſh* ones with the *Foreign* Occurrences, beſides Papers of Morality and Party-Diſputes. MY

112 *A Journey through* England.

My Bills of Exchange oblige me now and then to take a Turn to the *Royal-Exchange*, in a Hackney-Coach, to meet my Merchant. Thefe Coaches are very neceffary Conveniencies, not to be met with any where abroad : for you know that at *Paris*, *Bruffels*, *Rome*, or *Vienna*, you muft either hire a Coach by the Day, or take it at leaft by the Hour ; but here you have Coaches at the Corner of every Street, which for a Shilling will carry you any where within a reafonable Diftance, and for Two from one end of the City to the other. There are Seven Hundred of them Licenfed by Act of Parliament, and carry their Number on their Coaches ; fo that if you fhould chance to leave any Thing in a Coach, and know but the Number of it, you know prefently where to lay your Claim to it ; and be you never fo late at a Friend's Houfe in any Place of this great City, your Friend by taking the Number of the Coach, fecures your Safety home.

The *Royal-Exchange* is the Refort of all the Trading Part of this City *Foreign* and *Domeftick*, from Half an Hour after One till near Three in the Afternoon : But the better Sort generally meet in *Exchange-Alley* a little before, at Three Celebrated *Coffee-Houfes*, called *Garaway*'s, *Robin*'s, and *Jonathan*'s. In the Firft, the People of Quality, who have Bufinefs in the City, and the moft confiderable and Wealthy Citizens frequent. In the Second, the *Foreign Banquiers*, and often even *Foreign Minifters*.
And

A Journey through England. 113

And in the Third the Buyers and Sellers of *Stock.*

WHEN I entred into this laft, I was afraid I had got into *Little-Man*'s *Coffee-Houfe* again, for bufy Faces run about here as there, with the fame fharp intent Looks, with this Difference only, that here it is felling of *Bank-Stock, Eaft-India, South-Sea*, and *Lottery-Tickets*, and there it is all *Cards* and *Dice.*

YOU will fee Fellows, in fhabby Cloaths, Selling Ten or Twelve Thoufand Pounds in *Stock*, though perhaps he may'nt be worth at the fame time Ten Shillings, and with as much Zeal as if he were a Director, which they call Selling a *Bear*'s-*Skin* ; and thefe Men find Bubbles enough to get Bread by it, as the others do by *Gaming* ; and fome few of them manage it fo as to get pretty large Eftates.

NEAR this *Exchange* are Two very good *French* Eating-Houfes, the One at the Sign of *Pontack*, a Prefident of the Parliament of *Bourdeaux*, from whofe Name the beft *French* Clarets are called fo, and where you may befpeak a Dinner from Four or Five Shillings a Head, to a Guinea, or what Sum you pleafe. The other is *Kivat*'s, where there is a conftant Ordinary as abroad, for all Comers without Diftinction, and at a very reafonable Price.

I AM told, that while Policies were allow'd to be made on taking of Towns, and gaining of Battels, during the laft War, this *Exchange-Alley* was the fharpeft Place in the World ; but

I   the

114 *A Journey through* England.

the Abufe of Intelligence, Sham-Letters fpread upon the *Exchange*, and Private Letters coming before the Mails, made that Practice fo notorious, that the Queen and Parliament wifely thought fit to put a Stop to it; by a feafonable provifional Act againft it, as they have endeavoured to do by another Act againft exceffive Gaming, being both equally looked on as a Cheat, and Impofition upon the well-meaning Subject: However, fome great Men have not difdained to be deeply concerned in both, and have got good Eftates; for *Tricking* is not yet here reckon'd fo defpifeable a Quality as abroad, when it's cleanly done; therefore, my Friend, when you come here, play not in *England*, nor venture to lay Wagers, except you know your Company very well, or are fure of your Fact.

Lewis Theobald, 'No. 61: Coffee-House Humours Exposed (Tuesday, March 12)', *The Censor*, 3 vols (London, Jonas Brown, 1717), 8°. BL: 239.g.12. ESTC98529. Extract, II, pp. 210–16.

An essay on the coffee-houses of London, and the characteristics of their clientele in imitation of *The Spectator*. Theobald detects important differences between different kinds of coffee-houses and their clientele. He begins with the coffee-houses of the finer sort, where perfumed men of fashion gather in splendid gilt and mirrored interiors, before moving on to a more humble kind of coffee-house, where mechanic tradesmen and artisans are the more usual assembly. In both houses, he finds evidence of intellectual over-ambition and pretence: his satire turns on this concern for consistency of status and hierarchy.

Lewis Theobald (1688–1744) was a lawyer turned author who survived on his work as a librettist and occasional writer. Resident in Wyan's Court off Russell Street, he lived conveniently close to the literary coffee-houses of the day, and was a regular in Addison's circle at Button's Coffee-house. Theobald is best remembered today for his innovative work in Shakespeare editing and scholarship, especially *Shakespeare restored, or, A specimen of the many errors as well committed, as unamended, by Mr. Pope in his late edition of this poet* (London, R. Francklin, J. Woodman, D. Lyon and C. Davis, 1726). Theobald launched *The Censor* in 1715 as a column in *Mist's Journal* modelled on Addison and Steele's *Spectator*, running from 11 April to 17 June (Nos 1–30). It was then discontinued for eighteen months, before Theobald resumed the essay as an independent tri-weekly folio publication under its own title, running from 1 January to 30 May 1717 (Nos 31–96), costing two pence (a copy of No. 61 is in the Bodleian Library at Nich. newsp. 32A). Both sets were immediately collected and published in three volumes under the title *The Censor*, numbered continuously. It found some success, running to a second edition within the year. Nonetheless, in the 'Preface', Theobald lamented that his periodical had struggled to find its own place because it 'followed too close upon the Heels of the inimitable *Spectator*' (Preface, I, p. sig. A6r). The persona of the paper was named the 'British Censor' (one who exercises official or officious supervision over morals and conduct (*OED*)), a role that encompasses discussion of scholarship and literature, but also public morals and events – including some important essays on Shakespeare (see Peter Seary, *Lewis Theobald and the Editing of Shakespeare* (Oxford, Clarendon Press, 1990), pp. 32–40)

N° 6ɪ.   *Tuefday*, *March* ɪ2.

Occurfus hominum, cujus Prudentia *monftrat Summos* poſſe *viros*,———   Juven.

A S I am obliged, in order to ſee how the World runs, and gather Obſervations on the Humours of Man-kind, to make one at the Aſſemblies of the *beau Monde*; I conſtantly appear once a Day at the *Coffee-houſes* in Vogue, and where I expect to meet with moſt Matter for Speculation.   Were it not for theſe *Diurnal Circulations*, and the *Minutes* which I take from what occurrs there, I might find my ſelf ſometimes at a Loſs for Subjects to ſupply my Printer in Time; tho' there is eternal Room for Satire and Correction of thoſe Vices and Follies that, *Hydra*-like, ſprout up the faſter, and more numerous, for being lopp'd.

When I come into a *Coffee-houſe*, I labour to diſguiſe my Character from the Company by putting on an Air of Inad-vertence; and glean up the ſcatter'd

Papers

Nº 61.   *The* CENSOR.   211

Papers from every Table, as if I meant wholly to be taken up with the Contents of *Courants* and *Evening-Pofts*. Being feated, and like a profound Politician, with my Coffee half cold, feeming to nod o'er the refpective Interefts of *Europe*, I have the Advantage of perufing every fingle Figure that comes to the Houfe without any Views of Bufinefs or Information; of *fettling* their Heads with *fober Liquors*, or *difturbing* them with the Turns and Revolutions of Empires.

As I hunt chiefly after Objects of Entertainment, I avoid thofe Houfes where much Bufinefs is tranfacted in a *Smoke* and *Hurry*; and my Ears are affaulted either with *Reports* and *Demurrers*, or *Stock* and *Transferr*. To be free from this *Jargon*, I take care to refort to thofe Rooms, where the Society is compos'd of the *gay* and *fafhionable*; and where frequent Pannels of Glafs feem to multiply the *embroider'd Cuftomers*: tho' thefe Glafses, to ufe a Punn of *Shadwell*'s, make very *fevere Reflections*, when they return but the *Images* of *Shadows*.

To thefe Polite *Coffee-houfes* the Members flock merely to *fee*, and *be feen*; and they are Places of Rendezvous to the

brocaded

brocaded *Narciſſi*, from which they adjourn either to *Pawlet*'s, or the *Theatre*.
They are a ſort of *Drawing-rooms*, where
every diſtinguiſh'd Gueſt ſeems to keep
his *Levée*. Reciprocal Civilities are the
chief Things to be remark'd, Grimaces
of Satisfaction forc'd from the Conceit
of a Courtier's Wit, and Addreſſes of
Compliment inſtead of Applications of
Weight or Moment. The Flutter of
theſe fine Figures makes all common
Objects uſed with Diſreſpect, and ſerv'd
with Leiſure; and as the Smell of *Hercules*'s Club was reported, of old, to keep
the Dogs and Flies from the Chappel
where it was repoſited: So the Scent of
their Perfumes, and the Glare of their
Habits, deter an ordinary *Proteſtant*
from entering to drink a Mug of *Gill*,
and conſider the *Poſtman*.

There is another Rank of *Coffee-Houſes*, a little ſubordinate to theſe which
I have mention'd, where the Cuſtomers
are not of ſo *abſtracted* a Sett, but that
a *Man of Dreſs*, and a ruddy *Fox-hunter*
agree at one Table: At theſe Reſorts,
I have often ſat with Pleaſure to hear
the Nation ſettled, and the Wits arraign'd; and amuſe my ſelf with the
Variety of Converſation, which is ban-
dy'd

N° 61.   *The* C E N S O R.   213

dy'd by every diftinct Knot of Talkers.
I have heard a Country Squire over his
Pipe, at one Corner, fputtering about
the *Age* and *Strength* of his *October*; and
recommending the *Houfe-wifery* of his
Daughter *Penelope* At another, a Com-
pany of *Sparks* praifing the Beauty of a
Bar-keeper; and divided on the impor-
pant Queftion, whether She has not
One *intimate* Favourite. A Third Clan
would be canvaffing the *Sermons* and
Conduct of their *Parfon*; while the
Fourth has labour'd to explain the Ni-
cety of a Game at *Ombre*.

Thefe disjointed Topicks of Converfation, play'd off at one Time and in the
felf fame Place, put me in Mind of a
Simile, in *Horace's* Poeticks, of a *Sick
Man's Dreams*. If we were to fhut our
Eyes, and liften with the moft equal Attention we could to every thing faid;
the Confufion of the different Subjects
and Sentiments would prefent much the
fame huddle of *Idea's*, as proceed from
an ill Affection of the Brain, or irregular Fluctuation of the Humours.

I am as fully entertain'd fometimes
with defcending to Coffee-houfes of lefs
Note, and which are fituated in private Streets; where the Neighbouring
Mechanicks

Mechanicks meet to learn a little News, and, from their Politicks, to procure an Opinion of their Wisdom: It is pleasant to observe the Concern and Thought-fulness that dwell on each Face upon the *Arrival* of an *Express*, the coming in of the *Votes*, or the Publication of the *Session's-Paper*: There are generally some little Interests of a Wager depending, that give these News-mongers so much Sollicitude, or an Expectation of finding some agreeable Passage to divert their Wives with at their Return: But I must confess, at the same Time, it is provokingly ridiculous to hear a *Haber-dasher* descant on a *General's* Misconduct, and talk of an *Army's passing a River* with the same Facility as he himself could go over *Fleet-bridge:* The Zeal of Another, and his Opinion of his Suffi-ciency, tho' but a *Piece-broker* by Pro-fession, shall run over *Schemes* in *Parlia-ment* at Home, and the Measures con-certed in Foreign *Councils*. And a Third, sometimes more cautious of explaining himself, with Features scrued up to a grave kind of Sagacity, seats himself at your Elbow, and asks, *If there be any thing* particular *in the Papers*.

Among

N° 61.   *The* CENSOR.   215

Among the Provocations that are
daily found in thefe *Three-half-penny* Societies, none can be greater than your
Declaimers in Politicks.   Thefe are a
Set of Men that are precife in their Coffee-houfe Hours, where they by Cuftom
are intituled to a certain Seat, and are
the *Oracles* of the Cómpany.   I have
feen one of thefe, who, when he has
begun to open, has been furrounded by
a Convocation of *Lifteners*, who have admir'd, without underftanding him any
more than they would a Lecture of Mr.
Whifton's in *Aftronomy*, or *Hydroftaticks*.

It is frequent with thefe Gentlemen
to keep up their Harangue in a Stile and
Tract of Thought as abfurd, as unintelligible.   Their Method of explaining
Things is different from that with Men
of common Reafon; and the Subftance
of their Oration as foreign from the
Point as it is pompous, and affected. I
heard one of thefe Declaimers, upon
mention of the *Caimacan* of *Conftantinople's* Letter, begin a Differtation on the
Parity of the *Great Turk's* Preparations
with thofe of the *Perfian Xerxes*; and,
fomebody bolting out a Word by chance
of the Embarkment at *Gottemberg*, he
fell into the Queftion of how many
                                        Tran-

Transports *Julius Cæsar* made ufe of in his Invafion of *Britain*: And I doubt not, had I ftay'd long enough, I fhould have heard a *fuccinct* Account of what Veffels *Agamemnon* and his Confederates employ'd in the *Trojan* Expedition.

All that I have to fay of thefe Political *Oracles*, is, that if they are not to be filenc'd for the Benefit of the Houfes they ufe, their Declamations fhould at leaft be reftrain'd to a certain Duration: And, like the Orations of the *Grecian* Pleaders, be limited by the *Hour-Glafs*. Could this Reftriction once be fettled, I would allow them the Indulgence which thofe Gentlemen had; that if any One made an End of his Harangue before his *Glafs* was *run out*, he fhould have the Liberty to refign the *remaining* Part of his *Sand* to a fucceeding O-rator that fhould have Occafion for it.

EXPLANATORY NOTES

M. P., *A Character of Coffee and Coffee-Houses*

p. 5, l. 15: *Pantaloons*: men's loose breeches, a fashion introduced to London from France after the Restoration, and said to have been derived from the costume worn by the theatrical character of the same name, usually depicted as a foolish old man wearing Turkish slippers, loose red trousers and a skull-cap (*OED*).

p. 5, ll. 16–17: a la mode de France: French, 'in the French style'.

p. 6, ll. 1–2: The English-man ... both feet and face: misquoted from George Herbert, 'The Church-porch', iv, in *The Temple. Sacred poems and private ejaculations* (Cambridge, Thom. Buck and Roger Daniel, 1633), p. 1. Should be: 'O what were man, might he himself misplace! / Sure to be crosse he would shift feet and face'.

p. 6, ll. 3–4: *Hop, Malt, Cock, China, Rash-berry*: diverse ingredients used in drinks typically consumed in Britain: hops, the ripened cones of the female hop plant used to give a bitter flavour to beer; malt, barley prepared for brewing by steeping, germinating and kiln-drying; cock, the jelly and minced meat of a boiled cock infused in ale to make cock-ale; china, the fleshy rootstock of *Smilax China* (akin to sarsaparilla) used to flavour china-ale; and rash-berry or raspberry, the fruit of the common raspberry used to flavour ale or wine (*OED*).

p. 6, l. 11: *voraginous*: voracious, devouring (*OED*).

p. 6, ll. 15–16: Stygian *Lake*: pertaining to the River Styx, or more generally, to the infernal regions of classical mythology.

p. 6, l. 23: *Dryer*: in the humoural theory of physiology, a substance that removes moisture. For a full account of the effects of coffee expressed within the humoural account, see Walter Rumsey, *Organon Salutis*, Volume 4 of this edition, pp. 1–65.

p. 6, ll. 26–7: *highshoon*: one who wears high shoes, as rustics did, hence, a rustic boorish man (*OED*).

p. 6, l. 28: *Cruditie*s: an imperfect concoction (digestion) of the humours (*OED*).

p. 7, l. 7: Meagrim: headache, migraine (*OED*).

p. 7, ll. 12–13: *Academians of Bedlam*: literally, a member of the academy of the Hospital of St Mary of Bethlehem, outside Bishopsgate, London's main lunatic asylum.

p. 7, l. 16: *Neates-tongue*: ox tongue, as an article of food (*OED*).

p. 7, ll. 16–17: *a dish of Anchovaes, or a salt Bit*: a dish of anchovies or another kind of salty victuals.

p. 7, l. 22: Liber Pater: a Roman god of fertility, both human and agricultural.

p. 8, ll. 2–3: ad unum / Mollis opus: Horace, *Epodes*, XII.15: 'fit but for once'. Referring to the conventional view that men are able to perform coitus but once in each encounter.

p. 8, ll. 8–9: Hercules *in one night got fifty Women with Child*: sometimes included as one of the twelve tasks of Hercules.

p. 8, ll. 9–12: *a Prince of* Spain *was forc'd to make an Edict ... belike Men did exceed that proportion*: The anecdote is untraced, but was repeated in *The Women's Petition against Coffee*, see above, p. 114, ll. 7–9.

p. 8, l. 30: *Cataracts of* Nilus: the waterfalls on the river Nile, the first at Aswan.

p. 9, ll. 4–5: Hic fluvius Verborum, vix gutta Mentis: Latin, 'here's a flood of words with not a drop of sense'.

p. 9, ll. 9–10: Polewheel *runs division on the Base Viol*: A bass-viol is a stringed instrument played with a bow for playing the bass part in concerted music; to 'run division' is to execute a rapid melodic passage. Paul Polewheel (fl. 1650-60) was an English composer who achieved fame as a violinist during the Commonwealth.

p. 9, ll. 19–20: Who cannot rest ... dores his mind: George Herbert, 'The Church Porch', xxv, in *The Temple*, p. 6.

p. 10, ll. 4–5: *Mony!* Thou art the Man, and Man but Dross to thee: A rough translation of Juvenal, *Satires*, V.136–7: 'Money, you are the one he calls brother, the one he gives homage and honour' (*The Satires of Juvenal*, trans. by Rolfe Humphries (Indianapolis, Indiana University Press, 1958), p. 60).

p. 10, l. 17: *Suger-plum*: a sugar-plum, a small round sweetmeat or comfit, hence, something very pleasing and agreeable (*OED*).

p. 11, ll. 9–10: *as common, as Gold was once in* Ierusalem*, that is, as common, as Stones*: 2 Chronicles 1:15: 'And the king made silver and gold at Jerusalem as plenteous as stones' (KJV).

p. 12, ll. 6–7: *The Principles of a Popular Government at the* Rota: James Harrington (1611–77), English political philosopher, author of *Oceana* (1656), a utopian fiction on aristocratic republican principles utilising a rotating system of government known as the rota. In 1659–60, Harrington established a debating club to disseminate his ideas, popularly known as the

Rota, at Miles's Coffee-house in New Palace Yard, Westminster. See. Ellis, *Coffee-House*, pp. 42–55.

p. 13, ll. 4–5: *discoursing like a Parrat in the words of* Aristotle: referring to an uncomprehending and mechanical repetition of speech, like a parrot: an observation here attributed to Aristotle (384–22 BC), erroneously supposed to be the first author who mentions parrots.

p. 13, ll. 8–9: jurare in verba Magistri: Latin, follow implicitly. The phrase is well known from Horace, *Epistles*, I.14: 'Nullius addictus jurare inverba magistri', 'bound to swear as any master dictates' (trans. by H. Ruston Fairclough (Cambridge, MA, Harvard University Press, 2005), p. 252.

p. 13, l. 10: *Moderators*: arbitrators (*OED*).

p. 13, l. 21: Spartan: an inhabitant of Sparta, a Lacedaemonian, characteristically distinguished by simplicity, frugality and courage.

p. 13, l. 23: *Helot*: one of a class of serfs in ancient Sparta, intermediate in status between the ordinary slaves and the free Spartan citizens. Plutarch, *Lycurgus*, xxviii, states that on occasion the Helots were compelled to appear in a state on intoxication in order to excite a repugnance to drunken behaviour amongst Spartan youth.

p. 13, ll. 27–31: Utrum corpus est immateriale ... Utrum bestia honoranda sit: A series of scholastic coffee-house queries for disputation, all essentially quibbles: 'Whether the self is immaterial / Whether a million angels may sit on the point of a needle / Whether Rome or Christianity was founded first / Whether an animal should be accorded honour'. The second one quoted from William Chillingworth, *The Religion of Protestants a Safe Way to Salvation* (London, Leonard Lichfield for John Clark, 1638), 'Preface', p. [x]: 'Whether a Million of Angels may not sit upon a needle's point?'.

p. 14, l. 2: Orpheus *his Beasts did to his Charming Musick*: in Greek mythology, Orpheus was the son of King Oaegrus and the muse Calliope. Taught to play the lyre by Apollo, Orpheus played so beautifully that animals and trees were charmed by his minstrelsy.

p. 14, ll. 4–5: nam quae comoedia? Mimus Quis melior?: Juvenal, *Satires*, V.156–7. Juvenal recounts that Virro has entertained Trebius with a horrible meal, in order to mock him. In this quote Juvenal comments he prefers the spectacle of Trebius's discomfiture to the regular entertainments of dinner parties. 'What comedy ever, what mime, is so amusing' (*Satires*, ed. by Susanna Braund (Cambridge, Cambridge University Press, 1996), p. 73.

p. 14, l. 16: majore cachinno: Latin, 'excessive laughter'.

p. 14, l. 19: Aspice quid faciunt commercia: Juvenal, *Satires*, II.166: 'Just see what evil communications do!'.

p. 14, ll. 22–3: Virtuosi *and* Ingenuosi: a virtuoso was a learned person, a scholar or scientist; an ingenuoso a man with the education or culture befitting an honourable station. Both kinds of men were associated with the foundation of the Royal Society in 1660.

p. 14, l. 30: Verbum sat: Latin, 'a word is enough'.

Woolnoth, *The Coffee Scuffle*

p. 19, l. 7: Polipheme: Polyphemus, a Cyclops with one eye in the centre of his forehead, the son of Poseidon and Thoosa.

p. 19, l. 8: Don Quixot: the hero of the novel of the same name by Miguel de Cervantes (published 1605 and 1615).

p. 19, l. 10: *Noggin*: a small drinking vessel or mug.

p. 19, l. 22: *Hobedehoi*: hobbledehoy, a youth at the age between boyhood and manhood, a stripling (*OED*).

p.20, l. 4: *Prissians pate*: unclear, but 'Prissians head' is mentioned in Roger Boyle, *Mr Anthony: a comedy* (London, James Knapton, 1690), pp. 4–5.

p. 20, l. 7: Ovid's *great Nose*: Publius Ovidius Naso (43 BC–AD 17), Roman poet, author of the *Metamorphoses*, whose last name implied his family were known for large noses.

p. 20, l. 18: Euclid, Discartis: Euclid of Alexandria (325–265 BC), mathematician; Rene Descartes (1596–1650), French philosopher.

p. 20, l. 28: Mercuries: a person who brings news, hence newspapers.

p. 21, l. 12: Beza *and* Knox: Theodore Beza (1519–1605), a leading Protestant reformer in Geneva after Calvin's death; John Knox (1505–72), the founder of Presbyterianism in Scotland.

p. 21, l. 14: Blundel *and* Grotius, Arminius *and* Vossius: Calvinist philosophers: David Blondel (1591–1655), Calvinist historian, author of a dissertation on Pope Joan (published 1647) arguing the story is a myth; Hugo Grotius (1583–1645), natural law theorist and jurist of the Dutch Republic; Jacobus Arminius (1560–1609), Dutch theologian; Gerhard Johann Vossius (1577–1649), German scholar and Calvinist theologian.

p. 21, l. 17: Lockier, *sweet* Powel *and* Knocker: Nicholas Lockyer (1611–85), puritan divine; Vavasour Powell (1617–70), Welsh Baptist preacher; Knocker untraced.

p. 21, l. 18: Jesse *and honey mouth'd* Brook: Henry Jessey (1603–63), a Cambridge-educated Baptist from Yorkshire who led the Independent Baptist congregation in London; Humphrey Brooke (1618–93), physician and Leveller.

p. 21, l. 22: Taylor … Naylor: Thomas Taylor (1617–82), Quaker minister and writer; James Nayler (1618–60), Quaker preacher and writer.

p. 21, l. 24: Kiffin … Giffin: William Kiffin (1616–1701), a prosperous merchant who became a leader of the London Particular Baptists; Giffin not identified, perhaps Lewis Griffin (fl. 1661), Baptist preacher and controversialist.

p. 21, l. 20: Paul Hobs: perhaps Paul Hobson (d. 1666), Baptist who questioned the validity of infant baptism.

p. 22, l. 2: Teazar ... Keyser: not identified, perhaps Kaiser, meaning emperor.

p. 22, l. 3: Gildas: Gildas Bardonicus (fl. 5th–6th century) a British monk and historian.

p. 22, l. 7: Jack Straw *or* Wat Tyler: leaders of the Peasants' Revolt of 1381.

p. 22, l. 8: *Fifth-monarchy*: The Fifth Monarchists were a religious political movement prominent 1649–61 who saw the execution of Charles I as a precursor of the imminent coming of Christ's Kingdom on Earth. The Fifth Monarchists under Thomas Venner launched an uprising in January 1661.

p. 22, l. 9: Harringtons Rota *or* Boyls Vertuosa: notable coffee-house clubs of the late 1650s. For Harrington's see above, note to p. 12, ll. 6–7. Richard Boyle's club of virtuosi or scientists met at Tillyard's Coffee-house in Oxford in the late 1650s, and in 1662 formed the nucleus of the Royal Society.

p. 22, l. 12: *Wisson*: Whit Sunday, the seventh Sunday after Easter, observed as a festival in commemoration of the descent of the Holy Spirit on the day of Pentecost.

p. 22, l. 14: *Chimneys*: The Chimney or Hearth Tax, a parliamentary levy imposed by statute in 1661 (13 and 14 Car. II., c. 10) giving the king an hereditary revenue of two shillings annually upon every hearth in all houses paying church or poor rate.

p. 22, l. 17: *the Wind*: Pepys reports that in the coffee-house on 25 February 1662 'the great talk was of the effects of this late great wind' (*Diary*, vol. III, p. 35).

p. 22, l. 24: Robin *and* Jug: untraced

p. 23, l. 3: *Convocation*: the parliament of clergy in the Church of England, comprised of the synods of Canterbury and York.

p. 23, ll. 9–10: Corbet *and* Okey *And* Barkstead: Major General John Barkstead, Colonel John Okey and Miles Corbet, a lawyer. Regicide judges at the trial of Charles I in 1649 were excepted from the amnesty declared on Charles II's restoration. These three regicides were arrested in Delft and transported to London via Dover in March 1662, where they were tried and executed in April 1662.

p. 23, l. 17: *Sr.* Kenelms *powder*: Sir Kenelm Digby (1603–55), writer, diplomatist and scientist, promoted a 'powder of sympathy' which cured without coming in contact with the wound.

p. 23, l. 19: Ixion: In Greek mythology, Ixion was a mortal punished by Zeus for ingratitude by being bound to a winged wheel revolving in all directions.

p. 19, l. 15: *The Stocks*: a meat and fish market in London on the site where the city's stocks once stood, north of the church of St Mary Woolchurch and south of the junction of Cornhill, Threadneedle St and the Poultry. Removed in 1739 to make way for the Mansion House.

p. 25, l. 8: Gnomon: a rod which serves to mark the time of day by casting a shadow.

p. 26, l. 7: *muckle*: very (not in *OED*).

p. 27, l. 19: Memphian *god*: a figurine from the ancient Egyptian city of Memphis.

p. 27, l. 23: Crockedile, Pardus *and* Iaccall: African wild animals, specifically crocodile, leopard and jackal.

p. 28, l. 2: Socinian: a Protestant theology founded by Laelius Socinus (d. 1562 in Zurich) which denied the divinity of Christ and developed a rational account of sin and salvation.

p. 28, l. 19: Tully ... Demosthenes: Marcus Tullius Cicero (106–43 BC), Roman philosopher, statesman and orator, commonly known as Tully; Demosthenes (340–22 BC), Greek orator.

p. 29, ll. 19–20: *Captain* Mead ... *St.* Alhallows *Church*: All Hallows Church is the name of one of several in the City of London, the closest to the Stocks Market being in Lombard Street. Captain Mead may be Matthew Meade (1628–99), clergyman and ejected minister.

p. 29, l. 28: Heinsius *and* Schurman: Nikolaes Heinsius (1620–81), Dutch scholar of Latin literature; Anna Maria van Schurman (1607–78), Dutch poet and scholar.

p. 29, l. 29: Spanhemius, Barleus, Vanhelmont, Walleus: Dutch scholars: Fridericus Spanhemius, professor at Leiden who wrote a history of iconoclasm; Caspar Barlaeus (1584–1648), Latinist, scientist and founder of the Athenaeum Illustre at Amsterdam; Johann Baptista van Helmont (1579–1644), medical scholar and pioneer of chemistry and gases; Antonius Walleus, Calvinist biblical scholar at Leiden.

p. 31, l. 24: *Arminian*: a Protestant theology founded by the Dutch scholar Jacobus Arminius, which revised Calvinist doctrines of predestination.

p. 31, l. 27: *Runegado*: a person who has deserted his religion, an apostate (*OED*).

p. 33, l. 17: Cato: Marcus Porcius Cato (234–149 BC) was a Roman statesman and orator.

p. 33, l. 25: *Butterbox*: contemptuous designation of a Dutchman (*OED*).

The Tryall of the Coffee-Man

p. 37, l. 4: *Coffee-Man*: a man keeping a coffee-house (*OED*): this instance predates the first usage of 1673 noted in the *OED*.

p. 37, ll. 5–6: *Indicted, Arraigned, Convicted, and Condemned*: the narrative of criminal proceeding: to indict or bring a charge against a person for a crime; to arraign or call a person to answer for himself by interrogation or examination; to convict or prove a person guilty of an offence; and to condemn or give judicial sentence against someone, including execution.

p. 37, l. 7: Bacchus: the god of wine and drinking in Roman mythology, here imagined as the judge of the case.

p. 37, ll. 19–20: *Vintners, Brewers, Victuallers, Cooks, Ale-wives, Tapsters*: the traditional trades associated with drinking in England: vintners (merchants or innkeepers who deal in wines), brewers (those who brew malt liquors, especially beer), victuallers and cooks (keepers of eating houses, inns or taverns which sell food and drink), alewives (women who sell beer in alehouses) and tapsters (keepers of taverns that sell beer).

p. 37, l. 20: true Companions to the Pot, Pipe, and Can: drinkers of traditional English beverages, as defined by their characteristic drinking vessels.

p. 37, l. 21: *the* Arabian Kalender, *1662/3*: the Islamic calendar used to date events in Muslim countries, dated from the Hijra, Muhammad's emigration from Mecca to Medina. This is a joke referring to coffee's Arabic origins: in the Islamic calendar, 1662/3 would be rendered as 1072.

p. 39, l. 6: *my Trade being in it's prime near* Change-*time*: The Royal Exchange, the principle place of business for merchants trading in London, kept regular hours. In 1670 it met between 11 am and 12 noon and 5 and 6 pm: during these hours the Exchange was full of merchants 'Merchandizing, Shipping, Buying or Selling, and the like'. Coffee-houses in the vicinity were also busy at these times.

p. 39, l. 9: *Hell-broth*: coffee.

p. 39, l. 10: *good* Canary *lies by the* Lee: Canary wine, a light sweet wine from the Canary Islands which, through lack of business, is languishing in the barrels, where it throws a sediment or lees.

p. 39, l. 13: *Sack*: white wine from Spain or the Canaries.

p. 39, ll. 14–15: *a little fair Water replenish your loss*: the vintner suggests that when he vends his wine, each sale depletes his stock, but when the coffee-man sells coffee, he merely adds more water to the pot of coffee brewing on his stove. The accusation that coffee-men water or adulterate their beverage suggests both their fraudulent status and a level of ignorance about coffee production.

p. 39, ll. 16–17: *the crafty Whore of* Canterbury *was to the Lawyer's Clark*: Mary Carleton (née Moders), also known as the German Princess, a notorious impostor who pretended to be a noble German lady, and who in April 1763 married a lawyer's clerk called John Carleton, who himself pretended to be a wealthy gentleman. Her sensational trial for bigamy was celebrated in scandalous pamphlets such as *The Lawyers Clarke Trappan'd by the Crafty Whore of Canterbury* (London, John Johnson, 1663).

p. 39, l. 19: *cozen the Excize-man*: to cozen or cheat the officers of the Excise, employed to collect excise duties on beer and wine.

p. 39, l. 21: *to gage our Coppers*: the officers of the Excise determined the level of excise duty to be paid on each barrel of wine or beer by measuring the capacity of the vessels in which they were brewed or stored. A copper is a brewing pan made of that metal used in the making of beer, in which the wort and malt are boiled.

p. 39, l. 22: *througo*: through.

p. 39, l. 26: Tom Collins *Law*: Thomas Collins (fl. 1610–15) author of *The Penitent Publican* (London, Arthur Johnson, 1610).

p. 39, ll. 27–8: *there's more ways to the Wood than one*: proverbial expression: there is more than one solution to a problem. See John Ray, *A Compleat Collection of English Proverbs* (London, J. Torbuck, O. Payne and T. Woodman, 1737), p. 3967.

p. 39, l. 30–p. 40, l. 1: *nick ... froth lustily*: the wares of the vintner, brewer and victualler, such as wine and beer, froth up when served, allowing them to sell short measures.

p. 40, l. 16: *the* Brewers *Stoak-hole*: the stoke-hole (see above p. 44, l. 14): the space in front of a furnace where the stokers stand to tend the fires or the aperture through which the fire is fed and tended (*OED*): here used as a place of confinement.

p. 40, l. 17: *The Court*: a fictional court whose procedures parody those of criminal courts of the period. As women were not eligible for selection as jurors, the composition of the jury also wears a satirical aspect.

p. 40, l. 23: Don Ballingo Blackburn: the coffee-man's exotic name mixes a Spanish element (perhaps recalling the vogue for Spanish comedy in London in the Restoration) and a description of coffee. The character of Mr Black-Burnt the coffee-man is further used in *The maidens complain[t] against coffee* (see headnote, pp. 45–6).

p. 40, l. 26: *The Copy of the Indictment*: a parody of the legal diction of indictments.

p. 41, l. 2: Sconces: unclear, probably 'sconce', a term in fortification for a small fort or earthwork built to defend a ford, pass or castle gate (*OED*). In this usage, 'To enter their Sconces by way of Battery' suggests a siege using battery or siege guns, here carrying a venereal connotation.

p. 41, l. 4: *Felony*: a class of crimes considered of a graver character than misdemeanours (*OED*).

p. 42, l. 2: *as lank as a Dish-clout*: a clout or cloth used for washing dishes (*OED*); lank or shrunken, flabby. Dorothy claims Dick has been rendered impotent by drinking coffee.

p. 42, ll. 26–7: *smoaking their Noses like* Indians, *till their Inwards are like to a* Westphalia *Ham*: smoking tobacco, conventionally represented as an Amerindian habit, until their inwards or innards are smoked like the renowned hams of Westphalia, a part of the Duchy of Saxony in Germany.

These hams were smoked with juniper berries and beech wood, and, like prosciutto, were sliced thinly and eaten without further cooking.

p. 43, l. 5: *Islington, Holloway, Lambeth*: country villages on the outskirts of the city of London, to which the common people of the city would venture in the evening for recreation at inns and pleasure gardens. The maids complain they have been abandoned because the coffee-houses, to which the young men and bachelors have started to go, admit men only.

p. 43, l. 19: *Mistriss* Troublesome *our Fore-woman*: the principal juror who presides at the deliberations of the jury and communicates their verdict (*OED*). The character of Troublesome is further used in *The maidens complain[t] against coffee*, above, pp. 45–54.

p. 44, ll. 15–16: Brewers *Copper*: the vessel made of copper in which the wort and malt is boiled during the brewing process of beer.

p. 44, l. 20: *Bulls Engines*: the bull's-pizzle, the penis of the bull, formerly used as an instrument of flagellation.

p. 44, l. 20: Billingsgate: one of the gates of the City of London, near which was located the principal fish market, noted for the vulgar language of the market women.

p. 44, l. 22: *Ram-stones*: sheep's testicles.

Merc. Democ. [John Crouch], *The maidens complain[t] against coffee*

p. 47, l. 7: *Untyled*: untile, to strip a roof of tiles, here metaphorical, allowing the inside to be observed (*OED*).

p. 47, l. 9: *the Coffee-man*: a man who keeps a coffee-house (earlier than the first usage recorded in the *OED* in 1673).

p. 47, l. 9: *the Usurers man:* a workman or employee (man) of the usurer.

p. 47, l. 10: *Userer*: a money lender, one who lends money at interest, especially at an excessive rate (*OED*).

p. 47, l. 10: *Mountibank*: an itinerant charlatan who sold supposed medicines and remedies, frequently using various entertainments to attract a crowd of potential customers. Later an itinerant entertainer (*OED*).

p. 47, l. 11: *Apothecarier*: an apothecary was one who prepared and sold drugs for medicinal purposes. (*OED*)

p. 47, l. 16: Omnium gatherum: a gathering or collection of all sorts of people (*OED*). An allusion here to John Taylor, see note to p. 47, ll. 16–17, below.

p. 47, ll. 16–17: *the devout* Ironmonger *quotes it, in his Annotations upon* Toby *and his Dog*: a reference to a ferocious and obscene pamphlet war of 1642 between John Taylor the Water Poet (1580–1653) and Henry Walker (fl. 1638–60), an ironmonger turned parliamentarian, writer and Nonconformist preacher. Taylor's burlesque sermon entitled *A season-*

able lecture, or, A most learned oration disburthened from Henry Walker, a most judicious [...] iron monger (London, F. Cowles, T. Bates and T. Banks, 1642), was popularly known as 'Toby's Dog', and was addressed to 'Men and Women, Male or Female, Old and Young, Boyes and Girles, Lads and Lasses, Babes and Children, *Omnium gatherum*' (p. 1). Walker, who escaped punishment after the Restoration, was a recurrent topic of Crouch's ire.

p. 47, l. 18: *Merc. Democ.*: Mercurius Democritus, journalistic persona of John Crouch (*c.* 1615–*c.* 1680), writer and bookseller. See headnote, pp. 45–6. Democritus was a pre-Socratic Greek philosopher (460–370 BC) who wrote influentially on astronomy and mathematics. He was known as the laughing philosopher, in contrast to Heraclitus, the weeping philosopher.

p. 47, l. 18: at his Chamber in the World in the Moon: In 1638, the natural philosopher John Wilkins published an astronomical tract *The Discovery of New World, or, A discourse tending to prove, that ('tis probable) there may be another habitable world in the moon* (London, Micharl Sparke and Edward Forrest), which proposed that the earth was not uniquely different from other heavenly bodies. The notion of the world in the moon was seized upon by satirists as emblematic of the ridiculous excesses of Kepplerian astronomy in particular, and the New Science in general.

p. 47, l. 19: the mad-merry-conceited people under the Sun: 'mad-merry' meant wildly enthusiastic, 'conceited' meant clever, witty, amusing (*OED*). The phrase was repeatedly used on title-pages by Crouch.

p. 49, l. 19: *as safe as a thief in a mill*: a folk-saying current in the seventeenth century: a mill was a safe place for a thief, because all millers were considered to be thieves (of a portion of each consignment of grain sent to them).

p. 50, l. 1: *Ordinary*: an inn, public house, or (here) coffee-house where meals are provided at a fixed price. (*OED*)

p. 50, ll. 27–8: Consumption, Dropsie, Ptisick: consumption: a wasting disease, now applied specifically to pulmonary consumption; dropsy: a morbid condition characterised by the accumulation of watery fluid in the serous tissues or the connective tissue of the body; phthisic: a wasting disease of the lungs, pulmonary consumption. (*OED*)

p. 50, ll. 34–6: *fill the body with diseases ... corodes upon every part of the body*': satirical description of the physiological properties of coffee as described in the humoural system.

p. 51, l. 6: *Enter* Dorothy *and* Jane': women are generally regarded to have been excluded from the coffee-house: these working women (maids to the userer and broker) seem to have no scruples about entering the coffee-room.

p. 51, l. 10: *dry as a kix*: kex, the dry stem of various herbaceous plants, such as cow parsnip or wild chervil. Figuratively, a dried-up sapless person. (*OED*)

p. 51, l. 23: *making a chimney of his noddle*: smoking.

p. 51, l. 24: *fogh, fogh, fogh*: faugh, an exclamation of abhorrence or disgust (*OED*).

p. 51, l. 24: *a Jaques*: a jakes, a privy or latrine (*OED*).

p. 51, l. 33: *dry horson*: whoreson, a son of a whore, commonly used as a coarse term of reprobation, disgust or contempt (*OED*).

p. 51, ll. 34–5: *wrap my Maiden-head in my smock, and fling it into the Ocean to be bugger'd to death by young Lobsters*: a finely expressed but obscure saying, referring to something that is unlikely to happen.

p. 52, l. 20: Royal Exchange: The Royal Exchange or bourse, built by Sir Thomas Gresham 1566–8, and destroyed by the fire on 3 September 1666, on the corner between Cornhill and Threadneedle Street.

p. 52, l. 23: Lothbury: street occupied by merchants and bankers, north of the Royal Exchange, leading between Guildhall and Throgmorton Street.

p. 52, ll. 25–6: *Kattles, Skimers and Ladles*: utensils used in coffee preparation: kettles (a broad open pot for boiling), skimmers and ladles.

p. 52, l. 29: Moor-fields: an open space with tree-lined walks north of the City beyond Moorgate.

p. 52, l. 29: *Usurers Walk*: the habitual meeting place of usurers or moneylenders and their customers, in Moor-fields.

p. 52, l. 37: *the Great Turk*: the Ottoman sultan, resident in the capital of the Ottoman Empire, Constantinople (now Istanbul).

p. 53, ll. 1–2: *Kitching-stuff Tub*: a receptacle for kitchen waste (kitchin-stuff) (*OED*).

p. 53, l. 3: Bracket: bragget, a drink made of honey, ale and spice fermented together. Hannah Woolley, *The Accomplish'd Lady's Delight in Preserving, Physick, Beautifying and Cookery* (London, B. Harris, 1675), p. 122.

p. 53, l. 4, *a Maidens Pl—*: a placket, the opening or slit at the top of a petticoat, hence an obscene term for female genitalia.

p. 53, l. 9: *Landaberis*: Landabrides or Lindabrides, the name of a lady in *The Mirror of Knighthood*, a romance: hence, used allusively, a lady-love or kept mistress. Diego Ortúñez de Calahorra, *The Second Part of the First Booke of the Myrrour of Knighthood*, trans. by R. P. (London, Thomas Este, 1599).

p. 53, l. 10: Petty-France: street in Westminster so called because French wool merchants lived there (*LE*).

p. 53, l. 16: *fair* Hellen *of* Greece: in Greek mythology Helen of Troy was the notoriously beautiful daughter of Zeus and Leda, whose abduction by Paris caused the Trojan War.

p. 53, l. 18: Nunquam satis: Latin, 'never enough'.

p. 53, l. 20: Stygian Lake: pertaining to the River Styx, or more generally, to the infernal regions of classical mythology.

p. 53, l. 24: *Maycrel in* May: Mackerel, a fast-swimming pelagic fish, traditionally caught in vast shoals in May.

p. 53, l. 25: *the* Labour in Vain: a traditional name for a public house. One of this name was in Shadwell.

p. 53, ll. 28–9: Donpancratone, *the Spanish Postelion, and Monsieur* La Flamsted *the Plank-Weaver of* Tenebrosa: a postillion: one who rides a post-horse, a messenger. Tenbrose: dark, figuratively mentally or morally dark, obscure in meaning (*OED*). The particular individuals addressed here are untraced.

p. 54, l. 13: Gravel: urinary crystals recognizable by the naked eye, and the disease of which they are characteristic (*OED*).

p. 54, l. 25: *Nilus*: the River Nile.

A Cup of Coffee: or, Coffee in its Colours

p. 57, l. 4: *Colours*: the qualities or attributes of which objects present different appearances, hence, figuratively, outward appearance, show, aspect (*OED*).

p. 57, col. 1, l. 8: *Wax-Candle-Circles*: close associates (those close enough to someone to be seen within the light cast by a wax candle).

p. 57, col 1., l. 10: *scalding* Phlegeton: Phlegethon, one of the five rivers of Hades, which flows with fire and does not consume.

p. 57, col. 1, l. 13: Catiline's *Conspirators*: In 63 BC, having been elected consul, Marcus Tullius Cicero (106–43 BC) uncovered a treasonous plot, led by Catiline and five co-conspirators: the latter were immediately executed without formal trial.

p. 57, col. 1, l. 23: Ben Johnson: Benjamin Jonson (1572–1637), poet and playwright, the foremost living author after the death of Shakespeare. In 1616 Jonson was at the centre of a club of poets and writers that met at the Devil Tavern in Temple Bar.

p. 57, col. 1, l. 24: Beaumont *and* Fletcher: Francis Beaumont (1584/5–1616) and John Fletcher (1579–1625), playwrights who collaborated in over fifty plays in the decade after 1606.

p. 57, col. 1, l. 26: Castalian *Drop, nor Dew of* Helicon: the Castalian spring was located within the temple of the Oracle at Delphi, and was used to wash and purify male supplicants. Helicon was the name of a mountain in Boeotia, dedicated to the Muses, in which rose the springs of Agnippe and Hippocrene. Both springs were referred to allusively in reference to poetic inspiration.

p. 57, col. 1, l. 27: Sulphur, Liquid Fire: sulphur or brimstone is a crystalline substance found in volcanic regions; liquid fire refers to flows of volcanic molten rock (the term lava did not gain currency until the late eighteenth century).

p. 57, col. 1, l. 28: Cocytus: one of the five rivers of Hades, meaning 'river of lamentation'.

p. 57, col. 1, l. 28: Stygian Mire: mud from the River Styx, the 'river of hate' that separates the world of the living from that of the dead.

p. 57, col. 1, l. 33: Sirreverence: human excrement; an abbreviation of 'save reverence', an apologetic phrase introducing a criticism, contradiction, or some remark that might offend the hearer (*OED*).

p. 57, col. 1, l. 34: *Nuncle* Iohns *Kettle-house*: untraced.

p. 57, col. 1, l. 35: *Tripoly*: Tripoli, a city and port in North Africa, now the capital of Libya.

p. 57, col. 1, l. 37: Diurnal: a periodical published every day, a newspaper.

p. 57, col. 1, l. 44: Admirabilia: qualities to be admired, to be wondered at, or approved of.

p. 57, col. 1, l. 45: *gross Turky-shore*: gross denotes vices, errors, faults. The shore or common shore was the no man's land by the waterside, where filth was deposited. The Turkey shore was a cant term for the southern bank of the Thames, from Lambeth to Rotherhithe; see B. E., *Dictionary of the Canting Crew* (London, W. Hawes, P. Gilbourne and W. Davis, 1699).

p. 57, col. 2, l. 2: *Assafoetida*: a resinous gum with a strong onion-like odour, used in medicinal preparations and as a spice in food, prepared from *Narthex asafoetida*, a kind of giant fennel found in Central Asia. Sometimes called Devil's dung.

p. 57, col. 2, l. 9: Guaicum's ... Turpentine: medicinal preparations: guaiacum, the wood of or gum obtained from the lignum vitae tree (*Zygophyllaceae*), used in decoctions to treat a wide variety of diseases, but especially syphilis; turpentine, a term applied to various oleoresins which exude from coniferous trees, used in a number of medical preparations.

p. 57, col. 2, l. 12: Treacle-water: a cordial prepared with Venice treacle, an electuary composed of many ingredients and supposed to possess universal counter-poison and preservative properties (*OED*).

p. 57, col. 2, l. 14: Maiden Camphora: a vegetable oil having a strong and bitter aromatic taste, prepared by distillation and sublimation from common camphor (*Laurus Camphora*), reputed to be an antaphrodisiac (*OED*).

p. 57, col. 2, l. 15: Pharmacopeia: pharmacopoeia, a book containing a list of drugs, with directions for their preparation.

p. 57, col. 2, l. 21: *Grand-Signior*: the sultan of the Ottoman Empire.

p. 57, col. 2, l. 32: Morbum Gallicum: morbus gallicus, syphilis (*OED*).

p. 57, col. 2, l. 34: *Pocky*: marked with pocks or pustules, specifically infected with the pox (usually syphilis) (*OED*).

p. 57, col. 2, l. 35: Venus ... Bacchus: in Roman mythology, respectively the goddess of love and beauty, and the god of wine and intoxication.

p. 57, col. 2, l. 36: *dead drunk ... catching Fox*: proverbial: dead drunk, so drunk as to be insensible or unable to move; to catch the fox, to get drunk (*OED*).

p. 57, col. 2, l. 42: *Maggot-Meagroms*: a maggot, a whimsical or perverse notion or idea; meagrim, a migraine, but also a whim, fancy or fad.

p. 57, col. 2, l. 47: *Rimples*: wrinkles (*OED*).

p. 57, col. 2, l. 48: *Simples*: medical substances composed of one ingredient or element, uncompounded and unmixed (*OED*).

p. 57, col. 2, l. 51: the great *Mogul*: the great Mughal, the name given by the Portuguese, and subsequently by Europeans generally, to each of the successive heads of the Muslim dynasty ruling a large part of the Indian subcontinent from the sixteenth century.

p. 57, col. 3, l. 5: *Stew'd Prewen-mongers*: stewed prune merchants.

p. 57, col. 3, ll. 7–8: China-Ale ... Metheglin: diverse drinks: china ale, ale flavoured with China root (*Smilax China*, akin to sarsaparilla); stupone, untraced, but possibly a strong alcoholic liquor that brings on a stupor; virgin-wine, wine made from grape juice produced without pressing; mum, wheat beer flavoured with spices, Brunswick Mum (Braunschweiger Mumme) is a kind of beer from Germany, a dark lager beer with an opaque black colour, traditionally brewed in Braunschweig in Saxony; metheglin, a spiced mead popular in Wales (*OED*).

p. 57, col. 3, l. 13: *Perukes*: wigs, introduced to London by Charles II after the Restoration.

p. 57, col. 3, l. 19: *Piss and Cack*: urine and excrement.

p. 57, col. 3, ll. 20–1: Scythian Sack ... Fogofarto: nonsense drinks: Scythian Sack, white wine from Scythia, a region in the classical world to the north and north-east of the Black Sea, now Russia; Tantavelin, variant spelling of tantadlin, a lump of excrement, a turd; fogofarto, a combination of fogo (a disagreeable smell, stench) and fart (crepitus, breaking wind).

p. 57, col. 3, l. 30: *Hogo*: anglicized spelling of the French *haut goût*, high flavour, meaning a 'high', piquant or putrescent flavour (*OED*).

p. 57, col. 3, l. 37: *Novists*: a person given to novel opinions or habits, an innovator (*OED*).

p. 57, col. 3, l. 46: a *Leaguer*: a military force engaged in a siege (*OED*).

p. 57, col. 3, l. 51: *Turdy*: full of, befouled or defiled with ordure (*OED*).

The Character of a Coffee-House

p. 63, l. 10: *Signs*: shop sign-boards hanging over the road, typically with pictorial representations, many of which identified the kind of trade.

p. 63, l. 13: Culpepper: Nicolas Culpeper (1616–54), English herbalist and astrologer, in 1653 author of *Culpeper's Herbal*, a well-known book on herbs and their uses.

p. 64, l. 3: Morat: Murad or Amurath was the name of five sultans of the Ottoman Empire. It is not clear which one is being referred to here, although Murad

IV (reigned 1623–40) seems the most likely. The Great Coffee-house in Exchange Alley advertised coffee in the *Kingdom's Intelligencer*, 53, Monday 22 December 1662 'under the House Seal, *viz. Morat the Great*', inviting customers to visit 'the new Coffee house in *Exchange Alley*', at 'the Signe of the Great Turk' (p. 847).

p. 64, l. 4: *Shash*: a sash or band of fine material worn twisted around the head as a turban, from the Arabic.

p. 64, l. 6: *picture of a* Sultaness: a shop sign decorated with a portrait bust of a sultaness. In *Mercurius Politicus, comprising the sum of Forein Intelligence … for Information of the People*, 435, Thursday 23 September 1658, Thomas Garway (or Garraway) advertised 'That Excellent, and by all Physitians approved, *China* Drink, called by the *Chineans, Teha*, by other nations *Tay alias Tea*, is sold at the *Sultaness-head*, a *Cophee-house*, in *Sweeting's* Rents by the Royal Exchange, *London*' (p. 887).

p. 64, l. 9: Constantine *the* Grecian: A coffee-man named Constantine George is recorded trading in the 'Accompt of Coffee Houses in the severall Wards in May 1663', collated by the city magistrates (City of London Records Office: Alchin Coll. Box H/103.(12)). The same man advertised in *The Intelligencer, published for Satisfaction and Information of the People*, 8, 23 January 1664/5: 'One *Constantine* a *Grœcian*, living in *Thredneedle-street*, over against *St Christophers church London*, being licensed to sell and retail Coffee, Chocolate, Cherbet, and Tea, desires it to be notified, that the right *Turky* Coffee Berry or Chocolate may be had as cheap and as good from him the said *Constantine* at the place aforesaid, as is anywhere to be had for money: And that people may be there taught to prepare the Liquor *gratis*' (p. 51).

p. 64, l. 11: *the great* Bashaw: alternative transliteration of the Turkish title pasha, superior to that of 'bey', signifying a high official or military officer. The term 'great Bashaw' usually referred to the sultan in English sources.

p. 64, ll. 13–14: *a* Coffee-cup … Turkish pot: a popular shop sign was a hand holding an ibrik (a Turkish coffee pot), pouring coffee into a cup. Coffee-house tokens also reproduced these images; see George Williamson and William Boyne, *Trade Tokens Issued in the Seventeenth Century in England* (London, Seaby, 1967).

p. 65, l. 7: Worm *in his pate*: figuratively, a grief or passion that torments his conscience, or corrupts his reason; a perverse fancy, streak of madness or insanity (*OED*).

p. 65, l. 9: *Droptick belly*: dropsy, a morbid condition characterised by accumulation of watery fluid in the stomach (*OED*).

p. 65, l. 13: *Rhume*: obscure form of rheum, water matter secreted by the mucous glands or membranes, such as collects in or drops from the eyes, nose, mouth etc.: hence, an excessive or morbid defluxion of any kind (*OED*).

p. 66, ll. 19–26: Usurer, Furioso, Virtuoso, Player, Country Clown, Pragmatick, Phanatick, gallant: urban types representing cultural and political enthusiasms in Restoration culture: usurer, a money lender, one who lends money at interest, especially at an excessive rate; furioso, an enraged and easily angered person; virtuoso, a learned person, scientist, scholar; player, actor; country clown, an awkward country dweller; pragmatick, one who is busy and active, especially in other people's affairs; phanatick, one who is characterised by excessive or mistaken enthusiasm, especially in religious affairs; gallant, a man of fashion and pleasure (*OED*).

p. 66, l. 33: Aromaticum: the juices of pungent and aromatical fruits. Nicholas Culpeper's *Physicall Directory, or, A Translation of the London Dispensatory* (London, Peter Cole, 1652) lists five powders and cordials described as aromaticum, such as *aromaticum rosatum*, a powder prepared from rose, liquorice, aloe, sandalwood and spices.

p. 67, l. 16: prodigies: something extraordinary or marvellous from which omens or portents are drawn. In the early years of the Restoration numerous pamphlets describing prodigies and interpreting their meaning were published.

p. 67, l. 17: Norwich, Ipswich, Grantham, Gotam: Norwich, principal city in East Anglia, the second largest city in England at this time; Ipswich, principal city in Essex; Grantham, town in Lincolnshire; Gotam or Gotham, the name of a village proverbial for the folly of its inhabitants (later applied to Newcastle and New York).

p. 67, l. 33: *brim-fill'd* Nogans: a noggin, a small measure of alcoholic liquor, usually a quarter of a pint.

p. 67, l. 34: Hogan Mogans: a corrupt translation of the Dutch term signifying 'Their High Mightinesses', referring to the States-General of the United Provinces of the Netherlands; that is, a contemptuous term for the Dutch (*OED*).

p. 68, l. 34: in vino veritas: Latin, 'there is truth in wine'.

p. 69, ll. 9–16: *a* Knight, a grave old man, *a* Drawer, a dealer in old shoes and hats, *a bold* Mechanick: urban types cutting across conventional status hierarchies: knight, a gentleman representing a shire or county in parliament; a grave old man, one having weight or importance, respected, dignified; a drawer, one who draws drink (liquor, beer, coffee) for customers, a waiter; a dealer in old shoes and hats, a second-hand goods merchant; mechanic, one having a manual occupation, working at a trade, and characteristic of the lower social orders (*OED*).

p. 69, l. 31: Ague *fit*: an acute or malarial fever marked by successive fits or paroxysms (*OED*).

p. 70, l. 2: *a tester*: a slang term for a sixpence (*OED*).

p. 70, l. 6: Monsieur Mopus: a simpleton, a stupid person (*OED*).

p. 71, l. 1: *grutch*: begrudge (*OED*).

p. 71, ll. 6–14: spruce youngster, *Spanish* Don, *brisk* Monsieur, Dutchman: urban types revealing national stereotypes not normally represented as socialising together: a spruce youngster, a trim, neat, dapper young man; a Spanish Don, a gentleman from Spain, implying a man of high rank; a brisk monsieur, a smartly dressed Frenchman.

p. 71, l. 24: Non par ma foy: French, 'no, by my faith'.

p. 71, l. 26: Neen mynheer: Dutch, 'no sir'.

p. 72, l. 18: Caaco Caudle: chocolate.

p. 72, l. 19: Germans Mum, Teag's Usquebagh: German wheat beer and Irish whiskey.

p. 72, l. 20: Tredagh: an alternative name for Drogheda, a port town in Co. Louth, Ireland. The town was the focus of a series of strategic battles in the 1640s between Royalists and Parliamentarians. In 1649 the town was captured by Cromwell and the Parliamentary army, who subsequently massacred nearly all the inhabitants.

p. 72, l. 21: *Metheglin*: see above, note to p. 57, col. 3, ll. 7–8.

News from the Coffe-House

p. 75, l. 1: *COFFE-HOUSE*: a variant spelling of coffee, used frequently in the seventeenth century.

p. 75, col. 1, l. 9: *Battles and Sea-Fights*: referring here to the naval engagements of the Second Anglo-Dutch War of 1665–7, as discussed in the newsbooks and coffee-houses.

p. 75, col. 1, l. 13: *Minting-house*: an establishment where money is minted.

p. 75, col. 1, l. 21: Du Ruitters: Admiral Michiel Adriaanszoon De Ruyter (1607–76), commander of the Dutch navy in the Second Anglo-Dutch War.

p. 75, col. 1, ll. 25–8: *A* Fisherman ... Dutch: fishermen were repeatedly captured by both navies, and interrogated for information concerning fleet movements. For example, Pepys notes a fisherman taken by De Ruyter on 25 July 1667, who revealed that De Ruyter knew more than the Admiralty about the location of the two English fleets under Jordan and Spragg (entry for 29 July 1667, *Diary*, vol. VIII, p. 359).

p. 75, col. 1, l. 29: Yaw, yaw, yaw Myne Here: Dutch, 'yes, yes, yes, Sir'.

p. 75, col. 1, l. 31: Monck: George Monck, Duke of Albemarle (1608–1670), army officer and naval commander. He was appointed admiral of the fleet in March 1666, and commanded a fleet in key actions throughout the end of the Second Anglo-Dutch War, including the Four Day Fight (1–4 June 1666) and the St James's Day Fight (25 July 1666).

p. 75, col. 1, ll. 33–40: *Another Swears ... t'were true*: omitted in *The Coffee House or Newsmongers Hall* and *Triumphs of London*; see above, p. 73.

p. 75, col. 1, l. 35: French King: Louis XIV (1638–1715), king of France (1643–1715).

p. 75, col. 1, l. 36: *Flat-bottom'd boats*: repeated scares of French invasion forces were reported during the Second Anglo-Dutch War. Flat-bottomed boats were invasion craft that could operate in shallow water to land troops, artillery and material.

p. 75, col. 1, ll. 35–7: *a Girdle ... round about*: a belt or constraint encompassing England.

p. 75, col. 1, l. 45: *Lillie ... Booker*: William Lillie (1602–81) and John Booker (1602–67): the most renowned and prolific astrologers in England.

p. 75, col. 1, ll. 49–56: *They'l tell ... the Parish*: omitted in *Triumphs of London*; see above, p. 73.

p. 75, col. 1, l. 49: *Lady-ware*: genitals of either sex (*OED*).

p. 75, col. 1, l. 50: *light*: of persons and their behaviour, wanton and unchaste (*OED*).

p. 75, col. 1, l. 55: Jack Adams: a fool; see B. E., *Dictionary of the Canting Crew*.

p. 75, col. 1, l. 56: *Church-Warden of the Parish*: a lay honorary officer of the parish elected to help the incumbent clergyman in the discharge of his administrative duties (*OED*).

p. 75, col. 2, l. 3: *St. Peter's-street in* Rome: the piazza of St Peter's Basilica, Rome, the centre of the Roman Catholic world.

p. 75, col. 2, l. 4: Turnbull-street *in* London: unclear, possibly Turnmill Street, running north-south between Clerkenwell Green and Smithfield.

p. 75, col. 2, l. 5: Clerkenwell: during the Restoration a hamlet north of the City, once the home of the great houses of noblemen, but increasingly associated with wealthy merchants and craftsmen, particularly Huguenots (*LE*).

p. 75, col. 2, ll. 6–8: *What* Whore ... *Chain*: perhaps a reference to the Pope.

p. 75, col. 2, ll. 9–16: *At Sea ... believe it true*: omitted in *Triumphs of London*; see above, p. 73.

p. 75, col. 2, ll. 19–20: Colledge *and the* Court, / *The* Country, Camp*, and* Navie: seats of learning and authority, respectively: Gresham College, the King's Court, the political nation, the army and the navy.

p. 75, col. 2, ll. 21–4: *So great a* Vniversity ... *penny*: these lines are cited as the origin of the notion of the coffee-house as a 'penny university', first noted in W. H. Ukers, *The Romance of Coffee. An outline history of coffee and coffee-drinking through a thousand years* (New York, Tea and Coffee Trade Journal Co., 1948), p. 74, and celebrated in Aytoun Ellis, *The Penny Universities* (London, Secker and Warburg, 1956). The phrase does not appear to have been used in the seventeeth or eighteenth centuries.

p. 75, col. 2, ll. 25–32: *A* Merchants ... *doth know*: omitted in *Triumphs of London*; see above, p. 73.

p. 75, col. 2, l. 29: Articles *of* Peace: the conditions and terms of a peace treaty.

p. 75, col. 2, l. 35: *Like Women at a Gossiping*: a gossiping: a christening or christening feast, characterised by idle talk and chatter, and conventionally dominated by women.

p. 75, col. 2, l. 36: *double tyre of Tongues*: proverbial: a mouth with two tiers of teeth would talk more.

p. 75, col. 2, l. 37: *Broad-side*: a discharge of the whole array of guns on one side of a ship of war (*OED*).

p. 75, col. 2, ll. 41–8: *The Drinking ... then Wine*: omitted in *Triumphs of London*; see above, p. 73.

p. 75, col. 2, l. 42: *make a* Fool *a* Sophie: proverbial, to make a fool a wise man (a sophy).

p. 75, col. 2, l. 43: *the* Turkish Mahomet: Muhammad (AD *c.* 570–632), the Arab prophet and founder of Islam, who received his revelations progressively after 610 AD (well before knowledge of coffee in Mecca).

p. 75, col. 2, l. 46: *The Land of* Palestine: territorial region of the Ottoman Empire on the Mediterranean coast, administered from Jerusalem.

p. 75, col. 2, l. 50: *Perrywiggs*: The practice of wig wearing began after the Restoration, when it appeared as a sign of changed times. Pepys first wore a wig in 1663.

p. 75, col. 2, l. 52: *Novells*: news, tidings (*OED*).

A Broad-side against Coffee; Or, the Marriage of the Turk

p. 79, col. 1, l. 1: Turkish Renegade: an apostate from any form of religious faith (*OED*), in this case a Muslim who has become a Christian.

p. 79, col. 1, l. 3: *a Demur*: an objection (*OED*).

p. 79, col. 1, l. 5: *cold*: one of the four humours in ancient Greek physiology, as promulgated by Hippocrates, and influential though the writings of Galen (131–201 BC). See below, note to p. 79, col. 1, l. 7.

p. 79, col. 1, l. 6: Turkish Hymen ... *swet*: Hymen, in the Greek and Roman mythology, was the god of marriage, traditionally depicted as a man carrying a torch and veil. The name here makes a visual allusion to a Turkish man wearing a turban (Turbant), as was conventionally depicted on coffee-house sign-boards.

p. 79, col. 1, l. 7: Coffee *was as cold as* Earth: Coffee was typically described as cold and dry in humoural theory, and as such associated with black bile, earth, spleen and melancholy. See also below, note to p. 79, col. 1, l. 14.

p. 79, col. 1, l. 12: *Nymph*: in classical mythology a class of semi-divine spirits imagined as taking the form of a maiden (*OED*).

p. 79, col. 1, l. 14: *cold and moist*: water, as described in the Galenic humoural system.

p. 79, col. 1, l. 18: Newcastle's *bowels*: unclear, perhaps a reference to William Cavendish, 1st Duke of Newcastle (1593–1676), a playwright, patron of the arts and Royalist army officer.

p. 79, col. 1, l. 20: *the Slave* ... beaten: in the Turkish preparation coffee beans were not ground, but pulverised with a mortar and pestle.

p. 79, col. 1, l. 24: No ... Infidels: a doctrine established by the Crusades, dispensing with concepts of honour and justice in dealings with non-Christian peoples, and thereby allowing great brutality.

p. 79, col. 1, l. 26: Venetian Moor: Othello, a mercenary general employed in the service of the republic of Venice in Shakespeare's *Othello* (1604), and directed by the Senate to lead the Venetian forces against the Ottomans (III. i.48–9).

p. 79, col. 1, l. 27: *Asian Brat!*: an insignificant child from Asia, here noticing the short period of time that had elapsed since coffee first arrived in England from the Orient.

p. 79, col. 2, l. 1: *canting*: the practice of using thieves' cant, the secret language or jargon of thieves and professional beggars (*OED*).

p. 79, col. 2, l. 3: *Coachman*: The first coffee-house in London was opened by a Pasqua Rosee, a Greek servant of a Levant merchant named Daniel Edwards. No later than 1656, Rosee was joined in the business by one of Edwards's apprentices, Christopher Bowman, who is sometimes described as a coachman. See Markman Ellis, 'Pasqua Rosee's Coffee House 1652–1666', *London Journal*, 29:1 (2004), pp. 1–25.

p. 79, col. 2, l. 5: Me no good Engalash!: a humorous transliteration of Rosee's foreign accent.

p. 79, col. 2, l. 6: *plaid the Quack*: acted like a quack, that is one who boasts knowledge of wonderful remedies, a medical imposter (*OED*).

p. 79, col. 2, l. 7: Ver boon ... Ptisick: a transliteration of Rosee's speech, here stating that coffee is a boon (good, advantageous) remedy for the stomach, the cough, and phthisic (ptisick), or pulmonary consumption.

p. 79, col. 2, l. 8: *Physick*: medicine, especially a cathartic or purge (*OED*).

p. 79, col. 2, l. 9: a crust ... coal: a description of coffee flavour. A crust is a deposit or concretion left on the surface of something; to chark means to burn or char something to charcoal; a coal is a piece of burnt wood or carbon (*OED*).

p. 79, col. 2, l. 10: *Mock* China *bowl*: unclear, perhaps a reference to Bastard China, or *Smilax pseudochina*, a root from the Americas used in the preparation of China Ale, akin to sarsaparilla.

p. 79, col. 2, l. 12: Dives: Latin for 'rich (man)', and used generically for any rich man.

p. 79, col. 2, l. 14: *Blisters*: the efficacy of some medicinal preparations, such as the aphrodisiac cantharides, was measured by their ability to raise blisters. Coffee was notoriously consumed so hot as to blister the tongue.

p. 79, col. 2, l. 16: *Alembicks*: an apparatus used in distilling, used figuratively for something that turns one thing into another more valuable.

p. 79, col. 2, l. 20: Posset *or* Porrige: a posset is a drink made of hot milk curdled with ale, wine or other liquor, often with sugar and spices; a porridge is a soft food made of oatmeal stirred into boiling water or milk (*OED*). These two preparations were the principal hot drinks in England before the arrival or coffee, tea and chocolate.

p. 79, col. 2, l. 22: Noah's *Ark*: in the biblical tradition, the ark or ship in which Noah, his family and a pair of each of the animals were saved from the Flood (Genesis 6–8).

p. 79, col. 2, l. 23: *the Drench*: a medicinal, soporific or poisonous draught (*OED*).

p. 79, col. 2, l. 28: *a* Mountain *and a* Mouse: one of the fables of Aesop (No. 280): 'A mountain had gone into labour and was groaning terribly. Such rumours excited great expectations all over the country. In the end, however, the mountain gave birth to a mouse'; see *Aesop's Fables*, trans. by Laura Gibbs (Oxford, Oxford University Press, 2002), no. 280, p. 135. Cited by Horace, *Ars Poetica*, l. 139. The fable suggests that grand objects produce insignificant results.

p. 79, col. 2, l. 30: clap: gonorrhoea

p. 79, col. 2, l. 31: Mens humana novitatis avidissima: Latin saying, 'the human mind is eager for novelty'.

The Character of a Coffee-House, with the Symptomes of a Town-Wit

p. 85, l. 5: Lay-Conventicle: A conventicle is a meeting of Protestant Nonconformists for religious worship, prohibited by the 'Act to prevent and suppress seditious conventicles' in 1664. A lay-conventicle is an oxymoron suggesting a secular and non-clerical meeting of religious persons for seditious purpose (*OED*).

p. 85, l. 7: Toping: to drink in large draughts (*OED*).

p. 85, l. 8: Rota-room: a reference to the meetings of James Harrington's Rota Club, for which see above, note to p. 12, ll. 6–7.

p. 85, l. 11: Virtuosi: scientists, see above, note to p. 14, ll. 22–3.

p. 85, ll. 14–15: Gazets: gazettes or weekly newspapers (*OED*).

p. 85, l. 26–p. 86, l. 4: Unde quod est usquam ... in Orbem: Ovid's description of the house of Fame, located at the centre of the world, from *Metamorphoses*, XII.41ff.

p. 86, l. 28: Bedlam: Bethlehem Hospital in Bishopsgate, for the reception of mentally deranged persons, by extension, a lunatic asylum, mad confusion.

p. 86, ll. 30–1: Pluto's Diet-drink ... *Sacramental Vows*: In Roman mythology, Pluto is the god of the underworld. The description of the witches' brew recalls Glanvill's *A Blow at Modern Sadducism in some Philosophical Considerations about Witchcraft* (London, E. Cotes, 1668).

p. 87, l. 21: Pragmatick: busybody; see above, note to p. 66, ll. 19–26.

p. 87, l. 28: *Captain* All-man-sir: a sycophant, so named because he calls all men sir.

p. 87, l. 29: Eolus: In Greek mythology, Aeolus was the Keeper of the Wind: with Eos he had four sons, each of which was associated with a wind from each quarter of the compass.

p. 87, l. 37: Justin de Cynægiro: untraced. The events described by Captain All-man-sir are related to the Second Anglo-Dutch War.

p. 87, ll. 47–8: Gayland *and* Taffaletta: The English general Gayland was routed by Taffaletta, Emperor of the Moroccans, near Tangiers on 7 July 1666. The episode was made part of the subject of Elkenah Settle's tragedy *The Empress of Morocco* (London, for William Cademan, 1673).

p. 88, ll. 11–12: Sciunt id ... illi sciunt: Latin, from the Roman comic dramatist Plautus's (254–184 BC) *Trinummus* (*The Three Pieces of Money*), 207–9. Here slightly misquoted: it should read 'sciunt id quod in aurem rex reginae dixerit, / sciunt quod Iuno fabulatast cum Iove; / quae neque futura neque sunt, tamen illi sciunt': 'They know what the king whispered in the ear of the queen; they know what Juno talked about in conversation with Jupiter; that which neither is nor is likely to be, do these fellows know': *The Comedies of Plautus*, trans. by Henry Thomas Riley (London, G. Bell and Sons, 1912).

p. 88, l. 18: Fox, Stowe, *and* Hollingshead: English Protestant historians: John Foxe, *The Book of Martyrs* (London, John Day, 1563); John Stowe, *The Annales of England* (London, Raph Newberye, 1580); Raphael Holinshed, *Chronicles of England, Scotland and Ireland* (London, I. Harrison, 1577).

p. 88, l. 40: *two leaves of* Leviathan: Thomas Hobbes's *Leviathan, or the matter, forme, and power of a common-wealth ecclesiasticall and civill* (London, Andrew Crooke, 1651), the most important work of political theory to emerge during the Interregnum, offering a rational model for understanding the nature, purpose and justification of government.

p. 89, ll. 3–4: *Whatever is sacred ... fantastick* Buffoonery: S. Weiss, 'Joseph Glanvill and *The Character of a Coffee-house*', *Notes and Queries*, 197 (1952), pp. 234–5, points out parallels with page 143 of Glanvill's *Blow at Modern Sadducism*: 'everything that is sacred, or serious hath been exposed, and both Government, and Religion made the objects of idle, and phantastick buffoonery'.

p. 89, l. 22: Apostle of Malmsbury: Thomas Hobbes (1588–1679), born in Malmesbury. The name further recalls William of Malmesbury (d. *c.* 1143), the historian of England who wrote *Gesta Regum Anglorum* (*Exploits of the English Kings*).

p. 89, l. 45: Lullian Art: the rhetoric of Raymundus Lullius or Raymund Lull (*c.* 1232–*c.* 1315).

p. 90, l. 13: Jack-pudding: a buffoon.

p. 90, l. 19: O Brazile *(the Inchanted Island):* an allusion to the rapid changes of scene in Richard Head's (*c.* 1637–*c.* 1686) fictional Irish travel journal entitled *O-Brazile, or, The inchanted island: being a perfect relation of the late discovery and wonderful dis-inchantment of an island on the north of Ireland: with an account of the riches and commodities thereof* (London, William Crook, 1675).

p. 90, l. 29: *The* Ingeniosi ... Rehearsal: the ingeniosi are the wits, poets and writers. *The Rehearsal* (London, T. Dring, 1672) was a farce (dramatic satire) on learning, poets and Dryden by George Villiers, Duke of Buckingham.

p. 90, l. 43: Si quid nonisti rectius Candidus Imperti: Latin, 'If you know anything better than this candidly impart it', from Horace, *Epistles*, I.6.67.

Coffee-houses Vindicated in answer to the late published Character of a Coffee-House

p. 95, l. 14: Folio-Impertinence: referring to the large size of paper (a full sized sheet folded once) on which was printed Jonathan Edwin's *The Character of a Coffee-House, with the Symptomes of a Town-Wit*, for which see above, pp. 81–90.

p. 95, ll. 17–8: Billingsgate Rhetorick, *Dreggs of* Canting, *and such* Rubbish Language, *as* Bubbling, Bully-Rock, Fluxing, Gonorrhea, &c.: a description of the vulgar language of Edwin's *Character*. Billingsgate is scurrilous and vituperative abuse, so named from the flavour of the language at the Billingsgate fish market in London. Canting is the practice of using the secret or obscure language of thieves, professional beggars and prostitutes. The examples here instanced are bubbling (cheating or deluding), bully-rock (a bravo or hired ruffian), fluxing (a discharge of humours, blood or excrement) and gonorrhea (an inflammatory discharge of mucus from the genitals, now understood as a symptom of a sexually transmitted disease). (*OED*).

p. 95, l. 20: *Lay-Conventicles*: see above, note to p. 85, l. 5.

p. 95, l. 21: Solomans *double face'd advice*: Old Testament prophet who offered advice on wisdom in the Book of Proverbs.

p. 95, l. 23: Town-Witt: see above, p. 88.

p. 96, l. 3: Push-pin: a child's game played with pins, in which each player in turn pushes or fillips his pin with the aim of crossing that of another player (*OED*).

p. 96, l. 4: reading a Lecture to a Monkey: a pointless activity.

p. 96, l. 8: *the happy* Arabia, *Natures* spicery: Arabia Felix (the happy Arabia) was the name of one of three zones of the Arabian peninsula in classical geography, roughly corresponding to modern Yemen, an area long famous for cinnamon and other spices, and the origin of the coffee on the London market in the seventeenth century.

p. 96, l. 9: Aromaticks *and divers other Rarities*: spices (*OED*).

p. 96, l. 12: *good* plight, *and* eucrasy: good plight is a beneficial corporeal condition; eucrasy is, in the humoural physiology, such a due or well proportioned mixture of qualities as constitutes health or soundness (*OED*).

p. 96, l. 15: salutiferous Berry: coffee, a bean (not berry) that promotes or is conducive to health.

p. 96, ll. 16–17: *moderately* hot ... Quality: in the ancient physiology, statement of quality of humours in coffee. Here coffee is described as hot (not a reference to its temperature), dry (not a reference to its wetness), and being attenuating (something that makes the humours thinner) and cleansing (purifying).

p. 96, l. 17: decoction: boiling in water so as to extract the soluble parts of a substance.

p. 96, ll. 18–19: *Incomparable Remedy ... Stomach*: further description of the physiological properties of coffee. Crudities are imperfectly digested or concocted humours.

p. 96, l. 22: Mountebank: an itinerant charlatan who sold supposed medicines and remedies, frequently using various entertainments to attract a crowd of potential customers (*OED*).

p. 96, ll. 24–5: Phlegm ... *Countrey*: phlegm (mucus) is one of the four humours, traditionally described as cold and moist. The northern location of England associated residents of that country with the phlegmatic constitution.

p. 96, l. 29: exsiccant: drying, in the humoural theory.

p. 96, l. 31: voluntary Divels ... Drunkards: self-willed devils. Lord Cook is untraced.

p. 96, ll. 33–5: expelling Wind ... *kindnesses to Nature*: the wide range of physiological properties of coffee, articulated in the humoural theory. Coffee is effective in promoting wind, imparting vigour to the liver (the seat of passion), reanimating the heart (the seat of life), corroborating or strengthening the animal spirits (the vital principle), encouraging the appetite, assisting digestion and alleviating gall stones, rheums (watery matter secreted by mucuous glands) and defluxions (a flow or discharge of humours) (*OED*).

p. 96, l. 38: sottish: foolish, doltish, stupid (*OED*).

p. 97, l. 1: Tartars *and* Arabians: native inhabitants of areas where coffee was supposed to be habitually consumed: Tartary, the region of central Asia extending eastwards from the Caspian Sea to China, and Arabia, the Arabian peninsula.

p. 97, ll. 4–5: Shashes and Turbants: a shash or sash is a band of fine material worn twisted around the head as a turbant or turban: both a synecdoche for Islamic inhabitants of the Levant.

p. 97, ll. 8–15: Parkinson *in his exquisite Herbal* ... Verulam *in his* Natural History ... Sandy's *in his Travels'* ... Sir H. B. *both in his* Voyage to the Levant ... *Mr.* Howel ... *a Letter to Mr. Just. R. before his* Organon salutis: Coffee scholarship, making use of N. D., *The Vertues of Coffee. Set forth in the Works of Lord Bacon his Natural Hist., Mr Parkinson his Herbal, Sir George Sandys his Travails, James Howel Esq; his Epistles*; see Volume 4 of this edition, pp. 67–73. The texts referred to are: John Parkinson, *Theatrum Botanicum, the Theatre of Plants. Or, An Universall and Compleat Herbal* (London, Tho. Cotes, 1640); Francis Bacon, *Sylva Sylvarum: or A Naturall Historie. In ten centuries, Written by the Right Honourable Francis Lo. Verulam Viscount St. Alban* (London, J. H. for William Lee, 1627); George Sandys, *A Relation of a Journey Begun An. Dom: 1610. Foure Bookes* (London, W. Barrett, 1615); Sir Henry Blount, *A Voyage into the Levant. A Breife Relation of a Iourney* (London, I. [John] L. [Legat] for Andrew Crooke, 1636) and James Howell, 'To his Highly Esteemed Friend and Compatriot Judge *Rumsey*, upon his *Provang*, or rare pectoral Instrument, and his rare experiments of Cophie and Tobacco', in Walter Rumsey, *Organon Salutis*; see Volume 4 of this edition, pp. 1–65.

p. 97, l. 16: *puisne* Quiblers: puny or petty persons whose arguments rely on word play and verbal dexterity rather than substance.

p. 97, l. 19: Prince of Latine *Poets*: Publius Vergilius Maro (70–19 BC), Roman poet known in English as Virgil or Vergil, author of the *Eclogues*, the *Georgics* and the *Aeneid*.

p. 97, l. 22: Alba Ligustra ... Nigra Leguntur: Virgil, *Eclogues*, II.18; translated by John Dryden as 'White Lillies Lye neglected on the Plain, / While dusky Hyacinths for use remain', in *The works of Virgil: containing his pastorals, Georgics and Aeneis*, 3rd edn, 3 vols (London, Jacob Tonson, 1709), vol. I, p. 8. See also 'The white privets fall, the dark hyacinths are culled' from *Virgil: with an English translation. Eclogues; Georgics; Aeneid, I–VI*, trans. by H. Rushton Fairclough; rev. by G. P. Goold, Loeb Classical Library (Cambridge, MA, Harvard University Press, 1999).

p. 97, l. 24: Black Broath *of the* Lacedemonians: the black blood soup made by the inhabitants of Lacedaemon (Sparta). Although coffee was of wholly modern origin, early coffee scholars, beginning with the classicist George Sandys, erroneously suggested that this blood soup might be a classical antecedent for coffee. See George Sandys, *A Relation of a Journey Begun An. Dom: 1610* (London, W. Barrett, 1615), p. 66.

p. 97, ll. 29–30: *dull Planet ... amongst us*: the planet Saturn lies between Jupiter and Uranus (which was not discovered until 1781), and takes a little more than 29 years to make one revolution around the sun, meaning that the first coffee-house in London opened after 1644 (the mostly widely accepted date for this event is 1652).

p. 97, ll. 30–2: *how* numerous ... *Nation*: numbers of coffee-houses increased rapidly in London and across the country. See Ellis, *Coffee-House*, pp. 172–3.

p. 97, ll. 34–5: *A* Tavern ... *Purse-Consumption*: a bill of charges at a tavern; a wasting disease of the purse.

p. 97, l. 40: Hydroptick Stars: the symptoms or indicators (stars) of dropsy, a condition in which water or serous fluid accumulates in the cavities or tissues of the body.

p. 98, l. 10: *play the* Good-fellows: to act as an agreeable or jovial companion would (*OED*).

p. 98, l. 13: Aristotle: ancient Greek philosopher (384–22 BC).

p. 98, l. 13: Hobs: Thomas Hobbes (1588–1679), English philosopher.

p. 98, ll. 19–21: Discourse Is ... *Incentive of Ingenuity*: as translated here, the Latin tag is a commonplace, meaning conversation is food for the mind ('pabulum animi', Cicero, *Academica*, ii.41). A whetstone is a shaped stone for giving a smooth edge to cutting tools.

p. 98, ll. 21–2: Loquére ut te videam ... Phylosophers *Adage*: a proverb attributed to Socrates, translated here. John Dryden, in *An Evening's Love, or, The mock-astrologer* (London, T. N. for H. Herringman, 1671), renders it as 'speak that I may know thee' (p. 40).

p. 98, ll. 26–7: Pamphlet-monger *(that sputters out senceless* Characters *faster than any* Hocus *can vomit* Inkle): one of the conjuring tricks of Hocus, a generic name for a conjuror, was to produce from his mouth yards of inkle or linen tape. This mysterious production is here made an analogy with the hack writer or pamphlet-monger who produces large numbers of satirical characters.

p. 98, l. 34: *an* Excise-man *counting the number of dishes*: under the two Excise Acts of the Restoration (12 Car. II, c. 23 (1661) and 15 Car. II, c. 11 (1663)) coffee, chocolate and tea became subject to excise taxation, along the model of that levied on alcoholic beverages. The excise on coffee was regulated and assessed using the established corps of professional gaugers, who inspected equipment and facilities for the production and storage of coffee, and were reputed to make clandestine inspections of coffee-houses in search of illicit coffee.

p. 98, l. 39: In multiloquio non deest vanitas: Latin phrase, 'where there is much talk there will be no end of vanity'; rewriting Proverbs 10:19, 'in multiloquio non dest peccatum', given in the KJV as 'In the multitude of words there wanteth not sin: but he that refraineth his lips is wise'.

p. 98, l. 40: Royal Proclamation: a reference to *A Proclamation to Restrain the Spreading of False News, and Licentious Talking of Matters of State and Government*, dated 12 June 1672, which sought to control the publication and circulation of seditious information in print, manuscript and conversation 'not onely in *Coffee-houses*, but in other Places and Meetings' (see Volume 4 of this edition, pp. 89–92).

p. 98, ll. 41–2: Arcana Imperij: Latin, 'state secrets'.

p. 99, ll. 9–10: Pudor Subrusticus ... *Tully somewhere calls it)*: Latin phrase, 'boorish modesty', from Marcus Tullius Cicero (106–43 BC), known in English as 'Tully'. Cicero, *Epistles*, V.12.

p. 99, l. 21: Free-School of Ingenuity: a free (grammar) school (in Latin 'libera schola grammaticalis') was either a school in which learning was given without payment, or a school which gave a liberal education, perhaps because exempted from ecclesiastical or state control, or a school to which both of these conditions applied. In the seventeenth century the term became a poetic commonplace for an unregulated compilation or anthology, as in *Cupids Master-piece, or, The free-school of witty and delightful complements* (London, John Andrews, 1656).

The Grand Concern of England Explained

p. 105, l. 2: Mum: see above, note to p. 57, col. 3, ll. 7–8.

p. 105, l. 3: *These greatly hinder the Consumption of* Barley, Malt, *and* Wheat: these commodities were all central products of domestic British agricultural production, and were used in the brewing of beer and ale.

p. 105, l. 7: *vent*: the fact occasioned when commodities are disposed by sale or find purchasers (*OED*).

p. 105, l. 12: *two pence the Quatern*: a quarter of any measure, here presumably a quarter of a pint (*OED*).

p. 107, l. 21: *Silks, Stuffs, Ribbons, Laces, Points*: various kinds of textiles: stuffs are light woollen fabrics; ribbon is a narrow band of a fine material such as silk or satin; points are thread lace made wholly with a needle (also known as needle-point lace).

p. 24, ll. 14–15: *extraordinary husbands of their time*: a good husband can be held as someone who manages his affairs with skill and thrift (*OED*).

The Women's Petition Against Coffee

p. 111, ll. 14–15: the Right Honourable Keepers of the Liberty of VENUS: refers to those charged with the protection of the arts of love: libertines, rakes, courtesans and whores. During the English Republic (1649–53), and again during the Rump (1659–60), parliament abolished the kingly office and constituted itself as the 'Keepers of the liberty of England'; for which see 'An Act declaring what offences shall be adjudged Treason'(17 July 1649) in *The Constitutional Documents of the Puritan Revolution 1625–1660*, ed. by Samuel Rawson Gardiner (Oxford, Clarendon Press, 1906), p. 388. Venus is the goddess of love and the amatory arts.

p. 113, ll. 3–4: *Worshipful Court of* Female Assistants: prostitutes, courtesans, whores. A 'court of assistants' constituted the governing body of each of the City livery companies that regulated trade in London.

p. 113, ll. 6–7: *Buxome Good-women*: A goodwife or good-woman is the mistress of a house; buxom, full of health, plump, comely.

p. 113, l. 18: *Cock-sparrows*: the male of the sparrow, applied to men who show sparrow-like characteristics (*OED*).

p. 113, l. 19: Sa sa: English transliteration of the French exclamation 'ça ça', used to encourage and excite.

p. 114, l. 10: *dull* Lubbers: big clumsy stupid fellows (*OED*).

p. 114, l. 13: *Devoirs*: duties, here sexual (*OED*).

p. 115, l. 9: Cato: Marcus Porcius Cato (234–149 BC) was a Roman statesman and orator, here used as a byword for conservative rhetoric.

p. 115, l. 22: sapless *as a* Kixe: kex, the dry stem of various herbaceous plants, such as cow parsnip or wild chervil. Figuratively, a dried-up sapless person. (*OED*).

p. 115, ll. 27–8: *The Age of Man … Span*: misquoted from John Donne (1572–1631), *An Anatomy Of The World* (London, William Stansby for Samuel Macham, 1611) on the shortness of life: 'And as in lasting, so in length is man / Contracted to an inch, who was a span' (p. 7).

p. 115, l. 32: Stygian Tap-houses: Stygian means pertaining to the River Styx, or more generally, to the infernal regions of classical mythology. Tap-houses were small alehouses where beer is drawn from a tap.

p. 116, l. 10: *Quaker … Dispute*: a meeting of the Quakers held at the Barbican on 28 June 1674, defending themselves against recent allegations.

p. 117, ll. 7–9: *as what colour … Father in Law was*: quibbles of Biblical scholarship.

p. 117, l. 32: *Red Lattice*: a lattice painted red was the mark of an inn; hence also of an alehouse or tavern (*OED*).

p. 118, l. 2: *rare Langoon, and Racy Canary*: langoon was a kind of white wine, and canary a light sweet wine from the Canary Islands (*OED*).

p. 118, ll. 13–16: Tom Farthing ... Woman weary, &c: the first verse of a contemporary bawdy song in which a woman complains that Tom Farthing stays out too late, and when he gets home is too weary to have sex. See *A Perfect Collection of the Several Songs now in Mode either at the Court or Theatres* (London, n. p., 1675), p. 39. The name Tom Farthing was thereafter associated with silly and lewd song lyrics.

p. 118, ll. 29–30: Lusty nappy Beer, Cock-Ale, Cordial Canaries, Restoring Malago's *and* Back-Recruiting Chocolet: nappy beer was strong and foaming, having a head; cock-ale was mixed with the jelly or minced meat of a boiled cock, beside other ingredients; cordial canaries were hearty and health-giving sweet wines from the Canary Islands; malago was a white or red fortified wine from Malaga in Spain, also known as sack; chocolet or chocolate was supposed to have restorative powers (*OED*).

The Mens Answer to the Womens Petition Against Coffee

p. 123, l. 10: *Postures than* Aretine: *Aretino's Postures* (1524) was the name given to a well-known illustrated sex manual in verse, comprising sixteen sonnets by Pietro Aretine (1492–1556) and sixteen explicit engravings from drawings by Giuliano Romano, a pupil of Raphael, depicting various athletic sexual positions.

p. 123, l. 22: Italian *Padlocks*: chastity belts.

p. 123, ll. 26–7: *Commissioners of* Whetstones Park, *the Suburb Runners, and* Moor-fields *Night-walkers*: ironic reference to areas of London where prostitutes were commonly encountered. Whetstone Park was a street which lay between Lincoln's Inn and Holborn; Moorfields was an open area north of the city. A 'suburb sinner' was a loose woman, so named because the suburbs of London were associated with debased and licentious habits of life.

p. 123, l. 29–p. 124, l. 1: *preparations of Cantharides, spiced Meats, Anchoves, Cullises, Jelly-broths, Lambstones, Diasatyrion, Bononia Sawsages*: aphrodisiacs. Cantharides is Spanish Fly, a rubefacient and vesicant prepared from the dried beetle *Cantharis vesicatoria*; cullis and jelly-broths were both restorative strong meat broths; lambstones were lamb's testicles; diasatyrion was a medicinal preparation of which the principal ingredient was sanders or sandalwood; and bononia sawsages are a large kind of preserved Bologna sausage (salami). They, and most of the other aphrodisiacs here listed, are referred to in Henry Stubbe's *The Indian Nectar, or, a discourse concerning chocolate* (London, J. C. for Andrew Crook, 1662), pp. 136–7.

p. 124, l. 3: *Artificial Tranguin*: unknown

p. 124, l. 7: Solomon: Solomon (970–28 BC), king of the Israelites. Proverbs 30:16–17: 'There are three things that are never satisfied, yea, four things say not ... The grave; and the barren womb; the earth that is not filled with water; and the fire that saith not, it is enough'.

p. 124, l. 16: *the Turkish Woman straddling on their signs*: coffee-houses with depictions of Turkish women on their shop signs.

p. 124, l, 27: *Knights of the Bull-Feather*: a cuckold.

p. 124, l. 29: *Cace-daemon*: cacodemon, an evil spirit (*OED*).

p. 125, l. 5: *Catholicon,* Ens Naturae*, and* Aqua Tetrachymagogon: quack remedies. Catholicon is an electuary capable of relieving all humours, a panacea. The *ens natuarae* is a scholastic concept of being, created from nothingness. Aqua Tetrachymagogon was a liquid solution capable of purging the four humours at once, also satirised in Aphra Behn's comedy *Sir Patient Fancy* (London, Richard Tonson, 1678), p. 83.

p. 126, l. 1: *Grannum*: grannam, a grandmother or old woman (*OED*).

p. 126, l. 9: *Bonny Clabber*: milk naturally clotted on souring (*OED*).

A Brief Description of the Excellent Vertues of that Sober and Wholesome Drink, called Coffee

p. 129, col. 2, l. 10: Florescat Arabica Planta: Latin: blossom, Arabic seedling.

p. 129, col. 1, l. 26: *Country's called* Felix: Arabia Felix (Arabia the happy), the name of one of three zones of the Arabian peninsula in classical geography, roughly corresponding to modern Yemen.

p. 129, col. 1, l. 30: Phoenix: in ancient Egyptian mythology, the phoenix was a mythical bird with beautiful gold and red plumage, fabled to live five or six hundred years in the Arabian desert, after which it builds a nest of aromatic twigs which are ignited, consuming nest and bird, before the bird emerges with renewed youth.

p. 129, col. 1, l. 36: *By NATURE ... Dry*: a description of coffee in the humoural system: warm (one of the fundamental qualities, the opposite of cold), attenuating (making thinner), and dry (another fundamental quality, the opposite of moist). As something that was hot and dry, coffee would be associated with the choleric temperament, yellow bile, spleen and fire. See by contrast the description of coffee as cold and dry (melancholic black bile) in *A Broad-side against Coffee*, see above, note to p. 79, col. 1, l. 7.

p. 129, col. 1, l. 38: *Dropsie ... Gout*: dropsy, a morbid condition characterised by the accumulation of watery fluid in the serous cavities; gout, a disease characterised by the painful inflammation of the smaller joints (*OED*).

p. 129, col. 1, ll. 40–1: *Scorbutick Humours ... Catarrhs*: a list of ailments supposedly cured by coffee: scorbutick Humours pertaining to scurvy, characterised by swelling and bleeding gums; hypochondriack winds, melancholic spirits in the stomach or intestines expressed as flatus, flatulence; rheum, excessive secretion of watery matter from the mucous glands; ptisick (phthisic), a wasting disease of the lungs, pulmonary consumption; palsies (palsy), a paralysis or weakness of all or part of the body, sometimes with a tremor; jaundice, a morbid condition caused by obstruction of the bile and characterised by yellowness of the skin and tissues; coughs, fits of coughing; catarrh, profuse discharge from the nose and eyes during a cold, supposed to run down from the brain (*OED*).

p. 129, col. 1, l. 45: *Entercourse*: intercourse, communication between something, here the heart, liver and brain.

p. 129, col. 1, l. 48: *Microcosme*: the human individual in general (*OED*).

p. 129, col. 1, l. 49: *Peccant Humours*: morbid, unhealthy or corrupt humours that cause disorder in the system (*OED*).

p. 129, col. 1, l. 59: *Amorous Gallant*: a man of pleasure or fine gentleman dedicated to the arts of love.

p. 129, col. 1, l. 62: *Sweting-Tubs*: an open wooden vessel used to induce sweating or profuse perspiration, used as a medical cure (*OED*).

p. 129, col. 1, l. 64: *fumbling Doe-littles*: one who does little, a lazy person (*OED*).

p. 129, col. 2, ll. 13–14: *th'Impotent ... to a Misses Bed*: a complicated disparagement: a sot is one who dulls or stupefies himself with drink, here to the state of impotence, who must be induced to visit a young woman's bed, like a pickled or soused pig's head (an unwieldy and unrewarding dish).

p. 129, col. 2, l. 14: *Settle-Brain*: something that calms the brain (*OED*).

p. 129, col. 2, l. 21: APOLLO: a god in Greek and Roman mythology, the son of Zeus and Leto, the god of music, poetry and medicine, amongst other things.

p. 129, col. 2, ll. 31–2: *The* Rules ... *COFFEE-HOUSE*: an ironic title for a satire on coffee-house sociability. 'Rules and Orders' is a commonplace phrase in legal discourse, signifying the administrative regulations of certain judicial institutions, especially courts of law, or the body of rules followed by an assembly. See for example *Praxis utriusque banci, the antient and modern practice of the two superior courts at Westminster, viz. The King's Bench and Common Pleas together with the rules and orders of the said courts* (London, for J. Place and T. Bassett, 1674).

p. 129, col. 2, l. 34: Civil-Orders: the civil laws. A term in legal debate current in the period, as for example in Fabian Philipps's *Regale necessarium, or, The legality, reason, and necessity of the rights and priviledges justly claimed by the Kings servants* (London, for Christopher Wilkinson, 1671) p. 368.

p. 129, col. 2, l. 37: *Pre-eminence of Place, none here should Mind*: seats around the table in the coffee-room were not organized hierarchically, referring to the custom in coffee-houses, that each man should take the next free seat around the table.

p. 129, col. 2, l. 48: *Maudlin Lovers*: men who discuss their illicit gallantries and amours in a mawkish or sentimental manner, one of the ordeals of the coffee-house.

p. 129, col. 2, l. 52: *Affairs of State*: transactions concerning the state or nation, politics. The coffee-houses had come to be emblematic locations for debate on public affairs by those outside the court and ministry, where it was still assumed that ordinary people did not need to know about the state and its affairs.

p. 129, footnote: Coffee Mill *and* Tobacco-Roll: a mill for grinding coffee and a roll of tobacco (a roll of cured tobacco leaves sold in bulk, of varying weights around 100 pounds).

p. 129, footnote: *Chocolate, made in Cake or in Roll, after the* Spanish *Fashion*: chocolate is made from the fermented, roasted and ground beans of the cocoa tree (*Theobroma cacao*). Imported from Spanish America, chocolate was sold as a bitter paste made up into small cylindrical cakes or rolls, which were used in the preparation of hot drinks with the addition of water, sugar and sometimes eggs. Only in the nineteenth century was eating chocolate developed.

William Hicks, *Coffee-house jests*

p. 133, ll. 5–7: *This may be printed. March 30. 1677. Roger L'Estrange*: under the terms of the Licensing Act 1662 (14 Car. II, c. 33), all publications were submitted to the licenser Roger L'Estrange before publication, and required the license and licenser's name in the printed publication as proof, although the great majority of publications avoided these provisions.

p. 135, ll. 3–4: Oliver's *dayes*: Oliver Cromwell (1599–1658) was the effective ruler of England, first as lieutenant general of the army, and then from 1653 as Lord Protector, from the execution of Charles I in January 1649 until his own death in September 1658.

p. 135, l. 5: *persecuted and plundered*: In 1643 the Long Parliament reformed the clergy by instigating a systematic purge of scandalous ministers. This allowed local inhabitants to make complaints against clergy who failed to obey the Presbyterian religious ordinances enacted by Parliament. Such clergy were dispossessed of their churches, livings and rectories, a process known as being persecuted and plundered. The process was reversed in 1662. See John Morrill, 'The Religious Context of the English Civil War', *Transactions of the Royal Historical Society*, 5th series, 34 (1984), pp. 155–78.

p. 136, l. 16: *three such Kingdoms*: England, Scotland and Ireland.

p. 136, l. 28: *Rump Parliament*: after the purge of most members of the Long Parliament led by Colonel Thomas Pride in December 1648, the remaining parliamentarians comprised the Rump Parliament, which remained in office until the restoration of the Long Parliament by General Monck in February 1660.

p. 136, ll. 28–9: *St Edmunds Bury in Suffolk*: Bury St Edmunds, a town in the county of Suffolk.

p. 137, l. 2: grand Council: the Council of State was appointed by the Rump Parliament on 14 February 1649 after the execution of the Charles I, was modified in 1653 on the establishment of the Protectorate, and abolished in April 1660 on the restoration of the monarchy. In constitutional terms, the Council was the executive of the government, taking the place of the king and Privy Council.

p. 137, l. 18: the slip bestowed upon him: hanged.

p. 137, l. 20: *a great Cavalier*: gentlemen who supported the Royalist cause during the Civil War and Interregnum.

p. 137, ll. 22–3: *the County of* Chester: a county-palatine in north-west England, now known as Cheshire, which generally supported the Royalist cause in the Civil War.

p. 137, l. 28: Nantwich: a market town in Cheshire which supported the Parliamentary cause during the Civil War, and which was the site of a major battle on 26 January 1644, when the Royalist siege was broken by the Parliamentary Army under General Thomas Fairfax.

p. 138, l. 8: *Sir* William: Sir William Brereton (1604–61), major general of Cheshire, commander of the Parliamentary forces during the six-week siege of Nantwich (*ODNB*).

p. 138, ll. 15–16: a Muscatier or a Pikeman: kinds of infantry soldiers: a musketeer was a soldier armed with a musket, and a pikeman a soldier armed with a pike (*OED*). Both were used to man the parapets in the defence of towns, acting as sentries or sentinels.

p. 138, ll. 23–4: *Save-guards*: an outer skirt or petticoat worn by women to protect their dress when riding (*OED*).

p. 139, ll. 9–10: Tamberlain was and he was: Timur, the Tartar conqueror (1336–1405), ruler of the Timurid Empire in Central Asia, title character of Marlowe's *Tamberlaine* (1586).

p. 139, l. 28: *H* non est Litera: Latin, translated here as 'H is no letter'. In analysing the length of syllables 'according to the manner of the *Latines*', Thomas Campion 'noted that *h* is no letter', *Observations in the art of English poesie* (London, Richard Field for Andrew Wise, 1602), p. 37.

p. 140, l. 2: heat the Cawdle: a caudle was a warm drink consisting of thin gruel mixed with wine or ale sweetened and spiced, given chiefly to sick people (*OED*).

p. 140, l. 29: *a Crown*: a coin bearing the imprint of a crown, in Britain minted since the reign of Edward VI in silver, and of the value of five shillings (*OED*).

p. 142, ll. 2–3: *a Gossiping at* Limus *near* Ratcliff: for gossiping see above, note to p. 75, col. 2, l. 35. Limehouse and Ratcliff were neighbouring hamlets in Stepney, on the banks of the River Thames, home to substantial communities of mariners and their families (*LE*).

p. 142, l. 5: *an arch Jade*: a contemptuous name for a horse, used as a term of reprobation applied to a woman (*OED*).

p. 142, l. 10: a Tu— in your mouth: a turd in your mouth.

p. 142, l. 11: a pint of Sack: wine, see above, note to p. 39, l. 13.

p. 142, ll. 20–1: *two Modest and Civil* Whetstons-park *Women*: Whetstone Park was a lane lying between Lincoln's Inn and Holborn, notorious for street prostitutes. B. E., *Dictionary of the Canting Crew*: 'Whet-stones-park, a lane betwixt Holborn and Lincolns-Inn-Fields, fam'd for a Nest of Wenches, now de-park'd'.

p. 143, l. 4: a Groat: a coin to the value of four pence, first coined in 1351, that ceased to be issued for circulation in 1662.

p. 143, l. 15: Cut thy Girth: the girth was a belt of leather placed around the body of a horse and drawn tight, so as to secure a saddle (*OED*). Cutting the girth would mean the rider would fall off.

A Bridle for the Tongue: Or, A Curb to Evil discourse

p. 147, ll. 2–4: *a BRIDLE for the TONGUE*: figurative, a restraint, curb or check. An established phrase in Protestant rhetoric: see for example William Gearing, *A Bridle for the Tongue; or A Treatise of ten Sins of the Tongue. Viz. Cursing, Swearing, Slandering, Scoffing, Filthy-speaking, Flattering, Censuring, Murmuring, Lying and Boasting* (London, R. H. for Tho. Parkhurst, 1663), which was issued with the authority of the Bishop of London.

p. 147, l. 10: *With Permission*: under the terms of the Licensing Act 1663, writers were expected to apply for a license for their works to be printed. The unorthodox form of words suggests this text may be ironic or clandestine.

p. 150, ll. 1–6: God ordained Speech ... to Glorify God and to Benefit Mankind: a topic also discussed in the Anglican divine Richard Allestree's *The Government of the Tongue* (Oxford, At the Theater, 1667), pp. 1–6.

p. 150, ll. 12–14: *By our Words we shall be justified, and by our Words we shall be Condemned*: Matthew 12:36, 37.

p. 151, l. 18: Sir Thomas Moore: Sir Thomas More (1478–1535), humanist scholar and Protestant martyr, lord chancellor under Henry VIII (*ODNB*).

p. 151, l. 19: *distick*: two lines of verse which make complete sense in themselves (*OED*).

p. 151, ll. 21–2: *Quisquis amat ... esse sibi*: Latin, translated here as 'Let no man (absent) want a friend / His Name, and Fame, from slander to defend'. More revises St Augustine's well-known motto, recorded in numerous sources, including Caxton's printing of Jacobus de Voragine's *The Golden Legend* (*c.* 1229–98). According to this source, Augustine 'had these versus wreton at his table / Quisquis amat dictis absentum rodere vitam / Hanc mensam veti tam nouerit esse sibi / That is to saye / who so euer loue to missay ony creature that is absent / it may be said / yt this table is denyed to hym'. Caxton, *Legenda aurea sanctorum, sive, Lombardica historia* (London, William Caxton, 1483).

p. 152, l. 2: *Backbiters*: people who slander or traduce someone behind their back.

p. 152, ll. 11–12: *reforming Societies*: the writer proposes the establishment of societies for the reformation of manners, prefiguring those which were established in the 1690s in many cities in Britain. See T. C. Curtis and W. A. Speck, 'The Societies for the Reformation of Manners: a case study in the theory and practise of moral reform', *Literature and History*, 3 (1976), pp. 45–64.

p. 153, l. 1: Pharaoh: name given to all Egyptian kings in the Bible. The historical pharaoh of the Exodus was probably Seti II or Menepthah.

p. 153, l. 2: *Plagues*: Nonconformist divines often noted the bubonic plague of 1665 and the Great Fire of London of 1666.

p. 153, l. 3: Moses: Hebrew prophet who led the Israelites out of Egypt, whose life is recorded in the Torah, revered as a prophet in Judaism, Christianity and Islam.

p. 153, l. 8: *the Red-Sea of Gods wrath*: the sea between Egypt and Arabia, which according to Biblical narrative in Exodus, Moses and his people were able to cross when God divided the sea.

A Satyr Against Coffee

p. 157, l. 5: Satanic Tipple!: the strong drink or liquor of the devil (*OED*).

p. 157, l. 13: *Printing Libels*: A libel is a formal written statement, in civil law the statement by the plaintiff of his allegation or complaint. In the sixteenth century the term came to be used for a pamphlet or broadside posted up or publicly circulated that defamed the character of some specified person. Such libels became common in the Civil War. In 1647 Clarendon wrote that in 1640 'cheap, senseless Libels were scatter'd about the City, and fix'd upon Gates and publick remarkable places, traducing and vilifying Those who were in highest trust and employment', *The History of the Rebellion and Civil Wars in England*, 3 vols (Oxford, At the Theater, 1702), vol. I, p. 113.

p. 157, l. 13: *the Powder-plot*: the Gunpowder Plot of 1605, a conspiracy by a group of disaffected English Catholics to kill King James, his family and the members of the House of Lords by blowing up the Houses of Parliament.

p. 157, l. 18: Vespatian, *who impos'd Excise on Piss*: Caesar Vespasianus Augustus (9 BC–AD 79), Emperor of Rome AD 69–79. Among the many taxes he instituted or reformed was an excise on urine. The tax was levied on the urine that was collected from public urinals by artisans engaged in leather-tanning and cloth manufacture, who made use of the urine as a bleaching and cleansing agent.

p. 157, l. 19: smell of Lucre: a reference to an anecdote concerning Vespasian in Suetonius's *De vita Caesarum*. 'When his sonne Titus seemed to finde fault with him for devising a kinde of tribute, even out of urine: the monie that came unto his hand of the first paiment, hee put unto his sonnes nose: asking withall, *whether he was offended with the smell, or no,* and when he answered *No: and yet* quoth he, *it commeth of Vrine*', in *The historie of tvvelve Caesars emperours of Rom*, trans. by Philemon Holland (London, printed for Matthew Lownes, 1606).

p. 157, l. 20: *the common Sewer*: a drain through which all or a large part of the sewage of a town passes (*OED*).

p. 157, l. 21: *passes theough the Reins with Streams impure*: urine: the reins are the region of the kidneys, the loins (*OED*).

p. 158, l. 2: Malago: a fortified wine from Spain, shipped from Malaga.

p. 158, l. 3: sooty Surges *rise to* Charon's *Ferry*: in Greek mythology, Charon is the ferryman of the dead over the river Acheron.

p. 158, l. 6: the last Shift: the last resource (*OED*).

p. 158, l. 7: Whifflers: a trifler or insignificant fellow (*OED*).

p. 158, l. 8: *Convert your* Powder *into Irish* Snuff': a visual pun on the similarity between coffee powder and Irish snuff. Snuff is a preparation of powdered tobacco for inhaling through the nostrils: the 'Irish' preparation is dry, high roasted and very finely ground. James Howell noted in 1650 that 'The Spaniards and Irish take it most in powder or smutchin and it might-ily refreshes the brain', *Epistolae Ho-elianae: Familiar letters domestic and forren; divided into sundry sections, partly historicall, politicall, philosophi-call, vpon emergent occasions*, 2nd edn, 3 vols (London, printed by W. H. for Humphrey Mosely, 1650), vol. III, p. 12. Howell's term 'smutchin' is an English transliteration of the Irish *smuiteán*, meaning fine ashes or soot.

A dialogue between Tom and Dick, over a dish of coffee, concerning matters of religion and government

p. 163, l. 15: States-men: ironic, one who takes a leading part in the affairs of state (*OED*).

p. 163, l. 17: Petitions: on 7 December 1679 a petition signed by seventeen peers was presented to the King, asking him to recall parliament. This was the first of many petitions organised across the country, for which blank forms were printed, conveniently left in coffee-houses and taverns for men to sign. The petitions were answered by loyal addresses abhorring the petitions, and the years 1679–80 saw a vociferous debate between Petitioners and Abhorrers, a debate in which the terms Whig and Tory were first coined.

p. 164, l. 7: *politick Discourses: &* Further Discoveries: more Popish Plot tracts, typically given titles such as these.

p. 164, l. 13: Will Pryn: William Prynne (1600–69), Puritan pamphleteer and lawyer who wrote the official defence of Parliamentary actions in the Civil War, but was later imprisoned for three years for opposing the execution of the King and the Commonwealth. On the Restoration he was appointed keeper of the records in the Tower of London, where he was charged not only with reforming the organisation of the records, but also with writing a vindication of the privileges of the King's authority (*ODNB*).

p. 165, ll. 20–2: *That talk like* Aristotle ... Foplin: Aristotle (384–22 BC) is one of the two greatest ancient Greek philosophers, with Plato; Seneca (54 BC– AD 39) is one of the two greatest Roman orators, with Cicero; Sir Formal Trifle is a character given to empty oratory in Shadwell's *The Virtuoso*, subsequently noticed in Dryden's *MacFlecknoe* (1682); Sir Foplin is a petty fop, a foolish person interested only in his appearance. Sirs Trifle and Foplin thus fall well short of the classical antecedents.

p. 165, l. 28: Knaves: unprincipled men, given to dishonourable and deceitful practices; base and crafty rogues (*OED*).

p. 166, ll. 4–5: Algate *to* Temple-Bar, *in the City of* Westminster, *Burrow of* Southwark: from one end of the City of London to the other, and the outlying residential areas of Westminster and Southwark. This is closely modelled on the third paragraph of R. L'Estrange, *Citt and Bumpkin. In a Dialogue over a Pot of Ale, Concerning Matters of Religion and Government* (London, Henry Brome, 1680), p. 1. See above, pp. 159–60.

p. 166, ll. 7–8: buzing, *or rather* roreing *and* railing *up and down:* buzzing: whispering and muttering, full of busy talk; roaring: behaving in a riotous way; railing: abusing.

p. 166, ll. 11–13: *our* Gazets *too, our* Pamphlets, *our* Poems, *our* Intelligences, *our* Compendiums, *our* Coffee-tales: forms of printed news dissemination including gazettes (newssheets or periodical publications giving an account of current news), intelligences (newsletters in manuscript or print), compendiums (summaries or epitomes of complicated events such as the Popish Plot allegations) and coffee-tales (unregulated and unreliable news distributed in coffee-houses) (*OED*).

p. 166, l. 30: Sectaries: an adherent of a schismatic or extremist religious sect, most often referring to Protestant Dissenters (*OED*). Thomas Blount, *Glossographia* (London, Scolar Press, 1656): 'Sectary, one that follows private opinion in Religion, a Ring-leader of a Sect, a seditious, factious person'.

p. 167, l. 26: *Strangely*: gothic type was widely used to emphasise warnings and obscure prognostications in documents related to the Popish Plot.

p. 167, ll. 31–3: *He makes use of* ... Fire: a reference to the tale of a monkey belonging to Pope Julius II (1503–13) who used the foot or paw of a cat to rake roasted chestnuts out of the burning coals. *Notes and Queries*, 4:7 (1885), p. 286.

p. 168, ll. 9–10: *Narratives of* Dragons, Prodigies *and Strange Sights*: a reference to the large number of printed tracts interpreting extraordinary natural occurrences (such as meteorological phenomena or freakish births) as omens from which portents or prophecies could be drawn. An example is *Strange and wonderful news from Bull-and-Mouth-Street:, or, A faithful and true account how a child of five days old was heard to speak several words distinctly, and with a loud and manly voice; on Friday the 21 of this instant June, 1678* (London, printed for D. M., 1678).

p. 168, l. 28: Roysters, *the* God-dam-mees, *the* Jesters, *the* Fidlers: varieties of public behaviour: a roister (a swaggering or blustering bully); a God-damme (one who is addicted to swearing, applied by Puritans to Cavaliers); a jester (a mimic or buffoon); a fiddler (one who plays the fiddle, by extension, a trifler).

p. 168, l. 30: Hectors, *the* Bullies: a hector, a bully or braggart; bully, a blustering gallant, a bravo.

p. 168, ll. 31–2: *the* Court of Requests, *and* Westminster-hall: The Court of Requests in London offered jurisdiction for debts under forty shillings. Westminster Hall was a large hall erected in 1097 in the Palace of Westminster, primarily used in this period for judicial purposes, housing a number of important courts, including the Court of King's Bench, the Court of Common Pleas and the Court of Chancery.

p. 171, l. 24: Tun *at* Helderburgh: an extremely large cask or wine barrel used for storing wine at Heidelberg castle.

p. 173, l. 1: ô Brazell: Brazil, a large Portuguese colony in South America. See above, note to p. 90, l. 19.

p. 173, l. 2: *Rosicratians*: Rosicrucians, a secret religious order associated with the symbol of the Rosy Cross, which re-emerged in the early seventeenth century in a series of publications using obscure alchemical and mystical language to discuss moral and religious reform.

p. 173, l. 21: Seraphick Franciscan, *or a* Mouthing Dominican: the seraphic or exalted devotion of the Franciscan order of Catholic monks (the Order of Friars Minor), the pompous speech characteristic of the Dominican order of Catholic monks (the Dominicans or Order of Preachers had a mission to preach in vernacular languages in cities).

p. 173, ll. 29–30: Ship Stocking *Priests*: Nonconformist priests who wear short stockings or socks (known as slip-stockings). John Eachard's *The grounds & occasions of the contempt of the clergy and religion enquired into* (London, printed by E. Tyler and R. Holt for Nathaniel Brooke, 1672) narrates an anecdote of a clergyman who sermonized on the difficulty of taking off his slip stocking, as an example of how low or vulgar topics breed contempt for the clergy (pp. 70–4).

p. 174, l. 6: *Wanscote*: to wainscot, to line a wall with panel-work of wood (*OED*).

p. 174, ll. 10–11: *what* David *the* King *says*; The fool hath said in his heart there is no God: Psalm 14:1.

p. 174, ll. 30–1: toties quoties: Latin phrase, 'as often as', repeatable. The Catholic Church offered Toties-Quoties Indulgences, obtainable as often as desired.

p. 175, l. 8: Puther: dialect form of pother, a commotion, disturbance , or tumult (*OED*).

p. 176, l. 10: Godfrying: Sir Edmund Berry Godfrey (1621–78), magistrate. Godfrey was the magistrate who took the first depositions from Israel Tonge and Titus Oates concerning the Popish Plot. The discovery of the murder of Godfrey on 17 October 1678 near Primrose Hill was widely ascribed to papist assassins, although what purpose this would serve was not clear, and Royalist apologists later suggested he had committed suicide. The controversy occasioned by his murder and the subsequent enquiry did much to advertise the Popish Plot conspiracy: Godfreying (not in *OED*) is thus a term for fanning the flames of scandal (*ODNB*).

p. 176, ll. 23–4: *to take a* Dance *with* COLEMAN *at* Tyburn: Edward Coleman (1636–78), was a courtier and Catholic convert who was prominent in the Duke of York's (the future James II) circle. When his secret negotiations between the Duke's interests and French authorities were exposed in the enquiry following Titus Oates's allegations, they gave the best evidence that there was a Catholic plot against the King. Coleman was tried for treason at the King's Bench on 27 November, and executed at Tyburn on 3 December, amidst considerable tumult (*ODNB*).

p. 177 onwards: page numbers are given incorrectly in the original after p. 14, although text appears to be continuous (simply omitting page numbers fifteen and sixteen).

p. 178, l. 11: Bragadocio: a braggart, an empty or pretentious bragger.

p. 179, ll. 6–26: *First, Asperse boldly ... merit Pennance*: The list of the Citt's 'memorials' (memorandums) in Dick's commonplace book is an exaggerated and hostile account of Catholic practices of grace and Papal indulgence.

p. 179, ll. 30–1: Pater-Noster *or* Ave-Maria: the Lord's Prayer (Matthew 6:9–13) and the Hail Mary, a traditional Catholic prayer to Mary, mother of Jesus.

p. 181, l. 9: Fat-Gut Harry *the 8*th: Henry VIII (1491–1547), King of England and Ireland (1509–47). His characteristically large girth was widely used an emblem of his defence of national and protestant interests.

p. 181, l. 12: Oates, Bedloe, Dangerfield: the three principal men who made allegations concerning the Popish Plot: Titus Oates (1649–1705), William Bedloe (1650–80) and Thomas Dangerfield (1654–85). Whatever truth lay behind their Popish Plot allegations, all three informants were criminals, adventurers and frauds.

p. 182, ll. 3–4: Acts of Oblivion: The Act of Indemnity and Oblivion, which became law on 29 August 1660, restricting punishment for any actions that occurred during the Civil War and Interregnum to the regicides.

p. 182, l. 17: Company *of* Olivarians: the followers of Oliver Cromwell.

p. 184, l. 13: Reformed Lawn-Sleeves: sleeves made from lawn, a sheer cloth of linen or cotton, as worn by Anglican bishops when sitting in the House of Lords.

p. 186, l. 17: *Seven* Vials: Revelations 17:1: 'And there came one of the seven angels which had the seven vials, and talked with me, saying unto me, Come hither; I will shew unto thee the judgement of the great whore that sitteth upon many waters'. The Biblical prophecy of the decline and fall of Babylon in the Book of Revelations begins with seven angels carrying seven vials or cups, bringing seven plagues or disasters. The image was widely adapted in millennial prophecy.

p. 186, l. 20: Muskadine: a sweet wine made from Muscat grapes.

p. 188, l. 5: Lucian: Lucian of Samosata (AD 120–80), Greek rhetorician and satirist.

p. 188, ll. 20–1: *caress'd him just as* Joab *did* Abner: 2 Samuel 3. Joab killed Abner by smiting him under the fifth rib, motivated by revenge.

p. 188, l. 26: Man's Coffe-House: Man's Coffee-house, off Charing Cross near Scotland Yard, later known as Old Man's Coffee-house, established by a Scot, Alexander Man, *c.* 1666. After the withdrawal of the Proclamation of 23 December 1675 for the suppression of coffee-houses (see Volume 4, pp. 89–101), Man was reported to be the first to obtain permission from the crown to continue trading (many coffee-men ignored the requirement) and, as a result, the business was also known as the Royal Coffee-House. (Lillywhite 778).

p. 188, ll. 26–7: St. *Omerian* Companions: the College of St Omer, in St Omer in Artois, France, was the main institution for the education of lay English Catholics between 1594 and 1793, following Elizabeth I's outlawing of Catholic education in England.

p. 189, l. 23: Gaderine Swine: in the miracle of the Gadarene swine, Jesus performed an exorcism on a group of men possessed by evil spirits by transferring the demons to a herd of swine. The pigs then ran over a cliff into the sea, where they perished. Matthew 8:28–33.

p. 193, ll. 1–2: *Three Estates*: the three divisions of parliament, comprising the Lords Temporal (the peerage), the Lords Spiritual (archbishops and bishops), who meet in the House of Lords, and the Commons.

p. 193, l. 20: Prerogative: that special legal pre-eminence the king has in virtue of his regal state over ordinary persons: a body of customary authority, privilege and immunity recognised by the common law. An account of the prerogative occupies a whole chapter of Locke, *Two Treatises on Government* (London, printed for Awnsham Churchill, 1690), bk 2, ch. 14.

At Amsterdamnable-Coffee-House On the 5th of November next, will be Exposed to publick Sale these Goods following

p. 199, l. 4: *5th. of* November *next*: 5 November was the day on which the Powder Plot (the Catholic plot led by Guy Fawkes to murder the entire government by blowing up the Houses of Parliament) was commemorated. This was a notoriously riotous Whig celebration in which Catholics were burnt in effigy (especially the Pope).

p. 199, l. 6: *D. of* M*s.*: James Scott, Duke of Monmouth (1649–85), the illegitimate eldest son of Charles II, commander of the army, and the main rival of the Duke of York for the throne. During the Exclusion Crisis, Monmouth was a rallying point for the Exclusionists or Whigs, as he was the most obvious Protestant candidate for the succession. Many claims were advanced proving that he was a legitimate heir through a secret marriage, or could be made legitimate by the King, or Parliament. Monmouth was executed in 1685 after the failure of his rebellion of that year (*ODNB*). He was not an intellectual, so the idea of three volumes describing his political views is ironic.

p. 199, l. 10: Hobbs Leviathan: Thomas Hobbes (1588–1679), philosopher. His *Leviathan* became the most famous defence in political philosophy for legitimacy of the English republic. See also above, note to p. 88, l. 40.

p. 199, ll. 10–11: *the late E of S in his Retirements*: Anthony Ashley Cooper, 1st Earl of Shaftesbury (1621–83), one of the leaders of the Country Party (Whigs) in the Exclusion Crisis. In 1682 Shaftesbury was actively plotting against the Yorkist succession, determining to raise a rebellion to summon parliament to determine the succession. On 28 September 1682 Shaftesbury went into hiding in London, to escape judicial persecution by the newly elected Tory sheriffs, and in November he went into exile in Holland. In Amsterdam he became ill, and died there on 21 January 1683 (*ODNB*). The form of words used here suggests that the broadsheet was published at some time between late September, when he went into hiding, and 5 November 1682.

p. 199, l. 19: *Sir Tho. Armstrongs*: Sir Thomas Armstrong (1633–84), an army officer closely associated with the Duke of Monmouth. Elected MP for Stafford in March 1679 and again in the 1681 Oxford Parliament, Armstrong was active in organising against the Duke of York's succession. He was executed in 1684 for his role in the Rye House plot.

p. 199, l. 20: *the Mobile*: the mob, the rabble, the common people, short for the Latin phrase *mobile vulgus* (*OED*).

p. 199, l. 22: *Winding Hornes*: a horn making a sound; to wind the horn means to blow a blast on the horn (*OED*).

p. 199, l. 22: *K. of* Poland: John (Jan) III Sobieski (1629–96), King of Poland (1674–96). Since 1680 at least, Shaftesbury was known in Court satires as the King of Poland (in reference to his imagined support of an elective monarchy like that of Poland); see, for example, *A modest vindication of the Earl of S—y in a letter to a friend concerning his being elected King of Poland* (London, printed for Smith Bookseller in Chief to His Majesty Elect of Poland, 1681).

p. 199, l. 23: *M. Gray, Russel*: Ford Grey, Baron Grey of Warke (1655–1701) and William 'the Martyr' Russell, Lord Russell (1639–83). Both were central members of the Shaftesbury and Buckingham circle in the Exclusion crisis, supporting Monmouth's claim to the throne. Lord Russell was executed for his role in the Rye House Plot in 1683. After the 1685 Monmouth rebellion, Grey evaded punishment by testifying against his party.

p. 199, l. 30: *Sir W. W.*: identified as 'Sr: Wm Waller' in BL Sloane MS 1009, fols 142v–143r; for which see above, p. 198. Sir William Waller (*c.* 1639–99), a London magistrate notorious for his zealous pursuit of Catholics, including seizing property owned by Catholics in London. He was closely involved in the judicial enquiries into the Popish Plot allegations. In late 1682 he had fled into exile in Amsterdam.

p. 199, ll. 31–2: *the spawn of the Old Rump*: republicans and Nonconformists, associated with the Rump Parliament, the Puritan remnant of the Long Parliament which ruled 1648–53 and 1659.

p. 199, l. 33: *The Noble Peer's Speech, the Appeal, the Raree Show*: titles of Protestant pamphlets. Shaftesbury's *The Speech of a Noble Peer* (London, printed for F. S., 1681), John Nalson's *The True Protestant's Appeal to the City and the Country* (London, printed for J. B., 1681) and Stephen Colledge's *The Raree Show or the True Protestant's Procession* (London, printed for A. B., 1681).

p. 199, l. 34: *Seditious Libels, by C.C.*: a reference to publishers of Protestant pamphlets. The list is more explicit in the manuscript version (see above, p. 198) which refers to 'new loyall Libells by Carr Curtis Janeway Vile Baldwin and the rest of the loyall Protestant Pamphletteers'. These publishers are Henry Care (or Carr), Langley Curtis, Richard Janeway and Richard Baldwin (Vile is untraced). Their publishing activities are described in Mark Knight, *Politics and Opinion in Crisis, 1678–81* (Cambridge, Cambridge University Press, 1994), pp. 159–61.

p. 200, l. 3: *Two narrative Sham-plots of* Tapskies *own invention*: both factions traded accusations that the plots they discovered were fraudulent, describing them as sham-plots. Tapski or Potapski was a further Tory nickname for Shaftesbury, in reference to his earlier nickname of the King of Poland, current from 1681, perhaps as a wordplay on Jan III Sobieski. See Thomas D'Urfey's *Scandalum magnatum, or, Potapski's case a satyr against Polish oppression* (London, printed for J. Hindmarsh, 1682).

p. 200, l. 9: *Protestant Flails*: a weapon consisting of a short staff loaded with lead attached to the wrist by a strap, carried during the Popish Plot by persons who professed to be in fear of murderous assaults by Papists (*OED*).

p. 200, l. 13: *Two models of the Association, from the Cabal*: plans for a Protestant Association, which would bind members to protect the King's life and prevent James or any Papist from the succession, were raised repeatedly during the Exclusion Crisis, including in Parliament in 1680. During Shaftesbury's trial in 1682, a plan for an Association that had been allegedly found in Shaftesbury's closet was cited as evidence of his treason. The jury assessing this evidence brought their verdict of Ignoramus: that there was insufficient evidence for the trial to proceed; see K. H. D. Haley, *The First Earl of Shaftesbury* (Oxford, Clarendon Press, 1968), pp. 675–83. BL Sloane MS 1009, fol. 143r has 'Colchester Cabal'.

p. 200, l. 16: *Ells*: a measure of length, in England equal to 45 inches (*OED*).

p. 200, l. 16: *the Covenant*: Scottish Presbyterians adhered to their religious beliefs and ecclesiastical polity as articulated in a covenant or bond of agreement. The Solemn League and Covenant, signed in 1643, formed a military and religious alliance between Parliament and the Scottish Presbyterians. The Covenant was declared unlawful after the Restoration, and had to be formally abjured by all persons holding public office.

p. 200, l. 25: Be. *Dr. B. the Author of* Julian *the Apostate, the Ignoramus Dr.*: In BL Sloane 1009, fol. 143v this is given more fully as 'Amongst whom is Shts—bry, B—hm Sheriff Bethel th'Author of the Popish Successor & Julian th'Apostate, Doctr Burnet & th'Ignoramus Docteur'. These are the leaders of the Whig party. Samuel Johnson (1649–1703), Church of England clergyman and pamphleteer, was the author of *Julian the Apostate* (London, printed for Langley Curtis, 1682), a sensational political treatise attacking the Duke of York's succession, and arguing that the English could legitimately resist a popish prince. George Hickes (1642–1715) said that this tract was 'the pocket-book of all the party, carried to coffee-houses in triumph', for which see his *Jovian, or an answer to Julian the Apostate*

(London, Sam Roycroft for Walter Kettilby, 1683), p. 3. The Ignoramus Dr is untraced, but probably refers to a City magistrate who returned a bill of ignoramus on Court prosecutions of Shaftesbury and the Exclusionist party (when a bill of indictment was found to be unsupported by the evidence, it was endorsed 'ignoramus' on the reverse).

p. 200, l. 32: *Goodenough*: Richard Goodenough (fl. 1671–87), a Whig lawyer, at this time active in Shaftesbury's circle, engaged in defending Whig interests in court through his role of under-sheriff in London and Middlesex. In 1683 he was among the conspirators of the Rye House Plot to kill the King, and an important member of the Duke of Monmouth's party, acting as paymaster in the 1685 Rebellion (*ODNB*). The gothic type advertises his conspiratorial nature.

p. 200, ll. 34–5: The true Protestant Translator: a satirical title, referring to the allegations repeatedly made in Tory satires, that Titus Oates had converted to the Catholic Church in the early 1670s and then reconverted to the Protestant faith.

p. 200, l. 40: *Whiggs and Covenanters*: the term Whig emerged during the Exclusion Crisis as an abusive term for those who opposed the succession of James Duke of York, and became the name of one of the two dominant political parties of the long eighteenth century. Covenanters were adherants to the Solemn League and Covenant (see above, note to p. 200, l. 16).

J. C. B. [Aphra Behn?], *Rebellions antidote: or A Dialogue between coffee and tea*

p. 203, col. 1, ll. 17–8: Dido ... Æneas: Dido was the founder and queen of Carthage, who (in Virgil's *Aeneid*) fell in love with Aeneas when he visited Carthage. At the end of Book One, Dido commands Aeneas to relate his history, which he does over the following two books. When Aeneas departed Carthage to continue his quest, she killed herself on a funeral pyre: and subsequently her shadow spurned him in the underworld.

p. 203, col. 2, l. 6: Sham-ploting: the invention or publication of false conspiracies against the king or state.

p. 203, col. 2, l. 15: *Dish of* Twist: a slang or cant term for a beverage consisting of a mixture of two liquors or ingredients, as tea and coffee, gin and brandy (*OED*). B. E., *Dictionary of the Canting Crew*: 'Twist, half Tea, half Coffee'.

p. 203, col. 2, l. 16: *hit the Pin*: hit the target (a pin is a peg or nail in the centre of a target).

p. 203, col. 2, l. 17: *reverse the* Alewives *Oacen*: the flood of beer retailed by the alewives ('oacen' is a typographical error for ocean).

p. 203, col. 2, l. 18: Bacchus: the Roman god of wine.

p. 203, col. 2, l. 23: Acrostick: a short poem in which the initial letters of the lines, taken in order, spell a word or phrase (*OED*).

p. 203, col. 2, l. 25: *Obsequiens*: obsequious, compliant to the will of another.

p. 203, col. 2, l. 27: *Farthings four*: four quarter-pennies, hence a penny, the typical cost of a dish of coffee.

p. 203, col. 2, l. 28: *Enable all your mene*: In the seventeenth century 'mene' meant the main subject, the chief matter at hand (*OED*).

p. 203, col. 2, l. 33: *This may be printed*. R.L.S. 1685: licensed by Roger L'Estrange in 1685 according to the Licensing Act.

The School of Politicks: or, The Humours of a Coffee-House. A Poem

p. 207, l. 9: Tantúmne ... *Terent*: Publius Terentius Afer, known as Terence (fl. 170–159 BC), Roman comic playwright. The quote is from *Heauton Timoroumenos* (The Self-Tormentor), I.ii, written in 163 BC and translated in Burton's *Anatomy of Melancholy* (Oxford, L. Lichfield and W. Turner for H. Cripps, 1638) as 'have I so much leisure, or little business of mine own, as to look after other men's matters which concern me not? What have I to do with physic?'

p. 210, l. 7: Pluto: the Roman god of the underworld.

p. 211, l. 3: State-Conventicle: see above, note to p. 85, l. 5.

p. 211, l. 6: Babel: the city called Babylon by the Greeks, where according to Genesis 11:1–9 a great tower was built whose top was intended to reach to heaven. The plan failed when God confounded the languages of those building it, so they could not understand each other.

p. 211, l. 21: *affairs beyond the* Line: the merchant discusses affairs beyond the equinoctial line (the equator), such as events in the Cape or South America. The phrase is often used allusively for any distant colony over the sea.

p. 211, l. 23: Poetick Tom: untraced quack doctor, who advertised the efficacy of his pills.

p. 212, ll. 3–4: Lawyers *and* Clients, Sharpers *and their* Cullies, Quakers, Pimps, Atheists, Mountebanks *and* Bullies: a list of the miscellaneous people drawn to the coffee-house. Sharper, cheat, swindler, rogue; cully, one who is imposed upon or cheated; the pimp, a procurer who provides means and opportunities for prostitution; the mountebank, an itinerant medical charlatan and the bully, a blustering gallant.

p. 212, l. 8: Lilbourn: John Lilburne (1615–57), a leader of the Levellers during the Civil War. In the words of Richard Overton, Levellers believed that 'by natural birth all men are equally and alike borne to like propriety, liberty and freedom', and pressed for universal male suffrage, annual elections and complete religious freedom. Richard Overton, *An Arrow against all Tyrants and Tyranny* (London, Martin Claw-Clergy, 1646), p. 3.

p. 212, l. 9: Hotch-potch: in cookery, a dish containing a mixture of many ingredients; figuratively, a medly, confused assemblage (*OED*).

p. 212, ll. 22–3: *The* quick-eye'd … Popery: a sectary is an adherent of a schismatic sect, commonly applied to English Dissenters. Sleeves of lawn (a kind of fine linen cloth) formed part of the episcopal dress, and were used figuratively to appeal to Anglican bishops and their influence. Here the Dissenter argues that High-Church Anglicans were too close to Catholic forms of worship.

p. 213, l. 3: Close-stool: a chamber pot enclosed in a stool or box (*OED*).

p. 213, l. 5: Purge: a medical treatment which purges the body of ill humours, such as an emetic.

p. 213, ll. 25–6: Of *Sligo*, … and *Dundalk*: Irish locations, battles and sieges associated with King William's Irish campaign of 1689. Sligo was captured by the Jacobite army in October 1689; Ballyshannon, in Donegal at the mouth of the Erne, was attacked on 7 May 1689; Carrickfergus was captured by the Williamite army under Schomberg in August 1689; Dundalk, in Louth, was where the two armies halted less than half a mile apart for two weeks in September and October 1689 without joining battle. See J. G. Simms, *Jacobite Ireland 1685–91* (London, Routledge & Kegan Paul, 1969), pp. 123–35.

p. 214, l. 2: *Siege of* London-derry: Derry, or Londonderry as it was known to the Williamite forces, was invested by a Catholic army under the Earl of Antrim on 7 December 1688, and survived 105 days under bombardment. The Irish besiegers were joined by King James and his army on 18 April 1689, and the city was finally relieved by English ships on 28 July 1689. See Simms, *Jacobite Ireland,* pp. 95–113.

p. 214, l. 6: *Flanders*: in 1690 British forces joined the campaign of the League of Augsburg against the French in the Spanish Netherlands.

p. 215, l. 11 : *late* dreadfull Storm: the great storm of 12 January 1689. See *A True account of the great damages done by the late storm which happened between the hours of twelve and four of the clock on Sunday morning, January the 12th, 1689* (London, printed for W. F., 1689).

p. 215, l. 17: Noll th'Usurper: Oliver Cromwell died on 3 September 1658, on the same night as a storm caused considerable destruction. The twinned events were widely read as complementary. See for example Edmund Waller's *Upon the late storme, and of the death of His Highnesse ensuing the same* (London, printed for H. H., 1658).

p. 216, l. 5: the *Devil's Drop*: the remains of the second Roman lighthouse at Dover Castle, which was known as the 'Devil's Drop of Mortar'.

p. 216, l. 8: School-boy's *Gig*: a whipping top (*OED*).

p. 217, ll. 22–3: *Heads ... Hall*: the heads of those executed for treason were displayed on iron spikes over the door of Westminster Hall. The heads of the regicides executed in 1660 (and that supposed to be Cromwell's) remained for more than two decades.

p. 217, l. 25–p. 218, l. 1: the *Horse ... Stocks Market*: the equestrian statue to Charles II erected by Sir Robert Vyner. The statue was remodelled from an unfinished statue of Jan Sobieski, King of Poland, trampling on a Turk, in celebration of his relief of Vienna in 1683. Vyner had the head of Sobieski changed to resemble Charles II, and the head of the Turk that of Oliver Cromwell. The effect was not only ridiculous and sycophantic, but also historically inaccurate.

p. 219, l. 7: *Wittal*: a wittol, a man who is aware of and complaisant about the infidelity of his wife, a contented cuckold (*OED*).

p. 219, l. 15: *Whitson Ale* or *Christmas Liquor*: celebratory drinks brewed for holiday festivities, as at Whitsun (the seventh Sunday after Easter) and Christmas.

p. 219, ll. 24–5: Emperour ... *Alliance*: Emperor Leopold I (1640–1705), elected Holy Roman Emperor in 1658, King of Hungary and Bohemia. In 1686 he formed the League of Augsburg to defend the Palatinate from French aggression. In 1689, after Britain under King William joined, the league became known the Grand Alliance.

p. 220, l. 12: St. *Peter's Chair*: the Pope, the supreme head of the Roman catholic Church, beginning with Saint Peter, Bishop of Rome (d. AD 69). One of the trappings of the Papacy was the Papal throne or *sedia gestatoria*, a throne carried by twelve footmen in red uniforms.

p. 220, l. 15: *great Mogul*: the Sultan, absolute ruler of the Ottoman Empire.

p. 220, l. 19: the *Gazette*: *The London Gazette* was the official newspaper of record, published by the government through the secretary of state's Letter Office. Established in November 1665 as *The Oxford Gazette*, it was renamed *The London Gazette* in February 1666. It disseminated official news only, which is to say, intelligence was certified as official when it appeared in *The Gazette*.

p. 220, l. 21: *Jonathan's*: Jonathan's Coffee-house, established by Jonathan Miles around 1680, on the east side of Exchange Alley between Cornhill and Lombard Street, where it quickly established itself as a rival to Garraway's, and became a centre for stock-jobbers and the nascent insurance business (Lillywhite 656).

p. 221, l. 1: *Books* sold at *Tom's* by *Auction*: Tom's Coffee-house in Pope's Head Alley, running between Cornhill and Lombard Street, was the site of numerous auctions of books and paintings from 1687. See for example *Bibliotheca Maynardiana, sive, Catalogus variorum librorum bibliothecae selectissimae Rev. Viri D. Maynard, de Mayfield in comitatu Sussexiae quorum auctio habe-*

bitur Londini, loco vulgò dicto Tom's Coffee-house in Popes-head Alley, over against the Royal Exchange in Cornhill, June 13, 1687 (London, 1687).

p. 221, ll. 10–14: Francfort, March 29 ... Philipsburg: *The London Gazette*, 2545, 3 April 1690. Frankfurt am Main was a town on the river Main in Hesse (now in Germany); Philippsburg was a small town near Karlsruhe, in the Palatinate Bishopric of Speyer (Spires), now in Baden-Württemberg in Germany.

p. 222, l. 16: close Caball: a secret or private meeting, especially of conspirators or of a faction (*OED*).

p. 222, l. 21: *murmuring* Israelites: a Biblical phrase (for example Numbers 11:3; Deuteronomy 9:22) referring to the people Moses led out of Egypt.

p. 223, ll. 20–1: A lusty ... *Toby*: a bona-roba is a wench, a showy wanton (from the Italian, buonaroba, good stuff or dress); toby, the buttocks or posterior (*OED*).

p. 224, l. 15: *Usquebaugh*: whisky (derived from the Irish and Scottish Gaelic *uisge beatha*, the water of life or *aqua-vitae*) (*OED*).

p. 224, l. 16: *Lill' bullero*: the Lilli-burlero is part of the refrain (without meaning) of a song ridiculing the Irish, made popular from 1688 in ballads and songs associated with the Protestant forces under William. The tune is named after the third line, 'Lilli burlero, bullen a la', of the song first published in 1688: *A New Song* (London, n.p., 1688). The Irish writer Brendan Behan has claimed that the line was a corruption of the Gaelic 'An lili ba leir é, ba linn an lá', which translates roughly as 'The lily won the day for us'. See also, for example, *The False-hearted Glover, or, Fool and knave well fitted to the tune of Lilli burlero* (London, printed for P. Brooksby, J. Deacon, J. Blare, J. Back, 1688).

p. 224, l. 18: *Dum spiro spero*: Latin phrase, 'While I breathe, I hope'.

p. 224, l. 22: *Cham* of *Tartary*: the Cham or Khan of Tartary (Chinese central Asia).

p. 224, l. 23: fuddling *Cap*: a hat worn for drinking bouts; by extension, a way of referring to the act of getting drunk.

p. 225, ll. 1–2: *Drawers ... Corps du Guard*: waiters (drawers) will serve as my bodyguard (corps du guard).

p. 225, l. 4: *Link-boy*: a boy hired to carry a link or flaming torch to light passengers along the streets at night (*OED*).

p. 225, l. 6: *Privy Counsellours*: members of the Privy Council, the body that advises the monarch.

p. 226, ll. 13–22: *Papists ... amiss?*: The Dissenter blames a secret Jesuit plot for the execution of Charles I.

p. 229, l. 2: Great News from Ireland: news of the war between the Jacobite army and William's forces. There was no fighting in the winter and spring months of 1690, until the battle of Boyne in July 1690.

p. 229, l. 10: The *Bay of Biscay*: an arm of the North Atlantic Ocean that lies along the western coast of France and the north coast of Spain.

p. 229, l. 12: *K. J—'s Men*: the Jacobite army in Ireland was commanded by the deposed King James, who arrived in Kinsale on 12 March 1689.

p. 229, l. 25: my Dish of *Coffee* in your Face: not all coffee-house discussions were amicable and polite. This is perhaps a reference to the celebrated scuffle between Titus Oates and another gentleman in the Amsterdam coffee-house in July 1683, which concluded with Oates receiving a dish of coffee in his face (*CPSD*, 1 July–31 December 1683, pp. 351–2). See also the illustration 'The Coffehous Mob' in Ned Ward's *Vulgus Britannicus, or the British Hudibras*, above, p. 298.

p. 230, l. 3: *Glass of* Mum: wheat beer, see above, note to p. 57, col. 3, ll. 7–8.

p. 230, l. 4: Perriwig *and Point* Cravat: fashionable items of men's dress: a wig and an ornamental lace or linen scarf.

p. 230, l. 9: Garniture: ornamental trimming added to dress (*OED*).

p. 230, l. 11: *The Votes are come*: referring to the election of 1690. William III dissolved Parliament on 7 February 1690, and called for an election for a new Parliament to meet again on 20 March 1690.

p. 230, l. 21: Licens'd *Bread* and *Cheese*: referring to the debates on proposals to extend the excise to quotidien goods and commodities. The war in Ireland, and later in France, required a vast increase in Crown expenditure, which was funded by large votes of parliamentary supply. Many proposals were made by the Treasury to extend the range of excisable goods, although they were rejected by the House of Commons. Nonetheless, the existing excise on beer, ale and other liquors (including coffee) was doubled in 1690. See Peter Dickson, *The Financial Revolution in England, 1688–1756* (London, Macmillan, 1967), pp. 46–7.

p. 230, l. 26: *Royal Aid*: a pecuniary grant in aid; a grant of a subsidy or tax to the king for an extraordinary purpose (*OED*).

p. 231, l. 23: Bevii *cockt*: a hat made of beaver fur, worn cocked with a pronounced upward turn.

p. 232, l. 1: *Ev'ning's Frolick at the* Rose: the Rose Tavern, in Russell Street, Covent Garden. From its proximity to the theatres, it was much patronized by playgoers, and at night had the reputation of being a wild and dissolute house of entertainment (*LE*).

The Art of Getting Money by Double-Fac'd Wagers

p. 235, l. 4: *Double-Fac'd WAGERS*: a wager in which different results are predicted with different people, similar to the concurrent term to hedge, which means to secure oneself against a loss on a bet by making transactions on the other side so as to compensate more or less for possible loss on the first (*OED*).

p. 235, l. 6: *Cross and Pile*: heads and tails, so named from the cross or face of a coin, adorned with the royal effigy, and the pile, so named because it was on the pile side of the minting apparatus (*OED*).

p. 235, l. 6: *MONS*: the capital of the County of Hainaut, known as Bergen in Dutch, now in Belgium, and then part of the Spanish Netherlands. The city was an important fortress on the road to Brussels, garrisoned by Spanish troops under the Prince de Berghes.

p. 235, l. 8: Sharper *of the Town*: a cheat, swindler or rogue (*OED*). B. E., *Dictionary of the Canting Crew*, 'a Cheat, one that Lives by his Witts'.

p. 235, l. 9: *Jonathan's Coffe-House*: see above, note to p. 220, l. 21.

p. 235, l. 10: *Parturiant MONTES Nascitur ridiculus Mus*: Latin, Horace, *Ars Poetica*, l. 139, properly 'Parturient montes nascitur ridiculus mus': 'The mountains are in labor, and a ridiculous mouse is born'. See also above, note to p. 79, col. 2, l. 28.

p. 235, l. 12: Gentleman *in the* Band: a falling collar consisting of two strips hanging down in front, part of a conventional dress, especially clerical or legal. The citizen is presumably a lawyer.

p. 235, l. 14: *the* Presence: ceremonial attendance upon the king at Court, at the Presence-Chamber. The courtier has returned from Westminster bringing fresh news from the campaign in Flanders.

p. 235, l. 19: Pacolet's Flying Horse: a renowned flying horse owned by the enchanter Pacolet in the medieval romance *Valentine and Orson*, first printed in Lyon in 1489, but popular in English in a translation by Henry Watson *c.* 1550. The romance was frequently published in London in the late seventeenth century, with editions in 1683, 1688 and 1690, for example.

p. 235, l. 28: *a* little dipt: dipped, involved in debt (*OED*), here engaged in a wager or bet.

p. 236, ll. 1–2: *the Prince* De Bergue, *the Governour of the* Town: Phillipe François de Glimes, Prince de Berghes (1650–1704), governor of Hainaut.

p. 236, l. 4: Plimouth: Plymouth, a city in Devon in the south-west of England, an important port for the navy.

p. 236, l. 6: Opus *&* Usus: Latin phrase, 'work and experience'.

p. 236, l. 8: *the* Groom Porters: the Groom Porters were officers of the Royal Household, abolished under George III, whose principal functions were to regulate all matters connected with gambling within the precincts of the Court (*OED*).

p. 236, l. 9: Guineas: English gold coins, each to the value of 20 shillings, struck between 1663 and 1813 for the Company of Royal Adventurers of England Trading with Africa, made of such high quality African gold (11/12 fineness) that it circulated at 21 or 22 shillings value.

p. 236, ll. 15–16: *ten hard pieces of* Old Barbary Gold, *with the* Royal Effigies *upon them*: guineas. Ten guineas were worth ten pounds ten shillings. On the face of the guinea was an effigy of Charles II and an elephant.

p. 236, l. 24: *the* Gazett: *The London Gazette*. See above, note to p. 220, l. 19.

p. 36, l. 25: *little* Netherlandish Town, *not so big as* Rumford: that is, Mons. Romford was a small market town in Essex on the road from London to Colchester.

p. 236, l. 28: *Sparks*: a young man of an elegant or foppish character. (*OED*) B. E., *Dictionary of the Canting Crew*, 'a spruce, trim, gay Fellow'.

p. 237, l. 9: *since* Tuesday *the 31*st *of* March: Mons had capitulated on 29 March 1691. On 31 March a London newsletter commented that there was 'no certain news as yet from Mons, only the whole Court and town conclude it is in the French possession' (*CSPD*, May 1690–October 1691, p. 325). Contrary reports that Mons had been relieved by William III's army were still being received in London on 4 April and 7 April (*CSPD*, May, 1690–October 1691, pp. 329, 331), but *The London Gazette*, 2650, Thursday 2 April–Monday 6 April first reported the event on 6 April.

p. 237, l. 27: Myn heer Van Pickleherring: a Dutch gentleman, so named for the popularity of pickled herring in the Netherlands. Pickleherring was a humorous character in popular plays in Germany and Holland, known as 'Pickelhärings-spiele' (*OED*).

p. 237, l. 30: Northampton: a market town 60 miles north of London in Northamptonshire, destroyed by fire in 1675.

p. 237, l. 37: Whore of Babylon: an allegorical figure of supreme evil, mentioned in Revelations 17:1–2. Protestants used the phrase to refer contemptuously to the Roman Catholic Church from the Reformation onwards.

p. 237, l. 39: Bilboa Fleet: a convoy of ships supposedly trading with the Spanish city of Bilbao, although such ships were often conducting a clandestine trade with France using ports in the south of France.

p. 237, l. 42: *the* Peke *of* Tenariff: the mountain peak of the island of Tenerife in the Canary Islands in the Atlantic Ocean. El Teide is the third largest volcano in the world at more than 12,200 feet, and was a famous landmark for sailors.

p. 238, l. 1: *the* Insurance Office: the main office for marine insurance (which is what is referred to here) was at John's Coffee-house in Birchin Lane (Lillywhite 637). The insurance office later moved to Lloyd's Coffee-house, which moved to Lombard Street in 1691 (Lillywhite 736).

p. 238, l. 7: *the Bishop of* L— *Dr.* Scot, *Dr.* Grove: Henry Compton (1631–1713), Bishop of London (1675–1713), a staunch supporter of William and Mary, but after the revolution alienated from the Court party. Because he was in Holland, he did not attend the consecration of Tillotson as the Archbishop of Canterbury in 1691, nor his admission to the Privy Council, which may be the events noticed here (*ODNB*). Dr Scot and Dr Grove are untraced, but may be other disaffected High-Church Anglican clergy, probably John Scott (1638–95), rector of St Giles-in-the-Fields, and Matthew Grove, created Bishop of Chichester in August 1691.

p. 238, ll. 11–12: Algate *to* Newgate, *and from thence to* Tyburn: in 1685, Titus Oates (1649–1705), the main Popish Plot conspirator, was found guilty of false testimony, and sentenced to be whipped from one side of the city to the other, that is from Aldgate in the East, through Newgate to Tyburn in the west.

p. 238, l. 12: *to the Tune of Dr.* O—tes *his* Jig: a reference to one of the many ballads concerning the exploits of Titus Oates. Oates was released from prison after the revolution of 1688, but soon returned as a convicted perjurer, as he refused to give up his claim to a hold the degree of doctor of divinity from Salamanca.

p. 238, l. 21: Luxemburgh: François Henri de Monmorency-Bouteville, Duc de Luxembourg (1628–95), commander-in-chief of the French armies in Flanders in the campaign of 1690–5.

p. 238, l. 26: *Secretary's Office*: the Letter Office of the Secretary of State – the office which disseminated all official intelligence.

p. 238, ll. 40–1: Let Scraping … Brains: untraced.

The City Cheat discovered: or, A New Coffe-house Song

p. 241, l. 1: *City Cheat*: a trader or merchant made wealthy by forms of morally dubious commerce, as for example stock-jobbers. In thieves' cant, a cheat is a stolen thing, but, as Randle Holme noted in *The Academy of Armory* (Chester, 1689), bk 2, p. iii, 'the word cheat joined to others hath then a variable signification'. Robert Gould uses the term 'City-cheat' in the 'Prologue' to his *Poems chiefly consisting of Satyrs* (London, 1689). See also *The Complaint of all the she-traders*, above, pp. 243–5.

p. 241, l. 6: Lilli-bulero: doggerel. See above, note to p. 224, l. 16.

p. 241, col. 1, l. 5: *their Noddles*: the head.

p. 241, col. 1, l. 8: News Letters: a letter written specifically to communicate news, and distributed in manuscript or print to a specified list of correspondents, common in the second half of the seventeenth century.

p. 241, col. 1, l. 18: Tales of a Cock and a Bull: long, rambling idle stories (*OED*). James Howell notes 'Frivolous tales of a cock and a bull' as the English proverbial saying equivalent to 'Contes de la cicogne, viz. begauderies' in *Paroimiographia: Proverbs, or, Old sayed savves & adages in English (or the Saxon Toung), Italian, French, and Spanish* (London, J. G., 1659), p. 19.

p. 241, col. 1, l. 20: *Fire-ships and Friggots*: a fire ship is a vessel freighted with combustibles and explosives, and sent amongst an enemy fleet to destroy them; a 'friggot' or frigate is a small war vessel carrying from 28 to 60 guns (*OED*).

p. 241, col. 1, ll. 22–3: *The Mistriss ... hansome Women*: a night rail is a loose wrap or jacket worn after undressing. The satire suggests that the coffee-woman appears in lascivious revealing clothing, and invites prostitutes into the coffee-room.

p. 241, col. 1, l. 25: Kissing and Billing: billing is the caressing of doves (*OED*), and by extension the idle chatter of courtship and love.

p. 241, col. 1, l. 33: painting and Patches: use of cosmetic unguents, powders and patches (a small piece of black silk cut into a decorative shape) for adornment.

p. 241, col. 1, ll. 34–5: kissing and whineing ... hugging: whineing is a kind of 'squeaky crying' (B. E., *Dictionary of the Canting Crew*); tickling her womb suggests sexual intercourse, as do tugging, jugging and hugging.

p. 241, col. 2, l. 12: *Thorn-back maid*: the thorn-back is the common ray or skate (*Raia clavata*), a fish distinguished by several rows of short sharp spines along its back. The female young of the thornback is traditionally called a maid. This was a commonplace term of opprobrium for women 'said to be exceedingly provocative', B. E., *Dictionary of the Canting Crew*.

p. 241, col. 2, l. 26: a Pox on her Placket: a pox is a disease, usually venereal; and a placket is an opening or slit at the top of a skirt or petticoat, and by extension, a woman's genitals.

p. 241, col. 2, l. 32: *Sign of the* Shepherd *and* Fleece: not traced.

The complaint of all the she-traders ... against the city cheats, or the new coffee-houses

p. 245, l. 4: *She-traders*: slang term for prostitutes, as in 'Burdellos, T'encourage She-Traders and lusty young Fellows', in Alexander Radcliffe, *The Ramble: an Anti-Heroick Poem* (London, for the author by Walter Davie, 1680), p. 45.

p. 245, ll. 6–7: Rosemary-lane, Black-Mary's-Hole, Ratcliff, Dog-and-Bitch-Yard, Moor-fields, and Petticoat-lane: locations in London associated with dissolute sociability and prostitution. Rosemary Lane (now Royal Mint Street, E1) was the site of an old-clothes market, popularly known as Rag Fair. The area was surrounded by a network of alleys inhabited by large numbers of the very poor, especially Jewish and Irish immigrants. Black-Mary's-Hole was a well and pleasure garden which attracted a clientele of tradesmen, apprentices and their wives (now at the corner of King's Cross Road and Lloyd Baker Street), that had been leased by a black-haired woman called Mary Woolaston during the reign of Charles II. Ratcliff was a landing place on the Thames in Stepney, particularly inhabited by seamen and containing the brothels they used. Dog-and-Bitch-Yard was an alley off the notoriously rowdy Drury Lane, renamed Turnstile Alley by 1720, when Stow called it 'a most notorious Nest of Strumpets'; see William Stow, *Remarks on London: being an exact survey of the cities of London and Westminster* (London, T. Norris and H. Tracy, 1722), p. 80. Moor-fields, an open space with tree-lined walks north of the City beyond Moorgate, was much frequented by prostitutes at night. Petticoat Lane, an area inhabited by Huguenot and Jewish migrants, was so named from the street market for old clothes and other second-hand items that was held there on Sundays.

p. 245, ll. 7–8: Charing-Cross, Westminster, Covent-garden, Fleet-street: locations in the West End of London, which, by comparison with those named above, are associated with Court culture and new wealth. Charing Cross, at the junction of the Strand, Whitehall and Cockspur Street, was a wide open space where official proclamations were read.

p. 245, l. 9: To the tune of an *Orange*: so named for a tune used by a number of political ballads about William of Orange, the most important being *A New Song of an Orange, To that excellent Old Tune of a Pudding* (1688). 'The Pudding' was first published around 1682, but is itself a reworking of 'With a fading', a tune and refrain tag in James Shirley's *The Bird in a Cage* (London, printed by B. Alsop and T. Fawcet for William Cooke, 1633), iv.1. See Claude Simpson, *The British Broadside Ballad and its Music* (New Brunswick, NJ, Rutgers University Press, 1966), pp. 792–95.

p. 245, col. 1, l. 13: *Bantling*: a small child, or brat (often used as a synonym for bastard) (*OED*).

p. 245, col. 1, l. 16: *the* Star: untraced, perhaps referring to one of a number of coffee-houses whose sign and name was that of a star or comet. See for example The Star Coffee-house, by the Royal Exchange or in Exchange Alley, where a quack called Mr Wells advertised the sale of a nostrum called 'Lady Moor's Drops' (Lillywhite 1257).

p. 245, col. 1, l. 17: *where* Robin *has fix'd a Planet more fair*: unclear. A series of ballads popular in the 1680s features the courtship difficulties of Robin and Nancy. See for example *The Faithful Farmer, or, the down-right vvooing betwixt Robin and Nancy* (London, printed for Josiah Blare, 1685–8). There may be an obscure political dimension to this series.

p. 245, col. 1, l. 19: *old* Troy: a legendary city described in Homer's *Iliad* as the scene of the Trojan War.

p. 245, col. 1, l. 20: *brave* Nancy: the heroine of several courtship ballads of the 1680s. See above, note to p. 245, col. 1, l. 17.

p. 245, col. 1, l. 21: *flowr'd Sattin Gown*: a satin dress embellished with figures of flowers. Complaints against working women wearing dress associated with higher stations in life are a staple of conservative moralists of the period.

p. 245, col. 2, l. 17: *Quack who pretends to cure the Rein*: the reins are the kidneys, traditionally the seat of the feelings or affections (*OED*).

p. 245, col. 2, l. 19: *a George, may now for a* Sice: devalued. A 'George' is a slang term for a coin bearing the image of St George, 'a half-crown piece' (B. E., *Dictionary of the Canting Crew*, a silver coin worth two shillings and six-pence; a 'sice' or 'size' is the number six on a dice, used in this period as a slang term for sixpence (*OED*).

p. 245, col. 2, l. 21: *a Council*: the Common Council of the Aldermen of the City of London, an administrative body that, with the Lord Mayor, ruled London. The Common Council were frequently at odds with the Court at Westminster.

p. 245, col. 2, l. 24: Damaris Page: Damaris Page (*c.* 1610–69) was a notori-ous bawd and brothel keeper, who made a fortune first by keeping brothels catering to seafaring men in Stepney (amongst other places) at the Three Tuns, and later in property speculation, building several houses on Ratcliffe Highway. She was the subject, but not the author, of a number of scurrilous pamphlets and vulgar satires.

'Letter from a French gentleman in London to his friend in Paris ... Containing an Account of Will's Coffeehouse, and of the Toasting and Kit-Kat-Clubs'

p. 249, l. 3: Will's *Coffeehouse*: a coffee-house in Russell Street, Covent Garden, established *c.* 1660, where poets, critics and men of letters led by John Dryden assembled (Lillywhite 1548). See above, pp. 247–8 and, for those who were regularly present, below, notes to p. 250, ll. 13–16, 30–3.

p. 249, ll. 3–4: the *Toasting* and *Kit-Cat-Clubs*: the Kit-Cat Club, a Whig politi-cal and literary club, at which Whig statesmen, aristocrats and prominent writers would meet for sociability and mutual advantage. The Kit-Cat Club was probably founded around 1699, although it may have existed in secret before this date. The name is obscure: Edward Ward claimed that it was bor-rowed from its habitual repast, a large mutton pie, sold by Christopher 'Kit' Cat, a pie-man near Temple Bar. The club met in various locations, but was most famously associated with the Fountain Tavern on the Strand.

p. 249, ll. 6–7: en passant: in passing, in the course of a narrative (*OED*).

p. 249, l. 7: *of the Court of* England: the previous letter had described the entertainments and nobility to be found at the court of William III at Kensington Palace and St James's Park. See *Letters of Wit, Politicks, and Morality. Written originally in Italian, by the famous Cardinal Bentivoglio; in Spanish by Signior Don Guevara ... Done into English, by the Honourable H— H— Esq; Tho. Cheek, Esq; Mr. Savage. Mr. Boyer &c. To which is added a large collection of original letters of Love and Friendship*, ed. by Abel Boyer (London, J. Hartley, W. Turner, and Tho. Hodgson, 1701), pp. 210–15.

p. 250, ll. 4–5: *settled* Academies de Beaux-Esprits, *as we have in* Paris: the Académie Française was a learned institution established in 1635 by Cardinal Richelieu during the reign of Louis XIII. The Académie was given responsibility for the regulation of French grammar, orthography and literature.

p. 250, ll. 7–8: *promiscuous Company*: company that consists of members of different kinds grouped or massed together without order (*OED*).

p. 250, l. 11: Apollo: see above, note to p. 129, col. 2, l. 11.

p. 250, ll. 13–16: *the late Earl of* Rochester ... Wycherly: the first generation of poets who assembled at Will's, under the leadership of John Dryden (1631–1700), including John Wilmot, 1st Earl of Rochester (1647–80); John Sheffield, the Marquis of Normanby and 1st Duke of Buckingham (1647–1721); Charles Sackville, 6th Earl of Dorset (1643–1706); Sir Charles Sidley (1639–1701); Wentworth Dillon, 4th Earl of Roscommon (1637–85); Sir George Etherege (1636–92); and William Wycherley (1641–1716).

p. 250, l. 20: *Temple of the* Muses: in Greek mythology, the temple housing the Muses, the nine goddesses of the arts, poetry and letters.

p. 250, ll. 30–3: *Mr.* Wicherley ... *Mr.* Rowe: modern English poets who gathered at Will's Coffee-house: William Wycherley (1641–1716); Sir Samuel (Dr) Garth (1660–1719); William Congreve (1670–1729); the Honourable Mr Charles Boyle, later 4th Earl of Orrery (1674–1731); Colonel James Stanhope (1673–1721); Mr John Vanbruk or Vanbrugh (1664–1726); Mr Thomas Cheek (fl. 1697–1700); Mr William Walsh (1662–1708); Mr William Burnaby (1673–1706); Mr Nicolas Rowe (1674–1718). For Will's, see above pp. 247–8, and note to p. 249, l. 3.

p. 251, l. 3: Ben. Jonson: Benjamin Jonson (1572–1637), poet and playwright, famous also for cultivating a literary club at the Devil Tavern, known jocularly as the Sons of Ben.

p. 251, l. 3: Plain-Dealer: Wycherley's *The Plain Dealer* (London, printed by T. N. for J. Magnes and R. Bentley, 1677), a satire on the corruption of manners in the Restoration first performed on 11 December 1676. Some scenes are responses to Molière's *Le Misanthrope* (see note below).

p. 251, ll. 4–5: Moliere's Misanthrope: Jean-Baptiste Poquelin, known as Molière (1622–73), author of *Le Misanthrope* (Paris, chez Jean Ribon, 1667), a comedy satirising the social conventions of politeness and flattery in France.

p. 251, l. 10: *the* Country Wife: Wycherley's *The Country Wife* (London, printed for T. Dring, 1675), a comedy first performed at the Theatre Royal, Drury Lane on 12 January 1675, satirising the selfish desires that hypocritically lie below social conventions of honour and virtue.

p. 251, l. 30: *Mons.* Despreaux: Nicolas Boileau Despréaux, commonly called Boileau (1636–1711), a French poet and critic, author of *Le Lutrin* (1674).

p. 251, ll. 31–2: *the* Dispensary: Garth's *The Dispensary, a Poem* (London, John Nutt, 1699), a six canto mock-heroic satire on the medical profession, describing the battle between the physicians and apothecaries.

p. 251, l. 33: Lutrin: Boileau's *Le Lutrin* was a French mock-heroic satire on the clergy.

p. 252, ll. 13–15: Old Batchelour … Mourning Bride: Congreve's *The Old Batchelor* (London, Peter Buck, 1693), a comedy first performed at the Theatre Royal Drury Lane on 9 March 1693; *Love for Love* (London, Jacob Tonson, 1695), a comedy first performed at the new Lincoln's Inn Theatre on 30 April 1695; and *The Mourning Bride* (London, Jacob Tonson, 1697), a tragedy in blank verse first performed at the Lincoln's Inn Theatre on 27 February 1697.

p. 252, l. 16: *an Elegy*: Congreve's *The mourning muse of Alexis a pastoral lamenting the death of our late gracious Queen Mary* (London, Jacob Tonson, 1695), an elegy for Queen Mary written in 1694, for which he received £100 from the King.

p. 252, l. 19: Theocritus *and* Virgil: classical poets accepted as the established model for pastoral poetry: Theocritus (fl. 3rd century BC), whose Greek 'Idylls' influenced Publius Virgilius Maro, known as Virgil (70–19 BC), whose 'Eclogues' were written around 37 BC.

p. 252, ll. 23–4: *my Lord* Dorset, … *of the* English *Muses*: Charles Sackville, 6th Earl of Dorset and 1st Earl of Middlesex (1643–1706), poet and Whig politician, who as a patron cultivated a sociable group in his 'Poets' Parlour' and Knole; and Charles Montagu, Earl of Halifax (1661–1715), poet and Whig politician, a member of Dorset's literary circle (*ODNB*). Gaius Maecenas (70–8 BC) was a noted political advisor and patron of poets at the court of Augustus Caesar.

p. 252, l. 26: *the famous Earl of* Orrery: Roger Boyle, 1st Earl of Orrery (1621–79), politician and writer, a minister in Cromwell's Protectorate government, and a leader of radical Protestants in the Restoration (*ODNB*).

p. 253, ll. 1–4: *the Epistles of* Phalaris … Greek *MS*: while a student at Christ Church, Oxford, Charles Boyle translated the *Epistles of Phalaris*, a collection of letters supposedly written by a Sicilian in the fifth century BC. When his edition appeared in 1695, the preface remarked that the custodian of the King's Library at St James's Palace, Dr Richard Bentley (1662–1742), had hindered his research, sparking a literary controversy satirised by Swift in *The Battle of the Books* (London, J. Nutt, 1704). Bentley's two dissertations on the *Epistles*, and several rejoinders, followed. Although sometimes attributed to Boyle, the reply *Dr Bentley's Dissertation on the Epistles of Phalaris* …

examin'd (London, printed for Tho. Bennet, 1698) is probably not by Boyle (*ODNB*).

p. 253, l. 5: *Colonel* Stanhope: James Stanhope, later 1st Earl Stanhope (1673–1721), army officer, diplomat, politician, who published a translation of Demosthenes's third Philippic in 1701. See also above, p. 250, ll. 31–2.

p. 253, ll. 5–6: *Lord* Chesterfield: Philip Stanhope, 2nd Earl of Chesterfield (1633–1714), courtier and politician, grandfather of the author of Chesterfield's *Letters to his Son* (London, printed for J. Dodsley, 1774).

p. 253, l. 7: *Mr* Stanhope: Hon. Alexander Stanhope (1638–1707).

p. 253, l. 17: *Mr* Vanbruk: Sir John Vanbrugh (1664–1726), playwright and architect (his name had several variants, probably phonetic, including Vanbrook). See also above, p. 250, l. 32.

p. 253, ll. 20–1: *three Comedies ... Provok'd Wife*: Vanbrugh wrote three successful comedies in the 1690s. *The Relapse* (London, printed for Samuel Briscoe, 1697) opened at Drury Lane on 21 November 1696; *The Provok'd Wife* (London, printed by J. O. for R. Wellington and Sam. Briscoe, 1697) in April 1697 at Lincoln's Inn, and *Aesop* (London, printed for Thomas Bennet, 1697), adapted from the French of Edme Boursault's *Les fables d'Ésope* (*ODNB*).

p. 253, l. 26: *Mr.* Cheek: Thomas Cheek, writer of miscellaneous works. Cheek was the translator of Boileau's letters in Tom Brown's *Familiar Letters* (London, printed by W. Onley for Samuel Briscoe, 1697), and has a letter on wit in *Letters of Wit, Politicks, and Morality*, ed. by Abel Boyer, pp. 284–90. See also above, p. 250, l. 32.

p. 253, l. 32: *Mr.* Walsh: William Walsh (1662–1708), poet, author of *Letters and Poems, Amorous and Gallant* (London, printed for Jacob Tonson, 1692) and several other satires and panegyrics. See also above, p. 250, l. 32.

p. 253, l. 35: Voiture: Vincent Voiture (1597–1648), French poet

p. 254, ll. 1–2: *Dissertation ... Dryden*: Dryden's translation of *Virgil's Works* (London, printed for Jacob Tonson, 1697) included in volume I a 'Preface to the pastorals, &c.', defending René Rapin's neo-classical argument. The essay was by Dr Knightly Chetwood (1650–1720), but was widely attributed to Walsh (for example, in the 1782 edition of Dryden's Virgil).

p. 254, l. 3: '*Mr.* Burnaby: William Burnaby (1673–1706), playwright and translator. See also above, p. 250, l. 33.

p. 254, l. 5: The Reform'd Wife: *The Reform'd Wife* (London, printed for T. Bennet, 1700), a five-act comedy, was first acted at Drury Lane in 1700, one of the last of the so-called Restoration comedies.

p. 254, l. 9: *Mr.* Rowe: Nicolas Rowe (1674–1718), poet and playwright. See also above, p. 250, l. 33.

p. 254, ll. 10–11: *the* Ambitious Step Mother: The first of Rowe's tragedies, *The Ambitious Step Mother* opened in December 1700, and was published by Peter Buck in 1701.

p. 254, l. 30: Wittlings: a witling or Would-be-Wit is a petty wit, one who fancies himself a wit, a pretender to wit. The term was first used by Dryden in 1692 (*OED*).

p. 254, l. 33: Corneille: Pierre Corneille (1606–84), French playwright famous for his tragedies.

p. 255, l. 1: Racine: Jean Racine (1639–99), French playwright famous for his tragedies.

p. 255, l. 2: La Fontaine: Jean de La Fontaine (1621–95), French poet, author of *Fables Choisies* (1668).

p. 255, l. 20: Bossu *and* Dacier: René Le Bossu (1631–80), French critic, and André Dacier (1651–1722), French classical scholar.

p. 255, ll. 25–6: *upon the Stocks*: figurative phrase said of literary works planned or commenced, from the framework on which a ship or boat is supported while in process of construction, first used in this sense in 1669 (*OED*).

p. 256, ll. 12–13: *the three Unities* ... Drama: key terms of the neo-classical rules of drama derived from Aristotle's *Poetics*. The letter suggests the would-be-wit's criticism repeats these rules without comprehension.

p. 256, l. 24: Quibbling *and* Punning: a play upon words, technically paronomasia, a deliberate confusion of words that sound the same but have different meanings for comic effect. Punning was a favourite literary activity in the later seventeenth century amongst all orders, widely condemned by moralists as a form of equivocation.

p. 256, l. 29: Bear-Garden *Entertainment*: bear-gardens were arenas used for bear-baiting and other rough sports, figuratively, a scene of strife and confusion (*OED*).

p. 256, l. 32: Tom's *(a Coffeehouse adjoining* Will's*)*: Tom's was established *c.* 1700 in a house next door to Will's at No. 17 Russell Street by Captain Thomas West (Lillywhite 1366). It too attracted a literary clientele, until both it and Will's were overshadowed by Button's Coffee-house, across the road, established by Joseph Addison in 1712 in a deliberate attempt to wrest control of the literary institutions of the period. For Will's see above pp. 247–8, and note to p. 249, ll. 3–4.

p. 257, ll. 1–5: Politicians ... Beaux: politician, a politic person, a schemer, a crafty plotter (*OED*). Like '*Beaux*', one of the characteristic habitués of the coffee-house.

p. 257, l. 21: Knights of the Toast: a Whig drinking club of the 1690s, attended by figures from the world of politics and literature. The Order of the Toast wrote verses upon their drinking glasses, but little evidence remains of their members, meetings or discussions.

p. 257, l. 22: *the* Kit-cat-club: see above, note to p. 249, ll. 3–4.

Edward Ward, *The Humours of a Coffee House: a Comedy*

p. 261, ll. 6–10: *Levy ... Bohee,* the Coffee-man. *Whim,* a Projector: Ward's
characters all have type-names (names which recall their profession). For
example, the coffee-man's name, Bohee, refers to a kind of tea (bohea, a low
grade black tea from China).

p. 262, l. 1: *Hockstedt*: Höchstädt, a German town on the Danube. The plains of
Höchstädt were the field of combat for the Battle of Blenheim, fought on 13
August 1704, in which the French and Bavarian army under Tallard and the
Elector were defeated by the combined Austrian, British and Dutch forces
under Prince François-Eugène of Savoy-Carignan (1663–1736) and John
Churchill, 1st Duke of Marlborough (1650–1722).

p. 262, l. 11: *Banstead Downs*: on the North Downs near Epsom in Surrey, an
appropriate location, Ward imagines, for a battle with a French invader.

p. 262, col. 2, ll. 4–5: *St.* James's Park, Spring-Garden: public gardens in London,
places of resort for the upper stations of life.

p. 2, col. 2, ll. 16–20: *Duke of* Savoy ... Dauphine: a discussion of the fortunes of
the British forces in the War of the Spanish Succession. Prince Eugène, also
known as the Duke of Savoy, was the commander of the Austrian forces.
Dauphiné is the name of a province of France, now covered by the departments of the Isère, Drôme and Hautes-Alpes. The Austrian forces under
Prince Eugène undertook an inconclusive invasion of southern France in
1707.

p. 263, col. 1, ll. 47–52: *Battle of* Almanza ... *Lord* Peterborough ... *Lord* Galway:
In 1707 British forces under the Earl of Galway invaded Spain from Portugal,
and were defeated on 25 April at the battle of Almansa, near Valencia, by
a Bourbon-Spanish and French army led by King Philip V and the Duke
of Berwick (the illegitimate son of James II of England, who served in the
French army). Charles Modaunt, 3rd Earl of Peterborough (1658–1735),
once commander of British forces in Spain.

p. 264, col. 1, ll. 29–43: *King of* Sweden ... Saxony ... Silesia: Charles XII of
Sweden (1682–1718) led his army to Saxony in 1707, where he forced the
Elector Augustus II to renounce his claims to the Polish throne.

p. 264, col. 2, ll. 39–41: Post-Man, Post-Boy, Flying-Post, English-Post, *and*
Daily Courant: newspapers. See R. S. Crane and F. B. Kaye, *A Census of
British Newspapers and Periodicals, 1620–1800* (London, the Holland
Press, 1927).

p. 265, col. 1, ll. 3–4: Groom Porters*, and at* Marrow-Bone: Marrow-bone, or
Marylebone, was a village north of Westminster, at which there was a pleas-

ure garden famous for gaming. For Groom Porters see above, note to p. 236, l. 8.

p. 265, col. 2, ll. 5–6: *a Murrain take all* Astrologers: an imprecation invoking pestilence or misfortune upon someone, in this case, astrologers (*OED*).

p. 266, col. 1, ll. 29–30: *an* Oedipus: a person clever at solving riddles or puzzles, in allusion to Oedipus's deciphering of the riddle of the Sphinx (*OED*).

p. 266, col. 2, l. 13: Camisars: Calvinist radicals from the Cevennes and Dauphiné who rebelled against French rule in 1703. Some Camisars emigrated to England in 1707, where they established a reputation for enthusiastic preaching, miraculous cures and prophetic inspiration.

p. 267, col. 1, ll. 3–4: *Noli Prosequi*: Latin, 'unwilling to pursue'. In law it describes the prosecutor's voluntary dismissal of criminal charges.

p. 267, col. 1, ll. 43–5: Jo. J—bs, *that Raking* Draper-Trooper, *and now* Whisking Tubster: Joseph Jacob (1667–1722), an Independent minister who established his own church in 1698, preaching fiery political sermons and instigating a strict code of conduct, including compulsory moustaches for all his followers (*ODNB*).

p. 267, col. 2, ll. 2–50: a satire on the obscure rhetoric of astrologers and prophets.

p. 268, col. 1, l. 23: Bays: a conventional satirical name for a poet or critic, or one who acts in that character.

p. 268, col. 2, l. 37: *The British Court. A Poem*: Joseph Browne (fl. 1700–21), *The British court: a poem. Describing the most celebrated beauties at St. James's, the Park, and the Mall* (London, printed for Samuel Bunchley, and sold at the publishing-office in Dove-Court, near Bearbinder-Lane, 1707). A panegyric on the reigning beauties of the court of Queen Anne, published by the same bookseller as Ward's paper.

p. 269, col. 1, l. 4: Thoulon: Toulon, a strategic port city in southern France, a major base for the French navy fortified by the French military architect Vauban. Toulon was a target for Prince Eugène's campaign in July 1707, when it was attacked by the British fleet under Sir Cloudesley Shovell. Whim's wager is that the city will be taken by 1 August (see above, p. 285). It was not. See below, note to p. 279, col. 1, l. 47.

p. 270, col. 2, ll. 3–10: Guild-hall, Compter: part of a satire on the obscurity of legal language, and asinine pedantry of the law. A compter was a prison for debtors (London had the Poultry Compter and the Wood Street Compter).

p. 271, col. 1, l. 6: Occasionalists: an occasional conformist, that is, one who receives communion according to the rite of the Anglican Church solely for the sake of conformity, so that they may qualify for an official position in accordance with the Corporation and Test Act (*OED*).

p. 271, col. 1, l. 10: *the* Shortest Way: Daniel Defoe's *Shortest Way with the Dissenters* (London, 1702) was a popular satire which used the language of the High-Church Tories against themselves, and earned Defoe a large fine and the pillory for seditious libel.

p. 271, col. 1, ll. 15–16: *the* Archbishop *and the Lower House of* Convocation: reference to the conflict between Thomas Tenison (1636–1715), Archbishop of Canterbury, and the Convocation, the parliament of clergy of the Anglican Church, between 1701–7. As a Whig, Tenison was subjected to abuse from disaffected Tory ecclesiastics, who argued, somewhat ironically, that the lower house of Convocation, which represented ordinary clergy, should be independent of the bishops in the upper house. On several occasions, Convocation refused to comply with the Archbishop's adjournment.

p. 272, col. 1, ll. 25–6: Oneglia *to* Leghorn: seaports on the coast of Italy, Oneglia in Liguria to Leghorn (Livorno) in Tuscany.

p. 272, col. 1, l. 45–col. 2: *The Present State of Great Britain … The London Bell's … An Alphabetical List … 6d.*: recent publications by Samuel Bunchley: *The present state of Great Britain, under the auspicious government of Her Most Sacred Majesty Queen Anne* (London, S. Bunchley, 1707); Joseph Browne, *The London belles: or, a description of the most celebrated beauties in the City of London* (London, S. Bunchley, 1707); *An alphabetical list of the names of all those persons who have surrendred [sic] themselves to, or have been summon'd in to be examined by the commissioners, in the several commissions of bankrupt awarded against them* (London, S. Bunchley, 1707).

p. 273, col. 2, l. 2: Projection: a proposal, plan, design or scheme (*OED*).

p. 274, col. 1, ll. 3–5: The *British* Invalides: Or, an *Hospital* for *Superannuated* and *Disabled Dogs* and *Horses*: a satire on charitable projects, typically proposed by pious merchants, who raised money by subscription. The name recalls *Les Invalides*, a military hospital and home for old soldiers built in Paris between 1670 and 1676.

p. 274, col. 1, l. 32: *my* Green-Bag: a bag made of green material used by barristers and lawyers for documents and papers (*OED*).

p. 274, col. 1, ll. 38–41: Lap-dogs … Strephon: lap-dogs or toy dogs were repeatedly troped as unworthy recipients of affection and sympathy. Strephon was a conventional name for a shepherd in silly pastorals.

p. 275, col. 1, ll. 38–9: *the New* Play-House *in the* Hay-Market: the Queen's Theatre in the Haymarket, a street in St James's, was designed by John Vanbrugh, and opened in 1705. It was satirised in *The new Hospital in the Haymarket for the cure of folly* (London, Jacob Tonson, *c.* 1705), which may have provided a model for Ward here.

p. 276, col. 1, l. 1: *Colonel* Bilboe: bilbo, a sword noted for the temper and elasticity of its blade, and hence, a bully or swash-buckler (*OED*).

p. 276, col. 1, ll. 37–8: Si Populus vult decipi Decipiatur: Latin, 'If the people will be deceived, let them'.

p. 276, col. 1, l. 50–col 2: Advertisement ... Grace-Church-Street: Joseph Browne, *An account of the wonderful cures perform'd by the cold baths. With advice to the water drinkers at Tunbridge, Hampstead, Astrope, Nasborough* (London, J. How, R. Borough and J. Baker, 1707); *A trip to Spain: or, a true description of the comical humours, ridiculous customs, and foolish laws, of that lazy improvident people the Spaniards* (London, J. How, 1705); William Davenant, *Contemplations and reflections upon the several degrees and changes of human life* (London, John Morphew, 1707).

p. 278, col. 2, ll. 8–21: Mr. *Beauvilliers* ... Duke of St. *Aignan* ... Madam *Maintenon* ... Chamillard: Paul de Beauvillier, Duc de Saint-Aignan (1648–1714), one of Louis XIV's closest advisers; Françoise d'Aubigné, Marquise de Maintenon (1635–1719), second wife of Louis XIV; Michel Chamillard (1652–1721), secretary of state for war for Louis XIV.

p. 279, col. 1, l. 47: Sir *Cloudsley Shovel*: Sir Cloudesley Shovell (1650–1707), admiral of the Mediterranean fleet. Shovell's attack on Toulon, long in the planning, finally took place in July 1707. Shovell landed sufficient troops and cannon to overawe the French defenders, and burned many ships in the harbour. The siege however was raised on 23 August, after the French troops rallied.

p. 20, col. 2: *The Travels of an* English *Gentleman* ... *The Reformer*: A. F., *The travels of an English gentleman from London to Rome, on foot*, 2nd edn (London, J. How, 1704), there is no copy extant of the third edition advertised here; Edward Ward, *The Reformer. Exposing the vices of the age in several Characters* (London, J. How, 1700), there is no copy extant of the second edition advertised here.

p. 282, col. 1, ll. 8–9: Royal Society: the Royal Society for the Improvement of Natural Knowledge, founded in 1660. In the late seventeenth century its prestige was somewhat compromised, and it often stands as a byword for pedantry and dullness in satires of the period, although the appointment of Isaac Newton as president in 1703 suggested an upward turn in its fortunes.

p. 282, col. 1, ll. 32–41: Hippocrate *and* Galen, Æsculapius: ancient physicians, the fathers of medicine: Hippocrates of Cos (460–380 BC); Claudius Galenus of Pergamum (AD 131–201); and Asculapius, the god of medicine and healing in Greek mythology.

p. 282, col. 2, l. 3: Culpepper: Nicholas Culpeper, see above, note to p. 63, l. 13.

p. 282, col. 2, ll. 13–18: Pilula ex Pillorio ... Illerick *and* Icterick ... Histerick *and* Emmenanogogick: a medical satire describing a quack pill (pilula) with many different properties (*OED*).

p. 282, col. 2, l. 36: Scribblers Itch: writing.

p. 282, col. 2, l. 44: Cameronian: the name given to a sect within the Scottish Covenanters who followed the teachings of Richard Cameron, who formed their own church in 1690, taking the title the Reformed Presbyterians in 1743.

p. 282, col. 2, ll. 53–4: Turnitus: Or, a Tumutary Noise in the Head: tinnitus, a sensation of ringing in the ears.

p. 283, col. 1, ll. 5–6: Albumazar *and* Ptolemy*, and then* Cardan: the key philosophers in the astrological tradition: the Persian Ja'far ibn Muhammad Abu Ma'shar al-Balkhi (AD 787–886), the Greek Claudius Ptolemaeus (AD 85–165) and the Italian Gerolamo Cardano (1501–76).

p. 283, col. 2, l. 52: Monstrum Horrendum!: Latin, 'horrid monster'.

p. 284, col. 1, l. 25: *Priapus*: in Greek mythology, a god of fertility, gardens and male genitalia. This paragraph is for this period an unusually explicit account of transvestite sado-masochism, as it would now be called.

p. 286, col. 1, ll. 44–5: North Britain: Scotland. On 26 March 1707 the Acts of Union were passed, creating the new Kingdom of Great Britain.

p. 286, col. 2, l. 32: *Tongue Strappado*: a form of punishment, a strappado is a torture to extort confession in which the victim's hands were tied across his back and secured by a pulley, he was then jerked up and down.

p. 287, col. 2, l. 8: *Nantz*: brandy produced in the Nantes region of France, embargoed during the war.

Edward Arwaker, 'Fable XXIX: The Coffee-House: Or, A Man's Credit, is his Cash'

p. 291, l. 5: *Will's*: a coffee-house. See above, note to p. 249, l. 3.

p. 291, l. 26: Marlborough *and* Auverquerke: John Churchill, 1st Duke of Marlborough (1650–1722), commander of the British forces in Flanders; Hendrick Van Nassau, Count Overkirk (or 'Auverquerke') (1640–1708), commander of the Dutch army in Flanders in 1708. The battle the soldier brings news of may be either the battle of Ramilles, 23 May 1706, or more likely the battle of Oudenarde, 11 July 1708, in both of which these commanders figured prominently.

p. 291, l. 27: *Old* Lewis: Louis XIV (1638–1715), king of France.

p. 292, l. 19: *A Golden Snush-Box, with right* Vigo *fill'd*: a gold snuff box containing Vigo, a dark kind of snuff, probably from Vigo in Spain.

p. 292, l. 27: Charles: Charles VI (1685–1740), archduke of Austria, the contracted heir of the Spanish Hapsburgs, elected Holy Roman Emperor in 1711. After the Flanders campaigns of 1707, Archduke Charles was portrayed as the legitimate ruler of the Spanish Netherlands by the British and their allies.

p. 292, ll. 14–16: Quantum ... *Juven. Sat 3*: Juvenal, *Satires*, III.143–4: 'A man's word is believed in exact proportion to the amount of cash which he keeps in his strong box', *Juvenal and Persius*, trans. by G. G. Ramsay, Loeb Classical Library (Cambridge, MA, Harvard University Press, 1918), p. 43.

p. 292, ll. 17–18: contemnere ... *Ibid*: Juvenal, *Satires*, III.145–6: 'the poor man gives food and occasion for jest if his cloak be torn and dirty', *Juvenal and Persius*, trans. by Ramsay, p. 43.

p. 292, l. 19–21: plurima ... *Sat.5*: Juvenal, *Satires*, V.130–1: 'there's many a thing which a man whose coast has holes in it cannot say', *Juvenal and Persius*, trans. by Ramsay, p. 79.

Edward Ward, *Vulgus Britannicus, or, the British Hudibrass*

p. 302, l. 6: S.....l's *Name*: Henry Sacheverell (1674–1724), High-Church Anglican and religious controversialist. A fiery preacher, his sermons attacked Dissenters and Low Churchmen, the revolution of 1688, and all 'false brethren' who undermined the constitution of the Church and State. The controversy around his trial in 1710 caused riots across the nation, mostly directed against Dissenters and their places of worship.

p. 302, ll. 17–18: Low-Church ... High-Church: members of opposing wings of the Church of England. Low Churchmen held opinions that gave a low place to the authority and claims of the episcopate and priesthood, to the inherent grace of the sacraments, and to matters of ecclesiastical organisations. The religious politics of the Low Churchmen differed little from the opinions of Protestant Nonconformists; and in many respects, the term 'low-churchman' was synonymous with Whig. High Churchmen held opinions that gave a high place to the authority and claims of the episcopate, and to those points of doctrine, discipline and ritual that distinguished the Anglican Church from the Protestant Nonconformist churches. The term was often synonymous with Tory (*OED*).

p. 303, l. 20: *spiteful Asses would be braying*: a reference to Benjamin Hoadley, for whom see below, note to p. 305, l. 12.

p. 304, l. 13: *the two Good old* Cause Asserters: the Good Old Cause was the Protestant Republic, a name originally coined by the soldiers of Cromwell's new Model Army. The writers referred to are Benjamin Hoadley and Daniel Defoe; see below, notes to p. 305, ll. 11–12.

p. 304, l. 15: *the Saints*: an ironic appellation for Protestant divines employed in fomenting religious and political controversies.

p. 305, l. 4: Falsiloquence: false speaking, deceitful speech (*OED*). This usage is the first recorded by the *OED*.

p. 305, l. 11: *for* Scripture *read Reviews*: Daniel Defoe (*c.* 1660–1731), author of *The Review* (1704–13), the most important Whig newspaper during the Sacheverell crisis.

p. 305, l. 12: H...y's *Works*: Benjamin Hoadley (1676–1761), at this time Rector of St Peter-le-Poer, was, like Defoe, one of the most influential Low-Church Whig controversialists, publishing numerous tracts and sermons against Sacheverell. He was the subject of many Tory satires, and was typically portrayed with asses ears and two horns.

p. 308, l. 5: Esop's Satyr: on political opportunism. A tale in the *Fables* of Aesop (580–500 BC) related the story of a man who blew on his hands to warm them, and then on his porridge to cool it: his friend the satyr jokes that he will having nothing more to do with one who blows 'hot and cold out of the same mouth'. See Roger L'Estrange, *Fables of Aesop* (London, printed for R. Sare, T. Sawbridge, B. Took, M. Gillyflower, A. & J. Churchil, and J. Hindmarsh, 1692), p. 211.

p. 310, l. 2: Poppy Water: a soporific drink made from poppies (*OED*), such as laudanum, opium grains dissolved in alcoholic spirits.

p. 316, l. 1: *The Cheif of these whose* Books *of late*: Found guilty of 'high crimes and misdeamenours' at his trial in March 1710, Sacheverell's sentence, widely interpreted as ludicrously lenient, included having his sermons burned in the presence of the lord mayor and sheriffs of London and Middlesex.

p. 317, l. 4: *the* Alcoran: the Koran, the sacred book of the Muslims.

p. 317, l. 15: Pharisees: an ancient Jewish sect distinguished by their strict observance of the traditional and written law, and by their claims to superior sanctity (*OED*).

p. 319, l. 20: Perkenites *and* Traytors: Jacobite plotters. Sir William Parkyns (or Perkins) was a lawyer who conspired in a plot in February 1696 to assassinate William III and raise an army to welcome James's French army when he landed. Parkyns was executed at Tyburn on 3 April, in front of an enthusiastic crowd.

p. 323, l. 11: *their* Jewish *Liquor*: coffee.

p. 323, l. 18: *true* Blew Protestants: faithful, staunch and unwavering (*OED*).

p. 324, l. 7: *the* Mine adventure: the Company of the Mine Adventurers of England, a joint stock company founded in 1698 and organised on a lottery share arrangement to develop copper and silver mines in Neath, Glamorgan. By 1705 the company was beset with production and cash flow difficulties, and in 1709 the chief organisers were found culpable by a Commons enquiry.

p. 324, l. 16: *Sir* Mac: Sir Humphrey Mackworth (1657–1727), chief projector of the Mine Adventure, declared bankrupt in 1710.

p. 325, l. 8: *the Company call'd* Affrican: the Royal African Company, founded in 1662, held a monopoly in the slave trade until 1698, which they attempted to revive unsuccessfully thereafter.

p. 325, l. 13: *the* Junto: a body of men who have combined for a common political purpose: a cabal or faction (*OED*). Often used to describe the great Whig noblemen prominent under William III after the revolution of 1688.

p. 144, l. 17: Anna's: Anne (1665–1714), queen of Great Britain, reigned 1702–14.

John Macky, *A Journey Through England*

p. 335, l. 1: *the Street called* Pall-mall: Pall Mall was a fashionable street leading from Charing Cross to the north gate of St James's Palace, the residence of Queen Anne.

p. 335, l. 8: *great Mens Levees*: a levee is a reception of visitors on rising from bed, a morning assembly held by a person of distinction (*OED*).

p. 335, ll. 10–11: *the* Beau-Monde: the fashionable world (*OED*).

p. 335, ll. 12–15: *the* Cocoa-Tree *and* White's *Chocolate-Houses, St.* James's, *the* Smirna, *Mrs* Rochford's, *and the* British *Coffee-Houses*: grand coffee and chocolate houses near the court in Westminster usually frequented by high-status clientele: the Cocoa-Tree Chocolate-house, Pall Mall, founded *c.* 1698 (Lillywhite 262); White's Chocolate-house, St James's Street, founded 1693 (Lillywhite 1511); the St James's Coffee-house, St James's Street across from St James's Palace entrance, founded *c.* 1705 (Lillywhite 1131); the Smyrna Coffee-house, Pall Mall, founded *c.* 1702 (Lillywhite 1222); Mrs Rochford's Coffee-house, Charing Cross, founded *c.* 1713 (Lillywhite 1086); and the British Coffee-house, opposite Suffolk Street, Charing Cross, founded *c.* 1709 (Lillywhite 179). See above, p. 336, ll. 11–13, where Macky remarks that 'the Parties have their different Places' so that 'a *Whig* will no more go to the *Cocoa-Tree* or *Osinda's*, than a *Tory* will be seen at the Coffee-House of *St James's*'. Despite these partisan differences, the proximity to the Royal court meant that all these coffee-houses attracted an unusual clientele of erstwhile courtiers, nobility and politicians.

p. 336, ll. 6–7: Picket *or* Basset: card games fashionable in high society at which very large sums of money could be lost. Piquet is played by two persons with a pack of 32 cards. Basset was played by four hands (punters) and a banker (talliere), and was little more than a lottery.

p. 336, l. 12: Osinda's: Ozinda's Chocolate-house, St James's Street, founded 1692 (Lillywhite 961).

p. 336, ll. 16–19: *little* Coffee-Houses *much frequented* ... Sharpers: three smaller coffee-houses in the courts and yards around Charing Cross, Westminster, all operated by a man or woman surnamed Man. The first, opened by

Alexander Man *c.* 1666 in Charing Cross at the sign of the Golden Fleece near Scotland Yard (Lillywhite 778), was known as the Royal Coffee-house from 1676 when the proprietor claimed to have a Royal Warrant for the supply of coffee to the palace. When Mrs Hester Man opened another coffee-house in Charing Cross, near the equestrian statue of Charles I, *c.* 1701 (Lillywhite 1579), the two were known as Young-Man's and Old-Man's. Little Man's Coffee-house (Lillywhite 733) is only recorded in Macky, and probably refers to a coffee-house better known as Jenny Man's Coffee-house, Charing Cross, established *c.* 1712 (Lillywhite 624), which may have had premises in Tilt Yard.

p. 336, l. 22: Faro: a card game fashionable amongst high society, in which players (punters) bet on the order in which certain cards will appear when taken singly from the top of the pack.

p. 336, ll. 29–31: *Ordinaries* ... French: an ordinary was an eating house where meals were served at set times at a fixed price.

p. 337, l. 1: Suffolk-Street: Great Suffolk Street, off Cockspur Street between Charing Cross and Pall Mall.

p. 337, ll. 18–28: *two very Noble* Theatres ... *from the other*: Haymarket, for opera, Covent Garden for tragedy, and Lincoln's Inn for comedy (*LE*).

p. 337, l. 32: Shut-boxes: a seated compartment in a theatre, closed off by a door.

p. 338, ll. 2–3: *the* Parterre *(commonly called the* Pit*)*: the pit is the part of the auditorium of a theatre on the floor of the house; a parterre is a level garden occupied by a formal arrangement of beds and flowers. The term 'parterre' was commonly used for the pit in the early eighteenth century, and may be a corruption of 'parquet'.

p. 338, l. 22: Henry Purcell: Henry Purcell (1659–95), the greatest English composer of his time, held in especially high regard in the first two decades after his death (*ODNB*).

p. 338, l. 23: Lully: Jean-Baptiste Lully (1632–87), an Italian-born composer who worked in the court of Louis XIV, where he founded the French Opera.

p. 339: p. 111 is numbered as 109 in the printed original.

p. 339, ll. 3–4: *Mr.* Addison ... Cato: Joseph Addison (1672–1719), an editor and principal writer of *The Tatler* and *The Spectator*, completed his tragedy *Cato* in 1713. The play was first acted at Drury Lane on 14 April 1713, and was a great success, with Tories and Whigs identifying rival subjects for the satire.

p. 339, l. 9: Molliere: Jean-Baptiste Poquelin, known as Molière (1622–73), French playwright.

p. 339, l. 10: *Mr.* Cibber: Colley Cibber (1671–1757), comic actor, playwright and theatre manager, who was most famous in his role as a stage fop in Vanbrugh's *The Relapse* (1697).

p. 339, l. 19: Tom's *and* Will's Coffee-Houses: the two principal coffee-houses in Russell Street, Covent Garden, where poets, critics and men of letters assembled. Tom's Coffee-house, established *c.* 1700 (Lillywhite 1366), and Will's Coffee-house, established *c.* 1660 (Lillywhite 1548). See above, pp. 247–8, and note to p. 249, l. 3.

p. 339, ll. 22–5: Blue *and* Green Ribbons *and* Stars ... at Home: men wearing the insignia of high chivalric honours. A blue sash or ribbon was worn by members of the Order of the Garter, a green sash or ribbon by members of the Order of the Thistle (both orders were granted by the sovereign alone); a star was an ornament of precious metal in the shape of a star worn as part of the insignia of an order of a knighthood. Macky notes the distinctive egalitarian aspect of the coffee-house, but he also notes that rank is prominently advertised through displays of chivalric insignia.

p. 339, l. 28: *the Company of Ladies*: women of the same rank as these aristocratic men are not found in the coffee-house, but at assemblies in private houses.

p. 339, ll. 31–3: *the* Foreign *Prints* ... *Party-Disputes*: the range of newspapers in the coffee-house includes English papers which cover foreign news (such as *The London Gazette*), but also foreign newspapers themselves (such as *The Harlem Gazette*), as well as essay periodicals such as *The Spectator* (a paper of morality and party dispute).

p. 340, l. 1: *Bills of Exchange*: a written order by the writer or 'drawer' to the 'drawee' to pay a certain sum on a given date to the drawer, or to a third person named in the bill, known as a 'payee'. The bill of exchange is given in consideration of value received (*OED*).

p. 340, ll. 13–14: *Licensed by Act of Parliament*: Hackney coaches (four-wheeled coaches plying for public hire) were suppressed by proclamation in 1660, and then, when that measure failed, regulated by license in 1662.

p. 340, ll. 26–8: *in* Exchange-Alley ... Garaway's, Robin's *and* Jonathan's: the three principal coffee-houses for the market in stocks and shares in Exchange Alley off Cornhill. Garraway's Coffee-house, founded *c.* 1672 (Lillywhite 433); Robin's Coffee-house, founded *c.* 1702 (Lillywhite 1082); and Jonathan's Coffee-house, established *c.* 1680 (Lillywhite 656).

p. 340, ll. 31–2: *Foreign* Banquiers, *and often even* Foreign Ministers: a banquier or banker was one who changed money by dealing in bills of exchange, giving drafts and making remittances; a minister is an agent or representative of a sovereign state, ranking below that of an ambassador (*OED*).

p. 341, ll. 7–9: *selling of* Bank-Stock ... Cards *and* Dice: a list of the principal stocks, shares and gaming to be found in Jonathan's Coffee-house.

p. 341, ll. 14–15: *Selling a* Bear's-Skin: jargon of the stock market at Jonathan's Coffee-house. Someone who 'sells a bear-skin' is one who is speculating that the price of stock will fall, that is, someone who contracts to sell stock at a certain price in the future in the expectation that at that time he will be able to buy it at a lower price, and so make a profit on the falling market. Steele, in *The Tatler*, 38 (1709), remarks that 'I fear the Word Bear is hardly to be understood among the polite People; but I take the meaning to be, That one ensures a real value upon an Imaginary Thing, is said to sell a Bear' (ed. by Donald Bond, 3 vols (Oxford, Clarendon Press, 1987), vol. I, p. 273).

p. 341, ll. 20–6: 'French *Eating-Houses* ... Kivat's': French eating-houses renowned for their elite clientele of Whigs, noblemen and fops. Pontack (fl. 1666–1711) kept a tavern or eating-house (Lillywhite 1004) in Abchurch Lane (between Lombard St and Cannon St), renowned for its fine wines and luxurious dinners. He shared the same surname as Arnaud de Pontac (1599–1681), a president of the *parlement* of Bordeaux, but was not related (*ODNB*). By contrast with Pontack's expensive meals, a much more simple repast could be had at Kivat's (about which little is known). In the fifth edition (1732) this eating house is called '*Caveack's*' (vol. I, p. 197)

p. 342, ll. 1–3: *Abuse of Intelligence, ... the Mails*: all the various tricks of the gamblers on the stock exchange, as satirised, for example in *The Art of Getting Money by Double-Fac'd Wagers*, see above, pp. 233–8.

p. 342, ll. 7–8: *Act against excessive Gaming*: several measures were taken against immoderate gambling and deceitful practices like those noticed above in the period 1710–12, including the Act for the Better Preventing of Excessive and Deceitful Gaming (9 Ann, c. 14). In the fifth edition (London, R. Gosling and J. Pemberton, 1732), the following sentence was added: 'The fatal South-Sea Scheme, and the wicked Execution of it, proves what I foretold you to be too true' (vol. I, p. 198).

Lewis Theobald, 'Coffee-House Humours Exposed'

p. 345, ll. 2–3: Occursus ... *Juven.*: Juvenal, *Satires*, X.47–8: 'men of excellence, who will make great role models', *Satires*, ed. by Braund, p. 371.

p. 346, ll. 18–19: Reports *and* Demurrers: reports and demurrers are legal reports: in law, a demurrer is a pleading which admits the facts as stated in the opponent's pleading but denies that he is entitled to relief, and thus stops the action until this point be decided in court (*OED*). See Robert Gardiner, *The Doctrine of Demurrers* (London, for Tho. Bever, 1706).

p. 346, l. 23: *Pannels of Glass*: mirrors. Grand coffee-houses made extensive use of mirrors and gilt in order to give their interiors higher status. Theobald calls these places 'polite coffee-houses' on p. 346, l. 28.

p. 346, l. 25: *a Punn of* Shadwell's: Thomas Shadwell (1642–92), *Bury-Fair. A comedy* (London, James Knapton, 1689): 'Sir Hum[phrey Noddish]. Why, 'tis an ill-natur'd Looking-glass. *Wild[ish]*. How so? *Sir Hum*. Because it makes reflections; ha ha' (p. 30).

p. 347, l. 1: *brocaded* Narcissi: a person characterised by extreme self-admiration or vanity, a narcissist, from the name of a beautiful youth in Greek mythology who fell in love with his own reflection in water. Brocade is a rich fabric wrought with a flowered raised pattern.

p. 347, l. 2: Pawlet's: a chocolate house or ordinary; see George Farquhar, *Sir Harry Wildair* (London, James Knapton, 1701), p. 42.

p. 347, ll. 13–14: *the Smell of* Hercules's *Club*: a small tree called Prickly Ash or Club of Hercules (*Zanthoxylum clava-herculis*), whose leaves and fruit have a pungent aroma believed to deter dogs.

p. 347, l. 18–20: *deter an ordinary* Protestant ... Postman: Gill is a physic-ale brewed with ground-ivy: John Quincy, *Pharmacopœia officinalis* (London, A. Bell, T. Varnam and J. Osborn, and W. Taylor, 1718), p. 123. The perfume and gaudy clothes of the fops contrast with the simple Englishman drinking his bitter brew and reading his newspaper.

p. 348, l. 4: October: a kind of strong ale traditionally brewed in October (*OED*).

p. 348, l. 14: Ombre: a card game for three people using 40 cards (discarding the eights, nines and tens), in which players bid for the right to nominate a trump suit, and then attempt to win tricks (*OED*).

p. 348, ll. 18–19: *a Simile*, ... Sick Man's Dreams: Quintus Horatius Flaccus, known as Horace (65–27 BC), *Ars Poetica* or 'The Art of Poetry', a treatise on poetics. The allusion is to 'the foolish book / Where dream-like forms in sick delirium blend' (trans. by John Conington (London, Bell and Daldy, 1870), l. 11), like a man with the body of a horse and covered in feathers. Theobald is satirising the incongruity between the subjects discussed and the participants in the coffee-house.

p. 348, ll. 30–1: *the Neighbouring* Mechanicks: men engaged in trades which involve manual skill; artisans or tradesmen; hence, not gentlemen (*OED*).

p. 349, ll. 6–8: *the* Arrival *of an* Express ... Session's Paper: miscellaneous and ephemeral publications of raw news which excite debate in the coffee-house: an express or dispatch sent by an express messenger; a vote or printed list of the results of a division in parliament; or a session's paper, a monthly list of cases put down for trial at the sessions or judicial sittings (*OED*).

p. 349, l. 21: Piece-broker: 'Piece-broker, is a shopkeeper in London, who buys the shreds and remnants of all materials that go through the hands of the taylor, and sells them again to such persons as want them for mending cloaths; being generally decayed tailors, or some cunning men who have crept into the secrets of the trade': Richard Rolt, *A New Dictionary of Trade and Commerce* (London, T. Osborne and J. Shipton, 1756).

p. 350, ll. 2–3: Three-half-penny *Societies*: a club or society for which the entry and commons is three half pence, associated with the public entertainments of small traders and artisans.

p. 350, ll. 13–14: *a Lecture of Mr.* Whiston's: William Whiston (1667–1752), natural philosopher and theologian, Lucasian professor of mathematics at Cambridge, 1702–10. His *Praelectiones astronomicae* (London, B. Tooke, 1707) were published in English as *Astronomical Lectures* (London, R. Senex and W. Taylor, 1715), and his *Praelectiones physico-mathematicae* (London, B. Tooke, 1710) as *Sir Isaac Newton's Mathematick Philsophy More Easily Demonstrated* (London, J. Senex and W. Taylor, 1716). These works were written as undergraduate lectures, but offered a more accessible public route to Newtonian astronomy and hydrostatics (the branch of physics which treats of the pressure and equilibrium of liquids at rest) than Newton's own *Principia*.

p. 350, ll. 24–7: Caimacan *of* Constantinople's *Letter … the* Persian Xerxes: the Caimacan (more properly Kaimakam) was the deputy of the Ottoman grand vizier, and governor of Constantinople; the Great Turk was the Ottoman sultan; and the 'Xerxes' was the Greek transliteration of the Persian throne name Khshayarsha, meaning 'ruler of heroes'.

p. 350, l. 29: *'the Embarkment at* Gottemberg': Göttingen, a city on the River Leine then in the Duchy of Brunswick-Luneberg, one of the possessions of the Elector of Hanover (George I of England).

p. 351, ll. 1–2: Julius Caesar … Britain: Gaius Julius Caesar (100–44 BC), who invaded Britain in 55 BC. The satire here turns again on the incommensurability between these abstruse quibbles of scholarship and displays of pedantry and the lowly status of the coffee-house scholars.

p. 352, l. 5: Agamemnon: in Greek mythology, the hero and commander-in-chief of the Greek expedition to the siege of Troy.

p. 352, ll. 12–13: *Orations … limited by the* Hour-Glass: the speeches of Greek orators addressing the assembly or the law-courts were time-limited by water clocks. See Michael Edwards, *The Attic Orators* (Bristol, Bristol Classical Press, 1994), p. 5.